T5-DGQ-120
MARYLAND 20686

The Holocaust and Strategic Bombing

The Holocaust and Strategic Bombing

GENOCIDE AND TOTAL WAR IN THE TWENTIETH CENTURY

Eric Markusen
David Kopf

Westview Press
BOULDER • SAN FRANCISCO • OXFORD

All rights reserved. No part of this publication may be reproduced or transmitted in any form or by any means, electronic or mechanical, including photocopy, recording, or any information storage and retrieval system, without permission in writing from the publisher.

Copyright © 1995 by Westview Press, Inc.

Published in 1995 in the United States of America by Westview Press, Inc., 5500 Central Avenue, Boulder, Colorado 80301-2877, and in the United Kingdom by Westview Press, 12 Hid's Copse Road, Cumnor Hill, Oxford OX2 9JJ

Library of Congress Cataloging-in-Publication Data
Markusen, Eric.
The Holocaust and strategic bombing : genocide and total war in the twentieth century / Eric Markusen, David Kopf.
p. cm.
Includes bibliographical references and index.
ISBN 0-8133-7532-0
1. Genocide—History—20TH century. 2. World War, 1939–1945—Aerial operations. 3. Bombing, Aerial—History. 4. Holocaust. Jewish (1939–1945) I. Kopf, David. II. Title.
HV6322.7.M37 1995
304.6′63—dc20 94-32807
CIP

Printed and bound in the United States of America

The paper used in this publication meets the requirements of the American National Standard for Permanence of Paper for Printed Library Materials Z39.48-1984.

10 9 8 7 6 5 4 3 2

To Rabbi Harry Brown, who inspired me intellectually and spiritually when I was very young. Cousin Harry left for Eastern Europe in the 1930s to pursue advanced studies in theology. He never returned. We may never know whether he was a victim of the Nazi Holocaust, Stalinism, or a native form of fascism.

—D. K.

To the memory of my parents, Elizabeth and Raymond Markusen; to Jean Erickson, F. Wilmer Larson, and Robert L. Fulton; and to my family, Randi Ellen Markusen and Maria Claire Markusen.

—E. M.

To the memory and work of Leo Kuper.

Contents

Foreword

This book is a gift of decent, intrepid scholars who have dared to piece together the unbearable picture of enormous human death and suffering of civilian populations subjected to massive bombing in many countries in the 1930s and in World War II. These authors have the moral and intellectual authority to call human civilization to task for these crimes of genocide and hellish suffering. Their provocative, iconoclastic comparative analysis is likely to offend many readers with its conclusions that another project of mass killing had features in common with the Holocaust and that the Allied strategic bombing campaigns warrant being described as genocidal.

I do not envy the authors the criticisms they will receive from Holocaust scholars, centers, and institutions. I am also taking the position that the authors have made an important error in their choice of the metaphoric tool *Holocaust* as the symbolic machinery through which they wish to imprint on our civilization their important and valid assembly of information and interpretation of the murderous actions of governments in strategic bombing and total war. The authors argue persuasively that the underlying matrix of murder-enabling dynamics that has led government after government to make choices to kill, maim, and brutalize millions of innocent human beings in total war includes many of the same dynamic process factors in the mind collective that made the Holocaust possible. But I believe that that they go too far in the extent of their comparisons between the Holocaust and strategic bombing.

It is highly unconventional to criticize authors in a foreword to their book as strongly as I am doing. However, my criticism in this case also issues from my genuine convictions as to the excellence and significance of this work, to which I agreed, indeed am honored, to write the foreword. In effect, I say that I and many others are too small to join the authors in the greatness of their perception; and yet I also say that they have been somewhat insensitive to the symbolic wounds and needs that many of us have at this point in history, including those like myself who are fully in agreement with their basic thesis.

There is still another major ethical issue that this important book raises, which is whether in the battle against an intentionally genocidal power, genocidal mass murder of civilians is justified not as an outcome of a prejudicial-annihilatory policy but as an aspect of total war.

Part of me is seriously offended at the thought or suggestion that there should have been any turning back from overwhelming retaliation against both the government and people of the nation that committed the Holocaust against my people and brought about the ravages of World War II for so many other millions of victims. Yet I am also grateful to Markusen and Kopf for calling me back to ponder whether even military battle in very "just wars" must not be guided by clear moral perceptions that focus on *strategic destruction of the enemy and not on massive destruction of a people.* Even if it were possible to demonstrate that destruction of the other *people* brings about the necessary military victory over the monstrous, destroying enemy, one is still compelled to question the morality of bringing about the deaths and suffering of so many essentially innocent civilians. Moreover, the authors argue that the real dynamics leading to the decisions to fight civilians are not always pragmatic military choices but in their own right may reflect expressions of annihilatory, megalomaniacal human ambitions.

Overall, I cannot recommend this book more highly. The scholarship is deeply impressive and encompassing. It is written in the finest prose, to a point where, rare among scholarship on the Holocaust and genocide, the reader is swept into the dramas that the authors unfold in each of many case histories. Slowly but surely, these case studies are reconstructed as both historical events and psychological processes of the people and organizations that bring them about.

I challenge scholars of the Holocaust who do not understand that the monstrous systematic persecution, indescribable torture, and murderous extermination of the Jews in the Holocaust were events that go to the heart of *the nature of humankind and civilization,* that is, the penchant of our species and our societal organizations to destroy more and more of life. Jews continue to be the bellwether victims of this brutal nature of humankind.

Markusen and Kopf demonstrate how the processes of dehumanization, bureaucratic and organizational rottenness, killing under the guise of rationalizations of healing and the good of society, and other very dangerous processes that made the hated Holocaust possible were also responsible for runaway massive killings of civilians in various wars, and that those are dynamics we must fight wherever and whenever they appear in human life. Yet, as I indicated, I disagree with Markusen and Kopf in titling their book to compare strategic bombing and total war with the Holocaust.

Granted, the authors do note that there were several differences between the two. One major difference was the goal of the mass killing.

> It is widely accepted that the perpetrators of the Holocaust, after a period of experimenting with a variety of approaches to ridding the Third Reich of its Jewish population, eventually reached the point that they decided to intentionally and calculatingly exterminate the Jews and that such extermination was largely an end in itself. So vital was genocide as a primary goal during the war that the Nazis carried on their extermination program even when it interfered with their military campaigns against enemy soldiers. Moreover, had Germany won the war, its genocidal killing would have spread to additional areas that would have been conquered. In strong contrast, the political and military leaders responsible for the Allied strategic-bombing campaigns regarded the firebombing of German and Japanese cities as a means to the end of in-

> ducing the enemy to surrender. Their intent was not to kill *all* Germans and Japanese but to kill and injure and "dehouse" enough of them to induce their governments to give up the fight. Following surrender, the bombing abruptly ceased.

I also cannot fault Markusen and Kopf's powerful descriptions of masses of human bodies burning, indeed bursting into flames, and melting under the relentless massive incendiary bombings as not being very different from descriptions of the masses of human beings who found their deaths in the ugliest Nazi gas chambers and were then reduced to ashes in the huge crematoria. Thus, quoting from Caidin, "Whole families are in an instant set aflame, roasting alive in unheard paroxysms of screaming and pain as the terrible heat exploded the wooden doors and supports of the shelters into flame."

Yet I also argue that the adoption of the word *Holocaust* for the destruction of the Jews by the Nazis and their collaborators in World War II has, rightfully and importantly, taken on major precedent-shaping meanings and symbolic functions in the very memory of human civilization. The Holocaust was perhaps the first time that the cruel and indifferent nature of the collective human mind has been shocked and shaken to some meaningful extent by the facts of man's delight, talent, and unbelievable efficiency in destroying life.

There are constructive purposes to symbols. The Holocaust is a watershed event in the collective psychology-history of humankind. It is my judgment that at this point in collective human history, comparisons and relationships of other events to the Holocaust should be developed extensively, and generic implications for the development of new concepts in international law against all forms of brutalization, persecution, and mass killing should be scrupulously pursued. At the same time, once these new concepts have been adopted, the concept of *Holocaust* as a denotation of a specific event, namely the Nazi murders, especially of the Jews, should be reserved for that event as a shining light on the need to uncover relentlessly all other genocidal events and to uncover the genesis and organization of policies that bring about mass destruction of human lives.

In truth, I am very glad that the authors asked me to write this foreword. In my own scholarship and leadership in genocide studies, I have conveyed clearly for many years that the concern of all humankind must be with any and all instances of mass murder and genocide. I have even spoofed in satirical essays the days that will come when one will have to contend with definitions of events such as *planeticide* and that intergalactic committees will have to sit in judgment on the definitions of a whole variety of events of destruction of human lives, communities, nations, and then also planets and, who knows, maybe even galaxies. At what point will the insistences on the uniqueness of the Holocaust of the Jewish people fall into inconsequentiality in the face of events of history so large that the Holocaust, too, will take its place in the unbearable list of endless massacres of masses of human beings since the dawn of life? This does *not* mean that the Holocaust is, now or ever, to be minimized—none of the genocidal events should ever be taken so lightly—but that the Holocaust should no longer be treated as an inviolate, unique event that can be measured only in its own terms. If, in fact, virtually all of the component processes of the Holocaust have been duplicated in other events of genocide and if it is long since clear that many other peoples have suffered more than the Jews in terms of the proportion of their people killed, then the time is coming for a historiography and social science of genocide that seeks to examine *all* events of genocide.

I cannot recommend this book more highly to every scholar and human being who is concerned with understanding and knowing the truth about the specific events dealt with in this book and about the basic collective mind processes that bring about mass destruction of life.

I sincerely hope that the book will not suffer because of the angry criticisms that I predict will be heaped on the authors for their violation of a symbolic boundary, which I, too, have criticized. Notwithstanding what I believe is poor judgment in comparing strategic bombing with the Holocaust, the authors have given us an outstanding work on every level of scholarship, excellence of writing, and significance. I am tempted to fantasize that Markusen and Kopf are ahead of us and have come back to us in time from the twenty-first century. For their message about the madness and evil of human governments in their massive campaigns of destruction against civilians is obviously a message that we, as a planetary civilization, have been resisting. We will yet have to face it if we are to survive.

Israel W. Charny
Executive Director, Institute on the Holocaust and Genocide, Jerusalem
Professor and Director, Program for Advanced Studies
in Integrative Psychotherapy, Department of Psychology
and Martin Buber Center, Hebrew University of Jerusalem

Acknowledgments

This book uses a comparative analysis of the Holocaust and the Allied strategic-bombing campaigns during World War II in order to explore the relationship between genocide and total war as forms of governmental mass killing. It is a greatly revised adaptation of a doctoral dissertation in sociology ("The Holocaust and Strategic Bombing: Case Studies in the Psychology, Organization, and Technology of Mass Killing in the Twentieth Century") completed by Eric Markusen at the University of Minnesota, Minneapolis, in December 1985. In 1989, historian David Kopf joined Markusen in a collaborative effort to revise and extend the dissertation by incorporating newly available material and broadening the scope of the analysis to include the global context of violence during World War II. Both the dissertation and the present work reached the same conclusion—namely, that the line between war and genocide in the twentieth century is often very blurred and that much modern war can, and should, be described as genocidal.

Many individuals and organizations made important contributions to this project at its various stages. Any value that it has is due largely to their support, guidance, and encouragement. We take full responsibility, however, for any limitations or weaknesses.

The dissertation was initially inspired by Daniel Ellsberg's suggestion that Markusen investigate the 1945 incendiary bombing of Tokyo by the United States. Robert Jay Lifton's pioneering work on collective violence provided a crucial empirical and theoretical foundation for understanding genocidal killing, and Markusen's collaboration with Lifton on *The Genocidal Mentality* was an invaluable intellectual and personal experience (see the selected bibliography for these publications). Lifton also invited Markusen to be a regular participant in the annual Wellfleet Psychohistory Meetings, through which stimulating contacts with Norman Birnbaum, Margaret Brenman-Gibson, Daniel Ellsberg, Erik Erikson, Kai Erikson, Richard Falk, Robert Holt, Betty Jean Lifton, John Mack, Charles Strozier, and others were made possible. As will be evident from frequent citations in the text, this project is deeply indebted to the work of genocide scholars Israel W. Charny, Helen Fein, and Leo Kuper.

Student Pugwash USA, the Federation of American Scientists, and the Center for Energy and Environmental Studies at Princeton University all facilitated Markusen's early research, as did a doctoral dissertation fellowship and a special research grant from the University of Minnesota Graduate School and faculty development grants from Old Dominion University, Carthage College, and Southwest State University. A Travel to Collections Grant from the National Endowment for the Humanities enabled Markusen to make the first of four trips to Poland in order to visit Auschwitz and other relevant sites. The director of the Polish National Museum at Auschwitz, Kazmierz Smolen, and the director of the Polish National Museum at Majdanek, Edward Balawejder, gave Markusen full access to relevant archives. In Warsaw, Jola Bak and Danuta Jampolska provided important help with translations, arrangements, and accommodations.

Special thanks are due to Markusen's Ph.D. committee at the University of Minnesota, which included David Cooperman, chair, and Robert L. Fulton, Thomas Mackenzie, Don Martindale, Don MacTavish, and Mulford Q. Sibley.

Genya Markon, photo archivist at the United States Holocaust Memorial Museum, and John B. Taylor, archivist in the Military History Division of the National Archives, provided invaluable assistance.

A number of individuals read the draft manuscript in whole or in part and offered constructive criticism. They include Joseph Amato, Ronald Bee, Michael Carey, Israel W. Charny, Daniel Ellsberg, James R. Hayes, Herbert Hirsch, and Randi Markusen. Other friends, including Yonas Endale, Mark Holub, Jeff Kolnick, Kent Lee, and Greg Owen, provided stimulating discussion and encouragement.

Kopf wishes to give special thanks to Mary Lago, who organized the 1986 International Tagore Conference at the Commonwealth Institute, London, out of which emerged his first published article on nationalism, war, and genocide. Thanks are also due to the World History Association for providing a forum at the 1993 annual meeting in Hawaii on whether the British colonial wars in the nineteenth century were genocidal. Kopf also wishes to express his gratitude to Christopher Simmer, a graduate student in history at the University of Minnesota who has graciously shared in many discussions his special interest in Holocaust historiography.

Both Markusen and Kopf wish to thank the International Society for the Comparative Study of Civilizations, and Michael Andregg in particular, for providing opportunities to make presentations on this work as it progressed at annual meetings in Illinois, the Dominican Republic, Kentucky, and Ireland. We also thank the organizers of the international Remembering for the Future II Conference, held in Berlin, Germany, for inviting us to participate in the working group on genocide.

Several individuals associated with Westview Press, including Miriam Gilbert, Bruce Kellison, and Mick Gusinde-Duffy, helped make this book possible. Special thanks are due to Peter Kracht, senior editor, for his patience, advice, and encouragement. Brooke Graves and Diane Hess helped make the transformation from manuscript to book.

Eric Markusen
David Kopf

Chapter 1

Introduction

> The scale of man-made death is the central moral as well as material fact of our time.
>
> —*Gil Elliot (1972)*[1]

The Problem of Mass Killing

Of all the problems confronting humankind during the remaining years of the twentieth century and into the twenty-first, we believe that none is more urgently in need of solution than the deliberate killing of masses of defenseless people. One need only read the daily newspaper or watch the evening news on television to be inundated by a mind-numbing array of human-caused atrocities and tragedies—wars, famines, and genocidal massacres—occurring in many corners of the world. As this book goes to press in the last decade of the century, hundreds of thousands of people are dying—and millions more are at risk of dying—due to the direct and indirect effects of collective violence. From the tortured land that was once Yugoslavia come images of cities being reduced to rubble, innocent civilians lying on sidewalks in pools of blood, and emaciated prisoners in so-called detention camps— victims of an epidemic of social madness that has degenerated into reciprocal atrocities committed by Serbs against Muslims, Croats against Serbs, Muslims against Croats, Serbs against Croats, Muslims against Serbs, and even Muslims against Muslims. Far away from Europe, the towns and villages of Rwanda are littered with the bodies of thousands of men, women, and children who have been slaughtered in yet another genocidal tragedy. In the Middle East, reports of persecution and massacre of Shiite Muslims by military forces of the Iraqi dictator Saddam Hussein have compelled the United Nations to once again consider military intervention against Iraq. In 1992 alone, there were 19 major wars under way across the planet—more than in any other single year in recorded history. Moreover, war itself has become much more dangerous to noncombatants. In World War I, only 5 percent of the deaths were civilian; by World War II, civilians constituted 66 percent of the deaths; and in wars since the 1970s civilians have accounted for 80 percent or more of the deaths.[2]

And the future offers scant consolation. Despite the end of the Cold War, tens of thousands of nuclear weapons and other weapons of mass destruction remain in the arsenals of the United States, Russia, and other nations, and there is a real danger of their spread to additional nations and even terrorist groups.[3] In the final chapter of this book, we examine three trends that create a grave potential for further governmental violence, both genocidal and military, in the near future. First, we discuss structural violence, which refers to the creation or tolerance of unjust and harmful social conditions. Unlike genocide and war, this form of violence is not deliberate and direct, but it nevertheless causes millions of deaths each year and creates conditions conducive to the outbreak of war. Then, we address the growing tide of refugees in many regions of the world. Finally, we examine the dangers posed by the spread of chemical, biological, and other weapons of mass destruction into nations and regions made politically and militarily volatile by ethnic divisions and nationalistic aspirations.

Countless millions of men, women, and children have been slaughtered by their fellow human beings throughout history, yet there is persuasive evidence that the present century is the most murderous of all. Indeed, in his pioneering study *Twentieth Century Book of the Dead,* Scottish writer Gil Elliot estimated that more than one hundred million people were victims of "man-made death" in the first seven decades of the twentieth century alone.[4]

Moreover, the vast majority of men and women responsible for the slaughter of their fellow human beings have not been sadistic or psychopathic. As psychologist Israel W. Charny concluded from his extensive study of genocidal killing, "The mass killers of humankind are largely everyday human beings—what we have called normal people according to currently accepted definitions by the mental health profession."[5] Sociologist Everett C. Hughes suggested that such mass killers could in fact be viewed as "good people" doing the "dirty work" of their societies.[6] These are conclusions of major importance. How ostensibly normal, "good" people can be able and willing to contribute to atrocity is a question that merits serious study.

Neglect of the Problem of Mass Killing

Despite the vital contributions of scholars, human rights activists, and others from around the world, however, the energy and attention devoted to understanding and preventing governmental mass killing have been negligible when compared with the scale and urgency of the problem itself. To a large extent, this neglect reflects the default of the academic community. Our own, purportedly socially sensitive, disciplines of sociology and history have not been immune to the tendency to neglect the issue of mass killing. In her 1977 article "Is Sociology

Aware of Genocide?" Helen Fein (herself a sociological pioneer in this field with her 1979 study *Accounting for Genocide*)[7] reported on the results of a survey of the most widely used introductory sociology texts, whose authors attempt to examine important social issues of the day. Fein found that the majority of texts either completely omitted any mention of genocide or mentioned it only in a very superficial manner. "Until recently," Fein observed, "analysis and research of genocide has been almost nonexistent among sociologists."[8] To judge from the paucity of books and articles on genocide cited in *Sociological Abstracts* during the years following Fein's article, sociological attention to this topic has, at best, grown from almost nonexistent to barely existent.

Writing in 1989 specifically about the Holocaust, sociologist Zygmunt Bauman claimed that the contributions of sociologists to the understanding of this milestone in history have been "marginal and negligible."[9] And in their introduction to a special section of the *Sociological Quarterly* in 1985 devoted to the subject of nuclear warfare, Ronald Kramer and Sam Marullo decry the dearth of sociological work on the nuclear threat. "As a discipline," they stated, "we have failed to develop a body of knowledge concerning the threat of nuclear war in particular, and the problems of war and peace more generally."[10] (There have been notable exceptions to this trend of neglect: Sociologists who have studied the Holocaust include Leo Kuper, Helen Fein, Fred Katz, and Florence Mazian; and C. Wright Mills and Lester Kurtz have confronted the nuclear threat—all of the aforementioned are cited in the selected bibliography at the end of the book.)

Historians have also tended to avoid direct confrontation with the problem of mass killing as a subject in its own right. In their important 1990 book *The History and Sociology of Genocide*, historian Frank Chalk and sociologist Kurt Jonassohn point out a tendency among historians to neglect the darker side of world history:

> The coarseness and brutality of human existence throughout much of history was a subject that hardly ever appeared in ... our schools. The good news was reported; the bad news was not. The great massacres of the past lay beyond the range of telescopes designed to focus upon evidence that justice always triumphed. ... The authors of history textbooks hardly ever reported what the razing of an ancient city meant for its inhabitants. ...The fate of millions of human beings who died unnatural deaths as defenseless civilians was invisible.[11]

A case in point is provided by William McNeill's 1963 *The Rise of the West: A History of the Human Community*, which is the most successful and most popular world history textbook ever published in the United States. In the text, Hitler is given one line on a single page, and Auschwitz is not mentioned; nor are Stalin, his purges, his prison camps, or his man-made famine in Ukraine; nor are many of the horrors perpetrated by other infamous, charismatic heroes of twentieth-century totalitarianism.[12]

To be sure, specific genocides have been studied and written about, often by representatives of the ethnic groups that were victimized. Thus, Jewish scholars have written extensively about the Holocaust, and Armenian scholars have published on the genocide perpetrated by the government of Turkey against its Armenian citizens during World War I. And of course there have been abundant historical treatments of specific wars and battles, as well as sweeping overviews of the history of warfare. However, very few historians have attempted to examine the phenomenon of genocidal killing in comparative perspective. Nor has the potentially genocidal nature of modern war as a crucial and specific historical development been given the study it warrants. Our knowledge—both in the sense of scientific understanding and widespread awareness—of mass killing remains relatively rudimentary and dangerously inadequate.

Among those scholars who have focused on the problem of mass killing, there is little consensus on such basic issues as how to define crucial concepts, including "genocide." Some scholars question whether certain cases of genocide—notably the attempt by Nazi Germany to exterminate the Jews of Europe—are even comprehensible.[13] Others debate whether it is appropriate to make comparisons among different cases of genocide and genocidal killing. And controversy surrounds the issue with which this book is centrally concerned: the question of whether war and genocide are distinct, separate phenomena or whether they have important characteristics and causes in common.

Purposes of This Book

In the present study we seek to promote greater awareness and understanding of governmental mass killing by examining two major types—*genocide,* when a government slaughters its own citizens or subjects, and *total war,* when two or more governments slaughter each other's civilian citizens, as well as military personnel. The core of the book focuses on genocide and total war during World War II, but cases of mass killing from the distant past as well as from the postwar period are also discussed.

In this book we expose and examine mass killing in the recent past in the hope of providing insights about how to prevent similar tragedies from occurring in the future. Specifically, it attempts to provide at least beginning answers to such questions as the following: Is the twentieth century indeed the most murderous in history? If so, why? How have bureaucratic organization and advances in science and technology contributed to the scale of mass killing during this century? How can the willingness of apparently normal men and women to contribute to mass killing projects be explained? What psychological and social processes facilitate involvement in policies and programs that entail slaughtering masses of innocent, defenseless human beings? Why has the problem of mass killing not received the degree of attention that its scale and momentum warrant? What is the relationship between warfare and genocide? Should they be regarded as distinct, unrelated phenomena, or do they have important commonalities? Is it ever appropriate to define war as genocidal? Was strategic bombing genocidal? What are the prospects for further outbreaks of collective violence during the coming years and decades? And, perhaps most important, how can the study of such issues generate insights and actions needed to reduce the problem of governmental mass killing?

Although the conceptual framework, methodological approach, and subject matter of this book draw from a number of disciplines—including sociology, history, psychology, psychiatry, political science, national security studies, and international law—we regard our work primarily as a contribution to the small but growing field of genocide studies. By "genocide studies," we mean attempts to expose, comprehend, and prevent the phenomenon of genocidal killing as a subject in its own right and, ideally, in comparative perspective.*

Challenges Confronting the Study of Mass Killing

Mass killing as a subject confronts the scholar with a number of serious challenges. These include conceptual and definitional dilemmas, difficulties in obtaining reliable data, limitations of the human psyche when dealing with massive atrocities, political implications of such research, and resistances to a comparative approach. Each of them requires a brief discussion before proceeding.

Linguistic and Conceptual Dilemmas

A fundamental difficulty in genocide studies is created by the limits of language and by conceptual confusions. There is no single term accepted by a wide range of scholars that serves to define or characterize the overall phenomenon of large numbers of human beings killing masses of other human beings. Nor is there a widely accepted definition of genocide. What are the right words with which to discuss actions that are unspeakably atrocious and evil, such as the Holocaust and other clear cases of genocide? How does one label practices that entail mass mur-

*The field of genocide studies has yet to be comprehensively defined and delimited. Its essence, however, lies in a concern with the phenomenon of genocidal killing per se rather than with particular cases of genocide such as the Holocaust. There are, presently, several centers of genocide studies in the world, notably the Institute on the Holocaust and Genocide in Jerusalem; the Center for Genocide Studies in New York City; and the Montreal Institute for Genocide Studies in Quebec. Leading periodicals include the newsletter *Internet on the Holocaust and Genocide*, published by the Institute on the Holocaust and Genocide, and the journal *Holocaust and Genocide Studies*, published by Oxford University Press in association with the United States Holocaust Memorial Museum. Beginning in January 1995, the *Internet* newsletter will be published by the Centre for Comparative Genocide Studies at Maquarie University, Sydney, Australia. The Centre at Maquarie University will also initiate publication of the journal *Genocide Studies Quarterly*. A valuable introduction to genocide studies may be found in the journal *Social Education* (Vol. 55, No. 2, February 1991) and in the three volumes of *Genocide: A Critical Bibliographic Review*, edited by Israel W. Charny. (Bibliographic data for these volumes may be found in the selected bibliography.)

der of innocent human beings? Terms such as "slaughter," "butchery," and "massacre" come to mind and are used throughout the book. Gil Elliot used the term "man-made death" to emphasize the fact that so many people have been killed by their fellow human beings during this century.* We use this term repeatedly throughout the book as one of the core concepts. Another key term, "governmental mass killing," is used to reflect the fact that the vast majority of man-made deaths have been authorized and implemented by national governments or by factions within a nation-state that aspire to assume power.

Imprecise, inconsistent, and overlapping definitions characterize the field and help account for the fact that historians of war have regarded certain cases of collective violence as examples of war; genocide scholars regard the same cases as examples of genocide. This is true for the four cases of pre-twentieth-century mass killing that are briefly outlined in the next chapter. Thus, information on the Assyrians, the destruction of Carthage, the Mongol conquests, and the Thirty Years' War was found both in books on the history of war and in books on the history of genocide. Such dual identity is not limited to cases from the distant past. Twentieth-century cases of mass killing such as the slaughter of Southwest Africans by German colonizers in 1903–1908, the slaughter of Indonesian communists in 1965–1966, the Bangladesh War of Independence and accompanying genocide in 1971, and massacres conducted by Indonesian invaders of East Timor in 1975–1976 are regarded as examples of war by some scholars and as cases of genocide by others.

Limitations of Data on Mass Killing

Lack of reliable data creates an important methodological problem for the scholar of mass killing. Throughout most of history, the majority of those killed by their fellow human beings were simply not counted; as individuals, they were quite irrelevant. The value of a single human life was minimal. Even when military casualties were counted, the civilians who died as the result of disease, famine, and other consequences of war usually were not. Also, on the basis of extensive study of statistical data on war casualties throughout history, William Eckhardt concluded that as the scale of the killing increases, the accuracy of casualty estimates tends to decrease.[14]

Information about genocidal killing, which is even more sparse than data on wars, generally comes from refugee survivors and journalists who manage to escape censorship or is revealed when perpetrators are overthrown and their replacements capture documentary and other forms of evidence and expose it to the world. The latter occurred during the final weeks of the Holocaust, when the victorious Allied forces captured tons of German documents, many of which were

*Some may object to the fact that his term leaves out women, who have, to be sure, contributed to killing projects throughout history, but we feel that it is appropriate, since the overwhelming majority of mass killers have been men.

later used as evidence in the international military tribunal in Nuremberg, and also more recently when the Vietnamese overthrew the Cambodian government of Pol Pot in 1979 and discovered detailed records at the central torture-execution facility of Tuol Sleng.[15]

Reliability of data is also compromised by deliberate distortion. Perpetrators of mass killing usually have an interest in minimizing the number of victims, as well as in denying them altogether. This is exemplified during the twentieth century by Turkey's refusal to admit to the genocide of Armenians in 1915–1917 and the Soviet Union's reluctance, until very recently, to acknowledge the genocidal crimes of Joseph Stalin.[16]

Estimates of death tolls from specific wars, genocides, and other forms of mass killing are generally very imprecise. Writing of the Holocaust, political scientist R. J. Rummel noted: "Although the Germans are noted for their rule-following and record-keeping, and the relevant German archives were available after the war and participants could be systematically interviewed, there is still considerable disagreement—a range of over a million—among experts over the number of Jews actually murdered."[17] Another case in point involves the estimated death toll from the bombardment of the German city of Dresden by Great Britain and the United States during World War II. On the night of February 13, 1945, the British launched a massive incendiary bombing raid against the city, and then on the following day hundreds of U.S. bombers continued the attack. At that late point in the war (less than three months before the German surrender), Dresden was crowded with tens of thousands of uncounted refugees who were attempting to escape from the advancing Soviet army. This influx of people as much as doubled the normal population of 650,000.[18] Because there was no reliable count of the number of people in the city at the time of the bombing, and because a great many bodies were reduced to unrecognizable ash by the intense firestorm, estimates of the death toll vary widely from a low of 25,000 to as many as 70,000 or even more.[19]

Also complicating the attempt to count the victims of man-made death is the fact that many people die as the result of indirect effects of violence and many others die because of delayed effects. Throughout much of history the majority of civilian deaths from war have been caused by indirect effects, for example, disease and famine as a result of destroyed hospitals, burned crops, and disruption of transportation. Many such deaths occur months or even years after the actual conflict. For example, the atomic bombs dropped by the United States against the Japanese cities of Hiroshima and Nagasaki promptly killed approximately 140,000 and 70,000 people, respectively, but additional thousands died in the weeks, months, and even years after the war due to the delayed effects of radiation exposure. The death toll from the Nagasaki bombing, for example, doubled to 140,000 within five years of the attack.[20] Much more recently, large numbers of postwar deaths resulted from the Persian Gulf War of 1991, when U.S. and Allied bombers not only targeted specific military positions in Iraq but also destroyed the physical infrastructure of much of Baghdad, resulting in thousands of civilian deaths after the hostilities had stopped.[21]

Psychological Challenges to the Scholar and Student

Confronting the pervasive reality of mass killing—and identifying and counting its many vicims—is a profoundly distasteful but necessary task. It is far more pleasant to focus on the brighter side of human history—on exciting breakthroughs in knowledge, the creation of beautiful and enduring works of art, and examples of individual and social benevolence and altruism—than on the darker side, the side that demonstrates an ongoing proclivity of human beings both as individuals and as members of a collectivity to destroy each other. The student of man-made death must confront the fact that advances in the knowledge of how to save, prolong, and enhance life have been paralleled, and frequently overshadowed, by advances in the capacity and willingness to destroy it. Ironically, many millions of lives have been saved through the eradication of disease and the enhancement of food production; equally many, if not more, lives have been destroyed by new weapons of mass destruction, socially created famines, pogroms and massacres, torture, and other forms of calculated cruelty.

To study mass killing is to immerse one's mind in horror, to examine in detail the most atrocious behavior of which human beings are capable. The study of mass death and mass killing threatens to exacerbate the investigator's anxieties regarding his or her own death, as well as the deaths of loved ones. Psychiatrist and Holocaust survivor Bruno Bettelheim has observed that "Western man has relied on hiding stark death anxiety behind soothingly scientific and less threatening euphemisms." "But whatever man's psychological defenses against death anxiety," he went on to say, "they have always broken down whenever catastrophe struck and vast numbers of people were suddenly and unexpectedly killed in a very short period of time."[22] In the twentieth century—the age of unprecedented mass killing—maintaining psychological equilibrium with respect to death anxiety is particularly difficult.

There is a real danger that counting the dead may become an abstract intellectual exercise from which the human meaning is drained. No less a mass killer than Joseph Stalin noted a simple but immeasurably important fact when he reputedly observed that "a single death is a tragedy, a million deaths is a statistic."[23] Stalin recognized that large numbers can readily numb the mind to the existential horror of large-scale man-made death. As Elliot expressed it, "After a certain stage in assimilating casualties, the rest seems an indigestible piling-on of horror and numbers."[24] In Chapter 9, we explore the phenomenon of dehumanization—the process of regarding human victims of mass violence as nonhuman or less than fully human and therefore undeserving of customary empathic and moral considerations—as a fundamental facilitating factor in mass killing. But here it is important to point out that reducing human beings to numbers may also have the effect of dehumanizing them. As sociologist Zygmunt Bauman has noted, "It is only humans that may be objects of ethical propositions. ... Humans lose this capacity once they are reduced to ciphers."[25]

There is, ultimately, no ready solution to the natural tendency to become numb to the human meaning and horror contained within words, numbers, charts, and photographs that depict unspeakable suffering and tragedy. The subject of this book is intrinsically disturbing, especially when the reader appreciates the fact that man-made death is not merely a tragic feature of the distant past but also a current reality and future threat.

Anyone writing or teaching about this realm of human behavior must be sensitive to the danger of imbuing readers and students with a feeling of despair and fatalism. It is equally important to stress that thoughtful scholars have struggled with the question of how to confront and reduce the problem of mass killing. We examine a number of their valuable ideas in the final chapter of this book.

Political Dimensions of Genocide Studies

The study of mass killing is fraught with political implications and issues. It requires scholars and other citizens to look boldly at their own society, as well as other societies, and assess the role of mass killing in past and present national security policies. It is very clear that totalitarian governments are highly prone to resort to genocidal killing, but democracies also have engaged in the deliberate mass slaughter of civilians in pursuit of national security. The United States, for example, engaged in many incidents of genocidal killing in the process of removing the indigenous peoples from the path of settlement.[26]* Moreover, the United States, no less than the (former) Soviet Union, held for many years—and continues to hold—the entire world hostage to its policy of being able and willing to wage war with nuclear weapons. This is true also of democratic Great Britain, France, and Israel. Thus, to confront the problem of state-sanctioned mass killing is often tantamount to questioning, challenging, and striving to reform important policies of one's own government and, in democracies at least, facing the personal responsibility of having actively or passively supported such policies.

Identifying a particular action or situation as genocide or genocidal can have serious political ramifications. As we discuss in more detail in Chapter 4, the concept of genocide has frequently been appropriated by individuals and groups with political agendas. In a valuable essay on the concepts of the Holocaust and genocide, Henry Huttenbach has written, "Too often has the accusation of genocide been made simply for the emotional appeal or to make a political point with the

* Democracies such as the United States have also indirectly contributed to widespread torture and massacre through their support for totalitarian client states. We wish to thank Daniel Ellsberg for emphasizing this point. For a study of massacres conducted by client states of the United States, see Douglas V. Porpora, *How Holocausts Happen: The U.S. in Central America*, Philadelphia, Temple University Press, 1990.

result that the number of events claimed to be genocides rapidly increased to the point that the term lost its original meaning."[27] Thus, in his pioneering 1982 reader on genocide, sociologist Jack Nusan Porter noted that the label "genocide" has been misapplied to racial integration, methadone maintenance programs, certain features of the medical treatment of Irish Catholics, and the closing of synagogues in the Soviet Union.[28] And Helen Fein has pointed out that the Holocaust has frequently been politically exploited by individuals and organizations who seek to deny or diminish their own guilt for past genocides (e.g., the government of Turkey), to attract attention to an ongoing crisis, and for other motives. Fein has called the Holocaust "the paradigmatic genocide for political manipulation of images and revising the past."[29]

The Issue of Comparison

We recognize that comparing the Holocaust with the strategic bombing campaigns is a controversial scholarly undertaking. Looking at strategic bombing in a comparative context with the Holocaust will offend some Holocaust scholars, who assert the irreducible uniqueness of the Holocaust and resent its being compared with anything else. It will also offend others who resent the imputation that strategic bombing had anything at all in common with a universally condemned crime against humanity like the Holocaust, as well as those who may interpret our comparison as implying that we are equating the Holocaust with strategic bombing. In the remainder of this chapter, we will address each of these viewpoints, beginning with a consideration of the "uniqueness of the Holocaust" issue and then explicating the nature of comparative analysis as we employ it in this book.*

The question of whether the Holocaust is a "unique" historical event or whether it can and should be compared with other cases of mass killing is an important and divisive issue in Holocaust studies. In their valuable article "The Issue of the Holocaust as a Unique Event," Alan Rosenberg and Evelyn Silverman critically reviewed the literature on this contentious issue and identified three schools of thought: the "absolutists," who argue that the Holocaust is an incomprehensibly unique historical event; the "trivialists," who regard the Holocaust as simply one example of the phenomenon of genocide; and the "contextualists," who recognize that the Holocaust, like all historical events, has certain features that distinguish it from other, more or less comparable, occurrences but who also assert the validity and importance of examining the Holocaust in comparative perspective.[30]

*Among the sources on the comparative method that have been most helpful and influential to us have been Alexander George, "Case Studies and Theory Development: The Structured, Focused Method of Case Comparison," in Paul G. Lauren, Editor, *Diplomacy: New Approaches in History, Theory, and Policy,* New York, Free Press, 1979, pp. 43–68; and Theda Skocpol and Margaret Somers, "The Uses of Comparative History in Macrosocial Inquiry," *Comparative Studies in Society and History,* Vol. 22, April 1980, pp. 174–197.

The absolutist position is exemplifed by historian David Vital, who has claimed that "it is simply untrue" that the Holocaust "was of a class with other crusades, massacres, decimations, and slaughters."[31] Citing his statements that "the universe of concentration camps ... lies outside if not beyond history. Its vocabulary belongs to it alone" Rosenberg and Silverman also located Holocaust survivor and widely read author Elie Wiesel within the absolutist school.[32] One of the most outspoken scholars to stress the uniqueness of the Holocaust is philosopher-historian Stephen T. Katz. In two important articles, Katz compared the Holocaust to a number of other cases of mass killing in history, including pogroms against Jews during the Middle Ages; witch-hunts in Europe during the fifteenth through eighteenth centuries; the killing of North American Indians; slavery in the United States; the Nazi persecution of homosexuals; and the slave-labor and prison-camp system in the Soviet Union, primarily during the regime of Joseph Stalin. After summarizing the key features and death tolls of each of these cases, Katz compared them with the Holocaust and showed that none, however deadly, attempted or succeeded in killing such a large percentage of victims as did the Nazis in their campaign to exterminate virtually all of Europe's Jews. Arguing that such a "difference in degree is, ultimately, a difference in kind," Katz concluded that "the unmediated character of Nazi ideology is historically unique; of all the destructive belief systems its Judaeophobia alone demanded unlimited physical genocide. It is this fact that makes the 'Final Solution' an unprecedented and unparalleled event."[33]

In their discussion of the trivialist perspective, Rosenberg and Silverman included famed German historian Ernst Nolte, who in 1988 wrote an essay in which he argued that the Holocaust was not unique but was simply one in a number of cases of mass atrocity during the twentieth century. In that essay, Nolte asserted that

> it remains a striking deficiency of the literature on National Socialism that it is not cognizant (or does not wish to admit) the extent to which all those acts later perpetrated by the National Socialists—with the sole exception of the technical process of gassing—had already been described in a voluminous literature dating from the early 1920s: mass deportations and shootings, torture, death camps, the extermination of entire groups based on purely objective criteria, and public calls for the annihilation of millions of innocent human beings regarded as "enemies."[34]

Nolte's essay provoked a heated debate among other German historians, which has come to be known as the *Historikerstreit* (historians' quarrel or dispute). Nolte was criticized both for relativizing, and thereby diminishing the horror of, the Holocaust and for implying that Germany's national guilt was not unique but was comparable to that of other nations, such as Turkey and the Soviet Union, that had engaged in mass killing during the twentieth century.[35]

Our own position fits within the category that Rosenberg and Silverman label "contextualist." Although we strongly believe in the necessity of clearly recognizing the unique features of the Holocaust—including the fact that the Jews of Europe were the primary targets of the Nazi genocide and, with the exception of certain groups of Gypsies, were the only victim group targeted for total extirpation—we also believe that the Holocaust does share certain features with other cases of governmental mass killing. In this assumption, we are joined by Yehuda Bauer, who is widely regarded as one of the leading historians of the Holocaust. Bauer has written that "the worst massacres perpetrated by the Nazis have exact precedents, given the level of technical development, from ancient times to modernity."[36] (Bauer also, it is essential to note, has argued that certain specific features of the Holocaust, particularly the Nazi goal of exterminating virtually all Jews, are virtually unprecedented.)[37] We also believe that it is not only appropriate but essential to examine the Holocaust in comparative perspective. As Holocaust scholar Franklin H. Littell has emphasized, "The one who seeks to understand the Holocaust must risk entering the ground of comparison and analysis"[38] We believe that it is essential to study the Holocaust comparatively in order to discover what it may have in common with other cases of genocidal killing. Careful comparative analysis of the Holocaust may provide insights that can advance understanding of other genocides and instances of genocidal killing.

To those who are offended by our placement of the strategic bombing campaigns in the same analytic context as the Holocaust, we would emphasize that *comparing* two events is not the same as *equating* them or considering them as equivalent. Although *compare* is etymologically derived from the Latin *comparare,* which means equal, later usage includes a focus not only on similarities between two objects or events but also on differences. This simultaneous focus on *both* similarities and differences is emphasized by historian Charles S. Maier, who has written that "comparison is a dual process that scrutinizes two or more systems to learn what elements they have in common, and what elements distinguish them. It does not assert identity; it does not deny unique components." Maier went on to suggest that comparative analysis can "offer perspectives that the single case might not suggest [and] help reveal a wider historical process at work." Comparison, he continued, can make it possible "to discern a common causal mechanism otherwise unrevealed."[39]

One important difference between the two cases of mass killing that are comparatively analyzed in this book involves the relative danger to which the perpetrators of the Holocaust, on the one hand, and the bomber crews, on the other, were exposed. Service in the Nazi death camps, or in the paramilitary shooting squads that swept across the Soviet Union, entailed very little personal risk. Indeed, it was a far safer alternative to service on the front, particularly fighting against the Russian military. Only a handful of Germans died during the war as the result of being stationed in mobile killing units or at concentration and death camps. In strong contrast, the British and American bomber crews gravely risked, and very frequently lost, their lives during bombing attacks against Germany and Japan. More than 52,000 Americans were killed in the air war.[40] A study conducted by the

U.S. Army Air Forces in 1944 found that of every 1,000 men serving in the Eighth Air Force, "only 216 could be expected to finish twenty-five missions."[41] British losses were equally severe. According to one historian of the British strategic bombing campaign, of the 125,000 men and women who served in the British Bomber Command, about 56,000 were killed, about 28,000 injured, and 11,000 taken prisoner.[42]

Another important difference involves the intent of those policymakers who ordered the killing. It is widely accepted that the perpetrators of the Holocaust, after a period of experimenting with a variety of approaches to ridding the Third Reich of its Jewish population, eventually reached the point that they decided to intentionally and calculatingly exterminate the Jews and that such extermination was largely an end in itself. So vital was genocide as a primary goal during the war that the Nazis carried on their extermination program even when it interfered with their military campaigns against enemy soliders. Moreover, had Germany won the war, its genocidal killing would have spread to additional areas that would have been conquered. In strong contrast, the political and military leaders responsible for the Allied strategic bombing campaigns regarded the firebombing of German and Japanese cities as a means to the end of inducing the enemy to surrender. Their intent was not to kill *all* Germans and Japanese but to kill and injure and "dehouse" enough of them to induce their governments to give up the fight. Following surrender, the bombing abruptly ceased.

Yet another difference stems from the fact that the Jewish (and other) victims of the Nazi genocide had done absolutely nothing to threaten the national interests of Germany and warrant any reprisals, let alone massacre, whereas Germany and Japan were military aggressors against the Allies. Both Great Britain and the United States began the war with a clear policy *against* deliberate bombing of enemy population centers, but military atrocities committed by Germany and Japan helped create a process of reciprocal erosion of moral restraints.

Notwithstanding these and other differences, it is no less true that there were crucial similarities between the Holocaust and strategic bombing. These are examined in later sections of the book, but for present purposes we point out the following: First, and perhaps most fundamental, both strategic bombing and the Holocaust entailed the calculated, indiscriminate slaughter of masses of defenseless human beings, most of whom were innocent in the sense of having done nothing wrong (in the case of the Jews, Gypsies, and others) or having virtually no responsibility for aggression and crimes committed by their totalitarian government (in the case of most German and Japanese civilians). Nobody disputes the fact that the Jewish victims of the Nazis were both innocent and, in virtually all cases, helpless. It has been estimated that of the approximately 5 million Jews who were exterminated by the Nazis, between 1 million and 1.5 million were children.[43]

However, it is also the case that many of the victims of strategic bombing, both "conventional" incendiary area attack and attack with atomic bombs, were innocent and helpless. In his moral critique of strategic bombing, for example, theolo-

Captured American pilot being beheaded by a Japanese. SOURCE: Smithsonian Institution National Air and Space Museum

An American bomber shot from the sky over Europe. SOURCE: Smithsonian Institution National Air and Space Museum.

gian John Ford argued that many, if not most, of the civilians killed in bombing raids were "innocent noncombatants," especially children and the elderly, who made no contribution to the war effort and therefore could not be regarded as legitimate targets.[44] The same is true for the victims of the atomic bombs, most of whom were women and the elderly, as well as children who had not been evacuated to rural areas.[45]

In neither the Holocaust nor strategic bombing were the vast majority of victims killed because of what they had done as individuals. Instead, the Jews were killed because the Nazis regarded them as members of an enemy race, and citizens of Germany and Japan were killed because of where they lived and the fact that their totalitarian government had waged aggressive war against Great Britain and the United States. Even had an individual German or Japanese wanted to surrender, he or she had no influence over the government officials. Indeed, under the dictatorships that governed both countries, any citizen who questioned official policy faced arrest, imprisonment, and death.

Second, strategic bombing and the Holocaust were both national security policies. Both killing projects were authorized by the highest national leaders, rationalized as being in the service of the highest national interests, and implemented by duly authorized agents of their respective governments. In both cases, the killers regarded themselves not as mass murderers but as patriots performing a grim, necessary (and in the case of actually dropping the bombs, dangerous) task. In both cases, the slaughter of civilians was regarded as an acceptable means of obtaining a valued end.

Finally, neither project would have been possible without the contributions of psychologically normal individuals, many of whom were highly educated, scientifically brilliant, and culturally refined. This comes as no surprise to anyone familiar with the narrative of the Manhattan Project, which developed the atomic bombs that culminated the American strategic bombing campaign against Japan.* But it is also true of the Holocaust, in which members of numerous professions—including medicine, law, and education—played key roles as accomplices and perpetrators. As Franklin H. Littell has observed, "The Holocaust is also to be remembered as a rational program planned, supervised, and justified by professors and Ph.D.s."[46]

Organization of the Book

The remainder of the book is divided into three parts. The four chapters in Part 1 address the general problem of governmental mass killing in the contemporary

*German efforts to develop an atomic bomb also relied upon world-class scientists, most notably physicist Werner Heisenberg. For a detailed story of the German bomb project, see Thomas Powers, *Heisenberg's War: The Secret History of the German Bomb*, New York, Alfred A. Knopf, 1993.

era. Chapter 2 is a survey of mass killing throughout history. In it we evaluate the claim made by some scholars that the twentieth century is the most lethal in history. In Chapter 3 we examine what scholars have written about the concepts of total war and genocide and reveal some of the ambiguities and controversies surrounding these concepts. In Chapter 4 we take a close, critical look at the relationship between genocide and total war. In it we state our own position that genocide and total war do share many important common features and defend this position by examining a number of important commonalities. Part 1 concludes with a chapter that lays out a conceptual framework of psychological, organizational, and scientific-technological factors in terms of which cases of genocide and total war may be comparatively analyzed.

Part 2 presents the comparative analysis of the Holocaust and strategic bombing. Chapter 6 is a summary of the global context of violence that began years before September 1, 1939 (the date of the German invasion of Poland and the conventional starting point of World War II) and that was by no means limited to Nazi genocide and Allied bombardment of cities. Indeed, the chapter details many of the atrocities committed by the Japanese, as well as other participants in the war. In Chapters 7 and 8 we trace the evolution of the two cases of mass killing on which the book focuses—the Holocaust and the Allied strategic bombing campaigns, respectively. Then, in Chapter 9 we compare the Holocaust and the British and U.S. bombing campaigns in terms of a number of psychological facilitating factors. In Chapter 10 we do the same with respect to organizational and scientific-technological factors.

In Part 3, Chapter 11, we summarize the principal conclusions and provide our answer to the question, Was strategic bombing genocidal? Chapter 12 concludes the book with an examination of an important legacy of World War II in general and strategic bombing in particular: the preparations for nuclear war by the United States, the Soviet Union, and other nations. We also examine a number of dangerous trends in the post–Cold War world that point toward future outbreaks of genocidal violence. In the last section in Chapter 12 we explore some ideas concerning what can be done about the problem of governmental mass killing.

Part 1

The Problem of Governmental Mass Killing

Chapter 2

The Historical Ubiquity of Slaughter

History is a bath of blood.

—*William James (1910)*[1]

Both historians of war and scholars of genocide are in agreement with William James's bleak aphorism. For example, British field marshall Bernard Montgomery, who wrote military history from the perspective of a decorated war hero as well as a scholar, asserted that "war has been constant in human affairs since the earliest societies of which there is record."[2*] At the beginning of their book *The History and Sociology of Genocide*, historian Frank Chalk and sociologist Kurt Jonassohn acknowledged the "coarseness and brutality of human existence throughout much of history" and asserted that genocide in antiquity was "a relatively common event."[3]

In this chapter, we examine organized mass killing throughout history in order to document two important trends: first, the tendency of many conflicts to combine features of what we now think of as warfare and genocide, and second, the steadily escalating toll of conflict on both soldiers and noncombatants. The following section provides a sense of the barbarity of pre-twentieth-century conflict through brief vignettes of four illustrative cases. The next section is a survey of two nineteenth-century conflicts—the Napoleonic Wars of 1789–1815 and the American Civil War of 1861–1865—that presaged the total wars of the twentieth century. In the final section we examine the industrialized slaughter of soldiers and civilians in the twentieth century and evaluate claims that the twentieth century is the most murderous in history.

*It is important to note, however, that not *all* social groups or societies have engaged in warfare. For example, anthropologist Robert Dentan described the Semai in twentieth-century Malaya as nonviolent people who would prefer to flee rather than fight. And Margaret Mead described the Arapesh of New Guinea as people virtually without war. On the Semai, see Robert N. Dentan, *The Semai: A Nonviolent People of Malaya,* New York, Holt, Rinehart and Winston, 1968; on the Arapesh, see Margaret Mead, *Sex and Temperament in Three Primitive Societies,* New York, William Morrow, 1963 [1953], pp. 23ff. (We thank James Hayes for these references.)

The Barbarity of Pre-Twentieth-Century Conflict

To illustrate pre-twentieth-century conflicts, we have chosen two from the pre-Christian era: the conquests of the militaristic Assyrians, who ruled a vast empire in western Asia from 800 B.C. through 612 B.C. and the Roman destruction of Carthage in 146 B.C.; and two from the Christian era: the Mongol conquests in the twelfth and early thirteenth centuries, and the Thirty Year's War in Europe during the fifteenth century.

The Assyrian Conquests

Of all the empires that ruled Mesopotamia (in ancient times, the region between the Tigris and Euphrates Rivers), from the Akkadian in 2350 B.C. to the Persian Achaemenian in 550 B.C., none was as ruthlessly militaristic or as blatantly genocidal as the Assyrian (1100–612 B.C.). Incorporating the most advanced military technology of their day—which included an expert cavalry and light, manueverable chariots; siege engines and battering rams for use against enemy cities; and iron weaponry utilized by the most feared infantry in the "civilized" world at that time—the Assyrians easily destroyed a series of early rivals and carved out a monarchy in the upper Tigris valley, which was maintained by the closest thing in ancient times to a professional army.[4]

Sennacherib (705–681 B.C.), one of Assyria's most militarily successful and bloodthirsty warlords, destroyed the fabulous city of Babylon at the same time that he encouraged the growth of the Assyrian city of Nineveh as the chief imperial metropolis. If the following words attributed to him are true, then genocidal intent was certainly behind his orders to sack and burn the city: "The city and its houses, from its foundation to its top, I destroyed. I devastated, I burnt with fire. . . . Through the midst of that city I dug canals. I flooded its site with water, and the very foundations thereof I destroyed."[5]

In this manner, the Assyrians launched terroristic campaigns against their neighbors, which led ultimately to the conquest of not only the whole of Mesopotamia but also Syria, Phoenicia, Israel, Judah, and Egypt. They were unsparingly brutal to captive peoples. In the case of the Jews, the Assyrians wiped out all of the ten northern Hebrew tribes and all but two of the southern ones.[6]

Assyrian sculpture indicates that they valued war as a kind of national industry. Scenes of victorious combat are matched only by scenes of sadistic retribution against defeated foes, including women and children.

The Destruction of Carthage

The destruction of the great naval power of the western Mediterranean, Carthage, by an expanding Roman empire, has been called "one of the bloodiest episodes of ancient history."[7] It provides another example of how war and genocide frequently converged during the classical era. Originally a Phoenician colony, Carthage, or New City, became independent in the sixth century B.C., when Persia overran all of western Asia, including Phoenicia. The Persians moved eastward against Libya and across the sea to Spain, the Balearic Islands, Sardinia, and Sicily. Because Rome was also expanding its commerce, trade, and empire at the same time and in the same general area, it was inevitable that a confrontation between the powers would eventually take place.[8]

It finally did, in Sicily in 264 B.C., in what historians call the First Punic War (264–241 B.C.). There were two such wars before the Roman army was ready to demolish Carthage. In 146 B.C., after the conclusion of the Second Punic War, the Roman Senate decided that Carthage had to be eliminated in order to prevent future conflict. When the Roman army finally conquered Carthage after a three-year siege, its leaders allowed the soldiers to plunder the city. The resulting "total destruction" included burning the city to the ground and slaughtering 150,000 people out of a population of 200,000, with the survivors sold into slavery.[9] After several days of massacre and destruction by the Roman infantry, auxiliary troops were ordered to clean up the mess. According to an eyewitness, they "shoved the dead and those still living in pits in the ground, using their axes and crowbars and shoving and turning them with their tools like blocks of wood or stone. Human beings filled up the gullies. Some were thrown in head down, and their legs protruding from the ground writhed for a considerable while."[10] Finally, the ground was ploughed under and covered with salt.

The Mongol Conquests Under Genghis Khan and Tamerlane

For many, the very name Genghis Khan is synonymous with brutality, and for good reason. During and after his rule, A.D. 1206–1227, the hordes of nomadic Mongol horsemen from central Asia created one of the largest empires in the history of the world, first conquering China, then Persia, then most of Ukraine and Russia, and then Poland and Hungary.

The Mongols were no ordinary nomadic aggressors on the march. They regarded human life as far more expendable than the lives of their horses. In this respect, they were similar to other central Asian invaders of civilized states. Unlike other invaders of Europe throughout history, however, the Mongols under Genghis Khan and his successors despised what they perceived to be the corruption and dissolution of city life to the extent that rather than taking control over conquered cities, they frequently destroyed them without mercy. For example, during their conquest of western Asia, the Mongols demanded the surrender of the caliph of Baghdad. When he refused, in A.D. 1258 the Mongols captured the city, massacred 800,000 inhabitants, and razed the city, bringing the glorious era of Mesopotamian cities, which had begun in the fourth millenium B.C., to a brutal and abrupt end.[11]

Tamerlane, who claimed to be a descendant of Genghis Khan, continued Mongol depredations into the following century, invading India in 1398 and defeating the Turkish army at Ankara in 1402. Historian Arnold Toynbee portrayed Tamerlane as

> a militarist who perpetrated as many horrors in the span of twenty-four years as the last five Assyrian kings perpetrated in a hundred and twenty. We think of the monster who razed Isfarain to the ground in 1381; built 2,000 prisoners into a living mound and then bricked them over at Sabzawar in 1383; piled 5,000 heads into minarets at Zirih in the same year; cast his Luri prisoners alive over precipices in 1386; massacred 100,000 prisoners in Delhi in 1398; buried alive 4,000 Christian soldiers of the garrison of Sivas after their capitulation in 1400; and built twenty towers of skulls in Syria in 1400 and 1401.[12]

The Thirty Years' War

What historians have called "one of the most brutal and destructive wars of which we have record until the twentieth century" originally began in 1618 as a religious conflict between German Protestants and the Roman Catholic rulers of Austria.[13] However, as additional states entered the conflict for political as well as religious motives, the war evolved into a contest for hegemony in Europe. Eventually, the states of Austria, Spain, and Bavaria (the primarily Catholic imperialists) were arrayed against the primarily Protestant forces of France, Sweden, the Dutch republic, and a number of Protestant German states. After 30 years of a complicated course of battles, most of which took place on German territory, the Protestant forces defeated the Catholics, and the Treaty of Westphalia in 1648 brought the war to an end.

During the three decades of war, huge armies on both sides of the conflict plundered the German countryside for food and supplies. As was the case during the ancient years of Assyrian warfare, cities were besieged and their occupants slaughtered. By the end of the war, the population of Germany had declined from approximately 21 million in 1618 to about 13 million in 1648. In the Protestant German state of Bohemia, where the war began and where much of the fighting had raged, 29,000 out of 35,000 villages had been destroyed. Although many millions had fled the fighting, as many as 8 million Germans were killed during the war, of whom "only" about 350,000 were actual soldiers.[14] As military historian Gwynne Dyer observed, "It was a century and a half before there was another war in Europe that caused deaths on anything like the same scale, and fully three centuries—almost down to the present—before civilian losses again outnumbered the military casualties."[15]

The Tide of Violence Ebbs and Flows: The Thirty Years' War to the Twentieth Century

In the aftermath of the Thirty Years' War, a general trend toward more limited warfare developed, although there were many relapses and exceptions. For nearly 150 years, most European wars were fought between relatively small mercenary armies sponsored by absolute monarchs. Killing of noncombatants was significantly curtailed, and the casualty levels among soldiers were reduced, in part to keep the financial burden on the sponsoring monarchs as low as possible. Rather than ending in the annihilation of the loser, wars tended to end in settlements that left the structure of all societies largely intact. However, this respite from total war began to end at the close of the eighteenth century, when the French Revolution and the rise of Napoleon inaugurated an era of wars waged between entire nations.

The French Revolution and Napoleonic Warfare, 1789–1815

Napoleon utilized huge armies of conscripted soldiers, raised by means of the levée en masse on August 23, 1793. The mass armies fielded by France created pressures on its enemies to increase the size of their own forces. However, unlike the revolutionary French, the other nations were reluctant to disrupt the traditional system of paid soldiers, fearing that conscription might precipitate changes in their monarchical regimes. Thus, in order to compete with the French, England, in 1799, was required to institute the world's first national income tax on its citizens to defray the cost of paying for the expanded army.[16]

The effects of conscription spread throughout French society. Large numbers of citizens were obliged to leave their peacetime positions, often for the duration of the war. This had a disruptive effect not only on individuals and families, but also on the overall economy. It meant shortages of certain kinds of skilled workers whose talents were needed for the war effort. In order to harness the energies of the civilian population, a vast program of economic mobilization was undertaken. Citizens were taught how to make muskets and other necessary war materiel, skilled tradesmen converted their shops to produce needed war supplies, and lucrative prizes were offered for scientific inventions of use in the war.

Mass conscription affected not only the degree to which the nation of France as a whole was involved in the war but also the nature of the war itself. Casualties among combatants increased considerably in comparison with the preceding 100 years. As military historian J.F.C. Fuller has noted, "Conscription changed the basis of warfare. Hitherto soldiers had been costly, now they were cheap; battles had been avoided; now they were sought, and however heavy the losses, they could rapidly be made good by the muster-roll."[17] The vastly increased size of the revolutionary French army, which grew with conscription to include 750,000 soldiers, required changes in administration and logistics. The army was broken up into smaller, more mobile units, and long supply lines gave way to "compulsory requisition" of shelter and food, which often entailed officially sanctioned plunder of the contested territory—a practice that had largely been abandoned since the end of the Thirty Years' War.[18]

To maintain the morale of the conscripted soldiers and the support of the citizens at home, government propaganda was widely utilized. Such propaganda, which prominently featured vilification of the enemy nation, raised passions to the point that it became difficult to end the war on a basis that would promote a lasting peace. Fuller emphasized how difficult it was "for a conscripted nation—that is, a nation in arms—a nation fed on violent propaganda, to make an enduring peace."[19]

Following the final defeat of Napoleon at Waterloo in 1815, war-weary states in Europe entered another period of relative peace. In his survey of warfare over the centuries, sociologist Pitirim Sorokin found the overall intensity of war during the nineteenth century to have been exceptionally low.[20] Nations strove to prevent and limit wars through such efforts as the Vienna congresses, which, beginning in 1815, attempted to facilitate peaceful resolution of disputes, and the Rush-Bagot Agreement of 1817, in which the United States and England agreed to limit warships on the Great Lakes. The nineteenth century also witnessed a shift away from the huge national armies raised by conscription and a return to the smaller, professional armies characteristic of the early eighteenth century.

The American Civil War, 1861–1865

Although Europe was relatively peaceful during the first several decades following the defeat of Napoleon, the civil war in the United States had many features associated with what later became known as total war, including the use of conscription to raise vast citizen armies, new weapons technologies, and the growing tendency to regard civilians as legitimate military targets.

As in the Napoleonic Wars, conscription was used to assemble mass armies. Although both the Union and Confederate forces initially relied on volunteers, high losses on the battlefields forced the Confederacy to resort to conscription in 1862. A year later, the Union was obliged to follow suit. During the four years of warfare, more than 1.5 million men served in the Union army and more than 300,000 fought for the Confederacy.[21]

Propaganda was used by both sides to vilify the enemy and to intensify the hatreds between the warring parties. "Like the total wars of the twentieth century," Fuller wrote of the Civil War, "it was preceded by years of violent propaganda, which long before the war had obliterated all sense of moderation, and had awakened in the contending parties the primitive spirit of tribal fanaticism."[22] "This was not a war simply of hostile armies," military historians Richard Preston and Sydney Wise asserted, "but of hostile peoples, in which both sides were equally convinced of the absolute justice of their causes. … For both sides the objective was total. There could be no treaty, no compromises, no argument, no terms except unconditional surrender or separation."[23]

Many new weapons were introduced and tested in the Civil War, including new kinds of cannon, repeating rifles, land and marine mines, armored trains, flame projectors, submarines, and torpedoes—even hot air balloons used for aerial reconnaissance. According to Bernard and Fawn Brodie in their history of the evolution of weaponry, "The American Civil War was a colossal proving ground for improved weapons of all kinds. For the first time the achievements of the industrial and scientific revolution were used on a large scale in war."[24] Such weaponry, particularly the widespread use of the new rifles, resulted in massive death tolls among the soldiers. Of the 144,000 military deaths for which a definite cause was known, the vast majority of personnel (108,000) were killed by bullets, compared with "only" about 12,000 by shell fragments and 7,000 by bayonets and swords.[25] After a Confederate general lost 2,000 of his 6,500 men in a single attack against a Union position, he concluded, "It was not war—it was murder."[26] By the end of the war, more American soldiers had been killed (622,000 battlefield deaths) than was to be the case in World Wars I and II, the Korean War, and the Vietnam war combined.[27]

Economic warfare against civilians, including the northern naval blockade to prevent supplies from reaching southern ports and the practice of plundering and destroying enemy farms and homes, was an important feature of the war, especially in the latter years. Union general W. T. Sherman, for example, defended his scorched-earth campaign in Georgia with statements such as the following: "Until we can repopulate Georgia, it is useless to occupy it; but the utter destruction of the roads, houses and people will cripple their military resources. ... We are not only fighting hostile armies, but a hostile people, and must make old and young, rich and poor, feel the hard hand of war."[28]

The Twentieth Century: An Age of Violence

> The last volume of the *Cambridge Modern History* covering 1898 to the present is entitled *The Age of Violence*—which, considering the not inconsiderable violence of previous eras, is quite a distinction.
>
> —*Barbara Tuchman (1981)*[29]

> It is possible—in my view certain—that in a future perspective this explosion of human lives will be seen as the significant "history" of our period.
>
> —*Gil Elliot (1972)*[30]

As violent and murderous as pre-twentieth-century history has been, our present era has been as bad, or even worse. The bath of blood that William James found in his survey of many past centuries has become an ocean of blood in just a few decades.

The twentieth century, according to political scientist Roger Smith, "is an age of genocide in which 60 million men, women, and children, coming from many different races, religions, ethnic groups, nationalities, and social classes, and living in many different countries, on most of the continents of the earth, have had their lives taken because the state thought it desirable."[31] A partial listing of twentieth-century genocides includes the killing of more than 1 million Armenians by the Turks in 1915; the Holocaust, in which 5 million Jews and 4 million members of other victim groups were killed by the Nazis and their allies between 1939 and 1945; the slaughter of approximately 3 million Ibo tribespeople by other Nigerians between 1967 and 1970; the massacre of as many as 3 million Bengalis by the army of eastern Pakistan in 1971; and the killing of as many as 3 million Cambodians by the Khmer Rouge between 1975 and 1979.[32] An analysis of genocides and closely related forms of mass killing since 1945 found 44 episodes of genocidal violence that, collectively, took the lives of "between seven and sixteen million people, at least as many who died in all international and civil wars in the period."[33]

Just as the twentieth century has been described as an age of genocide, so has it been also labeled "the century of total war."[34] The scourge of warfare has been severe and widespread during the twentieth century. Of World War II—the most destructive war in history—historian of war Robert O'Connell has written: "Even taking into account such notable episodes of slaughter as the Mongol conquests and the Thirty Years' War, it is hard to point to a conflict more brutally fought than World War II, or to combatants more driven by the sheer urge to kill."[35] But World War II was only one, albeit the worst, of more than 200 wars (defined as "any armed conflict including one or more governments, and causing the deaths of 1,000 or more people per year") identified by William Eckhardt between 1899 and 1987.[36] Eckhardt also estimated the death tolls of 471 wars that have occurred since 1700 and arrived at a total of 101,550,000 fatalities.[37] Ruth Sivard, on the basis of Eckhardt's data, noted that "with 12 years to go [as of 1988], this modern century in which we live will account for over 90 percent of the deaths in wars since 1700."[38]

Industrialized Slaughter of Soldiers and Civilians

The advance of industrialization during the twentieth century dramatically affected the nature of warfare by increasing the extent to which national economic resources were exploited for the purposes of war. As the size of armies increased, and as armies became increasingly mechanized, the number of noncombatants needed to keep the army provided with equipment and supplies increased as well. For example, weapons and ammunition were used up in World War I at an astonishing rate. The nineteen-day British bombardment at Ypres in 1917 used 4.3 million artillery shells, which weighed more than 100,000 tons and represented an entire year's production of more than 50,000 armament workers.[39] Under such conditions, much of the adult population tended to be directly or indirectly involved in supporting the war effort. The coordination of the many sectors of the economy required greater centralization of governmental authority for economic planning. As Quincy Wright observed in his monumental book *A Study of War*, "Such a gearing-in of the agricultural, industrial, and professional population to the armed forces requires a military organization of the entire society."[40]

One implication of the extensive involvement of noncombatants in waging twentieth-century war has been a tendency to regard them as legitimate targets for attacks. This tendency, combined with tremendous increases in the lethality of weapons, has caused extreme levels of destruction and death affecting both soldiers and civilians.

In his classic study of the increasing rate of social change during the modern era, sociologist Hornell Hart documented several dimensions of the "accelerating power to kill and destroy." These included a tremendous increase in the killing power of the explosives that can be delivered to their targets. One measure that he used was deaths per ton of explosive. During the German bombing raids on London during World War I, for example, about 3 people were killed for each ton of high explosive bombs dropped. By World War II, the rate had risen precipitously. In the American incendiary bombing raid on Tokyo on March 9, 1945, for example, deaths per ton reached 50. By the end of the war, the invention of the atomic bomb had raised the death toll per ton of explosive even higher, up to "about 10,000 persons killed per ton of normal bomb load for the B-29 that made the raid."[41] Hart concluded his analysis of increased killing power by noting that "the five centuries from 1346 to 1875 saw several times as much increase in explosive power as had been achieved in the previous million years. The 70 years from 1875 to March, 1945, saw several times as much increase in explosive power as the previous five centuries."[42]

World War I offered a stark example of how advances in technology such as machine guns caused appalling casualties among soldiers. Artillery shells—another devastating technology that came into its own on the battlefields of World War I—were fired by the hundreds of millions across the no-man's-land into enemy trenches. According to Richard Rhodes, "The shells … produced the most horrible mutilations and dismemberings of the war, faces torn away, genitals torn away, a flying debris of arms and legs and heads, human flesh so pulped into the earth that the filling of sandbags with that earth was a repulsive punishment."[43]

Raymond Aron noted, "Trench warfare devoured hundreds of thousands of men every year. Stretched across hundreds of miles in frontal combat, the enemy armies slowly used up their men, without either side being able to break through the other front."[44] In the five-month Battle of the Somme in 1916, for example, the British lost over 400,000 men; German losses were equally great.[45] Such large numbers could be replaced only by a system of compulsory service. Thus, the draft was used to raise huge armies. In World War I, conscription enabled Germany to field an army of more than 13 million men. To compete against the massive German army, Great Britain, France, and the United States all resorted to conscription to assemble armies of 5 million, 8 million, and 4.7 million soldiers, respectively.[46]

Poison gas, another technological innovation in World War I, killed or wounded more than 1 million soldiers. The first major use of gas in the war took place on April 22, 1915, near the Belgian town of Ypres, when the German army opened the valves of 5,730 cylinders of liquid chlorine, which then formed a gas that drifted across a four-mile front. As many as 5,000 French-led soldiers were killed, and another 10,000 were wounded in that single episode of gas warfare. Again, to rely on Rhodes's vivid narrative, the victims, "surprised and utterly uncomprehending, staggered out of their trenches into no-man's-land. Men clawed at their throats, stuffed their mouths with shirttails or scarves, tore the dirt with their bare hands and buried their faces in the earth."[47]

It is little wonder, then, that World War I has been described by genocide scholar Richard Rubenstein as a "war of mass death in which massed men were fed for 1500 days to massed fire power so that more than 6000 corpses could be processed each day without letup." Rubenstein went on to state, "When it was over, 10,000,000 soldiers and civilians had been killed and mass death had become an acceptable part of the experience and values of European civilization."[48]

The blunting of psychological and moral sensibilities implied in Rubenstein's statement certainly began long before the hostilities ended and undoubtedly played a role in extending the carnage of war to civilians far removed from the battlefields and trenches. Thus, toward the end of the war, Germany used submarines to sink civilian ships. According to the Germans, the submarine campaign was necessitated by the British naval blockade of coastal cities, which prevented food and other imports from reaching Germany and caused an estimated 800,000 deaths among German civilians as the result of hunger.[49] Bombing of cities, which began early in the war, steadily escalated during its course. As military historian Lee Kennett has noted, "Aerial bombardment, still a novelty in 1914, had become by 1918 a vast undertaking employing hundreds of specially designed aircraft. Early in the war bombing began to reach beyond the actual battlefields of the contending armies, and the distinction between combatant and civilian began to blur."[50]

As we discuss in Chapters 6, 7, and 8, World War II was to prove far more lethal than its predecessor, for soldiers and even more for civilians. There is little doubt that World War I created a psychological and moral climate conducive to the many atrocities that were to be perpetrated during World War II. Holocaust scholar Yehuda Bauer has eloquently expressed this connection:

> World War I was evidence of the massive brutalization of the twentieth century; it was a major new departure in the history of mankind. For the first time in history had mass killing on such a scale taken place between civilized societies. The killing, mutilation and gas poisoning of millions of soldiers on both sides had broken taboos and decisively blunted moral sensitivities. Auschwitz cannot be explained without reference to World War I.[51]

Since the end of World War II, the advance of killing technology has made war even more lethal and destructive. Not only do armies have more "machines of destruction" ready to use against their enemies but those machines are capable of inflicting far greater damage. For example, Richard Gabriel traced the steady expansion of the "zone of destruction"—the area in which soldiers are at high risk of death or injury from enemy guns and artillery—from approximately 5 miles from the front in World War I to about 10 miles during World War II to more than 40 miles from the front by the late 1980s.[52] In many other ways, the lethality of modern combat has dramatically increased in the post–World War II era. These include the number of artillery pieces per division, the range of artillery shells, the accuracy of all types of weapons, the killing power of attack helicopters and attack aircraft, and new types of chemical weapons, to name just a few.[53]

A case in point was the war between Iran and Iraq from 1980 through 1989. Called by Anthony Cordesman and Abraham Wagner "one of the longest and bloodiest conflicts since World War II and ... one of the grimmest wars of attrition in modern times," the Iran-Iraq War featured the use of modern aircraft, ships, and surface-to-surface missiles, as well as chemical weapons and "human waves" of infantry composed largely of young men conscripted into the military forces of their respective nations.[54] During the nearly decade-long war, as many as 1 million people were killed, and an equal number wounded, and approximately 2.5 million people became refugees.[55]

Such "advances" in the technology of killing mean not only higher rates of death and physical injury but also higher rates of psychiatric casualties (a feature of war, Gabriel has argued, that has not been sufficiently appreciated). According to Gabriel, "War is not only becoming more lethal in terms of its ability to kill and maim; it is far more destructive in its ability to drive soldiers mad. Indeed, as the warriors among us improve the technology of killing arithmetically, the power to drive combatants crazy, to debilitate them through fear and mental collapse, is growing at an even faster rate."[56]

The destructive power of modern weapons, combined with the fact that many people are crowded into cities, can mean that even when efforts are made to avoid direct attacks against civilians, many noncombatants may nonetheless be killed or injured. An example is provided by the Persian Gulf War of 1991, in which the United States and about 30 other nations fought against Iraq in order to end the Iraqi occupation of Kuwait and destroy the Iraqi projects to develop and deploy nuclear, chemical, and biological weapons of mass destruction. Despite a U.S. and Allied policy of aiming only at military targets, many people were killed by the sheer destructiveness of the weapons used against strategic targets located in areas heavily populated by civilians. Although the media coverage of the war in the United States emphasized the success of high-technology, precision-guided munitions, they represented only a fraction of bombs dropped. In fact, only 7.4 percent of the 88,500 tons of bombs dropped were precision-guided. The rest, according to Paul Walker and Eric Stambler, were "very destructive conventional weapons."[57] Moreover, the U.S. Air Force, as reported in the *New York Times*, estimated that 70 percent of bombs dropped missed their targets, and presumably, some of them smashed and burned nearby buildings, including homes.[58]

No official U.S. estimate of the number of civilians killed has been announced to date, but one unofficial estimate put the toll at between 5,000 and 16,000 Iraqi civilians killed during the war and an additional 4,000 to 6,000 who died in the months immediately following the war as the result of untreated wounds and a lack of medical attention.[59] So great was the destruction of the capital city, Baghdad, and other cities that a UN report issued in March 1991 described the damage as "near apocalyptic" and stated that Iraq had been moved back to a "pre-industrial age."[60] Further evidence of the toll on civilians was gathered in May 1991 by a medical team from Harvard University that visited several Iraqi cities. It estimated that the destruction of hospital facilities and the general degradation of public services were likely to cause the deaths of tens of thousands of Iraqi infants in the coming months.[61]

The Most Violent Century in History?

In view of the mind-numbing number of wars and genocides and the number of victims during the twentieth century, it is perhaps not surprising that some scholars have concluded that this century is the most murderous in history. Writing of the 110 million victims of man-made death in this century, Gil Elliot asserted: "To set such a figure against the scale of violence in previous times involves the difficulties of comparing like periods and allowing for population increase. However, every attempt to do so shows the twentieth century to be incomparably the more violent period."[62] In this section, we review the work of a number of scholars who have attempted to compare the violence of the twentieth century with earlier periods of history.

Sociologist Pitirim Sorokin, one of the first modern scholars to trace quantitative trends in collective violence over the centuries, estimated the casualties (i.e., both deaths and injuries) of European wars from the eleventh century through 1925 and used population estimates to calculate the number of war casualties per 1,000 in the population for each century in each of the ten European nations under study.[63] He found that the estimated war casualties per 1,000 population during the first 25 years of the twentieth century—54—were considerably higher than in any other entire century (e.g., the war casualties per 1,000 of the population for the twelfth, eighteenth, and nineteenth centuries were 2, 33, and 15, respectively.[64] On the basis of such trends, Sorokin concluded that "*the curse or privilege to be the most devastating or most bloody war century belongs to the twentieth; in one quarter century it imposed upon the populations a 'blood tribute' far greater than that imposed by any of the whole centuries combined*" (emphasis in original).[65] In a later book, in which he extended the scope of his comparative study farther back and forward in time, Sorokin confirmed his earlier results, finding the twentieth century to be "the bloodiest and most belligerent of all the twenty-five centuries under consideration."[66]

Sorokin's conclusions have been supported by the more recent work of William Eckhardt, who continued the effort to quantify the human costs of collective violence. Eckhardt compared the number of wars and the number of war-related deaths from 3000 B.C. through the first half of the twentieth century. For estimates

TABLE 1 War-Related Deaths per 1,000 of the Global Population, by Century, Between A.D. 1000 and A.D. 1950

	Century A.D.									
	11	12	13	14	15	16	17	18	19	20[a]
Global pop. (millions)	320.00	360.00	360.00	350.00	425.00	500.00	545.00	720.00	1,200.00	2,500.00
No. of wars[b]	47.00	39.00	67.00	62.00	92.00	123.00	113.00	115.00	164.00	120.00
War deaths per 1,000 of the global population	.18	.36	1.14	1.43	2.07	3.23	11.21	9.72	16.19	44.37

[a]Eckhardt computed figures only for the first half of the twentieth century.

[b]He defined "war" as "any armed conflict, involving at least one government, and causing at least 1000 civilian and military deaths per year, including war-related deaths from famine and disease" (p. 1 of source).

SOURCE: William Eckhardt. "War-Related Deaths Since 3000 BC. Paper presented to the 1991 annual meeting of the International Society for the Comparative Study of Civilizations, Santo Domingo, Dominican Republic, 1991, p. 7. Used with permission.

of the global population, the number of wars, and the number of people killed in wars during each century, he reviewed a wide range of sources, including world population histories and military histories. Acknowledging the limitations of such data, particularly for earlier centuries, Eckhardt argued that rough estimates are still possible. His findings for the past ten centuries are summarized in Table 2.1.

Summarizing this research, Eckhardt states that "war-related deaths have been increasing over the past 50 centuries. When death estimates were divided by population estimates, this measure was significantly correlated with centuries, so that population growth alone could not explain the increase in war deaths over these 50 centuries. In other words, *war-related deaths were increasing significantly faster than population growth*" (emphasis added).[67] In an earlier study, Eckhardt eliminated the death tolls of World Wars I and II from the estimate of war deaths during the twentieth century and still found that the rate of war deaths has been increasing faster than the rate of population growth.[68]

These studies focused their quantitative historical comparisons on warfare. But what of genocide as another, ostensibly different, form of governmental violence? Unfortunately, the field of genocide studies has not yet produced its counterpart to Sorokin or Eckhardt. Nonetheless, some researchers have suggested that during the twentieth century, the death toll from warfare, as high as it has been, may be significantly lower than the death toll from genocide and genocidal killing. R. J. Rummel, for example, estimated that more than 35 million people "have died in this century's international and domestic wars, revolutions, and violent conflicts" and that more than 100 million have been killed "apart from the pursuit of any continuing military action or campaign," mainly at the hands of "totalitarian or extreme authoritarian governments" in "massacres, genocides and mass executions of [their] own citizens."[69] Similarly, Helen Fein has estimated that genocides between 1945 and 1980 killed more than twice as many people as did wars during the same period.[70]

To end this grim chapter, we simply reiterate that the problem of mass killing has afflicted humankind for many centuries, that many of the "wars" throughout history have had many features in common with genocide, and that there is abundant evidence to support the claim that our present century is the most murderous of all. In the next chapter, we turn to a review of what scholars have written about total war and genocide as two major forms of mass killing.

Chapter 3

The Historiography of Total War and Genocide

Though total war and genocide in the twentieth century have resulted in unparalleled levels of death and destruction, neither concept has been treated systematically within a given historical context. Without a clear presentation of both concepts historiographically—that is, analysis according to individual scholars in different historical periods—total war and genocide remain semantically unfocused and conceptually vague. Thus, it is not surprising that Berenice Carroll noted in her 1968 study *Design for Total War: Arms and Economics in the Third Reich*, that "'total war' is not a single, or 'unit' idea, but an accumulation of separable propositions, sometimes mutually contradictory, which have come to be associated under one term. The history of this composite of ideas remains to be written."[1] Similarly, in his critical review of many definitions of genocide, Ward Churchill concluded, "At the most fundamental level, it may be asserted that we presently lack even a coherent and viable description of the processes and circumstances implied by the term 'genocide.'"[2]

In this chapter, we examine the most provocative and important writing on these two forms of mass killing, beginning with the evolution of the concept of total war, and then turning to the concept of genocide.

The Evolution of the Concept of Total War

> If one side uses force without compunctions, undeterred by the bloodshed it involves, while the other side refrains, the first will gain the upper hand. That side will force the other to follow suit; each will drive its opponent toward extremes, and the only limiting factors are the counterpoises inherent in war.
>
> —*Carl von Clausewitz (1832)*[3]

A precursor to the modern concept of total war was the vision of modern warfare introduced by the Prussian general and military theoretician Carl von Clausewitz in his famous book *On War,* first published in 1832. Clausewitz was deeply influenced by the Napoleonic Wars of the late 1700s and early 1800s, which were far more destructive than any other European war during the 150 years that preceded them. In *On War,* he asserted that during and after the Napoleonic Wars, war "took on an entirely different character, or rather closely approached its true character, its absolute perfection."[4] According to Clausewitz, war is "an act of force to compel our enemy to do our will," and "there is no logical limit to the application of that force." He warned, "To introduce the principle of moderation into the theory of war itself would always lead to logical absurdity."[5] Historians of war Richard Preston and Sydney Wise wrote that "the core" of Clausewitz's teaching is that modern wars tend to become "absolute" and to involve "the full utilization of the moral and material resources of a nation to bring about, by violence, the complete destruction of the enemy's means and will to resist."[6] Similarly, sociologist Hans Speier, in his 1941 article "The Social Types of War," characterized absolute war by "the absence of any restrictions and regulations imposed upon violence, treachery and frightfulness."[7] As earlier examples of absolute wars, Speier mentioned the wars of the ancient Greeks against the barbarians and the wars between Christians and Muslims during the Middle Ages. In the latter case, weapons and methods that were prohibited in conflicts with other Christians were freely employed against the Muslim "heathens."

The conception of absolute war attributed to Clausewitz had a powerful influence on subsequent military officers and strategists. Carroll referred to "succeeding generations of military strategists" who were "hypnotized" by "his idea of 'absolute' war, in which the complete overthrow, or even destruction, of the entire enemy nation is the object, and unlimited effort and violence the means."[8] In "The German Concept of Total War," Speier discerned in the post–World War I writings of German general Erich Ludendorff ("the military dictator of Germany" between the two world wars) a number of assumptions about modern warfare that reflected the influence of Clausewitz. They included the necessity of extending the fighting to the entire territory of the enemy, rather than confining it to the battlefield; the need to involve the whole population in the war effort; the value of propaganda; and the importance of a strong, central authority.[9]

As have other military historians, however, Carroll warned against a simplistic interpretation of Clausewitz on this vital matter. She stressed that Clausewitz's observation of the absolute or total character of much modern war was not a recommendation that wars be waged without restraint. Indeed, he cautioned that the conduct of war should always be guided by political objectives, as in his widely quoted definition of war as "merely the continuation of policy by other means."[10] Most of the actual European wars during the remainder of the nineteenth century were in fact relatively limited both in size and destructiveness.

The term "total war" was not invented until 1918, when a French essayist, Leon Daudet, wrote what Carroll regarded as a relatively unimportant polemical book, *La Guerre Totale* (Total War). According to Carroll, Daudet's book and its title had been inspired by a far more important book by another French writer, Alphonse Seché, published in 1915. Seché's book, *Les Guerres d'Enfer* (The Hellish Wars), which Carroll considered as "the first full appreciation of the subject" of total war, outlined a vision of future wars derived from a consideration of the early months of World War I as well as the Napoleonic Wars of the 1790s.[11] Seché maintained that an era of total war began in August 1793 with the establishment of mass conscription and large national armies by the French government. The expanded size of the army increased the extent to which the entire nation was directly involved in the war, and the increased scale of warfare necessitated extensive mobilization of the economic resources of the warring nation. Thus, Seché wrote that "all means of production, the entire economic plant, must pass instantly into the hands of the State. … All industry, all commerce, all administration not essential for the militarized life of the country will suspend their operations, close their doors. No more superfluities."[12] Moreover, as the economy became integral to the war effort, the "division of forces into combatants and noncombatants" became "outmoded." Seché went on to ask: "The absolute communion of the nation, its total collaboration in the struggle—are these not an excuse for the brutality of enemy troops toward the civilian population?"[13] Seché also emphasized the role of science and industry in making modern wars increasingly destructive. Carroll quoted the following prophetic passages from his book: "With the appearance of scientific positivism, war becomes methodical, implacable, inhuman. … On the battlefield, as in the workshop, machines supplant men. Generosity is not to be expected of a machine. … The country fights with all its men, all its intelligence, all its military and economic equipment, all its gold. … Modern conflicts tend more and more to destruction, to extermination."[14]

The involvement of much of the nation in the war and the extremely high level of death and destruction have been emphasized in more recent definitions and analyses. Gil Elliot, for example, stated, "Total war is (theoretically) based on the complete dedication of a nation's energies to producing the means of war, and the readiness of forces in the field to destroy the enemy's men and materials to the completest extent."[15] Arthur Marwick and his colleagues included the "'nation in arms,' ideological warfare, horrendous battle casualties, and the extermination of civilian populations" as among the key characteristics of total war.[16] The notion of the "nation in arms" refers to the fact, as pointed out by Seché previously, that many economic resources of the nation must be dedicated to the war effort. It also implies that the impact of the war will be felt throughout the society rather than be confined to the soldiers or relatively limited sectors of the economy that design and build war materiel. The ideological nature of total war accounts for the widespread use of propaganda to maintain the morale of soldiers and the support of the civilians by engaging in what Speier termed "a general vilification of the enemy nation."[17] Such vilification of the enemy helps justify another feature of total war—"the conscious abandonment of most if not all restraints" on what and who is targeted and the kinds of weapons that are used.[18]

These features of total war, combined with highly destructive weapons available in a technological age, tend to result in wars in which the very survival of one or more of the belligerents is at stake. Accordingly, strategist Edward Luttwak defined total war as "a war in which at least one party perceives a threat to its survival and in which all available weapons are used and the distinction between 'military' and 'civilian' targets is almost completely ignored."[19] A similar point was made by Richard Hobbs, who stated, "Total war comes about when the object of war is to remove completely the enemy government or even to extinguish any trace of the enemy as a separate nation."[20]

Several analysts have argued that engaging in total war tends to blur the political, military, and moral distinctions between democratic and totalitarian nations. As Raymond Aron asserted bluntly, "Total mobilization approaches the totalitarian order."[21] Such mobilization requires a high degree of centralization and concentration of governmental authority and power.[22]

No recent war, even World Wars I and II, has been completely "total" in the sense that all of the available resources of the combatant nations have been devoted to the conflict or that the destruction of the enemy nation has been complete. Even during World War II, for example, Germany invested "only" 55 percent of its economic resources in the war effort, and the United States never committed more than 45 percent of its gross national product to the war.[23] As Marjorie Farrar noted in her article "World War II as Total War," "The term 'total' is absolute: only total and nontotal exist and degrees of totality are, strictly speaking, illogical. ... Totality can, however, be interpreted as one extreme in a spectrum of possibilities. Distinction is then made among degrees of totality. ... War is total in the degree to which it approaches the extreme of totality."[24]

In general usage, the label "total war" applies to conflicts in which either or both of these conditions—societal mobilization and destructiveness—exist to a sufficiently extreme degree. Frederick Sallagar clarified all this when he suggested that "what characterizes an all-out, or total, war is that it is fought for such high stakes that the belligerents are willing, or compelled, to employ, not *all* weapons they possess, but *any* weapons they consider appropriate and advantageous to them" (emphasis in original).[25]

For example, although poison gas was used by both sides in World War I—causing more than 1 million casualties, of which approximately 90,000 were fatalities—it was not used in the European theater of battle during World War II. (It was, however, used outside of Europe, by the Italians against Ethiopia and the Japanese against China.) Both Hitler and Churchill did direct their military and industrial leaders to prepare for extensive use of chemical weapons in World War II, but fear of retaliation in kind deterred both sides from actually employing them.[26] Nazi Germany, however, was not deterred from using deadly chemicals to exterminate millions of defenseless civilians in massive gas chambers.

For our purposes, a distinguishing feature of total warfare is the assault on civilians, whether as an inadvertent by-product of combat between soldiers (as when distribution of food is disrupted) or as a deliberate policy (as when cities are attacked by incendiary bombs). As noted in Chapter 1, the proportion of civilians injured and killed in wars of the twentieth century has steadily increased over time (leading one cynical scholar to title his book on modern war *Advance to Barbarism*).[27]

World War II and the Birth of Genocide Studies: Raphael Lemkin

> **In the present war … genocide is widely practiced by the German occupation. … Germany is waging a total war … not merely against states but against peoples. For the Germans … war thus appears to offer the most appropriate occasion for carrying out their policy of genocide.**
>
> —*Raphael Lemkin (1944)*[28]

The destruction of groups of people on the basis of their ethnicity, religion, or race was a common feature in the history of humanity for thousands of years before it was defined and conceptualized as genocide in the twentieth century. Etymologically, *genocide* is derived from the Greek *genos,* or tribe, and the Latin *cide,* or killing. Semantically, genocide in its current usage was invented in 1944 by a Polish jurist and victim of the Nazis named Raphael Lemkin in his landmark 1944 book *Axis Rule in Occupied Europe.*[29] The association between "genocide" and "the Holocaust" (invented as a word somewhat later in the late 1950s)* in the minds of many is not surprising when it is considered that Lemkin, a Jew who had lost 70 members of his family to the Nazis, should have established an inseparable bond between his idea of genocide and the bloody excesses of Nazi rule in Europe during World War II.[30] After demonstrating the various "techniques of genocide" Nazi Germany had practiced in the occupied countries through a "concentrated and coordinated attack upon all elements of nationhood," Lemkin wrote:

> The above-described techniques of genocide represent an elaborate, almost scientific, system developed to an extent never before achieved by any nation. … These practices have surpassed in their unscrupulous character any procedures or methods imagined a few decades ago. … Nobody at that time could conceive that an occupation would resort to the destruction of nations by barbarous practices reminiscent of the darkest pages of history.[31]

For those scholars concerned about the proliferation of government-sanctioned mass death in our time, Lemkin's concept of genocide is of unparalleled

*For a discussion of how the term "the Holocaust" became widely accepted and utilized, see Gerd Korman, "The Holocaust in American Historical Writing," *Societas,* Vol. 2, No. 3, Summer 1972, pp. 259–262. In this book, we reserve the term "Holocaust" for the Nazi genocidal campaign against the Jews of Europe.

importance. Nazi German colonization of Europe brings to mind the experience of the Spanish and Portuguese in the New World after Columbus or the Anglo-French imperialist victimization of Asia and Africa in the nineteenth century.* In his book, Lemkin opened the eyes of many to a dark world where peoples and cultures had to struggle for their survival against their own governments or the military machines of neighboring nation-states. Moreover, Lemkin was perhaps the earliest to distinguish genocide, or the deliberate and systematic annihilation of a people by a dominant culture in control of a state, from ethnocide, or the destruction of a culture without necessarily destroying the people.[32]

Lemkin identified eight specific ways in which Hitler implemented his genocidal policy. First, Hitler deprived people of self-determination, which destroyed the very political autonomy of a nation. Second, so-called inferior races were singled out for depopulation by means of segregation from "Aryans" and forced sterilization. Lemkin distinguished this "biological" aspect of genocide from the "physical," by which he meant actual murder. Third, there was the actual physical and biological annihilation of groups identified as races and held to be inferior by Nazi definitions. Economic mass murder was a fourth means, carried out by systematically starving captive peoples and otherwise impoverishing them. Fifth, the Nazis declared a war on religion by confiscating, pillaging, and destroying church property as well as by persecuting the clergy. Sixth, the social order was further undermined by identifying the intelligentsia, who were systematically hunted down and murdered. The totalitarian government, in a seventh approach, dismantled the community's moral principles, that is, its laws and other standards of proper behavior, which were to be replaced by the fascist code. The final assault was upon the total culture. The people were to be deprived of their national identity by means of ethnocide.[33]

Lemkin looked upon the twentieth century as an era of regression to barbarism. He could not separate genocide from war. The same German armies who invaded and conquered Europe also declared internal wars against targeted groups such as Jews, Poles, and Ukrainians. The killing of innocent noncombatants in World War

*The dubious distinction of conducting the earliest recorded mass killings as the result of Western expansion and colonization belongs to the Spanish, whose interaction with the Amerindian societies led to one of the worst examples of human destruction in history. Part of this, no doubt, was not the result of greed, ideological fanaticism, or sadism, but the impact of European microbes, against which the native population had little or no resistance. Spanish missionaries were also exuberant culture-killers who seem to have thrived on the ethnocide of pre-Columbian civilizations. One must not forget the impact of aggressive British migrants to North America, who expanded along a vast frontier at the expense of the indigenous population. There was also the ruthless dispossession and destruction of Australia's indigenous inhabitants, known as Aborigines, as a consequence of British colonization. On the impact of diseases on Amerindian peoples, see William H. McNeill, *Plagues and Peoples,* New York, Anchor Press, 1976, pp. 199–234. On the Australian Aborigines, see Tony Barta, "Relations of Genocide: Colonization of Australia," in Isidor Wallimann and Michael N. Dobkowski, Editors, *Genocide and the Modern Age,* New York, Greenwood Press, 1987, p. 237–251.

II reminded him of "Genghis Khan and Tamerlane ... or Carthage in 140 B.C. ... and the siege of Magdeburg in the Thirty Years War." The Hague Conventions of 1899 and 1907 suggested that a humane attitude might be emerging after "a long period of evolution in civilized society." War was to be "directed against armies, not against subjects and civilians." However, Germany had moved the clock back to barbarism by "waging a war against people."[34]

Lemkin's concerns about the rights and survival of human beings did not begin with the Nazi invasion of Europe. He was already an activist in 1933, when he proposed to an international conference in Madrid that "attacks on national, ethnic and religious groups should be made international crimes and that the perpetrators of such crimes should be liable to trial."[35] In that year, Jews were being deprived of their rights of German citizenship by Hitler, and to the east Ukrainian peasants were being deliberately starved to death by Stalin in a man-made famine.[36]

Before World War II, the League of Nations had turned a deaf ear to Lemkin's proposals. After World War II, the United Nations General Assembly passed a resolution on December 9, 1948, which clearly defined genocide and declared such acts as those described by Lemkin crimes under international law. Lemkin's idea of genocide became embodied in the Convention on the Prevention and Punishment of the Crime of Genocide, which was adopted by the UN formally in 1951 and declared the destruction of racial, religious, and ethnic groups illegal. However, the UN refused to extend the convention's definition of genocide to include political groups. As genocide scholar Leo Kuper observed years later, the political category was strongly resisted by many member states because of their "anxiety that the inclusion of political groups in the Convention would expose nations to external interference in their internal affairs."[37]

Unfortunately, Lemkin's struggle to prevent genocide, or, in the event that it did take place, to punish those responsible, did not succeed. There were many reasons the United Nations would not, or could not, deal with total war and genocide around the world. One important reason is the fact that some member states perpetrated attacks on their own citizens. Sri Lanka, India, Indonesia, Cambodia, Uganda, Nigeria, and Sudan are among those states in the post–World War II period that have slaughtered members of groups within their borders.[38] It was highly unlikely that so many members of the United Nations would either declare themselves criminals or punish themselves.

The Evolving Concept of Genocide: Gil Elliot and Richard Rubenstein

Even though cases of lethal violence against people were proliferating in the wake of decolonization and during the Cold War, social scientists generally ignored genocide as a subject for serious scholarly research. Not until 1972, when Gil Elliot published his *Twentieth Century Book of the Dead,* was the Lemkin idea of the inseparability of war and genocide resurrected, elaborated upon, and made the central focus of an ambitious contemporary world history of governmental mass killing.[39] Lemkin had spoken of war and genocide in global terms, but, empirically, his frame of reference remained Europe during World War II and particularly the Nazi Holocaust. Elliot's painstaking research on "man-made deaths" took him back in time to World War I and across the entire planet, where the grim death play of victims and victimizers was reenacted in varying geocultural contexts.

As did Lemkin, Elliot saw little difference between total war, that is, lethal violence directed at the innocent civilians of the enemy nation, and genocidal violence directed at a group of innocent civilians who have been declared enemies by the governing elite within a nation-state. In war, the enemy is often composed of individuals who were seized by conscription from their everyday lives and sent to the trenches to kill or be killed. Using World War I as an example, Elliot noted that

> the war machine, rooted in law, organization, production, science and technical ingenuity, with its product of six thousand deaths a day over a period of 1,500 days, was the permanent and realistic factor, impervious to fantasy, only slightly altered by human variation ... its function ... to destroy every organic thing ... man, a tree, a famous regiment, a closely-knit platoon, a strategic concept.[40]

Another important contribution to a global perspective on genocidal violence was made in 1975 by Richard L. Rubenstein in *The Cunning of History: The Holocaust and the American Future,* a series of essays dealing largely with the Jewish Holocaust under Hitler but in a perspective that was refreshingly comparative. Like Elliot, Rubenstein emphasized that in World War I "civilians were taken out of their normal occupations, supplied with weapons of unprecedented destructiveness and despatched to battle fronts."[41] Also, because the German, British, and French generals were strategically committed to "exterminating as many of the enemy as possible" and, in the process, sacrificing their own troops without mercy, Rubenstein concluded that "a giant step was taken towards the death camps of World War II."[42]

Rubenstein was among the first of the Holocaust scholars to acknowledge that the Turkish massacres of Armenians during World War I constituted "the first full-fledged attempt by a modern state to practice disciplined, methodically organized genocide."[43] He also compiled a list of genocidal events in the twentieth century that, whether intended or not, represented an extension of the Lemkin idea that genocide thrives best in conditions of total war and totalitarianism. Thus, Rubenstein cited the Sino-Japanese War of 1904 as foreshadowing World War I in the needless way both sides sacrificed human life to achieve illusive tactical gains. In his discussion of the Spanish civil war of 1936–1939, Rubenstein showed how human beings were treated like guinea pigs for the testing of modern military technology.[44] He exposed Stalin as a mass murderer before and during World War II, suggesting that totalitarianism of the left was as productive of genocide as that of the right.[45] Western strategic bombing and the American atomic bombing of Japanese cities were also included in his list of "twentieth century mass slaughters."[46] Therefore, concluded Rubenstein, "the Holocaust cannot be seen as an isolated and unique event." He went on to write that the Holocaust must be placed "within the context of the phenomenon of twentieth century mass death; never before have human beings been so expendable."[47]

In 1983, Rubenstein published *The Age of Triage: Fear and Hope in an Overcrowded World,* which was among the very best analytical and historical treatments of the preconditions and causes of genocide available up to that time. The work addressed the plight of the millions of human beings who had become a redundant population.[48] This category included unwanted minorities forced to migrate by their governments, refugees who managed to flee their unreceptive homelands, and the legions of displaced persons who spent their homeless existence in makeshift camps across endless frontiers leading nowhere. Because all these categories of what Rubenstein called "superfluous people" lacked the basic rights of national citizenship, they became vulnerable to national programs of mass killing.

Rubenstein argued that processes inherent in modernization—especially rationalization, or the application of rational (reasonable) principles to all fields of human endeavor; secularization, or the repudiation of religious influences on society and culture; and the Faustian ethic, or the "sense of mastery over nature and things"—created a situation in which whole segments of a population could become redundant and superfluous and, therefore, vulnerable to policies that called for their segregation, expulsion, or extermination.[49] Of critical importance to Rubenstein was how capitalism, technological development, and industrialism depersonalized and dehumanized relationships between elites and the masses of people who were subject to their leadership.

The Age of Triage offered several case studies that show how modernity and the birth of nation-states marginalized groups within a larger society by depriving them of their former means of livelihood and style of life, alienating them by enacting discriminatory policies, and then either forcing them out of the country or targeting them for extinction. Among the cases most effectively presented along these lines are the Irish famine of 1846–1848, the Armenian genocide of 1915–1917, the persecutions of Jews in nineteenth-century Eastern Europe and Russia, and Stalin's collectivization program in Ukraine in 1932–1933. Thus, England used starvation during the Irish famine to consolidate holdings at the expense of the native peasantry in order to maximize productivity and earn greater profits. The Armenians, as portrayed by Rubenstein, were the victims of the effort by the Young Turks to achieve ethnic homogenization throughout the Anatolian heartland, with World War I providing a perfect opportunity to carry out genocide as a strategic necessity. Rubenstein traced the anti-Semitic outbreaks in Europe back to the fact that Jews, who had played an important function as financiers and small businessmen in the precapitalist era, were being displaced and rendered superfluous in these areas during the nineteenth century. As for Stalin's bloody collectivization program in Ukraine, Rubenstein argued that the objective was not only consolidation under the state but also the utilization of grain for export to earn hard currency with which to industrialize the country. Ukrainian farmers and their families, rich and poor, paid dearly for the Soviet industrial revolution.

The Irish famine is Rubenstein's most original and provocative case in point, both in the sense of social triage during a natural catastrophe and as a precursor of twentieth-century genocide. The famine, which was caused by a potato blight that wiped out the principal food source for the Irish peasants, offered Thomas Malthus, the famed demographer who worked on the relationship between population growth and resource availability, an opportunity to test his theory under the most optimal conditions. Malthus, a priest in the Church of England, believed with the social Darwinists that the survival of the fittest was an expression of God's perfect wisdom. In his 1798 "Essay on the Principle of Population," Malthus argued that Providence ordained that "population should increase much faster than food."[50] The Irish poor were, in the eyes of Malthus, those whom Providence deemed unfit to live. According to Malthus, the poor multiplied without contributing anything positive to society, and in times of natural disaster, keeping them alive only drained the community's available resources, "leading to general scarcity and misery."[51] Malthus thus opposed the use of public relief funds to feed the starving Irish.

The Irish famine also brought into prominence Sir Charles Edward Trevelyan, who was placed in charge of the Irish relief effort. Trevelyan is, for Rubenstein, the ideal "proto-Eichmann," or that perfect embodiment of bureaucratic virtuosity with which we have become so familiar within the history of Nazi Germany's attempt to exterminate the Jews. (Adolf Eichmann was a principal bureaucrat in the process of transporting the Jews to the death camps.) According to Rubenstein, "We in the twentieth century have learned that a competent bureaucrat, skilled in the repression of feeling, incorruptibly committed to the performance of his official duties, is often capable of doing extra-ordinary harm to masses of human beings with an undisturbed conscience. Trevelyan was such a man."[52] Under Trevelyan during the years 1846–1848, Ireland lost 2.5 million people out of a total of 9 million—half that number through emigration to Canada and the United States and half through death from starvation.[53] "Trevelyan was not a Hitler," Rubenstein suggested, ordering the direct mass murder of the Irish, but he "knowingly committed himself to a policy the effect of which was to condemn them to death."[54] Trevelyan saw in the potato blight an "all-wise Providence" at work that was solving "the problem of Ireland's imbalance between population and food."[55]

Sociology Confronts Genocidal Killing: Irving Louis Horowitz and Helen Fein

In 1976, with the publication of *Genocide: State Power and Mass Murder,* Irving Louis Horowitz became one of the first sociologists to study genocide as a subject of serious scholarly attention in the social sciences. He began with the observation that there was too much systematic destruction of human beings in our century to ignore genocide.[56] Horowitz deplored the way his colleagues consistently avoided research into the realities of governmental killing.[57]

Of paramount importance in any organized attempt at destroying a group of humans, according to Horowitz, is the role of the state. A ruling elite that dominates the state utilizes power to annihilate a less powerful group. It need not be the numerical majority seeking to eliminate a numerical minority; South Africa has demonstrated quite the opposite as also being a likely possibility. Horowitz suggested that totalitarian states are more apt to commit genocide than democratic ones because so much power is already concentrated in the hands of a ruling elite that can easily manipulate the means of state control to wipe out an alleged enemy of the state. He readily acknowledged, however, that democracies have committed genocides abroad as imperialists. The British, Dutch, French, and Belgians have all been guilty of the most outrageous atrocities outside their own borders.

On a deeper level, Horowitz dismissed ideology as an adequate guide in predicting genocides because even though, for example, Germany and Italy both subscribed to fascism during World War II, they were poles apart in their attitudes toward anti-Semitism and the Final Solution. This mode of reasoning prompted Horowitz to construct a typology of societies according to how receptive they have been over time to tolerating pluralism and dissent, on the one hand, and their proclivity for evil, on the other.

Horowitz distinguished eight types of societies, arranged along a continuum with maximum social control on one end and complete tolerance on the other. Thus, a society can be *genocidal,* resolving problems by destroying a group; *deportation-oriented,* forcing the group to migrate; *incarceration-oriented,* imprisoning as many members of the group as possible; *torture-prone,* resorting to inflicting extreme forms of bodily and mental harm on the victims; *harassment-prone,* impeding a group's ordinary lifestyle and freedom of movement by a persistent series of annoyances; *shame-oriented,* tending to humiliate or disgrace the group; *guilt-prone,* inculcating in the group being persecuted a sense of collective self-reproach; *tolerant,* believing in the live-and-let-live policy characteristic of pluralist societies; or finally, *permissive,* protecting civil liberties and tolerating dissent.

As examples, Horowitz selected Germany and Uganda as genocidal and Cuba as a deportation society for having forced 1 million out of its 8 million people into exile after Castro's communist revolution in 1959. Brazil was seen by Horowitz as a torture society because its white citizens have been victimized by the state but generally have not been killed in the process. The indigenous people of Brazil, however, have been victims of genocide in much the same way that Native Americans suffered deprivation and death as a result of resettlement and expropriation of land. Shame and guilt are very close in China, Horowitz argued, because the government has tried to rehabilitate its dissenters through self-recognition of personal flaws—that is, shame—and the internalization of guilt. Great Britain was Horowitz's choice for an example of the permissive society.[58]

Of immense importance historiographically is a point raised later by Horowitz in his 1987 article "Genocide and the Reconstruction of Social Theory: Observations on the Exclusivity of Collective Death." This concerns his reaction to the question of whether there is or has been a genocide outside of the Jewish experience during the Nazi Holocaust. According to Horowitz, many Jewish scholars who identify closely with Jewish culture view their own Holocaust as the only true genocide because the Nazis aimed at exterminating all Jews simply because they were Jews. The victims were guilty of no crime other than being Jewish.[59] He suggested that Jews must learn to share their genocide with others who have suffered, such as Armenians and Cambodians. Ethnocentrism cannot be excused simply because people are survivors of a genocide. "I do not wish to deny Jewish victims of the Nazi Holocaust the uniqueness of their experience," wrote Horowitz, "but genocide is a process."[60] The twentieth-century landscape of history is littered with the victims of genocides and genocidal wars. Cambodia is a "holocaust" because, according to Horowitz,

> Those who share a holocaust share a common experience of being victims of the state's ruthless and complete pursuit of human life-taking without regard to individual guilt or innocence. It is punishment for identification with a particular group. … All too many people—Jews, Cambodians, Armenians, Paraguayans, Ugandans—have shared a similar fate for victims to engage in divisive squabbles about whose holocaust is real or whose genocide is worse.[61]

If Horowitz was the first major sociologist to assert that governmental mass killing is a subject worthy of study in his discipline, Helen Fein was the first sociologist to conduct serious monographic research on a specific genocide and to publish her results in a book. Fein's innovative 1979 book *Accounting for Genocide: National Responses and Jewish Victimization During the Holocaust,* although asking many of the same questions raised by Horowitz, provided different answers derived from years of intensive empirical study.[62] Like Horowitz, she refused to be consumed by a single-minded interest in the Holocaust but preferred instead the global approach to genocide with special interest in Armenia and the Soviets in Afghanistan. Her sustained interest in genocide in a comparative perspective, the sociology of genocide, and the theory of genocide were all neatly integrated in a book-length article published in *Contemporary Sociology* in 1990.[63]

Fein had no quarrel with Horowitz's definition of genocide as "organized state murder."[64] In *Accounting for Genocide* she also expressed interest in the process of excluding the Jews, Armenians, and others from what she eloquently labeled "the sanctified universe of obligation—that circle of people with reciprocal obligations to protect each other whose bonds arose from their relation to a deity or sacred source of authority."[65] For centuries, noted Fein, European Jews lived in constant fear of pogroms by Christians in the same way Armenians in the Ottoman Empire feared for their lives from collective acts of terrorism by Muslim Turks and Kurds. But Fein did not believe that genocides in our century are "simply the culmination of earlier traditions of collective violence."[66] To her, the rise of nationalism, totalitarianism, and modern warfare are all important contributing factors.

Like Horowitz, Fein addressed the relationship between specific societies and their varying propensities to commit genocide. From her own empirical work on the Jews of Europe, she asked why it was that some nation-states helped the Nazis eradicate the Jews and why others resisted these efforts. Why did the people of Austria, Poland, Estonia, Latvia, and Lithuania zealously participate in the Holocaust, whereas those of Italy, Holland, Denmark, and Bulgaria helped the Jews escape their fate? Horowitz placed societies ahistorically in a continuum from those blatantly genocidal to those that were permissive on the opposite end. The problem is that, historically, we find Bulgaria, for example, helping the Jews in the World War II period but committing ethnocide against its own Turkish citizens during the subsequent communist period.[67] Fein, who is much less of a rigid typologist and more of a historical relativist, discovered that the most anti-Semitic states were all in central and eastern Europe, that they developed late as nation-states, that they were exceedingly pluralistic, and that among the most visible newcomers in the 1890–1914 period were the Jews.[68] The data convinced her that "nationalism is the problem. New genocides occur among new nations. The dynamics of tribalism, like those of anti-Semitic agitation, are inexorably related to national development and ethnic conflicts. New nationalisms instigate new and previously suppressed groups to contest for power. They try to obtain a monopoly or quota of property and status through the state, using status-group politics.[69]

In the final analysis, Fein came to believe that genocide is largely an internal affair between the victim group and the state. As for the relationship between war and genocide, in her view, war was simply a pretext or a fitting opportunity for a Hitler to carry out his genocide against the Jews. Thinking also about the Armenians, Fein concluded that war reduced the deterrents against genocide because it "obscured the visibility of such action."[70] The perpetrators, she went on to argue, "invent post facto justifications of the program, accusing the victims of aiding the enemy, betraying them, or causing the war."[71]

War and Genocide as Global Phenomena: Leo Kuper

The publication of Leo Kuper's *Genocide: Its Political Use in the Twentieth Century* in 1981 represented another major advance in the field because, for the first time, episodes of state-induced mass murder in the Third World—especially those in

Africa—were depicted, analyzed, and cataloged in a very sensitive and scholarly manner.[72] More than anyone else before him, Kuper had a truly cosmopolitan outlook on peoples who had suffered from state terrorism and the murder of innocents. After him, it was difficult for anyone writing in the field to remain oblivious to genocides taking place around the world. Kuper was born in South Africa and practiced law there until World War II. Through documents available at the UN, which he could read with the eyes of a lawyer and to which he responded with the moral indignation of a social activist, Kuper immersed himself in the grim realities of decolonization.

The fact is that to anyone who lived through the 1970s with his or her mind open to the incredible atrocities being committed by governments across the globe, genocide could no longer be identified solely with the Nazi Holocaust, either from the point of the Jews being the chosen people to suffer or as an exclusive paradigm for genocides past and present. There were new Hitler and Stalin types to cope with, such as Mao Tse-tung of China, Idi Amin of Uganda, and Pol Pot of Cambodia, all of whom used the now-familiar agencies and instruments of state oppression and death such as the secret police and the death squads.

Kuper had to redefine genocide in a world where socially created famine and massacre had become common experiences and where the imposition of national unity on a pluralistic society only intensified lethal violence. The "wide range of genocide in the twentieth century [has taken] many forms," wrote Kuper.[73] It has happened to religious, racial, and ethnic groups; it has accompanied colonialism and colonization but was no stranger to the process of decolonization. It appeared in struggles for power but was also a consequence of a ruling elite's decision to wipe out a defenseless group. Hunters and gatherers or so-called indigenous populations have been targeted for genocide, but so have city people. We tend to associate it with modernization, but it is also present in the premodern context, where the instruments of torture and death are crude but effective. Nevertheless, as do other genocide scholars, Kuper believed that the "major arena for contemporary genocidal conflict and massacre is ... in the sovereign state."[74] And as Helen Fein had discovered in eastern Europe, Kuper now discovered in Africa that "genocide is partly a phenomenon of the plural society."[75]

Behind Kuper's effort to incorporate into the category of genocide an ever-widening variety of events embodying the intent to destroy human life is a dedicated activist career aimed at getting the United Nations to punish criminals, including heads of state, who engage in genocidal killing. Kuper was more concerned with the prevention of genocide or the punishment of those who perpetrate it than he was with playing the game of definition. To counter critics who may find his selection of genocides too all-inclusive, Kuper made use of the concept of genocidal massacre. He wrote: "I hope ... that the inclusion of genocidal massacre will reduce controversy over the selection of cases, so that the human concern for the prevention of genocide may prevail over the almost insuperable problem of precision in classification."[76] We shall examine the concept of genocidal massacre in some detail in the following chapter.

Kuper was, in many ways, Lemkin's true successor. As an activist, Lemkin worked to get the United Nations to formally declare itself against genocidal crimes; Kuper, decades later, tried to get the UN to actually carry out its mission. Kuper conveyed deep bitterness and anger with the world's only international forum supposedly empowered to expose and redress violations against human rights, arguing that the UN has been rendered impotent by member nation-states, each pursuing its own narrow self-interest. He painstakingly documented how the UN did nothing to prevent the millions of deaths resulting from genocide in places such as Bangladesh (1971–1972), Uganda (1972–1979), Cambodia (1975–1979), and East Timor (1975–).[77]

The ideas and manifestations of nationalism and territorial sovereignity have been held by the UN member states to be virtually sacrosanct. Lemkin's enormous struggle has not yet resulted in the protection of potential victim groups. "The United Nations provides no protection against genocide," argued Kuper. Indeed, "the Commission on Human Rights, though vested with a primary responsibility, actually condones the crime by delay, evasion and subterfuge." The commission "protects its fellow rulers, as a club or clique might protect its delinquent members."[78] In the following passage, Kuper both indicts the UN for complicity in the murder of millions of people and reflects on how they have been destroyed in the name of nationalism and the sovereign State:

> And one has to ask whether the slaughter of millions in Bangladesh, Biafra, the Sudan and now in Eritrea can possibly be justified by the interests of the Territorial State in the relatively unrestrained exercise of its internal sovereignty and in the preservation of the domains it has conquered or inherited? Or is there a need for the United Nations to abandon a dehumanized scale of values which effectively condones the sacrifice of human victims to the Territorial State?[79]

The Psychosocial Dimension of War and Genocide: Israel W. Charny and Robert Jay Lifton

Curiously enough, even though genocide as a global phenomenon was certainly terrifying from a psychiatric aspect, it received virtually no serious attention throughout most of the twentieth century. Then in 1982, an Israeli psychotherapist, Israel W. Charny, published *How Can We Commit the Unthinkable? Genocide: The Human Cancer,* in which he utilized an immense fund of scholarly sources, including recent studies on victimology. In spite of the fact that widely known Holocaust survivor Elie Wiesel wrote the introduction to the book and argued that the Holocaust could not possibly be compared with other genocides, Charny assumed a universalist posture based both on moral conviction and on scientific observation and research. In Charny's view, all peoples and cultures share alike the potential for doing good or evil. In Charny's own words,

> Everywhere I looked in history, it was the same. The Germans were essentially the same as all peoples—and ultimately so were the Jewish people. None of us are im-

> mune from the danger of possibly becoming mass killers, and none of us are entirely lacking in humanity and decency. Whatever it is that makes people monstrous destroyers is somehow potentially in all of us. The seeds of the cure, it seemed to me, were also potentially in all of us.[80]

After surveying mass killings since the Crusades, Charny expressed amazement at "man's bizarre destructiveness everywhere on the planet."[81] Charny's quest was for the "underlying rhythms, patterns, and meanings within the human mind, individually and collectively, that make it possible for us human beings to be drawn to the worst possible side of ourselves."[82]

One of Charny's most significant findings was that perpetrators are not recruited from the mentally ill in or out of institutions but from everyday "normal" people. Nazi bureaucrat Adolf Eichmann was pictured by Charny as a "normal" man embarrassed by sexual and emotional themes who sought to "reduce life to order, nonmovement, nonpassion so that all life would be controlled."[83] Like many of the Nazi bureaucrats, Eichmann saw himself as doing his job faithfully. He and his peers were ambitious, loyal, and strongly nationalistic. They saw themselves as loyal, patriotic citizens and loving fathers who did nothing improper or illegal.

To Charny, genocide, or "human destructiveness," is a "cancer of human experience" not so different from the dreaded disease that haunts "the physical existence of humans."[84] Quite possibly, speculated Charny, "physical cancer is ever present in a healthy organism," and under certain conditions, it breaks out of its innocuous and dormant state "to take over and swamp the healthy cell structure."[85] Charny went on to argue that the presence of cancer in each of us at all times suggests that the seeds of death are an integral part of human life. So long as we can maintain a balance between life and death, we can live healthy, "normal" lives. We have to learn to live with death in life and to build, pace, and channel our basic energy, which is always intense and volatile. When we defy our "pathetic limitations" and our energy process explodes with demonic fury, we get "Hitler and Vietnam: a rage against our impotence and a defiance against our animal conditions." We get genocides: "If we don't have the omnipotence of gods we can at least destroy like gods."[86]

Perhaps more than any other scholar in the field of genocide studies, Charny has dedicated himself to building a solid interdisciplinary network among scholars. He has edited three volumes of *Genocide: A Critical Bibliographical Review* in order to promote this endeavor.[87] He was also among the chief organizers of the first international conference on the Holocaust and other cases of genocide held in Tel Aviv in 1982. An institute and internationally circulated newsletter dealing with the Holocaust and genocide studies resulted from the conference.

Israel Charny came to genocide studies from psychology and psychotherapy; Robert Jay Lifton came to the field from a background in psychiatry and the synthetic field of psychohistory. (Psychohistory, according to Lifton, involves the "psychological study of contemporary or recent historical events" and combines "a depth-psychological approach with full intellectual immersion into the historical era studied.")[88] Beginning in 1961, with his first book, *Thought Reform and the Psychology of Totalism,* which explored brainwashing in communist China, Lifton has carefully studied the relevant testimonies of people who have survived mass violence, as well as those who contributed to such violence.[89] Subsequent books explored survivors of the Hiroshima atom bomb, the Chinese Cultural Revolution, American veterans of the Vietnam War, and Nazi doctors involved in the Holocaust.[90]

In all of these works, Lifton investigated what he called "shared themes," or psychological characteristics of particular groups who had participated in genocidal acts either as victims or victimizers.[91] Although acknowledging his debts to Freud and Erik Erikson, Lifton has been far more concerned than either scholar with the reality of death and the need to come to terms with it, both on an individual and collective level. During times of pervasive historical insecurity and crisis, in which death anxiety is exacerbated, people are often tempted to follow a charismatic leader with an ideology that promises relief from insecurity and restoration of both national greatness and personal well-being. Often, an important aspect of such an ideology is the identification of an enemy, within either the society or another nation, who is blamed for the troubles. Victimization of the enemy can become a means of attempted personal and societal salvation. For both individuals and entire societies, violence and victimization may be a means of attempting to restore a lost or threatened belief system that protects against death anxiety.[92]

In 1990, Lifton published, with Eric Markusen as co-author, *The Genocidal Mentality: Nazi Holocaust and Nuclear Threat.* In *The Genocidal Mentality,* with the Holocaust as a paradigm for what is most evil and destructive in our era, Lifton and Markusen compared the psychological and moral dimensions of the nuclear threat with certain forms of German behavior during the Nazi period.[93] Lifton and Markusen argued that earlier ideological considerations that divided a free world from a totalitarian world became blurred after World War II when governments in both camps decided to stockpile and deploy weapons with nuclear warheads. Reliance on the threat of nuclear war as the foundation for national security led to the construction of genocidal systems. "A genocidal system," contended the two authors, "is not a matter of a particular weapons structure or strategic concept so much as an overall constellation of men, weapons, and war-fighting plans which, if implemented, could end human civilization in moments and the greater part of human life on the planet within days or even hours."[94]

The Lifton-Markusen book demonstrated that war and genocide have become the Siamese twins of governmental lethal violence in the twentieth century. The nightmarish world depicted in *The Genocidal Mentality* is not about the "other's evil empire" but about ourselves, the so-called "normal" people, and about how twentieth-century modernization has brought us to the brink of self-destruction.

We are no less sick than were the Germans under the Nazis, and we use psychological mechanisms such as dissociation to live with the terror that has become an integral part of twentieth-century existence.

Genocide in World History: Frank Chalk and Kurt Jonassohn

In 1990, another important book on genocide appeared. Frank Chalk, historian, and Kurt Jonassohn, sociologist, published *The History and Sociology of Genocide,* which contained the first systematic attempt in print to present major case studies of genocides all across the world and from ancient times to the present. Chalk and Jonassohn acknowledged their debt to Lemkin and stated explicitly in their introduction that their book's main purpose was to use the "historic and comparative aproach to identify social conditions and situations in which genocide is likely to occur … as a first step in the prevention of future genocides."[95]

The differences between the work of Lifton and Markusen and that of Chalk and Jonassohn—both acknowledging indebtedness to Lemkin's profound legacy and both anxious to contribute to the prevention of future genocides—are, perhaps, more significant than the similarities. A primary difference is that however much Chalk and Jonassohn deplore war, they belong to the school that distinguishes genocide sharply from war. According to Chalk and Jonassohn, "Genocide is a form of one-sided mass killing in which a state or other authority intends to destroy a group, as that group and membership in it are defined by the perpetrator."[96] For them, the one-sidedness of the killing excludes "casualties of war, whether military or civilian" from the category of genocide because "neither side is defenseless."[97] We return to this issue in the next chapter.

The History and Sociology of Genocide was designed primarily as a collection of documentary sources—over two dozen—demonstrating that genocides have been with us from the genesis of civilizations as recorded and reflected in the earliest extant literature. Their first case, from antiquity, concerned the fate of the Trojans as reported in Homer's *Iliad.* While on the battlefield during the siege of Troy, Agamemnon observes that Menelaus seems reluctant to kill the enemy. He tells him: "My dear Menelaus, why are you so chary of taking men's lives? No, we are not going to leave a single one of them alive, down to the babies in their mothers' wombs—not even they must live. The whole people must be wiped out of existence and none left to think of them and shed a tear."[98] The Chalk and Jonassohn book was innovative because it went against the tradition of looking at world history as being simply a matter of inevitable progress from savagery to civilized states. Also, in no other book had anyone juxtaposed such diverse cases of genocide as the destruction of Carthage by the Romans, the Mongol invasion of Eurasia, the European witch-hunt, the annihilation of indigenous peoples on the American and Australian frontiers, the massacre of Armenians by Turks and Kurds, the massacre of Ukrainians by Russians, of Jews by the Nazi Germans, of Bengalis by the Pakistanis, of Cambodians by other Cambodians, and so on.

Chalk and Jonassohn were among the first to produce extensive documentation of genocide as a cross-cultural, cross-national, universal human problem. And they were pioneers in the field with their typology of genocide based on such a widely comparative, historical survey. From their historical review, they classified genocides primarily according to the motive of the perpetrator:

Type 1: to eliminate a real or potential threat;
Type 2: to spread terror among real or potential enemies;
Type 3: to acquire economic wealth; [or]
Type 4: to implement a belief, a theory, or an ideology[99]

Type 1 appears to have been the motivation behind the earliest genocides on record. The obliteration of Melos by the Athenians in 478 B.C. is offered as a case in point. The second type may go back to the Assyrians, who "probably deserve credit for realizing that the creation of terror is far more efficient [than outright slaughter] as well as effective."[100] Genghis Khan and the Mongols of the early thirteenth century were also adept at the use of terrorism as a form of psychological warfare. They expected surrender and, if disappointed, promised extinction. Type 3, genocide for economic gain, is one of the most universal forms of genocide from earliest recorded history to the more recent European expansion into America, Australia, Africa, and Asia, which left in its wake the destruction of entire peoples, cultures, and civilizations. The fourth type of genocide, which is perpetrated on behalf of an idea, is also, according to the editors, very old. Through the centuries, people have killed for Christ or Allah, for Stalin or for Mao, or for the purity of the Aryan idea of race. Even the burning of women as alleged witches in sixteenth- and seventeenth-century Europe to protect society from demonic witchcraft seems illustrative of type 4.

Although they concluded from their historical survey that there is very little new in genocide under the sun, they did stress that the ideological type "has increased dramatically in the twentieth century."[101] Essentially, however, Chalk and Jonassohn have concluded from their historical research that it is continuity of genocide for various motives that is more significant than any changes in how it has been perpetrated.

Chalk and Jonassohn have rendered an enormous service by countering the narrow, ethnocentric view of particular genocides through their portrayal of the phenomenon of genocide in comparative and global perspective. Such a perspective forces the scholar and student into new paths of logic and methodology. It calls into question claims of utter uniqueness of specific genocides. How can one argue, for example, that the Holocaust was completely unique unless it is carefully compared with other cases of genocidal killing, such as the Armenian genocide of 1915–1917, the Cambodian genocide of 1975–1979, and the slaughter of Tibetans by China since 1950? In a comparative perspective, moreover, uniqueness and commonality are not necessarily mutually exclusive. No one would seriously argue that there were not important differences between the pattern of genocide in Nazi

Germany against the Jews and, say, Pol Pot's Cambodia against other Cambodians, but few students of the subject would deny that there were important common principles and processes in the two cases. One should also add, for all of the cases mentioned in this paragraph, that there was an intimate relationship between war and genocide. We may, after careful comparative analysis, discover that war did not simply provide the setting for such genocides but may have been a principal causal factor—a causal factor that extends into the present in the case of the Yugoslavian civil war and its associated "ethnic cleansing" during the early 1990s.

Chapter 4

The Relationship Between Genocide and Total War

In the first three chapters, we explored a number of facts, issues, and themes concerning man-made death. In Chapters 1 and 2, we saw that despite the unprecedented magnitude of the problem of governmental mass killing, it has been woefully neglected relative to its significance. In Chapter 3, an overview of the historiography of total war and genocide revealed several points, including the rudimentary nature of this field of study, the number and variety of genocidal events that have occurred during our present century, and the variety of definitions that have been proposed by scholars for this phenomenon. In this chapter we examine in detail an important and as yet unresolved controversy: namely, the nature and extent of the relationship between genocide and total war as two ostensibly distinct forms of governmental mass killing.

After illustrating the opposing positions among scholars on this issue, we explore several possible reasons for the existence and persistence of the controversy. We then state our own position and propose that the concept of genocidal massacre can serve as a semantic and conceptual bridge between the phenomena of genocide and total war. Finally, several commonalities and connections between genocide and total war are examined. Briefly, they are

1. Total war often serves as a catalyst for genocide.
2. Both genocide and total war involve the deliberate massacre of noncombatants.
3. Both forms of mass killing are generally conducted by nation-states and rationalized as being in the service of national security.
4. Genocide and total war are antithetical to certain principles of democracy.

A fifth commonality—the fact that genocide and total war have both been facilitated by similar psychological, organizational, and scientific-technological factors—is examined in the following chapter. In Chapter 5, we develop a conceptual framework of shared facilitating factors that will be used in Part 2 to comparatively analyze the Holocaust as an exemplary case of modern genocide and the Allied strategic bombing campaigns during World War II as an exemplary case of total war.

Opposing Positions on the Controversy

The polarization among scholars on the question of the relationship between genocide and total war is quite striking. In the first major sociological study of genocide, Irving Louis Horowitz wrote that "it is operationally imperative to distinguish warfare from genocide" and asserted that the decision to emphasize the distinction between the two types of mass killing is "warranted by the weight of current empirical research that indicates that domestic destruction and international warring are separate dimensions of struggle."[1] Among the empirical research cited by Horowitz was a study by political scientist R. J. Rummel, who had reviewed several factor analyses of variables associated with both foreign and domestic conflict behavior and concluded that "*there are no common conditions or causes of domestic and foreign conflict behavior;* the genesis of domestic- and foreign-conflict behavior must be different" (emphasis in original).[2] (We shall see further on, however, that both Horowitz and Rummel have been inconsistent on this issue.)

More recently, Kurt Jonassohn (who, as noted in Chapter 3, eliminated civilian victims of war from the definition of genocide in his 1990 book on genocide with Frank Chalk) has asserted that

> nobody has yet shown that our understanding is enriched by comparing such unlike phenomena as wartime casualties and genocides. The fact that both war and genocide produce massive casualties is a terrible commentary on man's inhumanity to man, but it does not help to understand either phenomenon. We do not believe that there is anything to be gained analytically by comparing cases that have little in common except that they produce large numbers of casualties.[3]

In strong contrast to this view, sociologist Leo Kuper, widely regarded as the world's leading scholar of genocide in comparative perspective, steadfastly maintained that there is in fact overlap between genocide and warfare. In his pathbreaking 1981 book, Kuper wrote:

> The changing nature of warfare, with a movement toward total warfare, and the technological means for the annihilation of large populations, creates a situation conducive to genocidal conflict. This potential was realized in the Second World War, when Germany employed genocide in its war for domination, but I think the term must also be applied to the atomic bombing of the Japanese cities of Hiroshima and Nagasaki by the U.S.A. and to the pattern bombing by the Allies of such cities as Hamburg and Dresden.[4]

More recently, Kuper wrote, "Genocide may be committed against enemies. War crimes, crimes against humanity, and genocide are by no means exclusive categories."[5] We return to the question of overlap among these three categories of international crime later in this chapter.

Reasons for the Controversy

How is it possible that experts can be in such fundamental disagreement on such a basic issue? There are at least four reasons for the persistence of this controversy, which we now briefly explore.

The Variability of War and Genocide

First, the sheer variety of forms that both genocide and warfare have assumed complicates the effort to arrive at clear, consistent, and encompassing definitions of either phenomenon. Wars can vary according to the number of belligerent parties directly involved (from as few as two, as in the Iran-Iraq War from 1980 to 1988, to dozens, as in Operation Desert Storm in 1991). They can also vary in terms of scale. In the U.S. intervention in Grenada in 1982, 5,000 American troops fought against several thousand Grenadian and Cuban forces, whereas in World War II several million soldiers were engaged in combat.

Genocides, likewise, can vary widely. As Kuper has noted, "Given the great variety of historical and social contexts of acts of genocide, it would hardly seem possible to develop a general theory of genocide. ... Part of the problem is that there is no single genocidal process. The forms of genocide are too varied, with quite different sequences of action, and great differences in scale, raising different 'logistical' problems."[6] In terms of scale, genocides range from the killing of about 1,000 Guayaki (Aché) Indians in Paraguay between 1968 and 1972 to the killing of approximately 5 million Jews by Germans during World War II.[7] In recognition of the variability of motives, genocide scholars have developed typologies of genocide based on the presumed primary motive of the perpetrators. For example, Chalk and Jonassohn devised a fourfold typology that includes genocides intended "to eliminate a real or potential threat," genocides designed "to spread terror among real or potential enemies," genocides motivated by the desire "to acquire economic wealth," and genocides undertaken "to implement a belief, a theory, or an ideology."[8]

It should be noted that the project of devising typologies of genocide is not without its pitfalls. As Kuper has warned, "Some genocides defy easy classification. Indeed, the whole procedure of categorizing a type of genocidal state and filing genocides under it is decidedly cavalier. It reduces the enormity of cumulative human suffering to an abstract category and denudes the individual genocides of their unique qualities. Many genocides resist containment within preordained boundaries."[9]

The Political Nature of Genocide Definitions

A second factor that complicates definitions of genocide and thereby helps account for the persistent controversy over the relationship of genocide with warfare stems from the fact that labeling an event as genocide or genocidal is inevitably an emotionally and politically volatile act. In a paper presented to the first Raphael Lemkin Symposium on Genocide (at the Yale University Law School in February 1991), Israel W. Charny identified four "insidious types of political pressures on the definition of genocide that issue from entirely respectable intellectual circles." They include

1. Pressures to exclude certain events from the concept of genocide (including acts undertaken during warfare).

2. Pressures to avoid labeling a particular action as genocide in order to maintain positive political relations with the perpetrating nation (e.g., the reluctance of the U.S. government to formally acknowledge that the nation of Turkey, which is part of the North Atlantic Treaty Organization military alliance, committed genocide against its Armenian citizens during 1915).

3. Pressures to argue that a particular case of genocide is somehow more important or worse than others.

4. Pressures to engage in "blatant denials and revisionism of known historical events of mass murder" (most conspicuously, efforts to deny the reality and scale of the Holocaust).[10]

Leo Kuper, in his critique of the failures of the United Nations to enforce the provisions of the UN Genocide Convention, notes that there has been, within the relevant committees of the UN, a "psychological reluctance to use the term *genocide,* even when dealing with it" (emphasis in original). One of the reasons for this reluctance, he suggested, is that "charges of genocide immediately close off the possibility of discourse."[11]

The question of the relationship between genocide and war is particularly susceptible to political pressures. As Charny noted, "There are especially strong pressures by many countries to bar definitions of any military actions as genocide. … Reluctantly, most scholars of genocide back off from defining war and massive killing that goes on in war within the universe of genocide."[12] In her comprehensive review of the social science literature on genocide, Helen Fein suggested, "The question of whether killings of civilians in war are war crimes, consequences of acts of war admissible under the war convention, or acts of genocide has been clouded by the fact that genocide-labelling of wars today is often a rhetorical strategem for political delegitimation of specific wars which the labeller opposes."[13] We return to this issue further on.

Definitional Dilemmas

Both the variability of the phenomena of genocide and war and the political nature of definitions have created serious problems in developing widely accepted definitions that can serve as a consensual basis for analysis and comparison. Thus, as noted in Chapter 3, Ward Churchill concluded from a detailed analysis of many definitions of genocide there is no consensus on what constitutes genocide.[14] And Kuper, more recently, has echoed Churchill, stating that "there is no generally accepted definition of genocide. Definitions vary with the purposes of the analysis and the model accepted as the quintessence of the crime."[15]

It should be noted that some scholars have decried an overemphasis on definitional precision. For example, Charny has advocated more inclusive, rather than exclusive, definitions of genocide and has objected to what he calls "definitionalism," that is, "a damaging style of intellectual inquiry based on a perverse, fetishistic involvement with definitions to the point where the reality of the subject under discussion is 'lost,' i.e. no longer experienced emotionally by the scholars and therefore the real enormity of the subject no longer guides or impacts on the deliberations."[16]

Charny has identified an inescapable quandary in genocide studies, one that was pointed out in Chapter 1 in the discussion on counting the dead. There we noted that the student of man-made death must walk an intellectual and emotional tightrope between dehumanizing objectification of the victims of such violence, on the one hand, and the risk of becoming emotionally and spiritually overwhelmed by the horror, on the other. There is no ready solution to this dilemma, but as the still-fledgling field of genocide studies develops and matures, new conceptualizations and new forms of understanding may emerge.

One reflection of the unresolved definitional issues is that some conceptions of genocide explicitly include acts of war. Thus, Vahakn Dadrian, one of the first social scientists to specialize in the study of genocide, coined the term "latent genocide" to refer to cases where mass slaughter is the by-product of a policy that itself is not deliberately exterminatory. One type of latent genocide involves the forced relocation of minority populations that results in high death tolls, for example, the practice in U.S. history of uprooting Native Americans from their home territory and forcing them to march to reservations. The other type of latent genocide identified by Dadrian occurs when military activities cause high casualties among civilians, even if killing the civilians is not the primary objective. As Dadrian stated, "When the dominant group persists in these violent efforts and refrains from obviating the adverse, unintended consequences, such behavior may be termed genocidal."[17]

Other definitions of genocide also include motives and behavior that characterize warfare. For example, two of the types of genocide identified by Chalk and Jonassohn—those intended to eliminate a threat and those designed to spread terror among enemies—are based on motives frequently associated with war. Indeed, one of the most common justifications for the resort to war is to prevent or remove a threat. Also, many of the practices of modern war (including taking hostages, reprisals, and attacks against urban areas) are designed to intimidate and demoralize the citizenry of the enemy nation and thereby weaken its support for the war.

Moreover, some definitions of war appear indistinguishable from definitions of genocide. This is illustrated by the concepts of absolute and total war. Thus, in his discussion of absolute war, Hans Speier stated, "Peace terminating an absolute war is established *without* the enemy. ... Absolute war is waged in order to annihilate him" (emphasis in original).[18] According to Speier, absolute wars are characterized by a lack of moral restraint and the fact that at least one of the belligerents regards the other as inferior or even as subhuman. Speier included clashes between heavily armed colonizers and poorly armed indigenous peoples—clashes in which the latter have been slaughtered in great numbers—within his category of absolute war. This would appear to move an example of absolute or total war within the realm of genocide. Similarly, in his introduction to Clausewitz's classic *On War,* Anatol Rapoport noted that even though Clausewitz assumed that in absolute war the killing would be confined to the battlefield, "in the present political and technological environment, the actualization of Clausewitz's absolute war is total war, that is, genocide."[19]

Scholarly Inconsistency on the Issue

Finally, yet another reflection of the confusion surrounding the relationship between genocide and warfare—as well as a contributor to that same confusion—is the fact that some scholars have been inconsistent in their statements on this issue. Irving Louis Horowitz, for example, made contradictory statements within the same book. As noted previously, in his pioneering study he asserted that "it is operationally imperative to distinguish warfare from genocide," primarily because of "the weight of current empirical research that indicates that domestic destruction and international warring are separate dimensions of struggle."[20] Later in the same book, however, he contradicted himself when he stated, "The end of an era when formal declarations of war were made signifies the beginning of a new era in which the line between war and genocide becomes profoundly blurred."[21] As an example, he cited the U.S. war in Vietnam, an undeclared war that was alleged by some critics to have genocidal dimensions and by others to have been a case of actual genocide. After citing arguments on both sides of the question of whether the Vietnam War was genocidal, Horowitz stated, "The distinction between internal and foreign people who are being killed helps little, since it must be confessed that all genocidal practices involve a definition by the perpetrators of mass violence of those destroyed as outsiders."[22] Thus, he seemed to be acknowledging the existence of an important common process, depersonalization of victims, that occurs in both domestic and foreign conflicts.

A second example of inconsistency is found in the pioneering work of Israel Charny, who, despite his fervent advocacy of inclusive definitions, appears recently to have retreated from an earlier definition of genocide that did not explicitly exclude mass killing in warfare to a more exclusive definition that does so. Thus, in 1985, Charny proposed what he labeled a humanistic definition of genocide that greatly expanded the scope of genocidal killing from the restrictions of the United Nations Genocide Convention, as well as beyond the narrow, exclusive definitions proposed by some scholars. At that time, Charny defined genocide as "the *wanton* murder of human beings on the basis of any identity whatsoever that they share—national, ethnic, racial, religious, political, geographical, ideological" (emphasis in original).[23] More recently, however, Charny proposed a presumably even more broad, "generic" definition of genocide: "mass killing of substantial numbers of human beings, *when not in the course of military action against the military forces of an avowed enemy,* under conditions of the essential defenselessness and helplessness of the victims" (emphasis added).[24]

Later in his essay Charny moved back toward greater inclusiveness by proposing the concept of "genocide in the course of aggressive ('unjust') war" (e.g., the slaughter of civilians by Germany and Japan—both of whom engaged in aggressive, unprovoked attacks against their enemies during World War II). He continued, "In the present category, the issue of mass civilian deaths is unambiguously genocide. The deaths issue from an identifiably aggressive war, and the attacks on civilians are by such as Hitler, Hirohito, and Saddam Hussein; where there is no question that they are not at war in self-defense."[25] However, he then excluded comparable acts of civilian slaughter by nations conducting allegedly defensive, "just" wars from the realm of genocide and labeled them instead "war crimes against humanity" rather than genocides.[26] In other words, when civilians are slaughtered by an aggressor, it is genocide. But when they are slaughtered by a nation that has been attacked, then it is not genocide but something else.

A third example of inconsistency is provided by political scientist R. J. Rummel, who has moved in the opposite direction from Charny. As noted earlier, in 1969, Rummel asserted that genocide and war shared "no common conditions or causes."[27] As recently as 1990 in his book *Lethal Politics: Soviet Genocide and Mass Murder Since 1917,* Rummel proposed the concept of democide as a more inclusive alternative to genocide and defined it as "any actions by government ... designed to kill or cause the death of people ... because of their religion, race, language, ethnicity, national origin, class, politics, speech, actions construed as opposing the government or wrecking social policy, or by virtue of their relationship to such people."[28] In a discussion of "qualifications and clarifications" of his new concept, Rummel explictly excluded "the death of noncombatants killed during attacks on military targets (e.g., during bombing enemy logistics) or when targeted for militarily justifiable strategic or tactical reasons."[29]

By 1992, however, Rummel had changed his position to the point where he came to regard certain kinds of mass killing during war as forms of genocidal violence. Thus, in his 1992 book *Democide: Nazi Genocide and Mass Murder,* he stated: "However, in my work on China I became convinced by both the infamous terror bombing of Chinese cities by the Japanese and the world's reaction ... that democide should include this kind of slaughter."[30] In a different publication in the same year he suggested that "deliberately targeting civilians with explosive and incendiary bombs simply because they happen to be under the command and control of an enemy Power is no better than lining them up and machine gunning them, a clear atrocity."[31]

This discussion of inconsistencies is not intended as a criticism of the scholars mentioned, all of whom have made vital contributions to awareness and understanding of genocidal killing. Instead, it is meant to further underscore just how difficult it is to unravel the question about how much overlap there is between the concepts of war and genocide and the extent to which the two phenomena are interrelated and interconnected.

Our Position on the Controversy

Logically, there are two extreme positions possible on the issue of the relationship between genocide and total war. One extreme, which we have seen expressed by such scholars as Horowitz, Rummel, Chalk, and Jonassohn, holds that there is no relationship, that the two phenomena are distinct, discrete, and separate. The other extreme position would hold that war and genocide are indistinguishable, equivalent, equal. No one, to our knowledge, espouses this view.

Our own position falls between the two extremes but leans more toward the second than the first. Our review of the literature on both genocide and total war inclines us to regard them not as mutually exclusive phenomena but instead as forms of governmental mass killing that, in many but not all cases, are closely related and do in fact share important commonalities, which will be examined shortly. Moreover, specific instances of modern, total war may be appropriately regarded *genocidal,* if not actual cases of *genocide.* Both total war and genocide, in both preparation and implementation, may reflect a collective mindset that deserves to be labeled a "genocidal mentality."[32] This genocidal mentality is all too pervasive in the contemporary world.

The Concept of Genocidal Massacre

Before addressing commonalities, however, we first discuss the concept of *genocidal massacre* and suggest that the adjectival form of the word "genocide," if used with care and precision, can provide a semantic and conceptual bridge between the two extreme positions outlined previously.

Many scholars, including both those who argue against any overlap between genocide and war and those who assert that there is overlap, acknowledge that an action can be *genocidal* even if it does not constitute a *genocide* per se. As noted in

Chapter 3, Leo Kuper, while reluctantly relying on the UN Genocide Convention in order to identify cases of genocide, proposed the concept of *genocidal massacre* to characterize acts of mass killing that do not conform strictly to the criteria of the Genocide Convention but have some features that do fit it. He did not formally define the concept in his 1981 book, but he did provide a number of illustrative cases that suggest at least three criteria for classifying a particular case of mass killing as a genocidal massacre rather than as a genocide: the scale of the casualties, the intent of the perpetrator, and the nature of the perpetrator.

The closest that Kuper came to formally defining genocidal massacres was in his discussion of the ambiguity of the Genocide Convention on the question of how many people, or how large a percentage of a targeted group, must be destroyed in order for an action to be regarded as genocide. "I will assume that the charge of genocide would not be preferred," he stated, "unless there were a 'substantial' or an 'appreciable' number of victims."[33] When the numbers were neither "substantial" nor "appreciable," the action was considered by Kuper as a genocidal massacre rather than as a genocide. Among the examples of genocidal massacres according to this criterion of scale, he listed the French obliteration of Algerian villages during the period of the French colonization and the German destruction of the Czech village of Lidice during World War II in reprisal for the assassination of Nazi leader Reinhard Heydrich.

Shifting from a focus on scale to a discussion of perpetrator intent, Kuper again relied on the French actions against Algerian natives as an illustrative case. He noted Sartre's argument that the French colonists in Algeria could not adopt a policy of outright genocide because it would have been antithetical to their effort to economically exploit the natives. However, the use of brutal massacres was an effective means of maintaining the subjugation of the natives. Therefore, it appears that when the purpose of mass killing by a governing elite is not to completely eliminate a targeted group but rather to admonish and intimidate the majority of the group's members by killing a portion of them, the action is appropriately classified as a genocidal massacre rather than as a genocide.[34]

Finally, in his discussion of the mass killing that accompanied the partition of India into Hindu India and Muslim Pakistan following the withdrawal of the British in 1947, Kuper labeled the massacres of Hindus by Muslims and Muslims by Hindus as genocidal massacres rather than as genocide, apparently because they largely reflected spontaneous fury directed at one subnational faction by another instead of being organized as an official government policy.[35]

Helen Fein used the term "genocidal massacre" on numerous occasions in her 1990 critical review of the scholarly literature on genocide. Like Kuper, she suggested that the term is applicable to cases of mass killing in which the scale is relatively small and the intent of the perpetrators is not to murder all members of a group but only a portion of them.[36] Fein also used the term for "massacres that are not part of a continuous genocide but are committed against a particular ethnic or other distinguishable group."[37]

If the term "genocidal" may be used to characterize the aforementioned acts of mass killing that do not fit within a particular formal or legal definition of "genocide," then we suggest that it can also be used to describe certain kinds of warfare. In fact, different wars, and specific campaigns and battles within wars, vary according to the degree to which they are genocidal. Thus, wars may be differentiated in terms of such dimensions as the proportion of civilian to military casualties, the degree of dehumanization of the enemy, and the degree to which indiscriminate weaponry and tactics are used.

Total War as a Catalyst for Genocide

One connection between genocide and warfare, particularly total war, on which there is a wide consensus in the scholarly community is the tendency for war to create social and psychological conditions conducive to the outbreak of genocide and genocidal killing. Leo Kuper has noted that "international warfare, whether between 'tribal' groups or city states, or other sovereign states and nations, has been a perennial source of genocide."[38] Among his examples from the post–World War II era are the Chinese invasion of Tibet in 1950 and the invasion and occupation of East Timor by Indonesia in 1977, both of which entailed extensive genocidal killing.[39] Likewise, referring to the Armenian genocide of 1915–1917 and the Nazi Holocaust against the Jews, Vahakn Dadrian observed, "It is no accident that the two principal instances of genocide of this century coincided with the episodes of two global wars."[40] Civil wars also create the potential for genocidal killing. Indeed, Henry Huttenbach has warned that it is "probably one of the most likely settings for genocide in the future."[41]

Several dimensions of modern war expedite genocide. First, by posing a dire threat to the society, war serves, according to Dadrian, as "a cataclysmic agent of disequilibrium entailing manifold crises."[42] The presence of such a threat creates the potential for preexisting intergroup tensions in a culturally or racially diverse society to flare into violence directed by the majority against members of a minority group. The threat and disruption is not only blamed on the external enemy but can also be directed at members of a minority group within the society. The minority group may be accused of collaborating with the enemy or be used as a scapegoat for the frustrated aggression of the dominant group, especially when the war begins to go poorly.

Second, governments engaged in total war, whether they are democratic or totalitarian, tend to become more centralized, secret, and powerful. They commonly use official censorship and propaganda to increase support for their belligerent policies. This can take a variety of forms, including vilification of the enemy and cover-ups of mistakes or atrocities conducted by one's own forces. The result can be diminished popular awareness of, and resistance to, ruthless governmental actions against both external and internal enemies.[43]

Third, the government at war can utilize the military forces—men who have been trained to kill in the service of their nation—for the perpetration of genocide. This occurred in both the Armenian genocide and the Holocaust.[44] Other twentieth-century genocides in which soldiers and paramilitary personnel played key roles as killers include, but are not limited to, the following: the 1904 slaughter of more than 65,000 Hereros in German Southwest Africa (now the nation of Namibia); the killing of half a million southern Sudanese civilians by the Sudanese army between 1955 and 1972; the massacre of as many as 3 million Bengalis by the army of East Pakistan in 1971; the killing of tens of thousands of Timorese by the Indonesian army in 1975; and the slaughter of millions of their fellow Cambodians by the Khmer Rouge in 1975–1979.[45]

Fourth, just as conditions of war significantly increase the power of the government, they also tend to increase the vulnerability of the governmentally targeted victim groups, which tend to be, as Dadrian noted, "isolated, fragmented, and nearly totally emasculated through the control of channels of communication, wartime secrecy, the various sections of the wartime apparatus, police, and secret services, and the constant invocation of national security."[46]

Finally, a number of scholars have suggested that modern war creates a climate of moral and psychological numbing or desensitization that increases popular tolerance of cruelty, whether directed against an external or internal enemy. Thus, in his analysis of the role of the military in the Turkish genocide of the Armenians in 1915, James Reid found that earlier attacks by the Turkish army against civilians helped to psychologically facilitate their later involvement in the even more ruthless killing of Armenians.[47]

Similar Means: The Deliberate Massacre of Noncombatants

"Massacre," according to *The Oxford Universal Dictionary*, has a number of meanings, including, in the noun form, "a general slaughter (of human beings)" and "a cruel or peculiarly atrocious murder." As a verb, its meanings include "to kill indiscriminately" and "to murder cruelly or violently."[48] A fundamental commonality between genocide and total war is that both employ massacre of large numbers of innocent, helpless noncombatants as a means of obtaining their objectives.* In this section, we address the massacre of noncombatants in terms of two issues: the

*An important, but often overlooked, point needs to be made here about distinguishing between civilian and military casualties. Compilers of the statistics of death tend to separate civilians and military into two categories and usually place more moral abhorrence on the deaths of civilians. Indeed, the distinction between noncombatants and combatants, and the admonition against unnecessary harm to the former, is a basic tenet of the so-called just war tradition. (See, for example, Michael Walzer, *Just and Unjust Wars: A Moral Argument with Historical Illustrations*, New York, Basic Books, 1977, pp. 3–47.) One cannot deny that the killing of civilians is morally abhorrent, but one should not dehumanize military personnel, particularly in wars such as World War II, in which many of the military were simply young civilian men conscripted into uniform.

innocence and helplessness of the victims and the overlap among war crimes, crimes against humanity, and the crime of genocide.

The Innocence and Helplessness of Victims

One of the reasons for which genocide is universally reviled as a uniquely atrocious international crime is the innocence of its victims, the majority of whom are children, women, and the elderly. In their study *The Fate of Polish Children During the Last War,* for example, Roman Hrabar and his colleagues estimated that of the 6 million Poles (both Jewish and non-Jewish) killed by the Germans between 1939 and 1945, approximately one-third—about 2.2 million —were children.[49] These innocents were murdered in a variety of ways: by gunfire and bombs during the initial Nazi invasion, particularly the ruthless bombing of Warsaw; by being worked to death as slave laborers; because of starvation and disease in special concentration camps for children; and in the gas chambers of Treblinka and other death camps—to name just a few. Referring to the child victims of the Nazi genocide, Raul Hilberg has suggested, "That is what makes the Holocaust a holocaust!"[50]

However, it is essential to recognize that most of the victims of total war are also innocent in the sense of playing no direct role in the waging of the war or having absolutely no choice in the decision of their government to engage in war. Surprisingly, some scholars of genocide appear not to appreciate this crucial fact—or at least its staggering scale. For example, Barbara Harff, under the heading "Death in War and Genocide: The Means and Ends of Destruction," wrote that "during war civilians get killed, sometimes by the thousands."[51] We certainly agree with the first part of her statement; the second part, however, conveys but a pale hint of the actual scale of civilian casualties in wars of the twentieth century, particularly during and since World War II, when the vast majority of the millions killed have been civilians. Moreover, in the same book chapter from which we just quoted, Harff also claimed, "Most civilized states adhere to the rules of war, which proscribe the intentional killing of civilians during war. These principles rarely are applied fully, but the intent therefore is to avoid killing noncombatants."[52] Although we agree with Harff that most civilized states (i.e., democratic and nonaggressive states) do tend to adhere to the rules of war, we must also stress that such adherence is all too often violated. We would argue, for example, that such was the case during World War II, when both the United States and Great Britain carpet-bombed heavily populated enemy cities. Also, the sheer destructiveness of modern weapons makes it very difficult to avoid killing noncombatants. It is worth repeating in this context that civilians accounted for only 5 percent of the deaths in World War I; they accounted for more than 60 percent of the deaths in World War II; and in the wars of the 1970s and 1980s, civilians accounted for more than 80 percent of the deaths.

A number of scholars differentiate genocide and war on the grounds that the victims of genocide are helpless, but the victims of warring nations are far less so.

Fein, for example, has written that war "is ideally conceived of as a symmetrical conflict between two forces. Genocide, by contrast, is usually conceived of as an asymmetrical slaughter of an unorganized group or collectivity by an organized force."[53] Later in her paper, she reiterated that her "paradigm of genocide ... presumes a powerful perpetrator and relatively powerless victim."[54] Similarly, Chalk and Jonassohn stated that "when countries are at war, neither side is defenseless. Although individually the civilians may be defenseless, they are part of the group or nation that is at war." They noted also that in genocide, as opposed to war, "the victim group has no organized military machinery that might be opposed to that of the perpetrator."[55]

We agree that the victims of genocides are far less powerful than the perpetrators, but we also suggest that Fein, Chalk and Jonassohn, and others fail to sufficiently appreciate the fact that many wars are clearly asymmetrical rather than symmetrical. Indeed, aggressors are often stimulated to undertake invasion precisely because they believe that they can prevail with relatively low costs to their own nation. This was the case with Nazi attacks against Poland, France, the Netherlands, and other nations during World War II, and it was true also of the Iraqi invasion of Kuwait in 1991. Moreover, we also suggest that Fein and others do not sufficiently acknowledge the powerlessness of civilians under attack by modern military forces and weapons. For example, despite their formidable military forces, the governments of Germany and Japan were able to do little to spare their civilians from the ravages of strategic bombing by Great Britain and the United States. The reality is that in total war civilians become helpless pawns of their governments and, in many cases, defenseless targets of enemy artillery shells, bombs, and missiles.

Overlap Among War Crimes, Crimes Against Humanity, and the Crime of Genocide

Leo Kuper has asserted that "war crimes, crimes against humanity, and genocide are by no means exclusive categories."[56] To the extent that these three offenses contain overlapping provisions, a case can be made against the mutual-exclusivity position on the controversy over the relationship between war and genocide.

We follow two approaches to explore potential overlap among war crimes, crimes against humanity, and genocide. The first traces the historical evolution and provisions of each of these crimes in order to determine if they contain any common features. The second examines specific wars to determine if they involved any actions that might fit within the legal category of genocide.

The Historical Evolution of the Three Types of Crime. Although constraints on the practice of war, particularly the careful discrimination between combatants and noncombatants, have been a feature of international common law for several centuries, as well as a crucial feature of the Christian "just war" tradition, and even though the concept of crimes against humanity was first articulated in a legal forum in May 1915 (in response to Turkish atrocities against the Armenians), the legal status of war crimes and crimes against humanity was not firmly institutionalized until August 8, 1945.* On that date, the nations of the United States, the Soviet Union, Great Britian, and France signed the London Agreement, which established the Charter of the International Military Tribunal (IMT). They did so in order to provide a legal forum for the prosecution of Nazi leaders, both military and civilian, who had contributed to the many atrocities perpetrated by Germany during World War II.[57]

Three categories of crime were established by the IMT. *Crimes against peace* referred to the initiation and waging of a war of aggression. *War crimes* referred to "violations of the laws or customs of war," including "murder, ill-treatment or deportation to slave labor or for any other purpose of civilian population of or in occupied territory." This category also prohibited mistreating prisoners of war, killing hostages, plundering private property, and related acts.[58] The third type of crime, *crimes against humanity,* included a number of specific acts: "murder, extermination, enslavement, deportation and other inhumane acts committed against any civilian population, before or during the war, or persecutions on political, racial, or religious grounds in execution of or in connection with any crime within the jurisdiction of the Tribunal, whether or not in violation of the domestic law of the country where perpetrated."[59]

The category of crimes against humanity was designed to provide a legal basis for prosecuting the Germans for actions that had not been included in previous international laws concerning warfare. One major loophole, however, was that the charter applied only to crimes against humanity that had been committed in conjunction with other criminal actions in which Germany had engaged during the war, for example, the taking of civilian hostages or reprisals against civilians.[60] In order to include genocide per se as a crime under international law, a further step beyond the precedents established by the IMT charter was required, namely, the formal establishment of genocide as a crime.[61]

Thus, while the international military tribunal was conducting its trial of the major German war criminals, Raphael Lemkin, who originated the concept of genocide in 1944, was in the United States lobbying at the recently formed United Nations on behalf of a resolution that would clearly establish the offenses he had collected under the label of genocide as constituting an international crime. His efforts were initially rewarded on December 11, 1946, when the General Assembly of the UN unanimously passed a resolution affirming the charter and subsequent judgment. This important intermediary step in the legal evolution of the crime of genocide went beyond the Charter of the International Military Tribunal in as-

*As Daniel Ellsberg pointed out in a personal communication, it is ironic that this important date in the evolution of international law fell two days after the atomic bombing of Hiroshima and one day before the atomic bombing of Nagasaki. Both events, we argue in Chapter 11, arguably constituted both war crimes and crimes against humanity.

serting that the crimes against humanity that constitute the practice of genocide are illegal during both war and peace.

The next major step was the unanimous adoption by the UN General Assembly on December 9, 1948, of the Convention on the Prevention and Punishment of the Crime of Genocide, which codified the points made in the earlier resolution into a treaty open for ratification by the member nations.

The convention was explicit in listing specific actions that constitute the crime of genocide. Article 2 states:

> In the present Convention, genocide means any of the following acts committed with intent to destroy, in whole or in part, a national, ethnical, racial, or religious group, as such: (a) Killing members of the group; (b) Causing serious bodily or mental harm to members of the group; (c) Deliberately inflicting on the group conditions of life calculated to bring about its physical destruction in whole or in part; (d) Imposing measures to prevent births within the group; (e) Forcibly transferring children of the group to another group.[62]

The Genocide Convention was ratified by the requisite 20 member nations in 1951 and has since been justifiably regarded as a landmark in the quest to establish genocide as a heinous crime under international law. (However, the United States, despite being an early supporter of the convention, failed to ratify it until 1986 for a number of reasons, including a reluctance to give up national sovereignty.)[63]

Despite its widely acknowledged significance and value as a benchmark in international law, the Genocide Convention has been criticized on a number of grounds. These include the exclusion of political groups from those protected; the ambiguity surrounding the terms "intent to destroy, in whole or in part," which must be proven in order for the charge of genocide to be warranted; and the minimal potential for enforcement.

During the process of drafting the convention, efforts were made to include political groups along with racial, ethnic, and religious groups in the overall definition of genocide, as Lemkin had originally proposed. This would have meant that the domain of the crime would have been greatly expanded, as a greater number of cases of governmental mass killing would have fit within the definition. However, inclusion was strongly resisted by a number of nations, including the Soviet Union, Poland, and Iran.[64] The basic motive for noninclusion was political. Uriel Tal, for example, has cited the fear that the inclusion of political groups "would afford an opening for international bodies to intervene in what was termed the internal political life of individual countries."[65] The noninclusion of political groups is a serious loophole in the coverage of the convention. Some of the most egregious examples of governmental mass killing, such as the collectivizations and purges in the Soviet Union under Stalin, are excluded.[66]

In order for mass killing to fall within the jurisdiction of the Genocide Convention, not only must it be directed against one of the designated types of groups but there must also be evidence of "intent" to destroy that group "in whole or in part."

This provision excludes many acts that would otherwise be regarded as genocide. As an example, Kuper cited the case of Paraguay, whose government was accused by the International League for the Rights of Man in 1974 with complicity in the genocide against the Aché Indians, who were being hunted and killed, with some survivors being sold into slavery and others forcibly relocated to reservations. A spokesman for the Paraguayan government rebutted the charge of genocide by stating: "Although there are victims and victimizer, there is not the third element necessary to establish the crime of genocide—that is 'intent.' Therefore, as there is no 'intent,' one cannot speak of 'genocide.'"[67] By this, he meant that the government had no program to exterminate the Aché—only to remove them from economically valuable lands—and, therefore, there was no genocidal intent.

A final limitation of the Genocide Convention to be considered here is its lack of enforceability. The convention has defined the act of genocide as a punishable crime under international law, but to judge from the number of genocidal acts that have taken place since the ratification of the treaty, it has contributed little to either preventing or punishing the crime.[68]

Notwithstanding these and other limitations of the Genocide Convention, it is clear that it attempts to protect large categories of human beings, the vast majority of whom are civilians rather than soldiers, from governmental massacres. Thus, the crime of genocide shares with certain kinds of war crimes and with crimes against humanity the prohibition against killing civilians. In this respect, we suggest that genocide, whether perpetrated during a war or not, clearly overlaps with crimes against civilian populations that are committed during warfare.

In view of this overlap, we would also suggest that Charny's concept of war crimes against humanity, which, as discussed previously, was applied to deliberate mass killing of civilians by nations fighting "just," (i.e., defensive) wars, be relabeled "genocidal war crimes against humanity." The addition of the adjective is intended to announce and emphasize the *genocidal* nature of such warfare. An even bolder step would be to revise Charny's other new concept, "genocide in the course of aggressive ('unjust') war," which he uses to denote "genocide that is undertaken or even allowed in the course of military action by a known aggressive power," to simply state, "genocide in the course of war." Finally, in view of the undeniably genocidal nature of total war, whether fought by aggressors or defenders, might it not be appropriate to simply include all relevant cases of deliberate mass slaughter of innocent, helpless noncombatants during warfare under the rubric "genocide in the course of war"?

Genocide in Vietnam and Afghanistan? Further elucidation of the relationships among war crimes, crimes against humanity, and genocide may be gained by examining whether specific wars have featured genocidal actions or have even constituted cases of genocide per se. For example, in 1974 Hugo Adam Bedau published a widely cited evaluation of the accusation by a nongovernmental international war-crimes tribunal that the United States had committed genocide during its war in Vietnam by engaging in indiscriminate bombardment of Vietnamese civilians. Bedau concluded that although the practice of mass killing civilians was a common feature of U.S. war policy, it was not possible to prove that by doing so the United States intended to destroy the Vietnamese peasants as a group "in whole or part," as specified by the Genocide Convention. With the inability to prove genocidal intent, the charge of genocide could not be sustained, although Bedau did state that, "The gap between the results of the present discussion and a verdict of genocide is not very wide."[69]

A more recent comparative analysis was undertaken by Helen Fein and reported in her 1991 article "Discriminating Genocide from War Crimes: Vietnam and Afghanistan Reexamined."[70] Fein's article made an important contribution to the effort to comprehend genocide and modern war as forms of governmental mass killing, particularly because it provided a comparative perspective on two wars that pitted technologically superior superpowers against developing nations. Her goal was to "preserve the concept [of genocide] as an international norm" by proposing a paradigm that could be used to "distinguish genocide from war crimes and other mass killing" and thereby "distinguish putative cases from rhetorical misuses and specious claims."[71] Relying (as did Bedau) on the legal definition of genocide established by the United Nations Genocide Convention, her paradigm identified the following five propositions that spelled out "necessary and sufficient conditions to impute genocide." To quote from her article,

1. There is a sustained attack, or continuity of attacks, by the perpetrator to physically destroy group members.
2. The perpetrator is a collective or organized actor or a commander of organized actors.
3. Victims are selected because they are members of a collectivity.
4. The victims are defenseless or are killed regardless of whether they surrendered or resisted.
5. The destruction of group members is undertaken with intent to kill and murder is sanctioned by the perpetrators.[72]

Like Bedau, Fein stressed the critical role of *intent* in evaluating the charge of genocide in both cases. As she stated, "The judgment as to whether either action became genocide does not depend on the goals of either the United States or the Soviet Union, but it does depend on the intent and pattern of their use of force."[73] Essentially, she found that although both wars were characterized by massive bombing, the widespread use of antipersonnel weapons, and the deliberate destruction of crops and food supplies, there were important differences between the United States and the Soviet Union in terms of both intent and scale of these activities.

For example, although both wars involved "a sustained attack or continuity of attacks by the perpetrator" (Proposition 1), Fein argued that deliberate massacre of civilians was the exception in the American case (e.g., the infamous My Lai massacre, whose perpetrators were brought to military trial and punished), whereas Soviet soldiers "engaged in repeated massacres of Afghanis."[74] In the Soviet case, moreover, the perpetrators were not punished by their superiors but instead were actively encouraged to engage in such behavior.[75]*

Likewise, both the United States and the Soviet Union employed massive air bombardment. However, Fein stressed that the U.S. bombing campaign operated under constricting rules of engagement, but the Soviet bombing appeared "to have been purposely aimed at crowds and aggregates of people unlikely to attack soldiers, such as refugee caravans, weddings, funerals, religious gatherings, and civilian buses."[76]† Further, although both superpowers employed a variety of antipersonnel weapons, including fragmentation bombs and incendiaries such as napalm, the Soviet Union used "mines disguised as toys" that maimed and killed large numbers of innocent Afghani children.[77]

These and other differences examined by Fein help account for the different consequences of the fighting for the Vietnamese (of whom, according to Fein, less than 2 percent were killed between 1963 and 1974) and the Afghanis (of whom 9 percent were killed between 1978–1979 and 1988).[78]‡

On the basis of such considerations, Fein concluded that although the United States in Vietnam was probably guilty of war crimes, it was not guilty of genocide.[79] In contrast, she found that "a plausible prima facie case of genocide can be made against the Soviet Union and the DRA [the Democratic Republic of Afghanistan] in Afghanistan for its action from 1979–1988."[80]

In summary, both Bedau and Fein concluded that, under the terms of the Genocide Convention, the United States did not commit genocide during its war in Vietnam (although, as noted, Bedau acknowledged that it came very close). Fein, however, concluded that the Soviet Union did engage in genocide in Afghanistan. For our purposes here, the most important point is that Fein's analysis

*It should be noted, however, that of those involved in the My Lai massacre, only William Calley was brought to trial. He was later pardoned by President Richard Nixon. Moreover, as Daniel Ellsberg has pointed out in a personal communication, smaller massacres of Vietnamese civilians were not uncommon and generally went unpunished.

†Again, Fein's interpretation is open to question. As Herbert Hirsch has pointed out in a personal communication, the United States massively and secretly bombed Laos and Cambodia and bombed Vietnam massively. Indeed, the bomb tonnage dropped on Vietnam by the United States during the war vastly exceeded the tonnage dropped in both the European and Pacific theaters by all sides during World War II (Daniel Ellsberg, personal communication).

‡Other scholars put the Vietnamese death toll considerably higher. Ngo Vinh Long notes that the United States attacked Vietnam with a total of 12 million tons of bombs and artillery shells that displaced 10 million people from their homes and killed 2 million people out of an estimated population in 1972 of 19 million (Ngo Vinh Long, "Vietnam," in Douglas Allen and Ngo Vihn Long, Editors, *Coming to Terms: Indochina, The United States, and the War*, Boulder, CO, Westview Press, 1991, pp. 9–10). As Herbert Hirsch has noted, this death toll approximates the scale of killing by the Soviets in Afghanistan. (Herbert Hirsch, personal communication.)

reveals that in the specific case of the Soviet intervention in Afghanistan, war and genocide are not mutually exclusive, but the two types of mass killing can and have merged. Although other scholars may question the particulars of her analysis, as well as her conclusions about the nongenocidal nature of the Vietnam War, and although further comparative analysis of other wars is urgently needed, we suggest that her study lends support to our position, stated earlier, that war and genocide are frequently closely related and that modern war is very often genocidal.

The Nation-State as Mass Killer

Yet another commonality between genocide and total war is the fact that most modern genocides and wars are conducted by nation-states (or collectivities aspiring to become nation-states) and are rationalized as being necessary for the enhancement, protection, or restoration of national security.

Unfortunately, the concept of nation-state is as disputed and controversial as the concept of genocide. Indeed, the terms "state," "nation-state," and "nation" are often used interchangeably.[81] In his article on the state in *The International Encyclopedia of the Social Sciences,* Morton Fried acknowledged that "it is impossible to offer a unified definition of the state that would be satisfactory even to a majority of those seriously concerned with the problem."[82]

Nonetheless, a review of several definitions indicates a number of features that are widely accepted as being characteristic of this important form of large-scale social organization. In his lengthy study *The Nation-State and Violence,* sociologist Anthony Giddens defined the state as "a political organization whose rule is territorially ordered and which is able to mobilize the means of violence to sustain that rule."[83] Noting that the state originated as long as 7,000 years ago, Pierre van den Berghe defined it as "those individuals who, singly or collectively, manipulate to whatever ends the coercive apparatus for which they claim legitimacy."[84] Finally, Morton Fried stressed that states exercise control over a "defined and bounded territory," possess a "monopoly of paramount control in a society," are considered to be the legitimate possessors of that control and power, and are able to engage in violence on a large scale.[85]

The proclivity of states to use violence in order to protect their interests has been noted by a number of scholars. Van den Berghe, in the introduction to his edited reader on *State Violence and Ethnicity,* asserted that the state "has been the prime killer in human history. Killing is, in fact, in the very nature of the state. States are killing machines controlled by the few to steal from the many."[86] Chalk and Jonassohn, on the basis of a wide-ranging historical survey of genocidal killing, asserted, "Genocides are always performed by a *state or other authority.* In the twentieth century, the perpetrator is almost always the state because authority and power are highly centralized and the modern means of communication are so efficient that such centralization can be effectively imposed" (emphasis in original).[87] Warfare, likewise, is a tool of the state. Thus, historian Joseph Amato noted that war is among the "essential functions of the state."[88]

An important basis for rationalizing or justifying state violence is the ideology of nationalism, which was defined by Hans Kohn as "a state of mind in which the supreme loyality of the individual is felt to be to the nation-state."[89] According to van den Berghe, "The modern state kills mostly in the name of nationalism."[90]

What historian Arnold Toynbee called "the religion of nationalism" constitutes a common denominator in the justification of both genocide and war.[91] "Intense nationalism," wrote Horowitz, "is itself an essential characteristic of the genocidal society. It instills not only a sense of difference between those who belong and those who do not, but also the inhumanity of those who do not belong, and thereby the right of the social order to purge itself of alien influence."[92] Warfare has also been affected by nationalistic ideologies. Nation-states fighting for their very survival are willing to consider any means that promise to attain that end, and in the twentieth century such conflicts have become progressively brutal. Toynbee observed, "The increasing fanaticism of nationalism has exacted an increasing oblation of military human sacrifice."[93] Toynbee might have added that the sacrifice is by no means limited to the military but that noncombatants have been an ever-increasing proportion of the casualties of total war.

In some cases, the official claim of a threat to national security or even survival is clearly specious, as has been the case with recent genocides. For example, the Jews in Nazi Germany certainly did not pose a real threat to the German state. But to the extent that Nazi propagandists were able to convince German citizens that the Jews were to blame for Germany's many political and economic problems, the administrators of the Final Solution were able to secure both active complicity from some citizens and passive compliance from many others. In other cases, especially total wars like World War II, the threat to national survival posed by the enemy is real. But in both cases, specious and real, the ideology of nationalism is used by leaders to promote citizen participation in state-sanctioned mass-killing projects.

Nationalistic ideologies are powerful means of inducing members of one group to commit violence against outsiders. This power resides in at least three characteristics of such ideologies. First, they are very effective in defining the victims as outsiders and therefore undeserving of any compassionate considerations that would be warranted for members of one's own group. They feature explicit criteria in terms of which the identity of an enemy can be ascertained, for example, national or ethnic identity or residence within the borders of the enemy state. Second, nationalistic ideologies can create in the minds of the killers and their supporters a sense of "kill or be killed"—a mindset in which no act is too horrible if it reduces the alleged mortal threat to one's own national, religious, or ethnic group. Third, they enjoy the power residing in legitimate authority and the moral justification of being in the service of national security.

Thus, both genocide and total war have been justified as necessary responses to a threat to national security and survival; both have been authorized and legitimated by the highest national leaders and administered by officials to whom they have formally delegated authority; and both have been implemented by large numbers of citizens who regard their service as highly virtuous and patriotic. For example, in her comparative study of the Holocaust and the Armenian genocide, Fein noted that in both cases the security of the state had been threatened by a combination of political and economic crises and recent defeat in war. This in turn created the potential for preexisting intergroup tensions to flare into violence directed by the majority against members of a minority group that was blamed for the crisis.[94] The fact that the targeted victims were not responsible for the problems of the nation was quite irrelevant; what mattered was that government officials believed that they were responsible and were able to inculcate many citizens with that belief.

In total war, the source of the threat is another nation or organized group rather than a defenseless minority group within the nation. For example, during World War II, both the British and U.S. practices of attacking enemy cities with incendiary bombs evolved in the course of a bloody conflict with ruthless enemies and resulted from a reciprocal escalation of violence. Likewise, the U.S. decision to build the atomic bombs was spurred by the fear that the Germans would create and use them first; the decision to drop them on Japan was motivated primarily by the desire to bring the long war to a quick end and thereby save the lives of hundreds of thousands of American men who would have died in an invasion of the Japanese home islands.*

The policies of engaging in, or relying on the threat of, both genocidal and military killing are made and administered by government officials at the highest levels. For example, the Holocaust was directed by the SS, who were the elite guardians of the security of the Reich, and the decisions to target German and Japanese cities during World War II were made by top civilian and military leaders, as was the decision to drop the atomic bombs on Japan and as are plans (discussed in Chapter 12) for waging war with thermonuclear weapons.

The perceived legitimacy of the mass-killing project, be it genocide or war, is a very important element in securing the cooperation of the ordinary citizens who are needed in relatively large numbers to actually implement the killing project. Psychologist Herbert Kelman emphasized the role of legitimate authority in facilitating the breakdown of moral restraints. According to Kelman,

> The structure of an authority situation is such that, at least for many of the participants, the moral principles that generally govern human relationships do not apply. Thus when acts of violence are explicitly ordered, implicitly encouraged, tacitly ap-

*As we discuss in Chapter 12, recent scholarship has called into question the conventional assumption that so many lives were saved by the atomic bombs and that the dropping of the atomic bombs was the only feasible means to bring the war in the Pacific to a conclusion.

> proved, or at least permitted by legitimate authorities, people's readiness to commit or condone them is considerably enhanced.[95]

Finally, the lethal policies of genocide and total warfare are implemented by large numbers of individuals in many sectors of society. The majority of the people responsible for the massacre of innocent civilians in genocide and in total war are not psychopaths or sadists, but often loving parents who regard themselves as loyal, patriotic citizens serving the national interest.

Genocide and Total War as Antithetical to Democracy

Another important feature shared by genocide and total war is that both thrive in a totalitarian political environment. Put conversely, both forms of governmental mass killing are less likely to be employed by democracies than by totalitarian regimes. Perhaps the strongest case that democracies are less likely to engage in genocide than nondemocractic forms of government has been made by R. J. Rummel, who reported that of the estimated 151 million victims of "democide" (a term he coined that includes several forms of genocidal killing), between 1900 and 1991, "only" 1 million were killed by democracies; the remainder were slaughtered by nondemocratic governments. Rummel also found that the vast majority of wars during the twentieth century occurred between nondemocracies, or between democracies and aggressive nondemocracies, and concluded that "democracies don't make war on each other."[96]

Several features of democracy inhibit the resort to genocidal killing, whether in outright genocides or in total war. Since secret-police organizations in nondemocratic governments, such as the Gestapo in Nazi Germany and the NKVD (People's Commisariat of Internal Affairs) in the Soviet Union, are often among the chief perpetrators of genocidal killing, the absence of such agencies in democracies provides an important check against the resort to such killing policies. Moreover, power in democracies is distributed among more than one party or interest group, which decreases the likelihood that a single political faction that favors genocide will be able to dominate the entire state apparatus. Also, to the extent that democratic governments allow freedom of the press, infomation about mass killing, whether within the territorial boundaries of the nation or beyond them, is likely to be disseminated to the populace, giving them the basis for questions or protest. As Fein noted in her study of the U.S. war in Vietnam and the Soviet war in Afghanistan, the existence of such democratic institutions as a free press and a system of checks and balances among the branches of government put important limits on the potential escalation of the war in Vietnam. In the Soviet Union the absence of such "democractic checks" allowed the war in Afghanistan to "escalate to genocide."[97]

However, it would be a mistake to complacently assume that democracies are incapable of engaging in genocidal killing. One need only review the history of persecution and massacre of Native Americans in the United States and the eradication of Aborigines in Australia to realize that there have been tragic exceptions to the rule.[98]

Likewise, when democracies engage in warfare with totalitarian regimes, the political differences between the two forms of government tend to narrow as the centralization of political control required to wage total war encroaches upon democratic processes. For example, during World War II, Prime Minister Churchill and Presidents Roosevelt and Truman acquired vastly greater powers than incumbents of either office had ever attained before. According to Farrar, "Governmental authority was centralized and increased at the expense of individuals, parliaments, and the military in all of the belligerent states. As a result institutional and ideological distinctions among the belligerents were reduced and the democratic regimes increasingly resembled their totalitarian counterparts."[99]

Not only political but also military differences between democratic and totalitarian governments have tended to diminish during total wars of this century. As Quincy Wright observed, "the development of the airplane by the totalitarian states in the twentieth century first extended their empires and then compelled the democracies to adopt their techniques."[100] Thus, at the beginning of World War II, both Germany and Great Britain heeded the call by the then-neutral United States to abstain from bombardment of cities, but by the end of the war the democratic allies were deliberately setting the cities of Germany and Japan on fire, resulting in the deaths of tens of thousands of civilians.

Propaganda has played a crucial role in the total wars of the twentieth century, among both democratic and totalitarian nations. During World War I, government manipulation of information took the form not only of propaganda designed to demonize or vilify the enemy nation but also of the omission of information that might have reduced morale among the fighting men and their supporters on the home front. Not only the totalitarian nations but also the democracies resorted to concealment and distortion. In their discussion of World War I, the authors of a widely used American history textbook (*The Growth of the American Republic* by Eliot Morison and Henry Steele Commager, 1942) observed, "One of the most appalling revelations of the entire war was the ease with which modern technique and mass-suggestion enables a government to make even a reasonably intelligent people, with an individualistic, democratic background, believe anything it likes."[101] Governmental propaganda on all sides during World War II portrayed enemies—be they German, Japanese, Russian, or American—in vile, dehumanized images, and in the democracies, citizens were deceived about the actual nature of the strategic-bombing campaigns. Rummel conceded that "even in democracies, where Power can take root in particular institutions, remain unchecked and undisciplined, and hide its activities, it will murder en masse."[102]

The commonalities between genocide and total war that have been examined in this chapter lend support to the arguments of Raphael Lemkin, Gil Elliot, and Leo

Kuper that the differences between the two forms of mass killing may be less important than the similarities and that genocide and total war are frequently inseparable. The features examined in this chapter do not, however, exhaust the commonalities. The next chapter shows that genocide and total war are facilitated by several of the same psychological, organizational, and scientific-technological processes. A conceptual framework comprising such factors is then described in terms of which the Holocaust, as a case of genocide, and Allied strategic bombing during World War II, as a case of total war, can be comparatively analyzed.

Chapter 5

A Conceptual Framework for Further Analysis

In this chapter we examine another important connection between genocide and total war that was disclosed by our review of the literature, specifically that both forms of man-made death have often been facilitated by similar psychological, organizational, and scientific-technological factors. These factors are not themselves sufficient to cause perpetration of genocide or engagement in total war, but they can make it easier for both authorities and ordinary citizens to participate in the mass killing of innocent people. After identifying and discussing a number of such shared facilitating factors, we develop six of them into a conceptual framework in terms of which we can comparatively analyze the Holocaust as an exemplary case of genocide and the Allied strategic bombing campaigns during World War II as an exemplary case of total war. This comparative analysis is presented in Part 2 of the book (Chapters 6–10).

Psychological Facilitating Factors

Three factors operating at the psychological level to facilitate participation in both genocide and total war are the *dehumanization* of the victims; the use of *euphemistic language* in communications concerning killing projects; and the belief that killing others is necessary for, and justified by, the resultant protection or enhancement of one's own group, that is, the *healing-killing paradox*.[1]

Dehumanization

"Dehumanization," according to Leo Kuper, "might be conceived as the relegation of the victims to the level of animals or of objects or to a purely instrumental role. The denial of common humanity would seem to be an important component of any definition, since it emphasizes the element of exclusion."[2] Psychologist Herbert Kelman has suggested that dehumanization entails the removal of two fundamental qualities from the victim, identity and community; the individual identity of each victim is submerged in the group to which he or she belongs, and the group as a whole is considered to be subhuman or nonhuman.[3] A closely related concept, pseudospeciation, has been explored by psychoanalyst and psychohistorian Erik Erikson, who wrote, "The term refers to the fact that mankind, while one species, has divided itself throughout history–territorially, culturally, politically–into various groupings that permit their members at decisive times to consider themselves, more or less consciously and explicitly, to be the only true human species and all others (and especially *some* others) to be less than human" (emphasis in original).[4]

Genocide scholars have frequently noted the role of dehumanization.[5] Kelman, for example, observed that "the inhibitions against murdering fellow human beings are generally so strong that the victims must be deprived of their human status if systematic killing is to proceed in a smooth and orderly fashion. To the extent that the victims are dehumanized, principles of morality no longer apply to them and moral restraints against killing are more readily overcome."[6]

Total wars also rely on dehumanization to make it easier to engage in, or support, mass killing of enemy soldiers and civilians than might otherwise be the case. Governments engaged in total wars employ propaganda to maintain morale both on the battlefield and on the home front. Such propaganda tends to portray the enemy as unequivocally evil and one's own national cause as unequivocally just. Propaganda that dehumanizes enemies tends to weaken any potential moral or emotional hesitation against killing them by means that would ordinarily be regarded as unacceptable. In World War II, for example, the official German ideology regarded the Russians and other Slavic peoples as less human than Germans. Hence, when hundreds of thousands of Russian prisoners of war were deliberately starved to death, it was not as if men were being killed but rather that vermin were not allowed to live. Dehumanization has been observed to take place in more recent wars, such as the U.S. war in Vietnam. In his article based on interviews with U.S. soldiers who participated in massacres of defenseless Vietnamese civilians, former Army psychiatrist William Gault noted the frequency with which U.S. soldiers used such terms as "gook" and "slope" to describe their Asian enemies. Gault suggested that "these attitudes serve to psychologically soften the experience of killing Orientals, so that some soldiers feel that the individual dead enemy was 'not like you and me but more like a Martian or something.'"[7]

Euphemistic Language

A second psychological factor that makes involvement in a mass-killing project more emotionally palatable is the employment of euphemistic language that serves to conceal the true nature and goals of the project.[8] Again to quote from Kelman's pioneering work, "Moral inhibitions are less easily subdued if the functionaries, in their own thinking and in their communication with each other, have to face the fact that they are engaged in organized murder. ... The difficulty is handled by the well-known bureaucratic inventiveness in the use of language."[9] In the Holocaust, for example, deportation to the death camps was code-named "evacuation to the East," and the actual killing was termed "special action" and "special treatment."[10] Likewise, the deliberate firebombing of cities crowded with civilians in World War II was known as "strategic bombing," and the deliberate attacks on neighborhoods filled with German factory workers, which killed tens of thousands of women and children, was intended, in the official jargon, to "dehouse" those workers.[11] The Persian Gulf War of 1991 was no exception to the tendency to sanitize killing by the use of euphemisms. Hence, bombing raids were called "sorties"; inadvertent killing of civilians was "collateral damage"; bombs of various kinds were referred to as "ordnance"; and the accidental killing of American and British soldiers by their compatriots was termed "death by friendly fire."[12]

The Healing-Killing Paradox

A third psychological process involved in the facilitation of governmental mass killing entails justification of such killing by the claim that it is in the service of a noble, necessary, even heroic, cause. Robert Jay Lifton, in his study of Nazi physicians involved in the Holocaust, coined the term "healing-killing paradox" to denote this process. "In Auschwitz, too", observed Lifton, "killing was done in the name of healing. ... For the SS doctor, involvement in the killing process became equated with healing."[13]

Central to the healing-killing paradox is the conviction that killing outsiders is the only viable means of healing one's own people. The Nazi doctors believed that by killing the Jews they were actually healing various wounds that had been inflicted, allegedly by the Jews, on the German nation and its people. Scholars have noted a similar phenomenon in other genocides. For example, in his detailed study of the reciprocated genocidal massacres that occurred in the 1971 civil war between the government forces of West Pakistan and the secessionists in East Pakistan, in which as many as 3 million Bengalis were slaughtered, Robert Payne noted that those who ordered and carried out the massacres saw themselves as saviors. By exterminating members of the enemy groups, they ensured the security and survival of their own.[14] As Israel Charny has observed, "Incredible as it may seem, virtually every genocide is defined by its doers as being on behalf of the larger purpose of bettering human life!"[15] Similar processes operate in warfare, where leaders and soldiers regard killing of the enemy as a patriotic duty.

Organizational Facilitating Factors: Bureaucracy

A second contributing factor emphasized by analysts of mass killing is the pervasiveness of bureaucratic organization in contemporary society.[16] A direct connection between bureaucracy and the scale of mass killing during the twentieth century has been asserted by Richard Rubenstein in his essential study *The Cunning of History: The Holocaust and the American Future*, where he wrote:

> Usually the progress in death-dealing capacity in the twentieth century has been described in terms of technological advances in weaponry. Too little attention has been given to the advances in social organization that allowed for the effective use of the new weapons. In order to understand how the moral barrier was crossed that made massacre in the millions possible, it is necessary to consider the importance of bureaucracy in modern political organization.[17]

The role of bureaucracy in facilitating modern genocide has been noted by several scholars. Fein, for example, observed, "With the modern social organization of bureaucracies, characterized by hierarchy and a high division of labor, the important killers are white-collar criminals who command the diverse staffs that must be mobilized." She went on to suggest that "bureaucracy is not in itself a cause of the choice of destructive ends, but it facilitates their accomplishment by routinizing the obedience of many agents, each trained to perform his role without questioning the ends of action."[18] In his analysis of the Turkish genocide of the Armenians in 1915–1917, sociologist Vahakn Dadrian emphasized the crucial role played by "bureaucratic machinery" in significantly increasing the efficiency of the killing project.[19] Another example of the facilitating role of bureaucracy in genocide is provided by the more recent Cambodian genocide, in which, between 1975 and 1978, as many as 3 million Cambodians were killed by their government.[20] The communist Khmer Rouge perpetrators relied on bureaucracy in order to organize and implement their policies. As David Hawk has stated, "Murder-by-government under Khmer Rouge rule was so systemic and widespread that a large bureaucracy was required to eliminate the projected, suspected, and imagined opponents."[21]

Bureaucracy is also a crucial factor in modern total wars in which the economic, political, and military resources of complex nation-states must be harnessed in the service of a sustained struggle for survival or conquest. For every individual who is directly involved with the killing (e.g., the soldier on the ground or the crew member in the bomber), there are many others who must decide and promulgate the policies; design, build, and service the requisite machinery; coordinate the logistics of supply and transport; generate, distribute, and file paperwork; monitor and evaluate.[22]

Several specific features of bureaucratic organization serve to promote the overall efficiency of mass killing in both genocide and total war, as well as to enable participants to carry out their tasks with a minimum of questioning or doubt.

Hierarchical Structure

First, insofar as the positions within a bureaucracy are arranged in a formal *hierarchical structure*, individuals at the lower levels may tend to have a reduced sense of personal responsibility for either the policy they are helping to implement or its final outcome. They are, after all, only following orders that have descended through all the levels of the organization above their own.[23] This is particularly true of the military with its strongly indoctrinated tradition of unquestioning obedience to authority.

Division of Labor

Another feature of bureaucracy, *division of labor,* breaks down complex tasks into compartmentalized and specialized subtasks. Although such compartmentalization may contribute to greater efficiency and productivity for the organization, it may also tend to circumscribe the thinking and imagination of individual bureaucrats within the organization. As Robert Michels noted, "This tendency towards an exclusive and all-absorbing specialization, towards the renunciation of all far-reaching outlooks, is a general characteristic of modern evolution [of bureaucratic organizations]."[24] "Microdivision of labor," commented sociologist Don Martindale, "has made the goal of activity invisible, depriving it of meaning for the individual."[25] A similar point was made by Fred Katz in a noteworthy article analyzing the Holocaust from a sociological perspective. Katz observed, "The individual bureaucrat typically focuses on a particular task, without considering the wide implications, including broader moral issues."[26]

Organizational Loyalty

A third feature of bureaucratic organization with potential relevance to an understanding of peoples' willingness to participate in mass-killing projects is *organizational loyalty*—the tendency for loyalty to the organization to become an end in itself, even to the point of superseding moral or empathic considerations. As Max Weber noted, "The individual bureaucrat is thus forged to the community of all the functionaries who are integrated into the mechanism. They have a common interest in seeing that the mechanism continues its functions and that the societally exercised authority carries on."[27]

In their valuable analysis of bureaucratic politics in American national security policymaking, former National Security Council staff member Morton Halperin and his colleagues observed that "an organization favors policies and strategies which its members believe will make the organization as they define it more important."[28] Thus the maintenance or even expansion of the organization itself may become an overarching goal. In political struggles over alternative policy options, the interests of one's own agency may become a paramount concern. Parochial organizational interests may become the dominant perspective by means of which such alternatives are evaluated. If contributing to a mass-killing project is the price for occupational security or career advancement, then the functionary may become wholeheartedly devoted to the project, undistracted by doubt or guilt.

Amoral Rationality

The final characteristic of bureaucracies that we will consider—*amoral rationality*—involves preoccupation with the best means of attaining a particular goal or completing a given task while tending to ignore the moral or human implications of the goal or task. Bureaucracies deliberately strive to render moral and human considerations irrelevant with respect to the task at hand. As Max Weber noted, "a bureaucratic organization develops the more perfectly the more the bureaucracy is 'dehumanized,' the more completely it succeeds in eliminating from official business love, hatred, and all purely personal, irrational, and emotional elements which escape calculation. This is the specific nature of bureaucracy and it is appraised as its special virtue."[29] Such amoral rationality combines with the effects of the other features of bureaucracy to help create technically proficient functionaries who perform their specialized assignments with a minimized tendency to indulge in moral concerns.

Scientific and Technological Factors

Science and technology have affected mass killing in total war and genocide in several ways. Perhaps most obvious is the fact that scientists and technicians have played crucial roles in developing new forms of weaponry that have greatly increased the ability of killers to destroy and kill. Less obvious, but no less important, scientists have also provided rationalization for the mass killing itself. Moreover, new technologies—by imposing physical, emotional, and moral distance between the killers and their victims—have made the moral and emotional burdens of mass killing less onerous.

Scientific Rationalization

A vital characteristic of the twentieth century is the centrality of science as a means of understanding ourselves and our world. For many people, scientists have an authority and prestige that was once accorded to priests and other religious figures. Scientists play important roles in the formulation and implementation of public policies as well as in evaluating the implications of such policies.[30]

When science is used to legitimize a public policy, regardless of the nature of the policy, it runs the risk of losing the objectivity that is its hallmark. As Martindale noted, "In the instant that science undertakes the task of justifying one social arrangement rather than another, it ceases simply to be science. Whenever science becomes normative, and assumes tasks that exceed empirical explanation, it is, perhaps, best described as *scientism*" (emphasis in original).[31] In a society in which science enjoys great prestige and influence, there is always the danger that science may be exploited by advocates of a controversial policy to discredit dissenters and strengthen support. In such cases, it is used as a form of rationalization for policies that might otherwise provoke greater opposition.

The pervasive influence of science in contemporary public affairs has led to its having played an important role in the formulation and implementation of policies involving mass killing. In particular, science and scientists have been called upon to provide a rationale for such killing. Scientific authority has been invoked to justify the resort to killing as a means of promoting national security. Science has also been called upon to prove that mass killing is the best, or only, feasible means by which a particular goal can be reached. The costs entailed by such a policy are "scientifically" shown to be less consequential than the benefits.

Technical Distancing

Not only can killers annihilate great numbers of people in short periods of time, they can often do this without even seeing, hearing, or otherwise directly encountering their victims, be they enemy soldiers or civilians. In a seminal article on the impact of technology on modern war, sociologist Francis Allen notes that "the increasing tendency is to wage war at a distance. ... Modern scientific war thus becomes depersonalized."[32] His observation has been corroborated by other scholars of military history.[33]

In World War I, for example, heavy artillery pieces were fired across the no-man's-land into the area of enemy trenches rather than at individually sighted soldiers. During World Wars I and II, submarines sank both civilian and military ships from a distance with torpedoes; viewed at a distance through a periscope, the dying people looked more like frenzied ants than human beings. During World War II, many of the bombing raids against cities took place at night or when the targets were obscured by cloud cover or by the smoke rising from fires started by earlier attacks.

Technical distancing has been cited by analysts of genocide as an important facilitating factor. According to Horowitz, "The technological devices which permit collective death are also at work in creating a profound sense of total distance between victims and victimizers. ... Killing becomes a matter of policymaking rather than ethical decision. Thus the individual is reduced to the status of non-person not simply as victim, but with equal profundity, as victimizer."[34] Genocide scholar Kurt Jonassohn concurred with Horowitz, noting that modern genocides "often benefited from advances in technology" and that technology is "useful primarily for creating a distance between the killers and the victims." However, Jonassohn also cautioned that many modern genocides rely on "primitive" technology.[35] An example is provided by the Cambodian genocide of 1975–1978, in which the killers, rather than waste bullets, often used clubs and axes to slaughter their victims.

An important psychological effect of such technologically imposed distance between killers and victims is the increased dehumanization of the victim. "In general," stated sociologist Lewis Coser, "the perception of the humanness of the 'other' decreases with the increase in distance between perceiver and perceived."[36] As noted, such dehumanization erodes any moral or empathic restraints that might interfere with the effective performance of tasks by the killer.

Technology may also reduce sensitivity to moral dimensions of the task at hand. In a provocative article, "Technology and Genocide," philosopher Steven Katz suggested that "technology as such helps shape consciousness. ... It helps to redirect, to close off, the mind from larger, perennial considerations of the equation of ends and means, of objects and their use. This, in turn, produces a reconditioned mentality that is conventionally amoral."[37]

A Conceptual Framework for Further Analysis

The preceding examination of the literature has documented several important commonalities between genocide and total war as two forms of governmental mass killing. More work needs to be done, however. In her critical review of the social science literature on genocide, Helen Fein suggested that future research is needed to "assess the incidence, coincidence, and relationship between genocide, inter-state war, civil strife, and transitions of state power."[38] In the next major section of the book, we explore at least part of Fein's agenda—the relationship between genocide and interstate war. We do so by undertaking a comparative analysis of one exemplary case of genocide, the Nazi Holocaust, and one exemplary case of total war, the British and U.S. strategic bombing campaigns during World War II. We compare these two historical cases in terms of a conceptual framework of psychological, organizational, and scientific-technological facilitating factors that have been suggested by our review of the relevant literature.

The following conceptual framework identifies six facilitating factors that are hypothesized to play important roles in enabling people to participate in governmental mass-killing projects. These six facilitating factors do not presume to exhaust all of the processes that are potentially relevant to an understanding of mass killing. Instead, our conceptual framework represents a preliminary attempt to shed light on a relatively unexplored area of human behavior and to stimulate others to focus their scholarly attention on it.

Psychological Facilitating Factors

Dehumanization of Victims. Dehumanization involves converting the targets of mass-killing projects into outsiders for whom ordinary moral and empathic considerations do not apply. Indicators of dehumanization can assume a variety of forms. The official ideology of the government may define members of minority groups or citizens of enemy nations as sub- or nonhuman. Speeches by leaders may include dehumanizing labels applied to people targeted for government-sponsored violence. Laws can declare members of certain groups as less than fully human and therefore undeserving of civil liberties or rights. The mass media may be used to convey images of a particular group as less than human. Caricaturing them to look like animals or insects would be a clear example. The training of the functionaries for mass-killing projects may include lessons in which the dehumanized status of enemies or victims is emphasized. Deep-seated cultural traditions of racism may be called upon to help promote persecution of minorities or enemies.

The Healing-Killing Paradox. Lifton, Payne, Charny, and others have noted that many mass-killing projects have been justified by their perpetrators as being required for the security or even survival of their in-group. Indicators of the healing-killing paradox may be found in statements by individuals responsible for the killing project. Such statements may emphasize the need to kill members of a certain group in order to preserve one's own people from the malign influence of those targeted for killing. Alternatively, a practice that would ordinarily be considered as immoral or reprehensible may be justified as the most efficient means to attain a highly desired goal, often under exceptional circumstances. Questions about the evil nature of the means may be dismissed through reference to the benefits that those means help secure. The healing-killing paradox may also be manifested in official pronouncements by the government that sponsors the killing project. Official policy statements may justify the resort to mass killing by referring to the extremity of the threat confronting the nation or to the fact that mass killing is the only feasible means of attaining a needed objective.

Organizational Facilitating Factors

Compartmentalization of Tasks and Knowledge. One of the fundamental features of bureaucratic organizations is the division of labor into specialized tasks. In such an arrangement, the individual functionary may be preoccupied with only a small part of the overall project with which the organization as a whole is concerned. Such preoccupation may prevent the individual from thinking deeply about, or feeling personally responsible for, the end product of the organization. Compartmentalization of knowledge is closely related to specialization of tasks; functionaries in the project are permitted to know only what is regarded as necessary for them to perform their special duties.

Indicators of compartmentalization will be sought in descriptions of the organizational structure of the killing projects. To what extent were the various tasks broken down into specialized subtasks? What were the various occupational roles required for the project to succeed? For each individual engaged in direct killing, were there others who performed supportive functions? Or, in other words, what was the organizational infrastructure that facilitated the killing, whether in gas chambers or in firestorms? Also, was there evidence that individuals involved in the killing were deliberately misinformed about the nature of their tasks?

Organizational Loyalty. A second feature of bureaucratic organization with potential relevance to an understanding of people's willingness to participate in mass-killing projects is the tendency for loyalty to the organization to become an end in itself, even to the point of superseding moral or empathic considerations. Indicators of organizational loyalty will be sought in descriptions of the process involved in deciding to resort to mass killing as a government policy. Did specific organizations or agencies have incentives to promote such policies as a means by which to ensure their continuity or expansion? Is there evidence of competition among related or similar organizations for scarce resources, including money and personnel, whose allocation was contingent upon the willingness and ability to contribute to mass killing? Is it possible to identify key individuals whose loyalty to their organizations led them in the direction of mass killing as means by which to advance organizational interests?

Scientific-Technological Factors

Scientific Rationalization. Indications of scientific rationalization will be sought in accounts of the policymaking and implementation processes of the two mass-killing projects that are being analyzed in this study. To what extent did scientists play significant roles in justifying or promoting the killing policy? Did political or military leaders who advocate a killing project cite scientific support as an important element in their arguments? Were provisions made to subject the recommendations of the official scientific advisers to careful scrutiny by equally qualified peers who were not directly involved in the policy process? What was the quality of scientific evidence used to justify the killing policy? Reliance on evidence of questionable validity may suggest that the proponents of the policy were more interested in the legitimating image of scientific credibility than in an impartial assessment of available data.

Technical Distancing. Scholars of both genocide and war have noted the powerful impact of technology in creating physical distance between killers and victims and, by doing so, reducing psychological barriers to engaging in mass slaughter. Indicators of this factor will be sought in the historical record of the killing projects and in statements of individuals who participated in both the Holocaust and the strategic bombing campaigns.

Concluding Comments

In this chapter and in Chapter 4, a number of important dimensions of similarity and commonality between genocide and total war have been documented. In order to pursue this inquiry further, we now turn to a comparative analysis of the Holocaust and strategic bombing. Before we compare the two cases in terms of the conceptual framework, however, it is necessary to describe each case, which is done in Chapters 7 and 8. In order for the Holocaust and strategic bombing to be fully meaningful, they need to be placed within the larger context of violence that occurred during that period in history. Hence, we turn, in the following chapter, to the global context of genocide and total war in 1931–1945. Then we tell the stories of the Holocaust and strategic bombing in Chapters 7 and 8, after which, in Chapters 8 and 9, the conceptual framework is applied to each case.

Part 2

Case Studies in the Psychology, Organization, and Technology of Twentieth-Century Genocide and Total War

Chapter 6

The Global Context of Genocide and Total War, 1931–1945

Throughout the world
Everywhere we are all brothers.
Why then do the winds and waves
Rage so turbulently?

—*Emperor Meiji*[1]

This chapter focuses on certain atrocities committed by Asians and Europeans between 1931 and 1945.* First, we present several cases of Japanese brutality and cruelty against combatants and noncombatants. Then, the Italian fascist invasion of Ethiopia in the early 1930s and the combined German and Italian fascist military intervention in the Spanish civil war in the mid- to late 1930s constitute a second series of atrocities. Third, the Bengal famine of 1943 is examined as a case in which British policy during World War II caused massive suffering of innocent civilians. Fourth, we survey the non-Jewish victims of Nazi genocidal violence, including Soviet prisoners of war, Poles, Ukrainians, and Gypsies. Then we document genocides perpetrated by fascist allies of the Germans during World War II in Croatia and Romania. Finally, we expose a special category of mass murder that was perpetrated by Soviet dictator Joseph Stalin during World War II against his own people at the same time that Hitler had invaded and occupied the Soviet Union.

These cases document the fact that genocide and total war had become worldwide by the middle of the twentieth century. To be sure, the Nazis were masters of mass murder. It is difficult to match the ferocity and sheer magnitude of human destruction conjured up by such words as Auschwitz, Babi Yar, and Stalingrad.

*Although our focus is on World War II, we emphasize that World War I, "the war to end all wars," provided the psychological and technological precursor to the bloodbath that began in 1931. As Paul Fussell has written in his study of World War I, "The drift of modern history domesticates the fantastic and normalizes the unspeakable. And the catastrophe that begins it is the Great War." (*The Great War and Modern Memory,* Oxford, Oxford University Press, 1975, p. 74). We are grateful to Ronald Bee for stressing this point to us.

Though phrases such as Bataan Death March, Thai-Burma Death Railway, Rape of Nanking, Rape of Manila, and, recently, Unit 731—all to be discussed in this chapter—do not produce for many the same kind of recognition and revulsion as does the Nazi chamber of horrors, the Japanese, among others, committed atrocities sufficiently horrendous to be compared with those of the Nazis.

The truth might best be served if we saw the entire World War II period as one of the worst times in history, when war had become total and genocidal killing had become like a worldwide, uncontrollable fire consuming millions of people in Ethiopia, Spain, Britain, the Soviet Union, Poland, Romania, Yugoslavia, China, the Philippines, the islands of the South Pacific, and, of course, Germany and Japan. Some were victims of gas; others were burned to death when their shelters were bombed; still others were wiped out of existence by nuclear attack. Elsewhere, victims were machine-gunned and thrown into ravines or were half-buried alive and then slashed to pieces with knives or swords. The skillful use of the bayonet probably reached its high point as a genocidal weapon during World War II.

Japanese Militarism and the Evolution of World War II in East Asia

> Across the sea, corpses soaking in the water;
> Across the mountains, corpses heaped upon the grass.
> We shall die by the side of our lord.
> We shall never look back.
>
> —*Ancient Japanese poem*[2]

The first in a series of crucial events that precipitated war in East Asia was known as the Mukden incident, which occurred on September 18, 1931, when the Japanese dynamited a small portion of the South Manchurian Railway track north of the city of Mukden and then blamed China for a "warlike act." When a Chinese patrol showed up to investigate the source of the explosion, concealed Japanese artillery went into action while "all over south Manchuria Japanese troops who had been alert for days, began their surprise attack on Chinese garrisons."[3] During the next few days, Korean-based Japanese planes bombed scattered pockets of enemy troops while an army brigade crossed into Manchuria from its base in Korea.

On September 30, Henry Pu-yi, China's "last emperor," was installed as the head of the new state of Manchuko (the Japanese name for Manchuria). By November 1931, northern Manchuria fell to the superbly coordinated Japanese attack. Thus, four years before the Italians invaded Ethiopia and five years before the civil war began in Spain, Japan inaugurated World War II's first successful blitzkrieg operation.

Manchuria was probably as much an obsession to the Japanese ultranationalists as Ethiopia was to Mussolini and the Soviet Union to Hitler. Located to the south of the Soviet Union, to the north of Korea, and to the west of Japan, Manchuria was a vitally important Chinese province governed in 1931 by a warlord. Manchuria accounted for a fifth of China's total trade, most of which was in exports of coal, steel, and soy beans to Japan.[4] Zealously patriotic army officers in Manchuria were among the ultranationalists who "campaigned for government-sponsored emigration by Japanese farmers to the Manchurian countryside as the only solution to Japan's economic and agricultural plight." Manchuria was seen as an El Dorado that could "accommodate millions of new settlers."[5]

The Mukden incident of 1931 may be seen as the very beginning of World War II in East Asia. It was not simply the earliest use of lightning warfare, airpower, and modern weapons. Manchuria also represented a test of British, French, and U.S. determination to resist Japanese aggression. However, the only result of international pressure brought through the League of Nations was Japan's decision to leave the League on March 27, 1933.

Italian dictator Benito Mussolini, who followed events in Manchuria closely, was impressed with the fact that "Japan's Manchurian conquest remained unpunished."[6] As we discuss in a later section, Mussolini invaded Ethiopia, a League member, on October 3, 1935. Five days later, Italy was declared an aggressor by the League as Japan had been earlier. The British were instrumental in getting the League to impose sanctions that only drove Mussolini into a Rome-Berlin axis in February 1937 and the Japan-Germany-Italy Anti-Comintern Pact in November 1937. Mussolini's final and formal act of defiance against the "democracies" came in December 1937, when Italy left the League.

During the early 1930s, the more zealous faction of the Japanese military openly displayed a strong dislike for liberal Western values and institutions such as constitutional government and political parties, academic freedom, and freedom of speech or press. It sought to purify the government by ridding it of alien influences and enacting policies that would prepare the nation for "total war."[7] The ultranationalists glorified the Yamoto, or "pure" homogeneous Japanese race, with its "shining history" of 2,600 years.[8] They saw themselves as the true master race of Asia and the world.

The Shanghai incident, in March 1932, was similar to the Mukden incident in that the Japanese deliberately provoked the Chinese in order to justify military intervention. Of special interest in the history of military innovations during World War II was the experimental bombing of the city by planes launched from Japanese carriers. According to one source, the Japanese "bombed Chinese civilians in Shanghai causing several thousand deaths."[9]

Throughout 1932, the Japanese ultranationalists also conducted their crusade on the domestic front, murdering several liberals who had dared to promote the reduction of arms and international peace through the League of Nations. They even assassinated the prime minister. The event is significant in Japanese political history because from then on, prime ministers were no longer civilian party men but were all appointed by the emperor out of the ranks of the army or navy.[10]

As early as 1933, according to Joseph Grew, the U.S. ambassador to Tokyo at that time, maps used in Japanese primary schools "showed French Cochin China (South Vietnam), Thailand, the Straits Settlements, the Philippines, and the Dutch East Indies all under the Japanese flag."[11] It was no secret that the more radical wing of the military had long advocated the "strike south theory," which was designed originally to drive out the Western colonialists from Southeast Asia and save China from imperialism.

It was now only a matter of time before Japan would consider itself prepared to strike south into China. In September, Manchuria's government was reorganized and the local population was placed under the supervision of the brutal Japanese military police. By the end of the year a military document had been widely distributed among the Japanese people that began with the contemporary fascist promise that "war is the father of creation and the mother of culture." The authors deplored "Western individualism" and supported "national defense for total war."[12]

The Sino-Japanese War

Full-scale war broke out between China and Japan in 1937. By 1939, China had lost 800,000 soldiers and the entire coast, including six of China's seven major cities, to Japan.[13] Meanwhile, Chiang Kai-shek, leader of the Kuomintang Nationalist Party, had allied himself with his former enemy, Communist Party leader Mao Tse-tung, against a common enemy—the Japanese.

The Chinese were despised by the Japanese as the most inferior of all races.[14] According to the accounts of Japanese war criminals tried between 1945 and 1951, the army, navy, police, and administration all targeted the "people of Han" for abuse—torturing, burning, and massacring them by the tens of thousands.[15] The atrocity stories told by survivors at the war trials held in China after the war suggest that Japan's war against China was in many ways comparable with Germany's war against the Jews. From evidence presented at the Shanghai District Court in 1946, there were "30,000 cases of murder, torture, plunder and rape" alleged to have been committed by the Japanese against noncombatants in the city throughout the war.[16] This is precisely what the German troops did to civilians all over Europe. Again, the Japanese have the dubious honor of having been first to terrorize ordinary people after the shooting on the military front stopped.

Japan waged total war against the Chinese people. Ordinary persons in densely populated areas often found themselves trapped between armies "as the battlefield moved over them," and they became victims of the Japanese troops who looted, raped, and massacred them.[17] One source reports that 300,000 noncombatants lost their lives this way in the Yangtze Delta alone and that "a considerable proportion of these people were slaughtered in cold blood."[18]

The bloody aftermath of indiscriminate bombing by the Japanese was often photographed, showing "the dead bodies or their parts intermixed in grotesque piles on city streets."[19] These early images of "strategic" bombing shocked a world not yet hardened to the excesses of modern warfare. Japan was condemned for its bombing attacks by the League of Nations and the U.S. government. On September 27, 1937, the Department of State denounced Japan because "any general bombing of an extensive area wherein there resides a large population is unwarranted and contrary to the principles of law and humanity."[20] President Franklin Roosevelt deplored the new barbarism of bombing in his "quarantine speech" of October 5, 1937. A Senate resolution introduced in June 1938 singled out the Japanese as being the "major practitioners" of the "inhuman bombing of civilian populations."[21]

The Rape of Nanking

The atrocities committed by the Japanese on land were far more infamous than those committed from the air. The Rape of Nanking, for example, which started in December 1937 and continued through the early months of 1938, was perhaps the earliest full-scale bloodbath perpetrated on a defenseless people by a World War II army using deadly weapons of war. It was also the earliest such incident to be publicized widely because Nanking, the capital of China, was swarming with foreign service personnel, missionaries, and journalists. Though Japanese textbooks still deny that the incident ever took place, documentary evidence from all sides proving otherwise is overwhelming.[22] Also, the testimony given before the Allied Military Commission after World War II, which led to the execution of General Matsui Iwane, overall commander of ground forces on the Nanking front, and six other high-ranking officers, leaves no doubt at all that the Japanese troops acted in a barbarous manner.

The Japanese entered Nanking after fierce fighting with Chinese troops in Shanghai, 170 miles to the southeast. Later testimony revealed that Chiang Kai-shek employed his very best German-trained soldiers against the Japanese army.[23] Some 750,000 Chinese troops were pitted against 250,000 Japanese. The fighting for Shanghai went on for three months, until Japanese forces in a surprise maneuver encircled the numerically superior Chinese and forced them to retreat. It was General Iwane who then decided to pursue the defeated Chinese forces to Nanking. Meanwhile, dozens of bombing raids were conducted against Nanking between August and December.

As the bombing increased and the ground fighting came nearer to the city, an exodus from Nanking started. Among those who fled on December 7, 1937, was Chiang Kai-shek, who moved his government 250 miles southwest to Hankow.

The battle was won on December 13. On that day, Japanese field guns and aircraft were finally silenced. Pamphlets were dropped from Japanese planes seeking to reassure the populace that "the Japanese troops will assert themselves to the utmost to protect good citizens and enable them to live in peace."[24]

The Japanese troops entered the city on December 14, ostensibly to establish a new regime of law and order and to protect the citizens. They did just the opposite and subjected the Chinese people to an orgy of rape, torture, and murder that went on for four months. At least 100,000 men were massacred on the pretense that they were Chinese troops in civilian disguise. The most commonly accepted figure for women who were raped is 20,000. R. J. Rummel, who has carefully studied the death statistics on Nanking, offers the "prudent estimate" that a total of 200,000 people were murdered in four months.[25]

According to Japanese testimony at the postwar international military tribunal in Tokyo, their army was let loose in the city "to put the fear of God into all Chinese and to compel them to accept Japanese occupation as a more viable alternative to more Nankings."[26] Indeed, this was precisely the same excuse officially given for the bombing of cities. The Japanese needed a quick victory, and they believed that terrorist attacks on noncombatants would surely frighten the enemy into suing for peace.[27]

A very dark side of this affair was disclosed at the Allied trials when a Japanese general admitted not only to "having allowed his troops to rape, loot, murder and burn" but also to having "encouraged the sale of opium to destroy public morale."[28] Indeed, the military had a vested interest in the sale of drugs as a primary means of financing the war.[29] The ordinary soldiers lost all sense of decency and discipline as they ravaged the city.

Unit 731: Experiments on Human Guinea Pigs for Chemical and Biological Warfare

One atrocity that was not revealed at the Tokyo war-crimes trial or at any other postwar tribunal was the secret use of germ warfare by a Japanese army unit against Chinese civilians and prisoners of war captured by the Japanese. The infamous Unit 731, made up of scientists and medical doctors, deliberately infected human beings with dangerous germs and chemicals in order to determine their effectiveness in warfare. This gruesome affair was never brought to light or trial because the United States was itself involved in biological warfare experiments at the time and wanted access to the results of over a decade of research by the Japanese.[30] General Shio Ishii, director of Unit 731, bargained for full immunity in exchange for the data. American general Douglas MacArthur not only agreed but arranged for Ishii not to be prosecuted. In January 1946, Ishii came out of hiding, and two American scientists were sent to Japan to debrief him. Ishii himself "died of cancer at a ripe old age," but not before lecturing to U.S. Army specialists on chemical warfare at Fort Detrick, Maryland.[31]

When the Japanese began their invasion of Manchuria in 1931, Colonel Ishii was attached to the Army Medical College in Tokyo. His fame was derived from inventing a filter to purify water used by troops in the field. He was Major Ishii when he had demonstrated the effectiveness of his invention by purifying his own urine with the filter and then drinking it before Emperor Hirohito himself.[32]

Though Ishii's bacteriological experiments may have started as early as 1933, Hirohito did not fully sanction the Unit 731 project until 1936.[33] By 1939, Unit 731 was a cluster of laboratories, living quarters, and barracks with a staff of 3,000 scientists, technicians, and security personnel. The operation was secretly located 40 miles south of Harbin in Manchuria. For the thousands of Russians and Chinese "recruited" by the Japanese secret service, Unit 731 proved a death camp.[34] Later in the war, after the fall of the Philippines and Singapore, Unit 731 used U.S., British, Australian, and New Zealander prisoners of war "to see if the results would differ according to race."[35]

Ishii, a two-star general in 1939, set out to answer certain questions by direct empirical investigation. Was it possible, for example, to infect men in the same way that lice, mosquitoes, ticks, and fleas do? Where in the human body was it best to inject the infectious agent? Is delivery of bacteria by aircraft an effective means of causing epidemics? Can one kill more people by polluting the water supply?[36] The laboratories produced vats full of the bacteria of typhus, tetanus, anthrax, smallpox, and salmonella.[37]

Ishii's staff learned how to produce 300 kilograms of plague germs in a single month. With an inexhaustible supply of rats, they did intensive research on the plague bacillus in fleas.[38] They discovered, among other things, that "a flea normally ingests 5,000 plague organisms at one feeding from a rat which is suffering from an average dose of the disease."[39] These were no academic experiments designed to rid the world of a disease. Quite the contrary was true. The port of Ningpo south of Shanghai was attacked with plague germs "by scattering contaminated fleas by plane."[40] There were 99 recorded deaths from this incident. There were many such attacks in heavily populated areas, executed always with utmost secrecy.[41]

The human beings on whom experiments were performed were called *marutas*, or "wooden logs." From Japanese records, 3,000 such human guinea pigs lost their lives in grotesque experiments from which there was no escape.[42] Because syphilis was increasing among Japanese soldiers, female *marutas* were deliberately infected with the disease in order to test possible cures. Few survived the ordeal.[43] Trench foot was also studied because it was a common complaint among troops in the frigid north. Then there were the experiments in which blood was siphoned off and replaced with horse blood. Perhaps the greatest horror of all were the "anatomical studies" by a Dr. Kayo Okamoto and his colleague, Dr. Tachiomaru Ishikawa, who both practiced vivisection on living human beings. Later, the bodies were cut up and the specimens placed in hundreds of jars.[44] Again, neither Ishii nor any of his colleagues were brought to trial for their war crimes.

The Japanese Scorched-Earth Policy Against the Chinese Communists

The scorched-earth policy of the Germans in the wake of their invasion of the Soviet Union is well known. Much lesser known is the scorched-earth policy in northern China first implemented by Japan in 1941 against communist guerrillas and the peasants who supported them. Mao Tse-tung had taken great pride in the fact that "the peasants are the ocean in which the Red Army swims." The Japanese army was ordered to "drain the ocean."[45]

Officers commanded their men to "Loot all, Kill all, Burn all."[46] Total war was declared against the peasants. Villages were destroyed, crops were burned while the peasants starved in the ravaged land. When the peasants fled, the army pursued and killed them. When they fled to the caves, the army pursued them and then gassed them to death. "Vigorously obeyed," writes one statistician of man-made death, "the campaign reduced the Chinese population in the region from around 44 million to 25 million people."[47]

The Bataan Death March

On December 7, 1941, "the most modern, highly-trained and deadly naval air force in the world roared ... toward their targets."[48] The bombing of Pearl Harbor signaled Japan's determination to widen the war to include U.S. and West European interests in the South Pacific and Southeast Asia. At the end of 1941, except for General Erwin Rommel's weakening position in North Africa, German military forces were victorious everywhere. In the Soviet Union, Germans had already reached the outskirts of Leningrad and were moving steadily toward Moscow as Russian forces seemed to be collapsing on all fronts. Only Britain survived in western Europe. If ever there was a time when historical circumstances favored an all-out attack on Western colonialism in Asia, this was such a time.

The extension of total war was accompanied by fresh atrocities. In the Philippines, for example, the Japanese blitzkrieg proved so effective on the land, on the sea, and in the air that U.S. and Filipino troops were in complete retreat to the Bataan Peninsula and to the fortress of Corregidor only two weeks after the initial attack on December 8. Clark Field, the U.S. air base, which boasted 35 Flying Fortresses (B-17 long-range bombers), was totally devastated in four days, along with 75 percent of the planes.[49] American air force personnel who survived the attacks on Clark Field recall the amazing precision bombing and strafing by the Mitsubishi-built Zero, which, according to one analyst, was the "world's most advanced fighter plane" at the time.[50]

On April 9, 1942, after being totally defeated by Japanese forces, some 66,000 Filipino and 12,000 U.S. troops surrendered to the Japanese in Bataan, marking the event historically as the "heaviest numerical reversal ever suffered by an American force in a single engagement with a foreign foe."[51] The Japanese plan was to have the prisoners walk out of Bataan as far as San Fernando, a distance of 60 miles. The prisoners were to be shipped from there by train to camps in central Luzon. The evacuation was a disaster for the captive troops. It was so poorly planned, provisions for the sick and wounded were so neglected, and the attitude of the guards was so hostile that the operation rapidly degenerated into the infamous Japanese atrocity known in history texts as the Bataan Death March.

Accounts by men who lived through the ordeal reveal the horror. They were organized into groups of 100 and columns of 4 and forced to march. Most of them were suffering from malaria and some form of diarrhea or dysentery before they started out, but no special consideration was given to the wounded or sick. The guards kept the lines moving by beating the men on their heads with rifle butts. An unlucky prisoner might suddenly feel a long black snake whip around his neck or torso, after which he would be dragged behind a truck, never to be seen again.

Reports by those who survived unanimously depict the Japanese soldiers as totally cruel and barbaric. The Korean guards were even worse. Americans, whom the Japanese detested both on racial grounds and for surrendering rather than dying, were treated in a merciless and brutal way. They were beaten for the slightest breach of discipline with stalks of sugarcane three inches in diameter.[52] There was never compassion shown for the American sick and wounded. Typical is the story of the soldier with shrapnel in his shinbone who wrapped a white towel around his leg and walked the best he could. He noticed how the guards could not help laughing at the absurd way he moved about. One of them finally "took his rifle by the barrel and swung at me and broke my ribs on my right side. Then I walked with broken ribs and a wounded leg."[53]

Water was not permitted while the men marched under the hot sun all day long. If, as often happened, the men sighted a buffalo wallowing in the green scum, they might break rank and begin "drowning each other to try to get a drink."[54] The guards shot them immediately. Only at night, their "tongues thick with dust," were the prisoners allowed to have water. It was never sufficient. The Japanese provided adequate food and water for their horses, but not for the POWs.[55]

The nights provided no relief. After having walked all day from early morning to dusk the men were enclosed behind barbed wire. There were no toilet facilities of any sort. They simply sat in the filth and feces of those who had been caged in the same area on previous nights. The smell was indescribable. Most of the men had severe dysentery and during the march were not allowed to go off to the side of the road and squat. As one survivor recounted, "You would just release wherever you were … on yourself or somebody else. … Without food it was water more than anything."[56]

At San Fernando, on Bataan's southern tip, about 60 miles from the start of the forced march, the men sighted a train with boxcars. They were, at first, relieved because they were going to ride rather than march. But when the men were divided into groups of 100 for each car, their spirits sank. They were "jammed in—standing room only. Into the oven … the doors were closed. Men fainted with no place to fall … dysentery. … As the car swayed, the urine, the sweat, and the vomit rolled three inches deep back and forth around and in our shoes."[57]

The train took the men to prison camps, which for all practical purposes were death camps. Since the Japanese had not signed the Geneva Accords on POWs, Red Cross provisions never reached the prisoners. At a place like Camp

O'Donnell, formerly an American army base transformed into a prison camp by the Japanese, the guards paid little attention to the fact that their prisoners were dying frequently from malaria, dysentery, diphtheria, and dry beriberi.[58] Weeks went by during which the bodies could not be buried fast enough in holes that could not be dug deeper than four feet because water would seep into them. As it was, corpses were put into watery graves. As one American soldier on the burial detail remembered it: "While we shoveled dirt on them we had to hold them down with poles. Otherwise they'd float. At night the dogs went wild. They'd dig up the graves to get at the bodies."[59] Of the 132,134 Anglo-American prisoners taken by the Japanese during World War II, 27 percent—35,756—died in captivity.[60]

The Thai-Burma Railway of Death

Captured British soldiers were treated even more harshly than the Americans. The infamous Japanese atrocity known as the Railway of Death to the Burma frontier is, for the British, comparable with the Bataan Death March. In the same way that Americans looked upon Clark Airfield and the Corregidor fortress as military achievements to deter would-be aggressors in the Philippines, the British looked upon the port of Singapore as their "bastion of the East." Singapore, which the British founded in 1819, had a first-rate deep-water harbor of immense strategic importance because it controlled the movement of ships through the Straits of Malacca and defended the eastern means of access to India and the Indian Ocean. In 1941, two battleships, the *Repulse* and the *Prince of Wales*, had been dispatched to reinforce the naval defense of this allegedly impregnable fortress. The port of Singapore also boasted big guns pointed out to sea as a deterrent to any would-be aggressive sea power.

On December 10, just three days after the attack on Pearl Harbor, the Japanese bombed and destroyed both battleships, then defied British strategy and mystified British intelligence by threatening Singapore by land rather than by sea. General Tomoyuki Yamashita, henceforth called "the tiger of Malaya," had penetrated Malaya, then crossed into Singapore by its northern back door and captured the city with 30,000 troops.[61]

The Japanese had also bombed "everything that moved" on the island.[62] All the British Spitfires and Hurricanes, which might have stopped the Japanese blitzkrieg or slowed it down, had previously been flown to North Africa or western Asia to support British armies there. The Japanese also bombed the city, inflicting heavy losses on the mostly Chinese civilian population. After the city surrendered on February 15, 1942, it underwent its own ordeal. The army executed over 5,000 Chinese civilians in a few days of bayoneting, machine-gunning, and beheading.[63]

Following their surrender, British POWs were forced to serve as slave laborers for the Japanese army. To facilitate the Japanese invasion of Burma, they were put to work building a railway across 600 miles of Thai swampland, jungle, rivers, and mountains to the Burma border. Over 20,000 British troops—together with an indeterminate number of Chinese, Tamils, Malays, and other Asians—labored to build an average of 17 miles of track per day.[64]

The lack of compassion for the sick and wounded, the brutal punishment for the minor infraction of a rule, the sadistic behavior of the guards (mostly Korean), and the total disregard for internationally agreed-upon conduct by belligerents toward POWs seem to duplicate the Bataan Death March in every detail.[65] The high rate of death from starvation and dysentery was, no doubt, a result of the bad food fed to the slave laborers. Rice, for example, the staple food among the POWs, was composed of musty-smelling, dirty-gray granules with lime and, as was learned later, was "intended for digging back into the ground as fertilizer."[66]

The technology for building the railway was primitive. Rather than mechanical cranes, the primary tools were, according to one survivor, "weary aching muscles."[67] The Railway of Death, which stretched across Thailand, was built with picks and shovels and rusty axes. Machetes were used by the prisoners to make clearings in the jungle for temporary camps. In the rainy season these camps became "rat-infested sewers."[68] Malaria and dysentery spread through the ranks like an epidemic, but those dying of either disease were not excused from working 12 to 14 hours a day on the railway. And so, remembered one British soldier who lived through it all, "Foot by foot the Railway of Death edged towards the Burma frontier and the bamboo crosses multiplied daily in a score of jungle cemeteries."[69]

The most pathetic group was the captured Chinese, Tamils, Malays, and other Asians who were numerous among the never-ending columns of forced labor. They were not captured soldiers but old men, children, and mothers carrying their young. They plodded helplessly forward day after day, and as the following quotation graphically reveals, the British looked upon them with a deep sense of pity: "They knew, I am sure, that they were destined almost to a man, to die. This was the cruellest aspect in the long saga of Japanese bestiality. At all times, we had some sort of administration, some representation, some refuge for our sick. But these poor wretches had nothing and the Japanese were pitiless."[70]

For the victims, death became a great equalizer among the races. Whether Dutch, English, Australian, Chinese, or Malay, one died of dysentery in the same way. The flesh would melt away and the eyes would sink deep in the sockets; the teeth would protrude from the skull. During a severe cholera epidemic, a British detail collected corpses from each ethnic group. "We carried them all," a survivor recalls, "yellow and white, black and brown, into huge communal graves and spilt them one on top of another into a ghastly tortured heap. Day after day we lived, ate, worked and tried to sleep in the all-pervading stench of death."[71]

Japanese Military Misconduct in Hong Kong

Evidence of what happened in Hong Kong during and after the Japanese invaded the island suggests once more that army custom and training did not favor compassionate treatment of the defeated. Japanese planes deliberately bombed the crowded Kai-tek market in Hong Kong on December 8, 1941, "leaving 800 Chinese men, women and children bits of mangled flesh."[72] The Japanese army repeatedly committed acts of barbarism. The most infamous took place at St. Stephen's Hospital, where a Red Cross flag was totally ignored as Japanese troops forced their way into the building, bayoneted the doctors, then pulled the bandages off the wounded and killed 52 helpless patients. Next, they took the six nurses into a small room where they gang-raped them for 24 hours. The assault went on all of Christmas day and all of Christmas night.[73]

The Rape of Manila

One of the very worst cases of Japanese military violence against a helpless civilian population occurred in Manila, the capital of the Japanese-occupied Philippines, during February and March 1945, very late in the war. During this Rape of Manila, some 16,000 Japanese naval and 4,000 army troops suddenly turned against the people of the city in an orgy of torture, rape, and murder.[74]

General Yamashita, who commanded the Japanese troops around Manila and was held responsible for their behavior by the American army, claimed that he had ordered his forces out of the capital in December 1944 because there was no way of defending it. A special force was created to complete the evacuation, but the navy refused to cooperate. On February 13, 1945, according to General Yamashita, the navy was still "defending the city" even though they were hopelessly surrounded by the enemy.[75] The subsequent destruction of harbor facilities (the finest in Southeast Asia) was allegedly done against Yamashita's orders. In fact, he had lost all contact with the troops inside the city and did not know of the atrocities being committed there.[76]

It was during General Yamashita's trial at the international military tribunal in the Far East in 1946 that the atrocities committed by the Japanese troops were documented and publicized widely for the first time. Some 200 witnesses took the stand and reported to the court how the Japanese moved freely about the city, "beheading, bayoneting, clubbing, hanging and burning people alive."[77] One 13-year-old Filipino girl lifted her dress before the court to display 26 scars left on her body by Japanese bayonets.[78] During the trial, a mind-numbing catalog of abuses was revealed, including throwing babies in the air and catching them on bayonets.[79]

Out of the city's 700,000 inhabitants, 100,000 were killed in what historian John Dower has called a "blood lust in defeat."[80] Manila was so thoroughly destroyed that only Warsaw suffered a worse fate among the cities reduced to rubble in World War II. When the Americans finally entered the city, they found burned and slashed bodies littering the streets everywhere. The final scene was yet to come. It would be replayed again and again in Iwo Jima (February-March 1945),

Okinawa (April-June 1945), and elsewhere in the Pacific. The Japanese refused to surrender, preferring instead "gruesome, desperate acts of suicide."[81]

Mussolini's Invasion of Ethiopia

> **The Duce shall have Ethiopia, with or without the Ethiopians.**
>
> —*General Rudolfo Graziani*[82]

As noted earlier, Benito Mussolini, founder of fascism in Italy, studied the pattern of Japan's aggression carefully in the 1930s, noting the ineffectual opposition by the Western democracies and the League of Nations. Like the Japanese ultranationalists, Mussolini equated Italy's future well-being with the most ruthless kind of military conquest and imperialism. Like the Japanese military, he favored airpower and other weapons of modern warfare. And above all, he had no moral reservation about using his arsenal in a total war to achieve his ends.

Ethiopia, or Abyssinia as it was known to the medieval world, was the only independent state in East Africa and the only indigenous Christian state in all of Africa. Mussolini chose it as a prime target for conquest. It was a perfect choice for a colony because it bordered two Italian colonies in East Africa: Eritrea to the north and Somaliland to the southeast. The invasion would be launched from these colonies. Moreover, 40 years earlier, in March 1896, Italian troops had been beaten by Ethiopians in the Battle of Adowa, thus thwarting an attempt at conquest. Mussolini now hoped to avenge that defeat.

The pattern of aggression was familiar to those who had observed the Japanese. There was the incident at Wal Wal (December 1934), in which Somalis in the duce's service opened fire with tanks and aircraft on Ethiopians.[83] When the Ethiopians fired back, the Italians had their pretext for mobilizing their army for combat. Mussolini sent an expeditionary force to his colonies of 200,000 men, 7,000 officers, 6,000 machine guns, 1,700 pieces of artillery, 150 tanks, and 150 aircraft. The Ethiopians in 1935 had 350,000 men under arms with 400,000 rifles of various sorts and 200 antiquated pieces of artillery. Their air force was made up of three outmoded biplanes.[84]

The Italians crossed the Ethiopian frontier on October 3, 1935, but were forced back when winter began. The League of Nations ordered sanctions against Italy on November 2 in response to Mussolini's blatant aggression.

Fearing a repetition of what had happened to Italians the last time they had invaded Ethiopia, Mussolini agreed to the use of poison gas on December 26, 1935. Villages in the Takkaze ford area were drenched with mustard gas days later. News of the event was officially reported to the League on December 30.[85]

Starting in January 1936, the Italians intensified the brutality of their war against Ethiopia. Under ruthless military men such as General Rudolfo Graziani, the fighting became genocidal. General Graziani was especially chosen by

Mussolini for the Ethiopian theater because of the former's successful use of concentration camps in Libya to suppress a revolt there.[86] In Ethiopia, Graziani gained fame for the Battle of Ganale Doria on January 12, 1936, which was a veritable massacre. He had ordered nearly two tons of mustard gas to be sprayed on Ethiopian positions, and when the army tried to escape, they found that the Italians controlled all the available water in the wells and the river. As the Ethiopians reached the river and began begging for water, they were mowed down by machine-gun fire.[87]

War of annihilation was the pattern adopted by the Italians. They attacked towns and villages by indiscriminately dropping bombs and spraying the area with gas or machine-gun bullets. In one battle (at the Tokkaze fords) on March 3–4, 1936, 80 tons of high explosives and incendiary bombs were dropped on columns of Ethiopian troops struggling to cross a river.[88] Beyond the river, on the wooded slopes of Takkaze valley, bombers drenched the retreating troops with mustard gas. At one of the final battles of the war, on March 23 at Lake Ashangi, a deadly combination of artillery shells, bombs, and poison gas led to a disastrous defeat for 20,000 Ethiopian soldiers, who were then cut down as they fled for safety. The following describes more a massacre than a battle: "Throughout the day the planes continued to bomb the routed and demoralized force that no longer had any fire in its belly. Describing the scene, Halie Salassie said, 'It was no longer a war for the Italian airmen—it was a game. ... It was a massacre.' When evening closed in and the last planes flew back to ... base, the plain of Lake Ashangi was strewn with thousands of corpses."[89]

On May 2, Emperor Halie Salassie was on his way to Djibouti across the Danakil desert. His five years of exile had begun. On May 4, Italian troops entered the capital of Addis Ababa.

Intervention by the Totalitarian Powers in the Spanish Civil War

In 1931, the first municipal elections after eight years of dictatorship in Spain brought into power a republican form of government with moderate liberals at the helm. But in the next few years, the liberals were undermined by extremists of the left and right. Finally, in 1936, the government was taken over by the Popular Front—a coalition of left-wing republicans, socialists, and communists. They sent General Francisco Franco into exile in the Canary Islands, little realizing that he was involved in a plot by those on the right to retake power. Franco was Spain's most famous soldier, and in 1936, he looked upon the ideology of the Popular Front as a "foreign disease" threatening "civilization" with "barbarism."[90] Franco took command of Spanish forces in Morocco in July 1936, and led them in an invasion of Spain.

As early as July 19, 1936, Generalissimo Franco asked Mussolini for a dozen bombers. Days later, he asked Hitler for air transports. Ready assistance from both fascist powers enabled Franco to send arms and ammunition to one of his generals and to transport thousands of troops across the straits from Africa to Spain. By August, pro-Franco nationalist armies of the north and south were able to unite. Intervention from the totalitarian powers on the right—Hitler and Mussolini—had already turned the tide of the war.[91]

Franco now hoped that republican resistance would collapse. But the arrival of Soviet aircraft at this crucial time not only provided tactical air support for the republican army but suddenly gave them control of the air along most of the front. Then, Russian tanks appeared in Madrid and neutralized the struggle in that area. First fascist aid, then communist, prevented a quick decision on either side.

Intervention had the impact of polarizing the two warring sides among the Spaniards, which intensified their hatred of each other and made them prone to commit terrible atrocities. The Popular Front, following the models of the French and Bolshevik Revolutions, targeted the church as its chief adversary. Bishops, priests, monks, and nuns were murdered. Killer gangs of union workers, political cadres, and adolescent militants also sought out ordinary people suspected of traditionalist leanings. Altogether, the left may have murdered 55,000 civilians during the war.[92]

Nationalist killings of noncombatants were carried out largely by the military, who ferreted out republican sympathizers, often having them tortured, then executed. After capturing a city such as Granada, Seville, or Saragossa, they would round up the intelligentsia and have them shot. Even the world-famous poet Garcia Lorca was murdered, presumably because his brother-in-law was the Socialist mayor of Granada. The nationalists are credited with having taken the lives of 50,000 civilians.[93]

Spain proved a marvelous arena for the totalitarian armies who could and did utilize their military machines and hardware under optimum wartime conditions. Germany's 88-millimeter antiaircraft guns were very effective against republican air superiority in 1937. Hitler's most famous atrocity in Spain was committed by his Luftwaffe (air force) on April 26, 1937. On that day, 43 aircraft of the Condor Legion bombed the defenseless historical Basque town of Guernica. At least 1,000 people were killed and most of the buildings were destroyed.[94]

The Italians supported Franco with 50,000 troops and 660 aircraft and supplied him with some very expensive high-quality weapons. The Italians claimed that "they shot down 903 aircraft and sank 72,800 tons of Republican shipping."[95]

As far as Stalin's arsenal was concerned, it was the tank corps that surprised the nationalists most. Russian tanks were, according to one source, "heavier, better armed, faster and in every way superior to the German and Italian models."[96] For their part, the Russians learned about tank warfare in Spain, then utilized it against Hitler after the German invasion of their country in 1941. Stalin also aided the republican cause by sending them 1,000 pilots and 2,000 other military specialists.

In April 1937, a violent coup in Barcelona by the communists against other leftists Stalinized the republican government. From summer 1937 through spring 1938, Stalin's Spanish puppets tortured and murdered thousands of socialists and noncommunist leftists.[97] Spain's tragedy was compounded by becoming an extension of Stalin's "great terror," or widespread purge of communists all over the world in 1937–1938. Spanish Stalinists even had special concentration and death camps such as the Barcelona Convent of St. Ursula, which became known as "the Dachau of Republican Spain."[98]

On the nationalist side, postwar retribution was severe. Mussolini's son-in-law Count Ciano has been quoted as saying in July 1939 that "there are a great number of shootings. In Madrid alone between 200 and 250 a day, in Barcelona 150."[99] Tens of thousands of republicans died this way. The total given for those who were executed is 193,000. In time, Franco decided to halt the killings, commuting the death sentences into prison terms. By 1941, 33,375 persons were still imprisoned for their political "crimes" during the civil war.[100]

By the time war came to an end on March 28, 1939, with the fall of Madrid to Franco, nearly 200,000 Spanish soldiers had died, 90,000 on the nationalist side and 100,000 on the republican. The estimate is that 10,000 died in air raids. Besides the countless thousands who died of malnutrition, or were murdered behind the lines, the war produced 1 million cripples and 500,000 exiles.[101]

On March 28, 1939, the very day that Madrid surrendered to Franco, Hitler denounced Germany's 1934 treaty with Poland. A week earlier, Hitler had devoured Czechoslovakia. Spain proved a prologue to the European war that was both "inevitable and imminent."[102]

Winston Churchill and the Bengal Famine of 1943

> **The thousands who lost their lives in the great Bengal Famine of 1943 were ... as truly the victims of the Second World War as were the casualties in battlefields and bombed cities.**
>
> —*N.S. Venkataramani*[103]

From the cases presented thus far, it might appear that only the totalitarian powers were responsible for atrocities during World War II and that these atrocities were the consequences of deliberate governmental policies intended to terrorize populations and bring about quick victories. Actually, World War II witnessed cases of democratic governments behaving inhumanely and callously to people for whom they were responsible in a manner that brought about disasters that affected many people. Shortsighted tactical decisions, prompted by defeat in battle and threat of invasion, could and did lead to unanticipated catastrophic results.

Democracies did not often perpetrate deliberate, planned atrocities, but their method of resolving a crisis or their unwillingness to recognize it as such could and did have fatal consequences for whole populations.

For example, when Burma fell to the Japanese in May 1942, the British anticipated an invasion of India through the province of Bengal. The Andaman Islands in the Bay of Bengal had already been taken by Japanese troops a month earlier. Actually, the invasion of India never materialized in the disastrous way the British feared. The true disaster brought on by the Japanese conquest of Southeast Asia—the Bengal famine—was, surprisingly enough, never anticipated by the British, whose actions helped to create it.

On the eve of World War II, Bengal, no longer self-sufficient in rice production, depended on imports from French Indochina, Thailand, and Burma.[104] When Burma fell to the Japanese, the eastern Indian province of Bengal was suddenly "on the frontier of the war."[105] The British military proclaimed what it called a "denial policy," which it applied to rice and boats. The army removed rice paddies from certain coastal districts and, evidently without thinking of the consequences, removed all boats capable of carrying ten or more passengers from ports along the delta.

In Bengal, the largest river delta in the world, any deliberate restriction of the distribution of food grains by boat was bound to have serious consequences. Though the Famine Inquiry Commission, which later investigated the causes of the disastrous food shortage and subsequent starvation, did not see the denial policy as a primary cause of the famine, it did report that as a result of it, the military evacuated 30,000 families from the delta who were starving as a result of the policy.[106]

In January 1943, the first reports appeared in the American press on the difficult food problem eastern India faced. The *New York Times* and *Time* carried stories on how men, women, and children were being left to starve on Calcutta's streets. On January 11, "the American *charge d'affaire* in London informed the Secretary of State that the British Press had suddenly begun to give prominence to the food shortage in India."[107] However, at this very time (January 1943), Prime Minister Churchill decided to reduce sailings to the Indian Ocean by 60 percent even though the Ministry of War Transport suggested that "such a drastic reduction of sailings ... might result in 'violent' changes and perhaps cataclysms in the seaborne commerce of countries like India."[108]

The United States continued to receive information about the worsening situation. One important document published by the Board of Economic Warfare in July 1943, "Indian Agriculture and Food Problems," painted a very grim picture of the famine and predicted "hundreds of thousands of deaths from starvation" unless efforts were undertaken to relieve the situation.[109] On August 25, 1943, the *New York Times* printed an appeal from the mayor of Calcutta to the mayor of New York City and to President Roosevelt, which had been cabled to the newspaper: "Acute distress prevails in the city of Calcutta and province of Bengal due to shortage of foodstuffs. Entire population is being devitalized and hundreds dying of starvation. Appeal to you and Mr. Churchill in the name of starving humanity to arrange immediate shipment of foodgrains from America, Australia and other countries."[110]

British censors in India altered reports of American correspondents in India, removing such words as "starvation," "famine," and "corpses."[111] But by September, articles were appearing in U.S. papers on the exodus of starving persons from the rural areas to Calcutta, where many died on the roadside. It was estimated that by October over 100,000 destitute and starving people had "assembled in Calcutta—60,000 of whom were being fed daily at 220 free kitchens run by private organizations."[112] Calcutta's hospitals were filled to capacity. Interestingly enough, a month earlier, Churchill had been Roosevelt's guest in the United States and had attended meetings of various sorts that had dealt with everything from military strategy to feeding Allied soldiers. There is no evidence that the famine in India was even discussed. According to one source, "At the time when reports of starvation deaths began to arrive with sickening regularity at the State Department, Churchill was attending meetings at the American Cabinet and holding discussions with the President and his advisers on the progress of the Allied invasion of Italy."[113]

Food was, of course, of paramount concern to Churchill and the Roosevelt administration. But Europe and the Soviet Union were pivotal in their thoughts. The starving millions in India were of little or no consequence. In October 1943, when the Bengal famine was out of control, Vice President Henry Wallace delivered a major address before the National Consumers' Food Conference held in Cleveland. There was not a word spoken of the famine in India. The emphasis was clear enough when Wallace said, "The more food we can put into Russian stomachs, the more American blood will be saved."[114]

The Congress of the United States did, however, take the Bengal famine seriously enough to pass a bill in the House and Senate in February 1944, authorizing the United Nations Relief and Rehabilitation Administration (UNRRA) to include India within its scope as a recipient of urgently needed food supplies. But since Churchill had consistently denied that there was a famine in Bengal, the government of India refused to allow UNRRA funds to be diverted this way. UNRRA activities could not be forced upon a member nation. A deadly game was being played. Everyone knew that people were starving in Bengal, but the government of India (representing Churchill and British interests) refused to request UNRRA assistance. At the same time, the British in India paid UNRRA a contribution of $24 million, which made one of the poorest countries on earth the sixth-largest contributor.[115]

On April 29, 1944, Churchill, for the first time, admitted to Roosevelt that there was a famine in India and that he needed 350,000 tons of wheat immediately. Evidently, the supreme commander in the Southeast Asia Command, Lord Louis Mountbatten, and the Viceroy of India, Lord Archibald Wavell, had finally convinced Churchill of "the importance of averting a second ghastly round of mass starvation in India."[116] Churchill asked for "a special allocation of ships to carry wheat to India from Australia."[117] For reasons that are not altogether clear, during the period April 1944–March 1945, the U.S. government did not send any cereal to India; nor did it divert a single ship to transport food to the victims of famine in India. The human cost of the Bengal famine between 1943 and 1944 was 3 million lives.[118]

Hitler's Other Atrocities

Although the Jews were special victims of the Nazis, they were not the only victims, nor was their Holocaust the only genocide perpetrated by the Nazis. As the following sections show, Soviet POWs, Poles, Ukrainians, Russians, Gypsies, and others were butchered by the millions by the Nazis and their allies.

Soviet Victims in the Aftermath of Operation Barbarossa

On June 22, 1941, more than 4 million German soldiers invaded the Soviet Union at various frontier crossings, thus launching Hitler's long-awaited Operation Barbarossa. As with the Japanese in China, this was a total war waged by the Nazis not only against the military forces of the enemy but against the Slavic peoples who lived in the cities and villages of the Soviet Union.

The intense German hatred for Russians, Ukrainians, Poles, and other Slavs was expressed in one of the most horrendous bloodbaths in history. The war dead in the Soviet Union attributed to Nazi German mass murder is 17 million, divided evenly at 8.5 million each for civilians and combatants.[119] Between 1941 and 1943, 1 million people died in the attempted capture of a single city, Leningrad.[120] It has been estimated that the Germans murdered 4.5 million Soviet city dwellers, 3 million of whom were women, children, and the elderly.[121] As many as 10 million people from the Soviet republic of Ukraine were murdered by the Nazis throughout the war and occupation. Of that total, 900,000 were Ukrainian Jews.[122] The Germans also destroyed 8 million Soviet homes as well as all the livestock and crops they came across.

Hitler had elaborate plans for the fertile Ukraine that included the extirpation of the so-called *Untermenschen,* or inferior racial type, who presently occupied that land. He projected the settlement of 20 million "superior" German Aryans in that area within the next two decades. Eric Koch, Hitler's commissar of Ukraine, believed that the only justification for keeping Ukrainians alive was to serve their Aryan "masters" as "slaves." He was fond of equating Ukrainians with "Negroes."[123]

The Nazi treatment of Soviet POWs not only was a clear case of racism but also constituted a war crime. Soviet soldiers were not even considered POWs because, as Nazi officials argued, their government had not been a signatory to the 1929 Geneva Accords on the treatment of POWs. Alfred Rosenberg, Nazi minister of eastern affairs, declared that the prisoners were to be starved to death at the same time that he prohibited civilians from feeding them.[124] Most of the POWs, some 4 million of them, were captured in the first six months of the war, between June and December 1941.[125] Many were shipped to Poland and Germany as slave workers, where a substantial number ended up in factories located near death camps where they were "worked to death or liquidated." It is estimated that among those who labored in places such as Auschwitz, "500,000 Soviet POWs perished."[126]

From the accounts we have on how the Germans treated Soviet captives, a useful study could be made by a comparativist between the Slav POWs in Nazi hands and the Anglo-American POWs in Japanese hands. Hundreds of thousands of Soviet POWs starved to death during winter 1941–1942. At the prison camp of Kharkov, "as many as 100 men died every day."[127] As the experience at Camp Darnitsa indicates, the Germans were deliberately starving their prisoners to death. Outside the camp there were large collective farms with beetroot and potatoes that had not yet been dug, and "if anybody had been interested, the prisoners could have had all they wanted to eat."[128] The following passage vividly describes what happened at Darnitsa:

> The Germans brought huge cauldrons and began cooking beetroot. … Each prisoner was entitled to one ladle of beetroot water a day. … Those weak from hunger … had to crawl to the cauldron. … Officers and Jews were given nothing. … They had scratched over the whole of the ground and eaten what they could. By the sixth day, they were chewing on their belts and boots … on the ninth day … half-crazed with hunger … twelfth day … only a few left, out of their minds … who nibbled and chewed on their nails, looked for lice … stuffed them into their mouths.[129]

The Nazi War of Annihilation Against the Polish People and Their Culture

> **If I wanted to put up posters for every seven Poles shot, the Polish forests would not suffice to produce the paper for the announcements.**
>
> ***—Hans Frank, Nazi governor-general of Poland***[130]

The German invasion of Poland on September 1, 1939, was no simple declaration of war against a belligerent nation but was a total war against the Poles as a race, as a culture, and as human beings. Like the war against the Slavs and Jews of the Soviet Union, this war by the Nazis constituted an organized campaign of mass terror against the Poles. Civilians were the targets; Nazi fighter planes even strafed shepherds tending their flocks. As in Ukraine, the most fertile parts of Poland were to be Germanized. What this meant was clearly articulated by a high-ranking

Nazi bureaucrat in Poznan, who proudly stated, "In ten years, there will not be a single plot of land that is not German nor a single farm in the possession of anyone but one of our colonists. ... If God exists—it is He who has chosen Adolf Hitler to drive this vermin hence."[131]

The German army spread terror from village to village and from town to town. It began by rounding up priests, teachers, professors, judges, lawyers, journalists, and other members of the intelligentsia. Then it apprehended merchants and peasant leaders. In this way, the community's most-respected citizens were arrested, isolated, and then executed in the town square. Some villages were totally liquidated. The Nazis were especially severe with the clergy. By January 1941, some 700 Polish priests had been put to death; another 3,000 were thrown into concentration camps.[132]

The Nazis opened a training school in torture for the Gestapo at Fort VII in the Polish city of Poznan. Victims for the experiments in the latest sadistic techniques to extract confessions or inflict punishments were "recruited" from among the faculty at Poznan University or from among the intelligentsia in general. Techniques used globally today as routine torture practices were first perfected by the Nazis at these schools. For example, the practice of attaching a rubber hose to an air pump at one end and inserting the other into a victim's rectum was possibly first used effectively by the Gestapo. The objective was to inflate the intestines until they burst.[133]

Pursuing their ethnocidal policy, the Nazis regularly destroyed Polish statues or memorials honoring cultural heroes to eradicate pride or patriotism. It was very dangerous to display a Polish flag or sing a Polish song that glorified the ideals of nationhood. Poles who were deported to Germany as slave laborers were treated as untouchables. They were forced to wear a violet letter "P" with a yellow background on their clothes in order to discourage relations with German citizens. Poles could not enter German churches, theaters, or any other public buildings. Sex between Germans and Poles was an offense punishable by death. In spring 1941, 190 Polish agricultural workers were hanged for having sexual intercourse with German women.[134]

Though there was never a proclaimed "final solution" for Poles, the Nazis mass-murdered hundreds of thousands of Polish Christians at the Auschwitz death camp.[135] Indeed, the inmates at Auschwitz represented 50 nationalities. The Poles were, like the Jews, among the human guinea pigs used for medical research at Auschwitz. Polish women underwent surgical operations as part of a gynecological research program. They were also enslaved at military brothels.[136]

By the end of the war in 1945, the Nazis had managed to exterminate 6 million Poles, half of whom were Jews and half of whom were Christians.[137]

The Nazis Declare the Gypsies Unfit to Live

The Gypsies, most likely from India originally, lived a nomadic existence in Europe for centuries. They were among the first of the nationalities or ethnic groups to be rounded up in December 1942 and sent to Auschwitz.[138] Like the Jews, they had already been persecuted by the Nazis since the 1930s and had been pressured to migrate from German and Austrian soil. At Auschwitz, they were placed in a special section of the camp and were forced to wear a black triangle on their clothes with the word "asocial" on it. They then suffered the usual fate of those whom the master Aryan race deemed unworthy. First, they were worked to death as slaves; second, they were injected with typhus and spotted fever as human guinea pigs in a laboratory especially set up in the camp by the notorious Dr. Mengele; third, they were exterminated by being gassed to death. A conservative estimate is that the Nazis were able to wipe out 250,000 Gypsies by war's end.[139]

The Croatian Fascists (Ustashi) and Their Enthusiasm for Genocide

> **We have slaughtered here at Jasenovac more people than the Ottoman Empire was able to do during its occupation of Europe.**
>
> —*Vjekoslav Luburic, commander in chief of Croatian death camps*[140]

The spread of Nazi ideology that accompanied German conquest exacerbated existing ethnic and religious animosity in Europe, leading, in some cases, to genocide. Probably nowhere else was Nazi racism so warmly welcomed and earnestly domesticated than in Yugoslavia among the Serb-hating Roman Catholic Croats. This hostility had deep roots in the past. Resentment against Serbian dominance can be traced back to A.D. 900, when the Serbs ended Byzantine rule in the Balkans and, in the process, carved their own empire out of parts of Yugoslavia, Macedonia, and Greece. That dominance lasted until 1459, when the Balkans were absorbed into an expanding Ottoman Empire. In more recent times, Yugoslavia fell under the control of Austro-Hungary. Then it was declared a new nation after World War I. The Serbs had dominated Yugoslavia between the wars.

When Hitler overran Yugoslavia in April 1941, prior to Operation Barbarossa, he found a cooperative native fascist group under Ante Pavelic, who had long since established close contact with the fascist Mussolini in Italy.[141] Under Italian guidance, Pavelic had founded a terrorist organization known as Ustashi (Insurrectionists) in 1929, which the Nazis later established as the governing elite of an enlarged state called the Independent State of Croatia.

The Ustashi took over the government on April 16, 1941, and a week later began to massacre Serbs. Between 1941 and 1945, the Croats "doomed to extermination" as many as 750,000 Serbian men, women, and children simply because they "happened to belong to another ethnical and racial group and had inherited the Christianity of Byzantine rather than that of Rome."[142]

The genocide took many forms. In many villages and towns there were concentration camps that became killing centers. The Serbs, as well as Jews and Gypsies, were not simply killed quickly in some relatively painless way. They were tortured first and then slowly put to death. Characteristic of the way the Ustashi perpetrated genocide was the massacre of 331 Serbs in April 1941. People were cut to pieces with knives, and their remains were thrown into deep crevices. Hair and beards were pulled out; eyes were stabbed; people were buried half alive with the tormentors dancing around the victim, each in turn cutting off flesh as he passed.[143]

The Ustashi compressed in a single year what had taken the Nazis a decade to achieve in depriving unwanted citizens first of their civil rights and ultimately of their lives. Like the Nazis, the Croats promulgated laws prohibiting marriage between Croats and races deemed inferior. They also forced Serbs to wear a blue armband with the letter "P" and compelled the Jews to wear the Star of David on their backs. Neither these communities nor the Gypsies were allowed in public places or even to walk on the sidewalk. Posters were placed everywhere that read, "No Serbs, Jews, Nomads and dogs allowed."[144]

Pavelic's "final solution" was devised to eliminate 1.2 million Serbs in Bosnia-Herzogovina. His method was cost-effective and practical. The Ustashi turned to the natural surroundings of the area to facilitate their plan of mass murder. The Drina River flowed through a series of deep and grandiose canyons rather much like those in Colorado. Killing specialists known as the Black Legion performed their work here as the SS did in Poland. Approximately 800 to 1,200 people at a time were "tied two by two together with a wire and then connected with one long chain," after which they were taken to a deep crevice where they "were killed on the head with blunt instruments and thrown into the ravine among the rocks."[145] In this way, "these admirable sites would serve as cemeteries and slaughterhouses both at the same time."[146]

Amazingly enough, the Black Legion's atrocities were so extreme and excessive that the German military authorities felt it necessary to disarm and arrest an entire regiment.[147] German general Rendulic later confessed that he knew nothing of the persecutions by the Croats until August 1943, when he was informed that a half-million Serbs had been killed. Because the persecution "caused me no end of trouble," he wrote, "I finally had to put a stop to it with energetic measures and threats of force."[148] Whatever sympathy the Germans may have felt for the Serbs, they did nothing to interfere with the genocide of the Jews. Some 60,000 Yugoslavian Jews, alongside 20,000 Gypsies, perished.[149]

"Romanizing" the Hungarians of Transylvania

Romania had much in common with Yugoslavia in that both were multiethnic territories in eastern Europe that had been incorporated into an expansive Ottoman Empire, then won partial freedom in the nineteenth century when the Turks declined as a power, then became nation-states out of a dismembered Austro-

Hungarian Empire following World War I. Both countries also clearly illustrate the way in which war exacerbates ethnic hostility by redefining frontiers on the basis of the spoils of war rather than along the lines of linguistic and cultural identity.

In 1919, the Allies, without regard for the ethnic realities involved, gave Transylvania, a state largely inhabited by Hungarians, to Romania, a state composed of people who traditionally despised Hungarians. The gift was made in gratitude for military support by the Romanians against the Austro-Hungarians who had fought on the side of the Ottomans and Germans during World War I against the British, French, and U.S. forces. Between the wars, Romania did all it could to turn Hungarians into Romanians. At least 20,000 Hungarian families from Transylvania were forced to migrate across the border into Hungary.[150] Romania's policy was largely ethnocidal: cities, towns, and villages in Transylvania were renamed in a totally different language; the Hungarian language was forbidden in public places and was prohibited in schools. Meanwhile, publications in Hungarian were rigorously censored.

King Carol of Romania tried to keep his country neutral at the outbreak of World War II. However, in 1940 Stalin and Hitler imposed territorial modifications on his nation. Of special interest was Germany's insistence that the northern portion of Transylvania be returned to Hungary, thus "reuniting 1,200,000 Hungarians with their 'Motherland' still leaving about 600,000 under Romanian domination."[151] The Romanians, full of rage and resentment, retaliated with genocidal fury, killing an estimated 100,000 Hungarians between 1940 and 1945.[152]

Then things changed radically in 1944, when the Romanians came back to northern Transylvania behind the Soviet army. The price for reintegrating Transylvania into greater Romania (now communist) was another 100,000 Hungarians murdered by Romanian terrorist units between October and December 1944. One of the more infamous units was under the leadership of Gavril Olteanu, who excelled in destroying Hungarian villages and murdering every woman, man, and child who lived in them. The Romanian hatred of Hungarians reminds us of the Croatian hatred of Serbs. Olteanu's method was to decapitate the men "by the use of axes" or impale them in front of their families.[153] As with the Germans in Yugoslavia, the Russians in Romania did not approve of these terrorist units and actually arrested the "Olteanu-unit" and "handed them over to the Romanian police as common criminals."[154] But Olteanu never served more than two years in prison and, when released, was treated as a "national hero," receiving "a comfortable government job as 'hunting inspector.'"[155]

Anti-Semitism found a favorable soil and climate in the Romania just described. The country's 750,000 Jews experienced violation of their civil rights; exclusion from the society, economy, and culture of Romania; deportation into "reservations"; the Romanianization of Jewish property; and the Final Solution as victims of the Holocaust. Miraculously, 300,000 Romanian Jews survived fascism.[156]

Stalin's Mass Murder of Soviet Citizens During World War II

> These 10 million corpses must be added to the nearly 20,000,000 Soviet citizens that the Nazis likely killed. ... But an estimate of 29,625,000 ... killed overall still does not close the account for this most bloody period. To be added are ... 3,053,000 foreign civilians or POWs murdered by the Red Army or in NKVD executions, terror, deportations, and labor camps. Thus the Soviet wartime democide probably totals 13,053,000 people overall.
>
> —*R. J. Rummel (1990)*[157]

Of all the cases of governmental mass killing examined in this chapter, perhaps none was so blatantly cynical, brutal, and bloody as Stalin's widespread massacre of his own citizens in the course of World War II. The invasion of the Soviet Union by Hitler's troops was savage enough by any standards, but when one adds the fact that the Soviet people also endured a bloodbath caused by their own leader, the situation became incomparably catastrophic. As R. J. Rummel has aptly commented, "Had Ripley written a *Believe It or Not* of incredible tales of murder and death, the two-front war suffered by Soviet citizens and foreigners subject to Soviet occupation surely would provide prominent entries."[158]

Stalin used the NKVD (People's Commissariat of Internal Affairs), a special police unit, to murder or deport various groups in the same way that Hitler used the SS. Stalin had prisons emptied by the NKVD and the inmates shot. Gulags (slave-labor camps) were also evacuated, and the slaves were forced to march in columns against the Nazi positions at the front; the NKVD was poised behind them with machine guns ready to fire on those who moved backward rather than forward. The same victims were also compelled to clear minefields by marching through them. When Stalin's head of the Soviet military mission in Britain, General Ratov, was offered mine detectors by the British, he declined, stating that "in the Soviet Union we use people."[159] Though we may never know with any accuracy how many of the 10 million former gulag slaves died in this dubious form of service to their country, Rummel calculated that 8,518,000 Soviet citizens were "murdered in transit to or in the camps during the whole war period."[160]

We have already described how Soviet POWs suffered in German hands during the war. After the German surrender, some 5.5 million of those still alive were ultimately repatriated to the Soviet Union. Presumably because of the way they surrendered by the thousands to the Nazi armies in the early months of the war, Stalin treated them all as traitors. His viewpoint was once quoted by a journalist: "In Hitler's camps there are no Russian prisoners of war, only Russian traitors, and we shall do away with them when the war is over."[161]

Stalin sent 1.1 million of the repatriated POWs to labor camps, where they died a slow death while serving a 25-year sentence. At least 300,000 of them were immediately executed for the crime of having been German prisoners. Most of the men were used for forced labor. Rummel believes that roughly half of the POWs repatriated died unnatural deaths due to the sentences imposed upon them.[162]

Also, there were the Soviet deportations of ethnically and linguistically homogeneous peoples from places where their families had lived for centuries. The Crimean Tatars, Soviet Germans, and Meskhetians (Turkish community) were among several cultural groups forced to migrate en bloc from Soviet Europe to Siberia and central Asia during and after the war. Years after these deportations, Soviet courts found no evidence to support Stalin's charge that the groups had collaborated with the Nazi invaders.[163]

The Crimean Tatar ordeal may be taken as an example of how such communities were treated by Stalin in the deportation process. The Tatars, who had lived along the northern shores of the Black Sea (Crimea) for hundreds of years, were suddenly ordered to vacate their homes on May 18, 1944. Though large numbers of their community had fought in the Red Army or with local partisans, and several of them had been cited for bravery against the enemy, Stalin still accused them of aiding the Nazis.[164]

On May 18, six days after the last Germans had been driven out of Crimea, NKVD troops with sub–machine guns and bayonets on their rifles broke into Tatar homes and roused families from their beds. All families were ordered to leave their homes. The Tatars were given only minutes to collect their belongings and get into crowded cattle trucks. They were then transported several thousand miles to the Urals, Siberia, Kazakhstan, and central Asia. The trip took about four months to Kazakhstan, and according to one documentary source, "It was a journey of lingering death" like "mobile gas chambers." Many of the very old, young, and weak "died of thirst, suffocation and the stench."[165]

The worst was yet to come. Most of the 250,000 Crimean Tatars were ultimately taken to Uzbekistan, where they were greeted with "sullen hostility" by the indigenous population. One Tatar later recalled how his people were dumped in barracks half-starved, extremely sick from impure ditch water, and suffering from malaria and other debilitating diseases. The mortality rate was appalling. While analyzing the census figures for 1966, the Tatars concluded that 46 percent, or 110,000 of their people, died during the forced migration and the following eighteen months.[166] Rummel believes that among the "1,600,000 deported among eight nations (cultures), about 530,000 probably died."[167] This total includes the Tatars.

Evidence of this sort has compelled demographers to begin sorting out the grim details as to how many Soviets were murdered by Hitler and how many by Stalin. One Soviet scientist has estimated that 15 million were killed "through Soviet action."[168] The most accepted figure for Nazi killings of Soviets is 20 million.[169]

In conclusion, this catalog of horrors, which began with the Japanese invasion of Manchuria and ended with Stalin's war against his own people, suggests that genocidal killing in World War II was neither initiated by Hitler in his war against the Jews nor limited to the horrendous activities that took place in the Nazi death camps of eastern Europe. Looking at World War II Eurocentrically only narrows our vision and distorts the truth. Global processes such as the rise of totalitarianism and aggressive, fascistic nationalism exacerbated ethnic rivalries both within national frontiers and beyond. In the most cynical fashion, governments denigrated the rules of law that had afforded a measure of protection to citizens and violated rules of war that had constrained attacks against enemy civilians.

Hatred and violence only escalated with every new incident of massacre. Revenge was a crucial factor, as was dehumanizing the image of the enemy. As we will see in the following chapters, both of these factors were involved in the strategic bombing of cities with both incendiary and atomic bombs.

Chapter 7

The Evolution of the Holocaust, 1919–1945

> The passing of time has made it increasingly clear that a hitherto unbreachable moral and political barrier was successfully overcome by the Nazis in World War II and that henceforth the systematic, bureaucratically administered extermination of millions of citizens or subject peoples will forever be one of the capacities and temptations of government.
>
> —*Richard Rubenstein (1978)*[1]

The following summary of the evolution of the Holocaust focuses mainly on its primary victims, the approximately 5 million European Jews who were exterminated by the Nazis and their accomplices. However, although the focus of this chapter is on the Jews, it is essential to recognize that there were millions of other victims of genocidal killing by the Nazis. The other victims included as many as 10 million Slavs (including Poles, Russians, Belorussians, and Ukrainians); more than 3 million Soviet prisoners of war; approximately 258,000 Gypsies; 220,000 homosexuals; and more than 100,000 individuals with mental and physical disabilities in Germany itself.[2]

For present purposes, the evolution of the Holocaust is divided into four phases. The first includes the years between 1919 and 1933, during which Hitler and the Nazi Party successfully struggled for an increasing share of political power in Germany. The second phase began in January 1933, at which time Hitler became chancellor of Germany, and extended into fall 1939. During these six years, the Nazis experimented with several types of anti-Jewish measures, including random violence, economic boycott, and discriminatory legislation, all of which coerced many thousands of Jews to emigrate from the Reich. The third phase, from September 1939 through June 1941, involved a transition from the earlier policy of coerced emigration into one of forcible deportation to crowded ghettos and labor camps in Nazi-occupied Poland and finally into the policy of outright extermination. The fourth and final phase began in late summer 1941 and continued until the defeat of Germany. During this phase, the official policy of the Third Reich was to kill virtually every Jew in Nazi-dominated Europe.

1919–1933: The Nazi Rise to Power

In the aftermath of its defeat in World War I, Germany entered a period of social and economic disruption accompanied by personal stress and anxiety that was to prove advantageous to the Nazi Party and correspondingly disastrous to its self-declared enemy—the Jews. Having entered World War I confident of victory, and with armed forces still occupying large areas of territory at the time of surrender, Germans reacted to defeat with shock and humiliation. The humiliation was aggravated by the terms imposed by the victorious nations in the Treaty of Versailles, which required Germany to accept sole responsibility for starting the war, to relinquish territory that it had acquired through its early victories, and to make huge reparations payments to the victors. Adding to the trauma of defeat was the fact that nearly 6 million Germans—3 million soldiers and an equal number of civilians—had been killed in the war.

The early postwar years of the 1920s were marked by economic hardship and political instability. Widespread unemployment meant that many veterans were unable to find jobs, and inflation reached catastrophic levels. The democratic government (the Weimar Republic), which had been formed during the closing weeks of the war and had presided over the surrender negotiations, was very insecure, since its political base rested on a fragile coalition of moderate parties, no one of which enjoyed support by the majority of voters.

Such conditions created an emotional and political milieu conducive to two ominous trends. First, as had been the case in earlier periods of political and economic troubles in Germany and elsewhere in Europe, anti-Semitism became increasingly popular as a political ideology. The Jews of Europe, who for centuries had been subjected to prejudice, discrimination, and episodes of violence as religious outsiders and alleged economic competitors, provided a convenient scapegoat for the desperate, angry Germans.

The second trend was the emergence of numerous radical political factions in opposition to the Weimar government. They ranged from right-wing ultranationalists who claimed that Germany's defeat had resulted from being "stabbed in the back" by internal enemies—the Jews in particular—to left-wing communists who advocated overthrow of the capitalistic economic system. One of the radical parties that emerged after the war was the right-wing National Socialist German Worker's (Nazi) Party, which Adolf Hitler joined in 1919 several months after its founding. Like many of his fellow Nazis in the early days of the party, Hitler was a veteran of World War I. As an army corporal, he had served with valor. He had been wounded and gassed and awarded the Iron Cross, First Class. However, like many other returning veterans, Hitler failed to find a satisfactory niche in the troubled postwar German society.

Hitler rapidly rose to a position of power within the fledgling Nazi Party and played an important role in drafting the party platform in February 1920. Among its key planks was repudiation of the Treaty of Versailles, rejection of communism (the principal left-wing radical faction at that time), and disenchantment with liberalism and democracy. Two predominant features of the Nazi ideology were preoccupation with race in general and hatred of Jews, who were seen as the embodiment of all evil.

Hitler also promoted the use of terror and violence as political tools. In 1921, under his direction, a party paramilitary organization—the SA (Sturmabteilung, or storm troopers)—was formed to provide security at party gatherings and harass political opponents. The SA was put to use in November 1923 when, at the instigation of Hitler, the Nazis tried to seize control of the government in Munich. The attempted coup was quickly suppressed, however, and Hitler was convicted of treason and sentenced to five years in prison. He served only eight months due to the leniency of the court and sentencing judge. During his brief imprisonment, Hitler wrote *Mein Kampf* (My Struggle), published in 1925, which outlined in detail his political philosophy and goals. In its pages, he gave vent to his intense personal hatred of Jews.

After his release from prison, Hitler and the Nazis continued their quest for power, this time working within the democratic framework and seeking votes from German citizens. However, in the 1924 national elections, with the German economy improving, the Nazis did very poorly. As the economy continued to improve, support for the Nazis and other radical groups declined. Germans could dismiss the racist, anti-Jewish ravings of *Mein Kampf* as politically insignificant.

Then, in October 1929, the collapse of the U.S. stock market sent devastating reverberations throughout much of the world and hit Germany particularly hard, quickly reversing the improvements in the economy achieved by the Weimar government. The number of Germans who could not find jobs rapidly increased, reaching more than 7 million in winter 1932–1933.[3] Millions of Germans were dependent on government welfare programs. Dissatisfaction with the Weimar Republic intensified. Radical parties such as the left-wing communists and the right-wing Nazis enjoyed a resurgence of support. The Nazis portrayed themselves as an alternative to the communists, who were feared by German business interests, and also the democratic Weimar government, which they blamed for the financial distress that afflicted so many middle-class Germans.

The first election during this economic crisis was held in 1930. The Nazis received enough votes to become the second largest party in the nation. By the 1932 national elections, however, with the economy beginning to show signs of recovery, the Nazis did less well. Nonetheless, the disunity of the other parties reinforced the political power of the Nazis, who retained enough seats to disrupt the functioning of the Reichstag (German parliament). The seriously ailing President Paul von Hindenberg invited Hitler to become chancellor in an attempt to work out a compromise arrangement in the fragmented government. Hindenberg, the leader of a coalition of non-Nazi conservative factions, believed that by bringing Hitler into the government he could exploit the popular support enjoyed by the radical Nazis while maintaining control over Hitler. Hitler agreed and was appointed to the powerful position of chancellor on January 30, 1933.

January 1933–September 1939: The Search for a Solution to the "Jewish Question"

Hitler quickly eluded Hindenberg's efforts to control him and proceeded to transform the democratic government into a dictatorship. On February 27, 1933, the Reichstag building was destroyed in a fire that the Nazis blamed on the Jews and communists, but which some historians suspect had been set by the Nazis themselves as a pretext for usurping additional power.[4] On the following day, Hitler persuaded the Reichstag to issue an emergency decree that temporarily suspended civil liberties. On March 9, the first concentration camp, Dachau, was established outside Munich. Its first prisoners were communists and other political opponents of the Nazis. On March 24, Hitler's dictatorial powers were reinforced by the passage of the Enabling Act, which prolonged the suspension of civil liberties for four more years and gave Hitler the legal authority to govern by decree.

In late March 1933, the Nazis decided upon the first centrally organized action against the Jews of Germany, a nationwide boycott of Jewish shops and businesses. The boycott, which took place on April l, was organized by Joseph Goebbels, one of Hitler's close friends and a rabid anti-Semite. During the boycott, Nazi storm troopers blocked the entrances to Jewish enterprises, scrawled graffiti on the windows, and harassed customers. However, the boycott quickly degenerated into wanton violence, with windows smashed, stores ransacked, and Jews physically assaulted.

To Hitler and other top Nazis, the April boycott was a failure. Although it did provide an outlet for the violent impulses of radical Nazis, it also upset many other Germans, as well as foreign observers, and hurt the economy. In the aftermath of the boycott, the initiative for anti-Jewish measures shifted from the party radicals with their preference for overt violence to the Nazi legal establishment, which within a week of the boycott, drafted and passed the first of hundreds of laws designed to exclude Jews from economic and social participation in German society.[5]

On April 7, 1933, the Law for the Restoration of the Professional Civil Service dismissed non-Aryan, that is, Jewish, lawyers and judges from their government jobs. Later in April, similar laws forced Jewish physicians and teachers to leave their positions in government institutions. As the result of these laws, as many as

5,000 Jewish professionals lost their jobs, which were promptly filled by non-Jews. The legal onslaught against the Jews continued. On September 29, 1933, Joseph Goebbels was placed in charge of German cultural life and promptly proceeded to remove all Jews from positions with the press, radio, film, and publishing.

The combination of discriminatory legislation and the threat of street violence drove 53,000 of Germany's 500,000 Jews to emigrate to other countries in 1933.[6] Those who remained clung to the hope that such madness could not continue. Their hopes were seemingly fulfilled during the later months of 1933, when the flurry of legal measures began to abate. The respite from legalistic persecution continued into 1934, convincing many Jews that the worst was over and even inducing some of the émigrés to return to Germany.

Also in 1934, Hitler decided that the violence-prone SA, which by June had a membership of 4 million, had become a political liability and ordered its leader, Ernst Röhm, killed on what came to be known as the night of the long knives. Röhm and more than 80 other SA leaders were murdered in what historian Heinz Höhne called "the Third Reich's first mass murder."[7] The purge of the SA led to a temporary reduction in street violence, which further lulled the Jews into believing that the tide of persecution was receding. However, the purge also led to the growing power of another party organization, the Schutzstaffel (SS), or protective squads. The SS was an elite party organization that had originated in 1925 as a branch of the SA to serve as Hitler's personal bodyguards. It had won its autonomy in 1930 and became increasingly powerful after the purge of the SA in 1934.[8]

An ominous manifestation of growing Nazi boldness in anti-Jewish measures occurred on September 15, 1935, when the so-called Nuremberg Laws were adopted by a unanimous vote of the Reichstag after being hurriedly drawn up in response to a direct order from Hitler. The first of these laws—the Law for the Protection of German Blood and German Honor—prohibited marriage and extramarital relations between Jews and Aryan Germans. The law also applied to Gypsies, whom the Nazis also regarded as racially inferior.[9] The second Nuremberg law—the Law Respecting Reich Citizenship—decreed that Jews were no longer citizens of the Reich. The Nuremberg Laws dealt a devastating blow to all Jews and Gypsies in Germany, placing them in a position of social isolation and vulnerability to later measures.

In 1936, while Germany hosted the Summer Olympics in Berlin, there was another lull in the onslaught against the Jews. Despite worldwide concern over recent Nazi violations of the Versailles Treaty, including the military occupation of the Rhineland in March 1936, as well as over the widely publicized mistreatment of the Jews, athletes and spectators flocked to Germany, affording Hitler a very useful propaganda opportunity. During the weeks before the games, the Nazis removed anti-Jewish signs, soft-pedaled the Nuremberg Laws, and discouraged actions against Jews. As had been the case in 1934, many Jews were deluded into thinking that the period of persecution had finally ended.

Following the Olympics, Hitler went to his mountaintop retreat at Berchtesgarden to work on a four-year plan to prepare Germany for another war in Europe. Under the direction of Hermann Göring, the Four-Year Plan called for rapid mobilization of war-related industries. It also included provisions for the expropriation of Jewish property in order to help finance war preparations.

By winter 1937–1938, Hitler had purged most of the moderates in the Nazi government and in the armed forces, leaving those willing to support his plans for aggression against both internal and external enemies. With the German economy stronger than it had been in years, Hitler's popularity and support soared.

Nineteen thirty-eight was a year of stunning domestic and foreign policy triumphs for the Nazis and a year in which the plight of the Reich Jews rapidly worsened. In March 1938, following a campaign of terrorism by Austrian Nazis, Hitler coerced Austrian chancellor Kurt von Schuschnigg into accepting *Anschluss*, or union, with Germany. This move added an additional 200,000 Jews to the Reich—more than had emigrated out of Germany up to that time.

Meanwhile, the SS continued to increase its power in anti-Jewish policies. In spring 1938, Karl Adolf Eichmann, an ambitious young SS officer, took over the Jewish Emigration Office in Vienna. Using the threat of violence and concentration camps, and extorting money from wealthy Jews to finance the emigration of poor Jews, Eichmann drove out 100,000 Austrian Jews in one year. His success was due in part to the active complicity of many Austrians, who tended to be more anti-Semitic than most Germans. In Austria, the process of depriving the Jews of their civil rights and livelihoods, which had taken several years in Germany, was accomplished in several months.

Moreover, just as the SS was refining the techniques for coerced emigration and mass expulsion, the international community displayed unwillingness to provide refuges for the Jews. In early July 1938, representatives of several of the world's leading nations met at the request of the United States in Evian, France, to discuss the plight of European refugees. The Evian conference ended in failure. None of the participating nations, including the United States and Great Britain, was willing to significantly relax restrictive immigration quotas that created a major obstacle to Jews who sought to flee persecution in Germany and Austria.

In September 1938, Hitler achieved another major foreign policy triumph—the Munich Agreement in which England and France abrogated treaty obligations and acquiesced to the German annexation of the Sudetenland region of Czechoslovakia. Reinhard Heydrich, one of the top SS administrators of anti-Jewish policies, observed the Munich negotiations very closely and was impressed with the unwillingness of other nations to stand up to German aggression. Several days after Munich, Heydrich decided to expel thousands of Jews from Poland who had been living in Germany—many for as long as 20 or 30 years. More than 10,000 were packed into trucks and taken to the town of Zbaszyn, Poland, on the German-Polish border. The Polish authorities, however, at first refused to let the Jews into their country, and the deportees were forced to spend several days of appalling suffering in a no-man's-land at the border.

Shortly after this incident, one of the Jews described his wretched experiences in a letter to his 17-year-old son, Herschel Grynszpan, who was living at the time in France. Grynszpan then went to the German embassy in Paris and fatally shot a German diplomat, Ernst vom Rath, on November 7. The Nazis used the killing of vom Rath as an excuse to justify violent riots and attacks on the Jews of Germany and Austria on November 9, which came to be called Kristallnacht, or "the night of broken glass." By morning, nearly 200 synagogues had been destroyed, over 7,000 Jewish stores looted, 91 Jews murdered, and 30,000 Jews thrown in concentration camps.[10]

Soon after Kristallnacht, on November 12, Hermann Göring chaired an important meeting of representatives from numerous government agencies to evaluate the riots and to plan subsequent measures against the Jews. One of the measures decided upon was a further intensification of the Aryanization campaign.

Although the practice of Aryanization, that is, pressuring Jewish business owners to sell their holdings to Aryan Germans at a fraction of their worth, had begun as early as 1933, the pace and scale increased dramatically in 1938. Earlier concern about disrupting the economy had deterred attacks on large Jewish enterprises. At this time of robust economic growth, however, such caution was replaced by eager efforts of Aryan business concerns, including such huge corporate empires as Krupp and I.G. Farben, to take advantage of opportunities to cheaply acquire Jewish businesses.[11] Also, the German Jewish community was fined one billion *Reichsmarks* as an atonement payment for having allegedly provoked the riots.

On January 24, 1939, Göring ordered Reinhard Heydrich of the SS to organize the emigration of the remaining Jews in Germany, using the same methods that Eichmann had found so effective in Austria. With this decision, the SS moved a major step closer to becoming the predominant government agency in the efforts to solve the "Jewish problem." Six days later, in a speech to the Reichstag, Hitler warned that "Europe will not find peace until the Jewish problem has been settled. ... If international Jewry should succeed, in Europe or elsewhere, in precipitating nations into a world war, the result will not be the bolshevism of Europe and a victory for Judaism, but the extermination in Europe of the Jewish race."[12]

Nazi aggression continued. On March 15, 1939, the German army marched into Czechoslovakia and seized the provinces of Bohemia and Moravia. More than 120,000 Jews were thereby brought within the Nazi grasp. Four months later, Adolf Eichmann was transferred from Vienna to Prague with orders to organize the deportation of its more than 50,000 Jews. In August, tens of thousands of Czech Jews from the outlying areas were ordered to move into designated areas in Prague, as a prelude to expulsion. However, Eichmann's efforts were thwarted by the lack of places for the Jews to go. On May 17, 1939, the British government had issued a white paper announcing drastic reductions in the numbers of Jews who would be allowed to emigrate to Palestine, which had until then been one of the few available refuges for Jews. As historian Nora Levin stated, "The British were sealing up escape hatches at the very moment that Nazi officials were loosening them."[13]

Then, on August 23, 1939, the signing of the Non-Aggression Pact between the Soviet Union and Germany cleared the way for the German invasion of Poland on September 1. Two days later, Great Britain and France, honoring their treaty obligations to Poland, declared war on Germany, and World War II began.

September 1939–June 1941: Transition to Extermination

> **The narrow, crooked streets of the most dilapidated section of Warsaw were crowded with pushcarts, their owners going from house to house asking the inevitable question: Have you any room? The sidewalks were covered with their belongings. Children wandered, lost and crying, parents ran hither and yon seeking them, their cries drowned in the tremendous hubbub of half a million uprooted people.**
>
> —*Toshia Bialer (1943)*[14]

The German invasion of Poland was extremely brutal. In less than a month of fighting, 200,000 Poles were killed or wounded, and approximately 400,000 were captured as prisoners of war.[15] In the national capital, "eighty-five percent of Warsaw's substance was destroyed: all the bridges, and ninety-five percent of industry, hospitals, and buildings belonging to the health service."[16] When Poland surrendered to the Germans on September 27, 1939, approximately 2 million Jews fell into the Nazi grip.

On the day after the surrender, Reinhard Heydrich of the SS met with army leaders to arrange a more systematic campaign of violence in which special teams of killers, known as Einsatzgruppen (special-action squads), would locate and murder Polish intellectual and political leaders. This campaign, the A-B Aktion, killed as many as 10,000 non-Jewish Poles within the first 90 days of German occupation and continued until June 1940.[17] Although the Jews were not singled out for killing in this action, whenever they were snared by the Einsatzgruppen they were subjected to special brutality.

On September 21, 1939, however, Heydrich had called a meeting in Berlin of several of his top Einsatzgruppen leaders to plan measures focused specifically on the Jews of Poland. The decisions made in that meeting were recorded in a memo sent out the same day to SS officials throughout Poland, as well as to representatives of the army, civilian administrators of the occupied territories, and several major government departments in Berlin (Interior, Economy, Food), thus implicating and involving them in the campaign against the Jews. The Einsatzgruppen commanders were ordered to physically concentrate all Polish Jews within a few large cities, especially cities with extensive railroad connections.

The SS was also to compel each Jewish community to establish a Jewish council to provide for the welfare of the Jews and to put into effect later directives from the occupation authorities.[18]

The Search for a "Territorial" Solution

Beginning in October 1939, Heydrich's directive of September 21 was put into operation; Jews living in the western areas of Poland that had been incorporated into the Reich were forcibly moved into the Government General—a vast area of central Poland that was occupied by the Nazis and used as a dumping ground for Jews, Gypsies, and other "racially inferior" groups that were being purged from German lands. Also at this time, the first deportations began from Austria and the Nazi-occupied provinces of Czechoslovakia to the Government General. The destination of the deportees was the city of Lublin, which Nazi propagandists portrayed as a reservation where the Jews would be able to live and work together. The reality was a crowded slum in which the Nazis deliberately created inhumane living conditions. The hapless Jews were brutally rounded up by the Einsatzgruppen, transported in trucks and freight cars, often with only the clothes on their backs, and dumped on a street in the Jewish area. No food or water was provided on journeys that often lasted several days. Many died en route. By December 1939, nearly 90,000 Poles and Jews had been deported to the General Government area.[19] Also in late fall 1941, several thousand Gypsies had been forcibly deported from Germany into the Polish ghettos as part of a plan developed in September 1939 to eliminate all 30,000 of Germany's Gypsies from German soil.[20]

Deportations to Lublin continued for several months, with conditions deteriorating as overcrowding became progressively worse. Then, in March 1940, the deportations were halted, in part as the result of protests by local Nazi administrators who complained of so many Jews being dumped into their jurisdictions and in part in anticipation of the planned invasions of western Europe, which would require the railway resources used to transport Jews.

Just as the resettlement program was terminated, Odilo Globocnik, one of the top SS and police administrators of the area, proposed the creation of forced labor camps for the Jews. During summer 1940, he established more than 30 labor camps in the Lublin area in which overcrowding, underfeeding, and long hours of heavy labor soon created steadily rising death tolls.[21]

The shelving of the "Lublin plan" did not stop the search for a "reservation" onto which huge numbers of Jews could be dumped. Indeed, continued military triumphs by the Nazis made the search all the more urgent. On May 10, the German armed forces began their western European campaign, quickly conquering Holland, Belgium, and France and bringing 350,000 more Jews under direct Nazi rule. Just as the invasion of Poland gave rise to the idea of the Lublin reservation, so did the conquest of France stimulate Nazi thinking about another "territorial solution," this time the French island colony of Madagascar.

During summer 1940, the SS studied the possibility of shipping several million Jews to the island after the war had ended. By fall 1940, however, developments in the war effectively precluded any possible implementation of the Madagascar plan. On August 8, the Battle of Britain had begun, and on September 20, Hitler ordered his generals to draw up plans for the invasion of Russia. These developments meant not only that the war would be prolonged but also that several million Russian Jews would be brought under Nazi control.

Ghettoization of the Jews

With the abandonment of the Lublin and Madagascar plans, the Nazis resorted to an alternative means of solving the "Jewish problem." Rather than shipping all the Jews to one large territory far from the Reich, they returned to the practice of ghettoization, which involved forcing the Jews in large Polish cities to move into specified areas, or ghettos, and then relocating Jews from outlying areas of Poland and from other nations into the Polish ghettos. The first major ghetto had been established on May 1, 1940, shortly after the halt in deportations to Lublin, in the Polish city of Lodz. However, the main period of ghettoization in Poland began only after the Nazis gave up on the Madagascar plan, in October 1940, and lasted until April 1941.

The largest of the ghettos was in the city of Warsaw, whose 400,000 Jews made up a third of the population. On October 12, 1940, the Nazis decreed that all non-Jews living in a certain area of the city had to vacate their homes. Shortly afterward, Jews from the rest of the city and suburbs were forced to move into the ghetto, bringing with them only what they could carry or push in carts. By November 15, the entire ghetto was enclosed by a high brick wall, enabling the Nazi officials to control everyone and everything that left or entered the ghetto. No sooner had the Warsaw Jews been concentrated in the ghetto than the first of thousands of Jews rounded up in the surrounding countryside were driven into it. Within weeks, an area of the city that had once housed 25,000 people now held 500,000. As many as three families with their children were forced to share a single room. In the coming months, Jews from western Europe were transported to the ghetto. Similar operations took place in ghettos throughout Poland.

The Nazis maintained strict control over food and supplies entering the ghetto, which enabled them to begin a policy of deliberate mass starvation. Nazi officials held several meetings in which it was decided to limit the food available to the swelling ghetto population to levels that would guarantee starvation.[22]

Some Jews found work in German-managed ghetto factories and were able to obtain food. Others, whose wealth enabled them to purchase black-market food brought in at great risk by smugglers, were able to maintain at least a semblance of adequate nutrition. The vast majority, however, were dependent on the food supplied by the Nazis and distributed by Jewish welfare organizations. According to Yehuda Bauer, "In Warsaw the daily bread ration was less than 100 grams (3.5

Destitute Jews on the street in the Warsaw ghetto. SOURCE: U.S. Holocaust Memorial Museum.

ounces). The total caloric value of food supplied in Warsaw was 220, or about 15 percent of the normal daily requirement."[23] During the first year of the Warsaw ghetto's existence, Levin estimates that Jews were starving to death at the rate of 300 to 400 per day—more than 43,000 in all.[24]

The "Euthanasia" Program

While the Germans were shuttling trainloads of human cargo across Europe, in Germany itself another ominous development was unfolding. Initially directed at "Aryan" Germans, the so-called "euthanasia" program was to later make a crucial contribution to the Nazi effort to exterminate the Jews of Europe.

In October 1939, a month after World War II had begun, Hitler ordered the initiation of this program, which was designed to identify and kill adult Germans whose incurable mental handicaps rendered them, in the eyes of the Nazis, "life unworthy of life."[25] Several secret facilities were established where psychiatrists and other medical personnel supervised the killing. Shooting by pistol in the back of the head was the initial method of killing. But soon, under the guidance of the physicians, the more efficient "medical" method of lethal injection was employed. This involved use of a large syringe filled with poison and injected, in many cases, directly into the victim's heart.[26] Then, in either December 1939 or January 1940, the first known mass killing by means of poison gas was demonstrated at one of the secret "euthanasia" institutions. According to Michael Tregenza, "It was here during the course of these experiments that the idea of disguising the gas chamber

Corpses of Jews being laid in a mass grave by Jewish workers in the Warsaw ghetto. SOURCE: U.S. Holocaust Memorial Museum.

as a shower-room was first used and perfected, afterwards to be adopted on a grand scale at the huge Birkenau installation at Auschwitz."[27]

The "euthanasia" program also spawned the invention of a mobile gas chamber in the form of a specially adapted truck, or "gas van." According to historian Christopher R. Browning, "The victims were gassed, as chemically pure carbon monoxide, stored in the driver's compartment, was released from steel bottles through a hose leading into a specially constructed airtight compartment in which the victims were locked."[28] A special team of the SS used this gas van to exterminate thousands of patients in mental hospitals in areas of Poland that had been incorporated into the Reich.[29]

In the latter months of the "euthanasia" program's operation, Nazi efforts to maintain secrecy about it broke down, and increasing numbers of Germans protested the killing of their relatives. This popular resistance provoked Hitler to stop the killings. Between its inception in fall 1939 and its official termination in August 1941, the "euthanasia" program killed as many as 100,000 "Aryan" Germans, as well as thousands of Jewish and non-Jewish Poles.[30]

However, medically supervised mass killing did not cease with the official termination of the "euthanasia" program. Since summer 1940, it had been extended into Nazi concentration camps under the auspices of a program known as 14F13, which involved medical "experts" from "euthanasia" institutes visiting the concentration camps and screening the inmates, usually by cursorily reviewing their files, to determine which were incapable of strenuous work. Those who failed the screening were sent to the nearest "euthanasia" killing center, where they were gassed. The 14F13 program was coordinated by Hitler's Chancellery, which also administered the "euthanasia" program, and by the SS, which ran the concentration camps. The program continued to operate throughout most of the war. According to Robert Jay Lifton, "The 14F13 program is thought to have killed more than twenty thousand people, but the concepts and policies it furthered contributed to the death of millions."[31]

Preparing for a "War of Extermination" Against the Soviet Union

At the same time that Polish civilians were being hunted down and killed by Einsatzgruppen, Jews and Gypsies were being forcibly relocated to ghettos in central Poland where they were being worked and starved to death, and German mental patients were being gassed, plans were under way for the invasion of the Soviet Union. As early as July 1940, Hitler had set in motion preliminary planning for what was to be his crowning achievement, and on December 18, 1940, he signed Directive 21, which set the date for invasion on May 15, 1941—though it was later postponed to June 22. Hitler code-named the attack Operation Barbarossa, after a tenth-century emperor who had united the diverse lands of Germany and advocated expansion to the east.

As the date for invasion neared, Hitler and his top generals ensured that the war against the communist Soviet Union would be far more brutal than the campaigns in western Europe and even more devastating than the attack against Poland. On March 13, 1941, Field Marshal Wilhelm Keitel, the head of the armed forces, issued a directive that authorized the collaboration of SS leader Heinrich Himmler's Einsatzgruppen with the German military. The Einsatzgruppen were authorized to engage in certain "special tasks … entailed by the final struggle that will have to be carried out between two opposing political systems."[32] These tasks involved rounding up and murdering any civilians suspected of anti-German sentiment or action. At the end of March 1941, Hitler told a gathering of his top military officers that the coming war in the east would be a "war of extermination."[33] On June 6, 1941, less than a month before the attack, the infamous Commissar Order was issued by Hitler to authorize summary execution by the German military of certain types of political officers attached to the Soviet army. As German historian Jürgen Förster has noted, "Hitler was determined to convert the Wehrmacht [German military] into an instrument of extermination alongside the SS by erasing the line between military and political-ideological warfare."[34]

Operation Barbarossa was conceived as an ideological crusade against a racially inferior enemy for whom traditional ethical and legal constraints did not apply. Hitler and most of his top generals regarded Jews and communists as inseparable.

Thus, on May 19, 1941, the army leadership issued "Guidelines for the Conduct of the Troops in Russia," which called for "ruthless and vigorous measures against Bolshevik inciters, guerrillas, saboteurs, Jews, and the complete elimination of all active and passive resistance."[35]

Also in May 1941, 3,000 men were assembled for the training and indoctrination needed to carry out the tasks assigned to the SS during the war.[36] As is discussed in the next section, they were to constitute four Einsatzgruppen who would accompany the invading German military into the Soviet Union and slaughter millions of Jews, Soviet prisoners of war, and others deemed dangerous or undesirable.

By early 1941, several conditions were in place that facilitated the eventual mass slaughter of the European Jews, as well as millions of other victims of the Nazis. The stunning military successes in Poland and western Europe had brought millions of Jews within the Nazi grip while at the same time foreclosing emigration as a means of ridding themselves of those same Jews. Earlier persecutions of the Jews, both in Germany and elsewhere in Europe, had provoked no substantial resistance by the rest of the world. The Jews themselves had been weakened and demoralized by social isolation, poverty, hunger, and physical brutality and were being confined in ghettos and labor camps throughout German-occupied Europe. After a period of infighting among Nazi factions vying for control over Jewish policy, the SS had emerged in a position of clear predominance. The emigration and ghettoization programs had provided experience in forcibly shipping masses of human beings over great distances. Both the A-B Aktion n Poland and the "euthanasia" program in Germany had permitted experimentation with techniques for direct mass killing and the recruitment and training of personnel adept at employing them. Finally, the "war of extermination" against the Soviet Union was about to create a context in which the genocidal impulses of the Nazis could find free expression.

June 1941–May 1945: The Final Solution

On June 22, 1941, Germany invaded the Soviet Union. Within a month, the Wehrmacht had crushed nearly 90 divisions of Soviet troops, destroyed one-half of the Soviet air force, taken more than 600,000 Soviet prisoners of war, and conquered territory in which millions of Jews lived.[37] Following closely behind the German army, the Einsatzgruppen began fulfilling their delegated duties of "general pacification. This meant gathering political and economic intelligence, liquidating hostile and suspect elements, and preventing the organization of resistance behind the lines."[38] Nazi brutality to both Soviet military and civilians stimulated partisan resistance, which was ruthlessly countered by both the German army and the SS. On July 16, 1941, Hitler announced that "the partisan war gives us the possibility to exterminate everyone who opposes us."[39] On the following day, the

High Command of the Wehrmacht reached a formal agreement with the SS whereby the army would turn over certain categories of Soviet prisoners of war to the Einsatzgruppen for "special measures."[40] During late summer 1941, the SS combed through the vast prisoner-of-war camps and summarily murdered thousands of Soviet soldiers who had surrendered. Civilians in areas occupied by the Nazis were also at great risk. Anyone even suspected of engaging in or supporting resistance efforts was likely to be killed. Rather than entering homes or buildings in which partisans were believed hiding, troops were told to simply set the structures on fire.[41]

"Military" Mass Killing by the Einsatzgruppen

By the last week in July 1941, the German advance had begun to slow down as the result of stiffening Soviet resistance. At about the same time, in the late summer of 1941, the Einsatzgruppen began a genocidal campaign of slaughtering as many Russian Jews as they could get their hands on.[42] The 3,000 "soldiers," who in May had received intense ideological indoctrination on the need to eliminate the racially inferior Jews and others, were dispersed into four main groups and began their hunt. The killers took full advantage of the speed with which the German army had seized vast tracts of land and of the fact that Soviet authorities had not publicized the atrocities against the Jews that had occurred in Poland during the first 22 months of German occupation. In many cases, they obtained lists of Jewish residents of towns and villages from the leaders of the Jewish communities themselves, who had no idea of the use to which they would be put. Often, the community leaders were the first ones killed in order to reduce the possibility of organized resistance. Whenever possible, local Jew-haters were recruited to participate in the capture and slaughter of their Jewish neighbors.

The chief method of killing was mass shooting. The killers would round up their victims, often in the middle of the night, and either march or drive them to the edge of the town or village. There they would be forced to undress and walk in small groups to freshly dug pits, where they would be shot. As historian Leon Poliakov noted,

> Every action group and squad had its preferred methods. Certain squads forced their victims to lie face down and fired a pistol point blank into the back of their necks. Others made the Jews climb down into the ditch and lie on top of the bodies of those already shot so that the pile of corpses steadily mounted. Still others lined the victims up along the edge of the ditch and shot them in successive salvoes; this way was considered the "most humane" and the "most military."[43]

Although shooting was the most popular method, it was by no means the only one. The killers demonstrated ghastly initiative and creativity in taking advantage of local conditions. When the Jews lived near large bodies of water or wide rivers, they were often loaded on barges that were towed a suitable distance from land

Einzatzgruppen at work in the Soviet Union in the vicinity of Kraigonev. SOURCE: U.S. Holocaust Memorial Museum.

and then sunk. There were reports of the Einsatzgruppen killers forcing the Jews to dig a mass grave and then burying them alive. In October 1941, Romanian counterparts to the Germans herded 19,000 Jews of Odessa into a fenced-in square, sprayed them with gasoline, and set them afire.[44]

Such methods were very effective. For example, after capturing the city of Kiev on September 19, 1941, and seizing more than 650,000 prisoners of war, the German army permitted one of the Einsatzgruppen units to slaughter by mass shooting more than 33,000 Jews on September 29 and 30 at the ravine known as Babi Yar.[45] "Within five *weeks* of the German invasion of Russia on June 22," noted Martin Gilbert, "the number of Jews killed exceeded the total number killed in the previous eight *years* of Nazi rule" (emphasis in original).[46]

During late summer 1941, Heinrich Himmler, who was the supreme leader of the SS and in overall charge of the killing project, decided to visit one of the squads in the field. However, as he stood at the edge of the pit watching a group of Jews being shot, pieces of brain from one of the victims splattered his boots, and he would have fainted into the pit had he not been held up by his aide. When he recovered, Himmler made an impassioned speech about how difficult, but also how essential, was the work that these men were doing. Shortly after this experience, he gave orders to his officers to search for a less disturbing means of mass killing, particularly of women and children.[47] The SS experimented with two alternatives to mass shooting—dynamite and mobile gas chambers. According to Christopher Browning, "An explosives test proved unsatisfactory; it required two

German soldiers standing by while Soviet civilians are forced to dig their own grave prior to being murdered. SOURCE: U.S. Holocaust Memorial Museum.

explosions to kill all the victims, a group of mental patients locked in a bunker, and left parts of bodies strewn about and even hanging from nearby trees. The gassing test was more successful; five mental patients were killed in a sealed room by introducing exhaust gas through a hose from a car and truck parked outside."[48]

Thus, the killers began to use gas vans similar to those used earlier by personnel of the "euthanasia program," but with a number of technical improvements. The vans looked like busses (with windows painted on). Death was caused by carbon monoxide piped from the engine to the airtight chamber in the back. The Jews were told that the trucks would transport them to a labor camp. Instead, they were driven slowly along country roads while the victims died and then backed up to pits in which the bodies were buried. Several units of Einsatzgruppen used the gas vans during the fall of 1941 but found that they presented their own problems. Frequently, it took an hour or more for the victims to die, and on numerous occasions, people were still alive when the vans were unloaded. Also, the Nazis found the task of unloading the vans unpleasant. Ultimately, mass shooting proved to be the most "productive" and favored method used by the Einsatzgruppen.[49]

By late fall 1941, the Einsatzgruppen had penetrated 600 miles into the Soviet Union and murdered an estimated 500,000 Jews—approximately 100,000 per month.[50] Then the cold weather hampered the work of the killers, and there was a lull in the killing actions during which the surviving Russian Jews were herded into ghettos much like those established earlier in Nazi-occupied Poland. There

Mass grave of 7,000 Ukrainian Jews slaughtered in January 1943. SOURCE: U.S. Holocaust Memorial Museum.

they would be confined and utilized as slave laborers until the Nazis augmented the killing teams and prepared for a second sweep.

Escalating Mistreatment of Soviet POWs

As was discussed in the preceding chapter, the German army became deeply implicated in mistreatment of prisoners of war and Soviet civilians. In October 1941, the Wehrmacht gave the Einsatzgruppen greater access to prisoner-of-war camps, and tens of thousands were summarily executed. Later in October, the official allowable ration for POWs was lowered to 500 calories, with the predictable result that many tens of thousands starved to death.[51] According to Omer Bartov in his study of the "barbarisation of warfare" on the eastern front, mass starvation was "a consequence both of a lack of any organization and of a deliberate policy of 'elimination.'"[52] The German army also "went out of its way to turn over Jews to the Einsatzgruppen, to request action against Jews, to participate in killing actions, and to shoot Jewish hostages in 'reprisal' for attacks on occupation forces."[53]

On September 19, 1941, Hitler issued orders for the assault against Moscow—code-named Operation Typhoon—to begin on October 2. As was the case with the initial invasion on June 22, the Germans at first enjoyed great success, advancing as much as 30 miles per day, capturing approximately 650,000 prisoners, and getting to within 20 miles of Moscow by late November.[54] However, in October and November, the German army experienced its first "serious setbacks" as the lengthy supply lines, weary German troops, bad weather, intensifying partisan activities, and tough Red Army defenses all created formidable obstacles.[55] By early December, the German advance was halted, and the Soviet forces launched a devastating counteroffensive that decisively turned the tide of war against the Germans on the eastern front.

The military setbacks provoked what historian Arno Mayer has termed "the spiraling mistreatment of Soviet prisoners of war."[56] By the end of the war, approximately 3.3 million of the nearly 6 million Soviet prisoners of war captured by the Germans were dead—many as the result of direct killing (including gassing), but many more as the result of starvation and disease.[57]

From Mass Shooting to "Medicalized" Mass Murder in Gas Chambers

While the German army and the Einsatzgruppen were slaughtering Russian Jews and prisoners of war with bullets and other means, an alternative method of mass killing was evolving. Rather than sending the killers into the territory where their victims lived, the victims would be shipped from their homes to several special camps in which they would be killed by poison gas.

During late fall 1941, personnel from the "euthanasia" program, along with some of the gassing equipment, were transferred from Germany to the General

Government area of Poland, where they began setting up death camps to which the millions of Polish Jews who had already been captured and confined in ghettos could be transported and killed. Gas vans that had been used by the Einsatzgruppen in Russia were brought to the Polish village of Chelmno, located near the teeming Lodz ghetto. On December 8, 1941, Chelmno became the first death camp to operate. Several gas vans, each with a capacity of between 80 and 90 victims, were used to begin the process of "liquidating" the ghetto. Chelmno operated longer than any of the other five extermination camps—until January 18, 1945. It has been estimated that during this period, more than 300,000 Jews were murdered there. Only three Jews are known to have survived Chelmno.[58]

Also in fall 1941, related developments were occurring at Auschwitz, a concentration camp located in the southwestern corner of Poland on territory that had been incorporated into the German Reich. During summer 1941, the commandant of Auschwitz, Rudolf Höss, had been summoned to Berlin by Himmler, told of Hitler's decision to extend the Final Solution to the Jews of western Europe, and ordered to prepare the camp for use as a mass-killing center. On September 3, 1941, Auschwitz officials carried out an experimental mass gassing using Zyklon B, a commercial insecticide that was on hand in large quantities for the purpose of disinfecting barracks and clothing.[59] Historian Leon Poliakov has provided a description of this experiment:

> Mass killing was tried on 250 patients from the hospital and about 600 prisoners of war in the underground shelters of Block 11. The windows of the shelter were covered with dirt. An SS man wearing a gas mask threw the contents of cans of Cyclone B through the open door, which was then closed. The next afternoon, SS man Paltisch, again wearing his mask, opened the door and noted that many prisoners were still alive. More Cyclone was added and the door shut until the following evening. This time all the prisoners were asphyxiated.[60]

In November of the same year, Höss had begun work on a vast extension of the Auschwitz camp, which came to be called Birkenau and later featured several massive gassing and cremating facilities.

By the end of 1941, the decision to exterminate the Jews of Europe had been made, and most of the technical details needed to implement the Final Solution had been worked out. What remained was the formidable task of working out the organizational and administrative details.[61]

Thus, on January 20, 1942, a crucial meeting was held in the Berlin suburb of Wannsee to coordinate the administrative arrangements for the Final Solution. Reinhard Heydrich chaired the meeting, with detailed minutes taken by Adolf Eichmann. In attendance were representatives of major agencies that were to be directly involved in the mass-killing project. They included officials from the Department of State, Interior, and Justice; the Government General of Poland; the Foreign Office; the Reich Chancellery; and several agencies of the SS. Reference

The lakeshore villa in the Wannsee suburb of Berlin, in which the Wannsee conference was held. Of the 14 invited participants, 8 held doctorates or comparable university degrees. SOURCE: Eric Markusen.

was made to Hitler's order for a final solution, and an estimate of the total number of Jews in German-occupied territory targeted for killing—about 11 million—was announced. Then the conferees discussed the question of how to carry out the Final Solution in the countries controlled or dominated by Germany. Heydrich's plan was to "comb" Europe from "west to east" and ship the Jews to labor camps in the east. To quote from the minutes of the meeting as recorded by Eichmann:

> Separated by sex, the Jews capable of work will be led into these areas in large labor columns to build roads, whereby doubtless a large part will fall away through natural reduction. The residual final remainder which doubtless constitutes the toughest element, will have to be dealt with appropriately, since it represents a natural selection which upon liberation is to be regarded as a germ cell of a new Jewish development.[62]

Although the "appropriate" treatment for those Jews who did not die in the labor camps and ghettos was not spelled out in the minutes, there is little doubt that all of the participants knew exactly what was meant. By the time of the meeting, the Einsatzgruppen had completed their first sweep of Russia, the gas vans at Chelmno had been in operation for more than a month, and work on five other death camps was moving forward. According to Yehuda Bauer, "The importance of Wannsee lies in the fact that at that place and at that time the entire German bureaucracy became involved in the conscious effort to murder a nation."[63]

Even as the Nazi officials were discussing the administrative details of the Final Solution at the Wannsee conference, the second and final sweep of the Einsatzgruppen had begun in Russia. The second sweep was even more brutal then the first, as the elements of surprise and ignorance that had enabled the killers to deceive their victims into a measure of cooperation and passivity during the first sweep were no longer present. Heavily armed Einsatzgruppen, aided by auxilliary forces recruited among local Jew-haters, surrounded the Jewish ghettos and rounded up their victims in house-to-house searches.[64] The inhumane conditions deliberately imposed by the Nazi authorities in the ghettos had succeeded in demoralizing and weakening most of the Jews, thus reducing the chances for organized resistance.

By the time of the second sweep, Nazi efforts to keep the mass killing secret had broken down. German soldiers captured by the Allies were found with snapshots of mass graves and piles of bodies. Jews who had escaped the roundups, and even a few who had been only wounded and had managed to crawl out of the pits before being buried, were spreading the terrible news as rapidly as possible. In June 1942, Himmler gave orders that all traces of the mass burial pits throughout Russia be removed. A special commando was formed for this purpose, and Jewish concentration camp inmates were forced to perform the actual work of digging up hundreds of thousands of rotting bodies and disposing of them. Under the control of former Einsatzgruppen officer Paul Blobel, the commando began by digging up the mass graves that had accumulated at the Chelmno death camp. At first, they tried to destroy the bodies by means of dynamite but soon discovered that burning was the best way. Blobel and his Jewish workers, most of whom were periodically killed and replaced by others, traveled from site to site, retracing the steps of the killing squads. One of the few survivors of this commando provides a glimpse of what he and his comrades endured:

> Today a large group is scheduled to start on a new working site, a place located about thirty feet from the ravine. The graves here are about two months old. The ground is moist, and the workers soon find that the corpses have disintegrated. For this reason the work takes much longer. Instead of pulling out an entire body, one pulls out parts of it; usually the heads are severed from the bodies. We count only the heads. Bodies without heads are not tallied—they are too disintegrated for accurate counting. … The work is gruesome. The inmates are up to their knees in puddles of foulness. With bare hands, they toss the remnants into buckets; they carry the contents over to the fireplace, and toss the contents into the fire.[65]

Later, the methods Blobel developed were put to use at the largest of all the killing centers, Auschwitz, when the pace of killing exceeded the capacity of the crematory ovens, and bodies had to be burned in large pits.

Most of the killing actions of the Einsatzgruppen had been committed by late 1942. By then all of the extermination camps had commenced operations. On the basis of meticulous records kept by the killers and sent to several different offices in Berlin after major actions, it has been estimated that during approximately 18 months of actual killing operations, the Einsatzgruppen had destroyed nearly 1.4 million Jewish men, women, and children.[66]

By spring 1942, three more killing centers—in addition to Chelmno—that had been set up by personnel from the "euthanasia" program were ready to begin "clearing" the Polish ghettos. These camps were under the supervision of SS officer Odilo Globocnik and relied chiefly on large gas chambers into which carbon monoxide was pumped from internal combustion engines. Belzec, the first of the three to begin killing operations, was located near the Lublin ghetto and opened in March 1942. At the peak of its performance, Belzec had six gas chambers, each of which could hold 750 people at one time. Belzec operated until June 30, 1943. Of the estimated 600,000 Jews who were shipped to their deaths in the Belzec gas chambers, only two are known to have survived.[67] Belzec was followed by Sobibor, which operated from May 1942 until its inmates revolted on November 30, 1943. Sobibor was also used to "clear" the Lublin ghetto, though Jews from the Netherlands, France, and other nations were also killed there. Sixty-four inmates survived by fleeing into the forests during the revolt.[68]

The biggest camp under Globocnik's control was Treblinka, located about 50 miles from the huge Warsaw ghetto. It operated from June 1, 1942, until November 30, 1943, when a revolt by its inmates closed it down. During a seven-week period from July 22 to September 12, 1942, 265,000 Jews were shipped from Warsaw and gassed at Treblinka, a rate of 4,000 per day. A description of the gassing process at Treblinka has been provided by one of its few survivors, Yankiel Wiernik:

> Between 450 and 500 persons were crowded into a chamber measuring 25 square meters. Parents carried their children in their arms in the vain hope that this would save their children from death. On the way to their doom, they were pushed and beaten with rifle butts and with Ivan's [one of the Ukrainian guards] gas pipe. Dogs were set upon them, barking, biting, and tearing at them. To escape the blows and the dogs, the crowd rushed to its death, pushing into the chamber, the stronger ones shoving the weaker ones ahead of them. The bedlam lasted only a short while, for soon the doors were slammed shut. The chamber was filled, the motor turned on and connected with the inflow pipes and, within 25 minutes at the most, all lay stretched out dead or, to be more accurate, were standing up dead. Since there was not an inch of free space, they just leaned against each other.[69]

It has been estimated that as many as 750,000 people were killed at Treblinka during the 400 days of its operation.[70] There were only 40 known survivors of the death factory.[71]

The other two killing centers—Majdanek and Auschwitz—were originally concentration and slave-labor camps that were later also used as death camps equipped with gas chambers. Majdanek, located near the Lublin ghetto, was adapted for extermination in fall 1942 and continued gassing Jews until late July 1944.[72] During a three-year period, an estimated 360,000 victims were slaughtered by guns and gas at Majdanek.[73]

The largest and most infamous of all the death camps was Auschwitz-Birkenau. Auschwitz had opened as a conventional concentration camp in June 1940 but began adapting for extermination operations in summer 1941. As noted previously, the first experimental gassing, using the pesticide Zyklon B, took place in September 1941, followed by construction of an extension of the Auschwitz camp, which came to be known as Birkenau and where the bulk of the mass-killing actions were carried out.

In February 1942, Nazi officials decided to build four huge crematoria–gas chamber complexes at Birkenau, a process that was to take over a year to complete. In two of the new complexes, underground gas chambers with a capacity of 2,000 people at one time were planned.[74] While the new facilities were being built, killing was done in a gas chamber at the Auschwitz camp and in two small huts at Birkenau that had been converted into gas chambers. Although transports to Auschwitz began to arrive in early 1942, the four new crematoria were not all ready at Birkenau until mid-July 1943. When the first of the new facilities was ready for action, the camp authorities staged a celebration. According to two inmates who witnessed the festivities before escaping from the camp,

> Important visitors came specially from Berlin for the inauguration of the crematoriums, and a special feast was provided for them in the shape of the gassing and burning of 8,000 Cracow Jews. The visitors, both military and civilian, watched the whole process of gassing and burning through a special opening, and were highly satisfied with the results. They expressed their appreciation to the Camp Administration.[75]

The killing process at Birkenau resembled an assembly line. On arrival by train, often after several days of riding in crowded boxcars with no food or water, the Jews would form two lines—one with men and boys and the other with women, babies and small children, the elderly, and the infirm. Both lines would file past Nazi doctors, who would perform "selections," choosing a small percentage to enter the camp as slave laborers. The rest would be told that they were going to be given baths and were told to walk to the "baths and disinfection" facility. They would find a large building with a tall chimney surrounded by carefully maintained grass and flowers. Often, there would be an orchestra playing. They would be greeted by an SS officer who repeated that they would be given baths. An eyewitness account is provided by Filip Müller, a Slovakian Jew who was forced by the Nazis to work in the gas chambers and crematoria and who survived the war to write his story, *Eyewitness Auschwitz: Three Years in the Gas Chambers.* According to Müller, the SS officer

> asked the people to get undressed because, in their own interest, they had to be disinfected. "First and foremost we shall have to see that you are healthy," he said. "Therefore everyone will have to take a shower. Now, when you've had your showers, there'll be a bowl of soup waiting for you all." Life flooded back into the upturned faces of the men and woman listening eagerly to every word. The desired effect had been

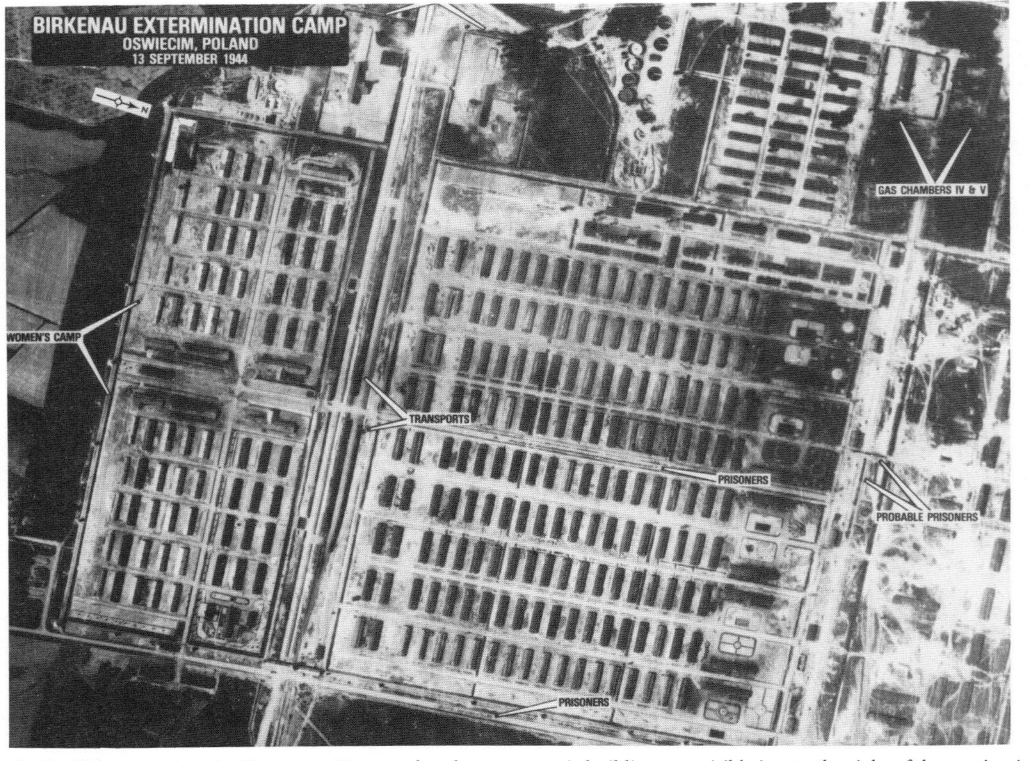

An aerial overview of Auschwitz-Birkenau extermination camp. Two gas chamber-crematoria buildings are visible just to the right of the caption in the upper-left corner of the photo. Details of one of these buildings follow, in photos 11 through 15. The other two gas chamber-crematoria buildings are in the upper-right corner of the photo, labeled "Gas Chambers IV & V." Below the caption "Transports" is the railroad track used for trains bringing in shipments of Jews and others to the camp. The numerous rectangular shapes in the center of the photo are barracks used to house prisoners, each of which held as many as 1,200 inmates. The camp population reached its peak of approximately 100,000 inmates in 1943. This picture was taken by a U.S. Army Air Forces photoreconnaissance plane. SOURCE: U.S. Holocaust Memorial Museum.

> achieved; initial suspicion gave way to hope, perhaps even to the belief that everything might still end happily. Hoessler [the SS officer] sensing the change in mood quickly began to speak. In order to invest this large-scale deception with the semblance of complete honesty, he put on a perfect act to delude these unsuspecting people. "You over there in the corner," he cried, pointing at a little man, "what's your trade?" "I'm a tailor," came the prompt reply. "Ladies or gents," inquired Hoessler. "Both," the little man replied confidently. "Excellent!" Hoessler was delighted. "That's precisely the sort of people we need in our workrooms. When you've had your shower, report to me at once." ... All the people's fears and anxieties had vanished as if by magic. Quiet as lambs they undressed without having to be shouted at or beaten. Each tried his or her best to hurry up with their undressing so that they might be among the first to get under the shower.[76]

The undressing room was carefully designed to reinforce the illusion. Again to quote Müller:

> This underground room could accommodate more than 1,000 people. They entered from the yard down wide concrete steps. At the entrance to the basement was a signboard, and written on it in several languages the direction: *To the baths and disinfecting rooms.* The ceiling of the changing room was supported by concrete pillars to which many more notices were fixed, once again with the aim of making the unsuspecting people believe that the imminent process of disinfection was of vital importance for their health. Slogans like *Cleanliness brings freedom* or *One louse may kill you* were intended to hoodwink, as were numbered clothes hooks fixed at a height of 1.50 meters. Along the walls stood wooden benches, creating the impression that they were placed there to make people more comfortable while undressing. There were other multi-lingual notices inviting them to hang up their clothes as well as their shoes, tied together by their laces, and admonishing them to remember the numbers of their hook so that they might easily retrieve their clothes after their showers.[77]

From the undressing room, the people would walk to the "shower room." Often, one group would have to wait there while another went through the charade in the undressing room. Finally, when the gas chamber was filled to capacity, the doors would be shut and locked, the lights would be turned off, and an SS "disinfection officer," who had arrived in an ambulance marked with a red cross, would pour the gas crystals into the chamber. According to Müller,

> As soon as the Zyclon B crystals came into contact with air the deadly gas began to develop, spreading first at floor level and then rising to the ceiling. It was for this reason that the bottom layer of corpses always consisted of children as well as the old and the weak, while the tallest and strongest lay on top, with middle-aged men and women in between. No doubt the ones on top had climbed up there over the bodies already lying on the floor because they still had the strength to do so and perhaps also because they had realized that the deadly gas was spreading from the bottom upwards.[78]

After a Nazi doctor, peering through a peephole, determined that the victims were dead, special ventilating fans were turned on in order to purge the gas from the chamber. Then, special teams of Jewish inmates (like Müller) entered with

A transport of Hungarian Jews undergoing selection by Nazi doctors at Auschwitz-Birkenau. Visible at the upper-left of the photo is a line of Jews who have "failed" the selection and are walking to the gas chamber. At the upper-right, a truck is being loaded by prisoner-laborers with the belongings of the Jews who arrived on the train. SOURCE: Yad Vashem.

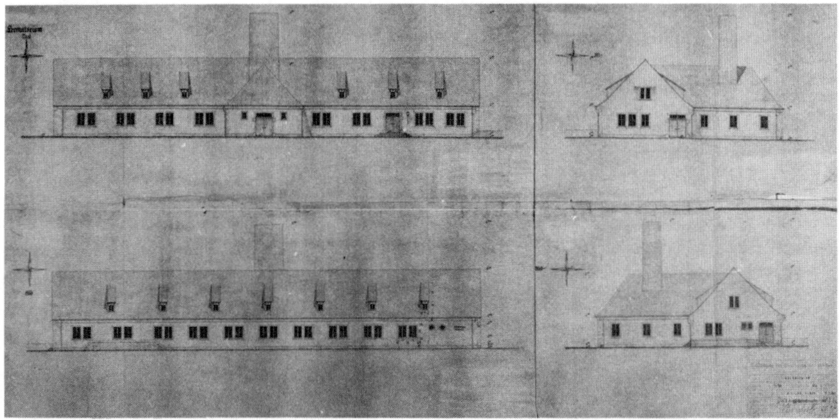

An architect's drawing of the gas-chamber building shown in the sketch in photo 12. During the closing months of the war, the Nazis attempted to destroy all evidence of their extermination policy, but one file drawer containing architectural drawings and blueprints was inadvertently untouched. SOURCE: Polish National Museum at Oswiecim (Auschwitz).

TOP: A sketch of one of the gas chamber–crematorium buildings at Auschwitz-Birkenau, drawn in 1945 based on the architect's drawing shown in photo 11. The cremation ovens were located on the ground floor. The attic area was used as housing for the Sonderkommando and also for drying hair shorn from the heads of gassed women (later to be shipped to Germany for industrial uses). At the lower-left corner of the sketch is the roof of the underground undressing room. SOURCE: Polish National Museum at Oswiecim (Auschwitz).

LEFT: Inmates constructing the roof of the underground undressing room for one of the gas chamber–crematorium buildings at Auschwitz-Birkenau. The aboveground part of the building, housing the ovens, is clearly visible. The photo was taken by an SS photographer on either January 25 or 26, 1943, as part of a series on the construction of the building. SOURCE: Polish National Museum at Oswiecim (Auschwitz).

Close-up of the model of a gas chamber–crematorium building, showing a line of people moving into the undressing room as well as those already inside it. The model is on display at the Polish National Museum at Oswiecim (Auschwitz). Although it contains some minor inaccuracies, it does provide a clear impression of the layout and scale of the building. SOURCE: Polish National Museum at Oswiecim.

Close-up of the model of a gas chamber–crematorium building, showing people being killed in the gas chamber, as well as inmates in the Sonderkommando working at the ovens on the ground floor. SOURCE: Polish National Museum at Oswiecim (Auschwitz).

Hungarian women and children gathered in the forested area near one of the gas chambers, waiting to be killed. This photo was taken by the same photographer of the same transport of Hungarian Jews shown in Photo 10, this chapter. SOURCE: Yad Vashem.

powerful hoses to wash off the urine, feces, and menstrual blood that had been expelled in the victims' death agonies. After these teams pried the bodies apart, individual corpses were inspected for gold teeth and valuables hidden in body cavities, and the dead womens' heads were shorn of their hair, which would be shipped back to Germany for industrial uses. Only then were the bodies taken to the crematoria furnaces. Later, the ashes were scattered in a nearby river.

The most intensive period of killings at Auschwitz-Birkenau occurred during summer 1944, following the Nazi occupation of Hungary during March of that year. Between May 15 and July 19, 1944, Eichmann and his assistants arranged to have nearly 440,000 Hungarian Jews deported to Auschwitz, the vast majority of whom were killed on arrival. Such a volume of killing taxed even the resources of Birkenau. Even though the crematoria were operated around the clock by more than 800 inmates, camp officials had to resort to the use of huge outdoor burning pits, the smoke from which was visible 30 miles away.[79] Once again, we rely on Müller for an eyewitness account:

> Under the ever-increasing heat a few of the dead began to stir, writhing as though with some unbearable pain, arms and legs straining in slow motion, and even their bodies straightening up a little, hesitant and with difficultly, almost as if with their last strength they were trying to rebel against their doom. Eventually the fire became so intense that the corpses were enveloped by flames. Blisters which had formed on

> their skin burst one by one. Almost every corpse was covered with black scorch marks and glistened as if it had been greased. The searing heat had burst open their bellies; there was the violent hissing and spluttering of frying in great heat. Boiling fat flowed into the pans on either side of the pit. Fanned by the wind, the flames, dark-red before, now took on a fiery white hue; the corpses were burning so fiercely that they were consumed by their own heat. The process of incineration took five to six hours. What was left barely filled a third of the pit.[80]

Between November 1941, when mass gassings began, and November 1944, when the approach of the Russian army forced camp officials to stop gassing, dynamite the crematoria, and begin marching the surviving inmates to camps further west, as many as 1.3 million Jews were killed at Auschwitz and Birkenau.[81]

The Holocaust has been aptly called the "ultimate and archetypal genocide,"[82] but it was certainly not the first, nor was it the last. Moreover, as Yehuda Bauer has warned, "It is essential to realize that we live in an era in which Holocausts are possible, though not inevitable. The Holocaust was produced by factors that still exist in the world, factors such as deep hatreds, bureaucracies capable and willing to do the bidding of their superiors, modern technology devoid of moral directions, brutal dictatorships, and wars."[83] Some of these factors are explored in Chapters 9 and 10. But first, we turn, in the following chapter, to the story of strategic bombing.

Chapter 8

The Evolution of Allied Strategic Bombing, 1939–1945

Whoever fights monsters should see to it that in the process he does not become a monster. And when you look into an abyss, the abyss also looks into you.

—*Friedrich Nietzsche (1886)*[1]

On September 1, 1939, the day on which Hitler invaded Poland, President Franklin Delano Roosevelt issued an appeal to Great Britain, France, and Germany to abstain from using airplanes to attack cities and innocent civilians. Referring primarily to the air bombardment of cities during World War I, which had killed thousands of noncombatants, Roosevelt wrote, "The ruthless bombing from the air of civilians in unfortified centers of population during the course of the hostilities … has sickened the hearts of every civilized man and woman, and has profoundly shocked the conscience of humanity." He urged "every Government which may be engaged in hostilities publicly to affirm its determination that its armed forces shall in no event, and under no circumstances, undertake the bombardment from the air of civilian populations or of unfortified cities."[2] In response, two weeks later, British prime minister Neville Chamberlain told the House of Commons: "Whatever the lengths to which others may go, His Majesty's Government will never resort to the deliberate attack on women and children and other civilians for purposes of mere terrorism."[3]

By the end of the war, however, both the United States and Great Britain resorted to the very practices they had earlier repudiated as being unworthy of civilized, democratic nations. Both nations started the air war with a policy of carefully avoiding civilian casualties, and both ended by using incendiary bombs to deliberately set crowded enemy cities on fire.

The Evolution of British Bombing Policy and Practice

Both Britain and Germany Demonstrate Restraint

At the beginning of World War II, British bombing policy was rigorously discriminating—even to the point of putting British aircrews at great risk. Only obvious military targets removed from population centers were attacked, and bomber crews were instructed to jettison their bombs over water when weather conditions made target identification questionable. Several factors were cited to explain this policy, including a desire to avoid provoking Germany into retaliating against nonmilitary targets in Britain with its then numerically superior air force. British officials feared that such attacks might paralyze public morale and support for the war—a view that had been espoused in the period between the two world wars by such highly influential theorists of air warfare as England's Sir Hugh Trenchard and Italy's Guilio Douhet.[4] British war planners lacked the planes, in terms of both numbers and capabilities, to wage a major air offensive against Germany. They hoped that a period of mutual restraint would give them time to build up the capacity of British air forces. Finally, moral considerations such as those articulated by Prime Minister Chamberlain also exercised a restraining influence on early policy and practice.[5]

When Great Britain did initiate offensive aerial warfare, on September 4, 1939, 19 bombers attacked German naval installations on the North Sea coast that could be readily differentiated from population centers. Seven British planes were lost in this raid.[6] In subsequent raids, also conducted in daylight in order to ensure positive identification of military targets, the British incurred 50 percent losses from German defenses.[7] Despite such losses, the British continued the daylight, precision-targeting policy. In turn, the Germans in their air attacks against England showed similar discrimination.

This mutual restraint between Great Britain and Germany lasted from September 1939 until mid-May 1940—the period widely known as the "twilight war" or "phoney war."[8] Duing this period, the war in the west was largely dormant, with each side carefully observing the other and gearing up for later hostilities. Both British and German air operations remained limited to conducting reconnaissance flights, dropping propaganda leaflets, and occasionally attacking each other's coastal naval facilities.

In the east, Poland suffered terribly under German air bombardment. On September 17, 1939, the German air force (Luftwaffe) began bombing and strafing the capital city of Warsaw, which had stubbornly refused to surrender. Much of the city erupted in flames as "German bombers crisscrossed over it while their crews threw out incendiaries by the shovelfull, stoking the mighty furnace ten thousand feet below."[9] The air offensive was in support of a massive invasion. In what became known as blitzkrieg, or "lightning warfare," 1,250,000 German soliders in 60 divisions struck Poland from the north, west, and south. The Luftwaffe coordinated its attack with speedy armored columns of the German army. In less than six weeks, 66,000 Poles were killed, 200,000 were wounded, and some 694,000 Polish soldiers were taken prisoner.[10] Within two weeks, Poland surrendered to Germany.

Although the Germans regarded their air attacks as aimed at military targets within a city that had chosen not to surrender, the British regarded the attacks as a direct violation of the Roosevelt appeal. On October 16, 1939, Great Britain decided that it would no longer be bound by the restraint called for by the Roosevelt and Chamberlain declarations. "Henceforth," wrote historian Lee Kennett, "British air policy would be governed by expediency."[11] Notwithstanding that decision, actual practice remained characterized by the targeting of precise, military objectives as the "phoney war" in the west persisted for eight more months.

Then, on May 10, 1940, Germany launched its western offensive against the Netherlands, Belgium, and France. This brought the "phoney war" in the west to an abrupt end and provoked the resignation of British prime minister Neville Chamberlain. Chamberlain was replaced by Winston Churchill, who was a strong advocate of aggressive bombing policies.

The Erosion of Mutual Restraint

During the western campaign, the German air force used its dive-bombers as tactical support for the ground offensive. Cities were bombed only when they contained active military forces and refused to surrender. The goal of the bombardment was to induce surrender rather to deliberately kill civilians and destroy their homes.

Then, on May 14, 1940, German bombers launched a massive attack on the Dutch city of Rotterdam. Erroneous reports quickly spread through Europe claiming that as many as 30,000 civilians had been killed and that the city had been attacked after it had surrendered. The reality was quite different; about 1,000 people died, and the attack occurred after German authorities who had been negotiating surrender terms with Dutch officials had tried unsuccessfuly to signal the planes to abort their mission.[12]

The British government, however, interpreted the attack as a deliberate effort to kill civilians and an egregious repudiation of the mutual restraint that had been exercised to that point in the war. In retaliation, Churchill ordered the Royal Air Force to undertake a nighttime mission on May 15 against several cities in the German industrial region of the Ruhr. Although the targets were officially designated as military and industrial facilities, the poor accuracy and darkness resulted in substantial damage to residential areas. Nine days after the British attacks, Hitler ordered his air force to prepare for a full-scale air offensive against England both as a reprisal for the Ruhr attacks and as preparation for a planned cross-Channel invasion of the British Isles.[13]

The German air offensive against England, known as the Battle of Britain, began in June 1940. Initially, the German air force attacked during daylight and aimed its bombs at British air defenses. Hitler had explicitly forbidden attacks on London and other cities. Similarly, the British air force, although it continued to bomb at night in order to reduce losses to German fighter and flak defenses, aimed its bombs at specific military and industrial targets. The German capital of Berlin was deliberately spared. Some British policymakers were impatient with the relatively limited results of the "precision" bombing policy, however. In his history of the air war, R. J. Overy wrote, "Churchill and some of the Air Staff favoured an indiscriminate offensive, partly in retaliation, partly because it was by no means clear that night attacks could be made with enough precision to ensure that targets could be hit, let alone destroyed."[14]

As the German losses during daylight raids against Britain began to mount, the Luftwaffe also began attacking at night. This meant that many German bombs missed their targets and fell instead in residential areas. Much like their counterparts in Britain, the Luftwaffe leaders insisted that they were aiming at precise military targets and that any bombs that fell on residential areas were unintentional. The net result, however, was a rapid, reciprocal erosion of mutual restraint.

Then, on the evening of August 24, 1940, about a dozen German bombers that had been ordered to attack oil storage tanks and other military targets on the outskirts of London veered off course and accidently dropped their bombs on central London, starting a number of fires and destroying many homes.[15] In retaliation, Churchill ordered British bombers to attack the German capital, Berlin, for the first time during the war. Shortly thereafter, a British night attack by 81 bombers was launched against specific industrial sites in Berlin.[16] Although the British raid caused relatively little damage, Hitler was infuriated, telling a mass rally about a week later, "If they attack our cities, we will simply rub out theirs."[17] In reprisal for the Berlin attack, Hitler ordered Hermann Göring, the head of the Luftwaffe, to begin a series of raids against London and switch from military targets to the city itself. These intentional city attacks, which became known as the Blitz, began on September 7, 1940, and continued, sometimes intensively and other times sporadically, until mid-May 1941.

The change in tactics by Germany allowed the beleaguered British Fighter Command to marshal its forces for an effective defense against subsequent German attacks. It has been suggested, in fact, that Churchill's order to attack Berlin was a deliberate effort to provoke the diversion of German bombers from their previous focus on bombing British fighter bases.[18] Another result was an inexorable movement in the direction of deliberate destruction of cities by both sides. According to Frederick Sallagar, who carefully studied the process of reciprocal escalation of the air war, "On September 7 [1940] the Germans sowed the wind of which they were to reap the whirlwind some years later. It was the start of indiscriminate air warfare—the end of the road to total war."[19]

During the nine months of the Blitz, more than 45,000 Londoners were killed by more than 50,000 tons of high explosive and incendiary bombs.[20] More than 3.5 million homes were destroyed or seriously damaged.[21]

Under this onslaught, there was heated debate among government officials and military leaders about the best use of the British bomber force, which was Britain's only effective means of taking the war to German territory. Some military and political leaders continued to favor attacks against precise military and industrial targets like oil refineries and other facilities whose destruction, it was argued, would disrupt the German economy and, hence, the Nazi war machine. Others argued that attacks against the homes of German workers would more effectively disrupt the economy by depressing their morale and patriotism. As a compromise, Bomber Command (the branch of the Royal Air Force responsible for strategic bombing operations) decided to aim both high explosive and incendiary bombs against "precision targets in residential areas."[22] Thus, on October 30, 1940, Bomber Command was ordered to target German industrial installations surrounded by densely populated residential areas in order to maximize damage to residential areas inhabited by civilians. In the words of the official directive, the planes were to use incendiary bombs to raise massive fires and then successive sorties of bombers were to "focus their attacks to a large extent on the fires with a view to preventing the fire fighting services from dealing with them and giving the fires every opportunity to spread."[23] According to the official historians of the British air offensive, any pretense of precision military targeting was officially abandoned, and the practice of deliberate "area" or "saturation" bombing was officially endorsed.[24]

Pressures toward area bombing were further intensified on November 14, 1940, when a German raid on the city of Coventry, England, left over 500 civilians dead and 20,000 homes destroyed. In his history of Bomber Command, Max Hastings observed that at one Bomber Command base, an officer "pinned photographs of blitzed London, Coventry, Southampton on the wall of the operations room and stabbed his finger at them them as he briefed the crews 'Go now and do likewise to the Hun!'"[25] The intellectual rationale for area bombing was augmented shortly after the Coventry debacle, when photoreconnaissance flights disclosed that the high levels of accuracy and damage previously assumed to have been obtained by precision bombing of targets in Germany had actually been grossly exaggerated.[26]

Much to the relief of the British fighter crews and the citizens of England, the Blitz ended in May 1941, when the Luftwaffe was diverted to prepare for the impending German invasion of the Soviet Union. During summer 1941, after the Blitz had ended, the British air force attacked a variety of targets, such as oil refineries and factories surrounded by heavily populated neighborhoods. However, Bomber Command was still divided over the best approach to targeting. The precision attacks did not appear to be reducing the German capacity to wage the war. On August 18, a British government commission that had analyzed the photographic records from earlier bombing raids reported that the inaccuracy was even greater than had been feared, and the damage to the German war effort was considerably less significant than had been assumed. Moreover, German fighters and antiaircraft guns were proving very damaging to the British bombers. Renewed and intensified debate on the value of civilian morale as a target for the bombers ensued. On July 9, 1941, Bomber Command was directed to attack transportation facilities in urban-industrial areas. Bombs that missed the railway stations and switching yards would fall on the nearby homes of German workers. During this same period, British bomber crews were ordered to drop their bombs on targets of opportunity if they were unable to reach their primary target.

Despite the expansion of targeting to maximize collateral damage to civilian areas, the heavy losses of aircraft and crew, combined with the disappointing results from the raids, induced the top British war leaders, on November 13, 1941, to order Bomber Command to drastically curtail its activities. The resulting lull in the strategic air offensive lasted until February 1942. The high hopes entertained for strategic bombing were dashed, and morale in Bomber Command plummeted.

Bomber Command Targets the Morale of German Citizens

After considerable debate on targeting policies and jockeying for leadership positions within Bomber Command, the British bomber offensive resumed in February 1942 under the guidance of a new directive that explicitly stated: "It has been decided that the primary objective of your operations should now be focussed on the morale of the enemy civil population and in particular, of the industrial workers."[27]

Shortly thereafter, on February 20, Sir Arthur Harris was placed in charge of Bomber Command. Harris was a staunch disciple of Hugh Trenchard, the British "prophet of strategic bombing," who had advocated, after World War I, the development of a long-range British bomber force for use in a future war.[28] Harris strongly shared Trenchard's belief that physical destruction of enemy cities held the key to victory.[29]

Shortly after Harris assumed command, an important memo advocating "dehousing" German workers as an expeditious means of destroying German morale was issued by Frederick Lindemann, Churchill's chief science adviser and close confidant. Lindemann wrote:

> Investigation seems to show that having one's house demolished is most damaging to morale. People seem to mind it more than having their friends or even relatives killed. At Hull [an English city that had been bombed by the Germans] signs of strain were evident, though only one-tenth of the houses were demolished. On the above figures we should be able to do ten times as much harm to each of the fifty-eight principal German towns. There seems little doubt that this would break the spirit of the people.[30]

This report provided crucial support for those who favored incendiary attacks on German cities, notwithstanding the fact that its allegedly scientific rationale was severely criticized at the time of its release.

For the remainder of the war, the principal thrust of Bomber Command was to be direct attacks against German cities, with success measured in terms of how many acres were destroyed. "The fundamental goal," asserted Kennett, "was physical destruction."[31] At times, the bombers were diverted from the city-destroying mission by the exigencies of the larger war, as was the case when they were ordered to attack more traditional military targets such as German naval bases in anticipation of the Allied invasion of Normandy, France, in June 1944. The bulk of the bomb tonnage, however, fell on cities.[32]

In late March 1942, Harris put his ideas into practice with a massive incendiary attack on the German town of Lübeck, which had been selected specifically because its crowded, wooden buildings were highly flammable rather than because of its military or industrial significance. According to the official historians, "The inclusion of such a relatively unimportant place as Lübeck, which happened to be especially inflammable, in the target lists, showed the extent ... to which a town might become a target mainly because it was operationally vulnerable."[33] The attack involved 234 bombers releasing 300 tons of bombs (about half high-explosive and half incendiary) and was considered a great success and a vindication of Harris's staunch belief in the value of incendiaries as opposed to high-explosive bombs as the most efficient means of destroying enemy cities.[34]

Shortly after the Lübeck attack, the Luftwaffe initiated a series of reprisal attacks on scenic, historic British cities with no important military significance, including Oxford and Exeter. These attacks, which became known as the Baedecker raids (named after a series of famous tourist guides to Europe), further hardened British determination to take the war to German civilians.

On May 30, 1942, Harris orchestrated another stunning success for Bomber Command, a raid with nearly 1,000 bombers against Cologne. By dropping approximately 1,400 tons of bombs (two-thirds incendiaries), the bombers managed to raze 600 acres within the city. According to one account of the raid, "Bombs fell with grim impartiality on industrial buildings, empty city offices, crowded hospitals, empty churches, hastily abandoned homes and crammed air raid shelters."[35] Thanks to extensive civil defense preparations, casualties were kept relatively low (at least by comparison with later raids): several hundred people killed and several thousand wounded. In the weeks following the raid, survivors went back to work producing materiel for the war. Both the incendiary attack on Lübeck and the "thousand raid" on Cologne provided Bomber Command with vital experience for later raids against such cities as Essen and Bremen, which would combine the extensive use of incendiaries with very large numbers of bombers.

Between January 14 and 24, 1943, British and U.S. military and political leaders met in the Moroccan city of Casablanca to plan a combined air offensive against Germany. Roosevelt and Churchill decided that for the time being, bombing was the only feasible means by which the Allies could directly aid the Russians, who were suffering heavy casualties in ground combat. They also decided that air supremacy over Germany was essential for the anticipated land invasion by Allied forces. The British tried to persuade the Americans to adopt their nighttime area-bombing techniques, but the Americans insisted on a daylight, precision approach. In the end, the British decided to continue their night offensive, and the Americans bombed by day.[36]

Under the direction of Harris, the British continued to focus their attacks against German cities. From March through July 1943, Bomber Command staged 43 raids against important manufacturing cities in the Ruhr area of Germany, as well as raids against Berlin.

Operation Gomorrah: The Fire Raid Against Hamburg

Between July 24 and July 28, 1943, British and U.S. bombers combined forces in a series of devastating attacks on the German city of Hamburg. Code-named Operation Gomorrah, the official intent of the attacks was "the total destruction" of the city.[37] In keeping with the division of labor established at the Casablanca conference, the American bombers conducted daylight raids aimed at precise military-industrial targets. They achieved only modest results, accounting for only about one percent of the destruction. However, the British night area attacks, particularly on the evening of July 27–28, killed 45,000 people, which was the single greatest death toll in a bombing raid thus far in the war.[38]

A number of factors contributed to such a devastating result. For the first time in the war, British bombers used a device known as "window" (strips of tin foil dropped from the planes) to disrupt the German defenses, allowing the nearly 800 planes to drop their 1,200 tons of incendiaries with optimal accuracy and concentration. The flammability of the city of Hamburg, with its many wooden buildings built closely together, had been recognized for some time. Finally, the weather conditions were highly conducive to the creation of what has been called "the war's first great firestorm."[39]

Unlike previous incendiary raids, the Hamburg attacks created what was, in effect, a tornado of fire in the heart of the city. The countless fires started by the thousands of incendiary bombs converged to form "a concentrated mass conflagration that burned with increasing intensity."[40] The air above the fires became so hot that it created a powerful suction that drew fresh air from outside the burning area into the core of the fire, thereby intensifying the heat and expanding the area of the firestorm.

A description of the Hamburg firestorm is provided by Horatio Bond, an official of the United States National Fire Protection Association who, like many of his colleagues during the war, had consulted with the U.S. air forces on the best ways to create large fires in enemy cities:

> Incendiary bombs started fires which spread particularly in thickly inhabited parts of town in a very short period of time. Thus in several minutes whole blocks were on fire and streets made impassable by flames. The heat increased rapidly and produced a wind which soon was of the power and strength of a typhoon. The typhoon first moved into the direction of the fires, later spreading in all directions. In the public

squares and parks it broke trees, and burning branches shot through the air. Trees of all sizes were uprooted. The "firestorm" broke down doors of houses and later the flames crept into the doorways and corridors. The "firestorm" looked like a blizzard of red snow flakes. ... The heat turned whole city blocks into a flaming hell.[41]

From the air, the crews in the bombers looked down in amazement at what they had created. One airman recalled, "As far as I could see was one mass of fire. 'A sea of flame' has been the description and that's an understatement. It was so bright that I could read the target maps and adjust the bomb-sight." Another stated, "As I looked down, it was as if I was looking into what I imagined to be an active volcano. There were great volumes of smoke and, mentally, I could sense the great heat. Our actual bombing was like putting another shovelful of coal into the furnace." A third was "amazed at the awe-inspiring sight of the target area. It seemed as though the whole of Hamburg was on fire from one end to the other and a huge column of smoke was towering well above us—and we were on 20,000 feet! It all seemed almost incredible and, when I realized that I was looking at a city with a population of two millions, or about that, it became almost frightening to think of what must be going on down there in Hamburg."[42]

On the ground, the conditions were hellish. In his book *The Night Hamburg Died,* Martin Caidin posed the questions: "How can you describe the heat in Hamburg tonight? How do you describe temperatures that reach to more than 1400 degrees Fahrenheit? At this temperature lead becomes a bubbling fluid, aluminum has long since run as a liquid. This is a heat so great that it explodes wood subject to its murderous touch."[43]

People died in many different ways. The majority succumbed to carbon monoxide poisoning or suffocation. According to Gordon Musgrove,

In the firestorm it actually hurt to breathe; the air was hot rather than merely warm, and it was drawn in down a parched throat into lungs which were straining for oxygen but being fed smoke and often phosphorus fumes. At a time when the brain required richly oxygenated blood to help it perform the clearest thinking, it was receiving an increasingly polluted supply. As conditions worsened so the ability of the individual to deal with them decreased.[44]

Others were turned into human torches by the intense heat. There were reports of babies being torn by the high winds from their mothers' arms and sucked into the flames. Many died trapped in the burning wreckage of buildings. Upon entering many basement air-raid shelters, would-be rescuers found nothing but bones suspended in congealed fat. One eyewitness recalled,

Women and children were so charred as to be unrecognizable; those that had died through lack of oxygen were half charred and recognizable. Their brains tumbled from their burst temples and their insides from the soft parts under the ribs. How terribly must these people have died. The smallest children lay like fried eels on the pave-

> ment. Even in death, they showed signs of how they must have suffered—their hands and arms stretched out as if to protect them from the pitiless heat.[45]

Some people managed to make their way to the numerous waterways and canals that crisscrossed the city of Hamburg, but even that did not guarantee survival. Treading water, or standing in neck-deep water, they were still assaulted by the intense heat. According to Caidin,

> Despite their efforts, these people suffered severe burns on their necks and faces. Buried in water up to their chins, they are dying from the heat! ... The heat radiation sucks away their life. The skin blisters and reddens and begins to swell horribly. Their eyes protrude until the bulging is beyond belief. Great water blisters appear and burst unfelt, cascading the bile of ruptured skin along their cheeks and over their open, gasping mouths. Standing thus, they die, their life ebbing away until finally, eyes staring sightlessly, they are swept away by the moving current, lifeless hulks that drift like flotsam along the greasy, heated surface.[46]

The bombers deliberately hampered fire-fighting efforts by mixing various types of high-explosive (HE) bombs among the incendiaries. Musgrove quotes from the postraid report by the police president of Hamburg: "This constantly alternating dropping of HE bombs, land mines, and incendiary bombs made possible an almost unimpeded spread of fires."[47]

Operation Gomorrah succeeded in burning 13 square miles of the city of Hamburg.[48] Of the 45,000 people killed, it has been estimated that 50 percent were women and children and many of the men killed were elderly, above military age.[49] For weeks after the raids, survivors were plagued by "droves of vicious rats, grown strong by feeding on the corpses that were left unburied within the rubble as well as the potatoes and other food supplies lost beneath the broken buildings."[50]

In November 1943, the British launched the Battle of Berlin, a series of 16 major bombing raids against the German capital that lasted until March 1944. Unlike the Hamburg raids, however, German fighters and flak prevented the British from causing significant damage. In the final attack in the Battle of Berlin, more than 9 percent of the British bombers were lost as the result of German fighters, antiaircraft fire, and midair collisions.[51]

During summer 1944, the Germans began to strike London and other British cities with their so-called vengeance weapons—the V-1 buzz bomb and the V-2 ballistic missile. About 5,000 V-1s and about 1,000 V-2s reached Great Britain, killing several thousand people, though only a fraction the number killed during the Blitz in 1940–1941.[52]

The British bomber offensive developed a powerful momentum during the last year of the war in Europe. According to Kennett, "In its scope and intensity it dwarfed anything seen before." In a ten-month period, "fifty of Germany's great cities were reduced to rubble and ashes."[53]

The Torching of Dresden

The British air offensive against German civilians culminated in February 1945, when British and American planes bombed the city of Dresden in eastern Germany. For a number of reasons, the Dresden raid was among the most controversial Allied actions of the entire war. Some analysts have questioned whether the city had enough military or industrial importance to warrant a massive incendiary and high-explosive attack so late in the war. Historian David Irving has written:

> Not endowed with any one great capital industry like those of Essen or Hamburg, even though Dresden was of comparable size, the city's economy had been sustained in peacetime by its theaters, museums, cultural institutions and home industries. Even by the end of 1944 it would have been difficult to have singled out any one plant of the kind of major importance which occasioned air attacks on other less fortunate German towns and cities.[54]

Even Sir Robert Saundby, one of the highest-ranking officers in Bomber Command during the war, wrote in the foreword to Irving's book: "That the bombing of Dresden was a great tragedy none can deny. That it was really a military necessity few, after reading this book, will believe."[55] At that late point in the war in Europe, Dresden had been largely spared from air attack, persuading many of its leaders and citizens that its strategic insignificance would continue to protect it and prompting the military authorities to transfer most of its antiaircraft defenses to other German cities whose military and industrial importance made them far more likely to be hit.

At the time of the bombing, Dresden was swollen with hundreds of thousands of refugees from the eastern areas of Germany—men, women, and children fleeing from the advancing Soviet army. The normal population of about 650,000 was at least doubled by the refugees, many of whom had no place to live and were not assigned to public air-raid shelters. That the planners of the Dresden raid were well aware of the tide of refugees is indicated by the following wording from the official directive authorizing fire raids against "Berlin, Leipzig, Dresden and associated cities where heavy attack will cause great confusion in civilian evacuation from the East."[56] In addition to the masses of homeless German civilians, there were also, unbeknownst to the British and American planners of the raid, as many as 26,000 British and American prisoners of war in the vicinity of Dresden, some of whom were killed in the raid.[57]

The raid was deliberately planned to create a massive firestorm and consisted of three waves of attacking bombers. Typically, the British attacked at night with incendiaries, and the Americans struck with far less effect during the day, mainly with high-explosives. The first wave, consisting of nearly 250 British bombers carrying both high-explosive and incendiary bombs, hit Dresden at 10:00 P.M. on February 13. Three hours later, a second wave of more than 500 British bombers, carrying more than 650,000 incendiary bombs, struck again. Ten hours later, at about noon, 316 American bombers attacked, dropping nearly 500 tons of high-explosive and 300 tons of incendiary bombs. Also included in the American bomb loads were bombs with delayed-action fuses designed to explode while rescue workers and firefighters were at work.[58] Accompanying the American bombers were fighter planes that used machine guns to strafe masses of survivors trying to leave the burning city.[59]

As in the raids against Hamburg, the aircrews were astonished by what they witnessed from their planes over the burning city. One British pilot interviewed by Irving remembered, "The fantastic glow from two hundred miles away grew ever brighter as we moved into the target. At 20,000 feet we could see details in the unearthly blaze that had never been visible before; for the first time in many operations I felt sorry for the population below." A crew member on a different British plane told Irving, "It was my practice never to leave my seat, but my skipper called me on this particular occasion to come and have a look. The sight was indeed fantastic. From some 20,000 feet, Dresden was a city with every street etched in fire."[60]

The situation on the ground was very much like that at Hamburg, only on a far greater scale. The force of the wind was even stronger. A survivor recounted many years later, "Because of the fire-storm, at first it was possible to give help only at the periphery of the fires. I had to look on, helpless, as people who were clinging to iron railings were seized mercilessly by the suction [of the wind] and plucked off into the flames. And not human beings only, but all sorts of things, even prams, were seized by this force and sucked into the sea of fire."[61] For days after the raid, the city was littered with thousands of corpses, some burned down to unrecognizable lumps of charcoal and others who had died of carbon monoxide poisoning or suffocation looking relatively normal. For weeks, the city reeked of decomposing bodies and the acrid stench from huge fires in which the remains were cremated prior to burial in mass graves.

The precise number of people killed in the 14 hours of the Dresden raid will never be known, since many thousands were reduced by the intense heat into nothing but ash and since nobody knew just how many people were actually in the city at the time of the firestorm. On the basis of careful analysis of available information, Alexander McKee concluded that 70,000 is a reasonable estimate.[62] The considerably higher figure of 135,000 was accepted by Ira Eaker and Robert Saundby, top officers of the wartime American and British bomber forces, respectively.[63]

Following the German surrender of May 7, 1945, Bomber Command was effectively retired from action. Winston Churchill, who had been an outspoken advocate of city bombing during most of the war, appeared to reverse himself shortly after the war and refused to issue a customary campaign medal for the crews of Bomber Command. Harris was embittered by this postwar treatment of his courageous crews, 50,000 of whom had given their lives in the air offensive against

Workers collecting bodies after the Dresden fire raid on February 13–14, 1945. Note the pyre of burning bodies in the background. SOURCE: Saechsische Landesbibliothek, Dresden.

Germany, and left England for South Africa. Some scholars have suggested that Churchill and the other British wartime leaders were ashamed of the anticivilian practices in which Bomber Command had engaged during the war.[64]

U.S. Strategic Bombing Against Germany

Like the British, the Americans began air combat in World War II committed to a policy of daylight, precision bombing of specific military and industrial targets, with maximal effort made to avoid civilian casualties. However, also like the British experience, this initial restraint was to steadily erode during the course of the war, culminating in the practice of deliberately setting crowded cities on fire.

American preparations for the air war began years before the Japanese attack against Pearl Harbor on December 7, 1941. As early as September 1938, during the Munich crisis, the United States initiated a rapid expansion in the production of military aircraft. By 1940, and even more in 1941, massive quantities of planes and other equipment were sold to Great Britain under very favorable terms and ferried across the Atlantic by American crews. Although in pre–Pearl Harbor days there existed a strong isolationist sentiment among the American citizenry, many of the top military and political leaders, particularly President Roosevelt, felt that U.S. entry into the war was inevitable. Accordingly, contingency plans for a U.S. air offensive were made. In an address on May 16, 1940, to a joint session of Congress,

Close-up of a pile of bodies at Dresden, before being set aflame. The absence of evident burns suggests that many of these people died of carbon monoxide or asphyxiation in their bomb shelters. SOURCE: Saechsische Landesbibliothek, Dresden.

President Roosevelt called for U.S. industry to produce "at least 50,000 planes a year."[65]

The first formal talks between the United States and Great Britain on strategy for combined air operations took place during March 1941. It was concluded that a massive air offensive against Germany would be a necessary prerequisite for an eventual Allied land invasion of Europe. President Roosevelt's enthusiasm for air warfare helped pave the way, in June 1941, for a reorganization of U.S. military forces, including the creation of the Army Air Forces, which gave the air arm of the military more autonomy and priority than it had previously enjoyed.[66]

Commitment to Daylight, Precision Bombing

U.S. strategic bombing policy crystallized during July 1941, when a newly formed U.S. Army Air Forces task force called the Air War Plans Division developed a comprehensive plan for the use of American airpower to help defeat Germany. The resulting plan, known as AWPD-1, specified that the U. S. contribution to victory would be attained through daylight, precision bombing of carefully designated military and military-industrial targets. One goal would be to neutralize the German air force, but the highest priority was the destruction of the German economy, particularly power plants, transportation resources, and oil facilities. AWPD-1 envisioned an assault by 4,000 U.S. bombers that would "in six months bring much of her [Germany's] vital industry to ruin."[67] It was assumed that bombing would pave the way for an Allied land invasion of the continent, although some air force planners felt that after a successful bomber offensive "a land offensive may not be necessary."[68]

As early as January 1941, British air force officers had informally suggested that the U.S. employ area bombing should war occur, but the American planners rejected the notion. According to the official historians of the U.S. strategic air offensive, one factor in the decision was the perception of "widespread antipathy toward attacks on 'civilian' objectives."[69] On December 4, 1941, AWPD-1 was described in detail in newspapers throughout the United States.[70] However, although the official, public posture of the U.S. air forces focused on precision bombing of specific military-industrial targets in Europe, some air-war planners were in fact advocating incendiary, area attacks against Japan. On November 15, 1941—before the Japanese attack against the U.S. naval base at Pearl Harbor—General George C. Marshall, chief of staff of the U.S. Army, told a group of reporters, after swearing them to secrecy, that if war with Japan broke out, "we'll fight mercilessly. Flying fortresses [the four-engined B-17 bombers used by the United States against targets in Europe] will be dispatched immediately to set the paper cities of Japan on fire. ... There won't be any hesitation about bombing civilians—it will be all-out."[71]*

Early Precision Attacks Against Germany

The U.S. began air-combat operations in Europe on August 12, 1942, when 12 bombers of the Eighth Air Force launched a daylight attack against railroad yards in Nazi-occupied France. Subsequent raids were launched against such targets as railroad junctions, factories that produced war products, and German submarine bases in Nazi-occupied Europe. Though the U.S. bombers did encounter resistance by German fighters, losses were relatively low, reinforcing the belief in the value and feasibility of precision attacks.[72]

Also during August 1942, U.S. and British planners held further discussions on the conduct of combined air operations. These discussions led to the second major U.S. air-war directive, known as AWPD-42, which replaced AWPD-1 and specified that the United States would continue its daylight raids and that the British air force would continue its night operations. This arrangement was then reaffirmed when Roosevelt and Churchill met for the Casablanca conference in January 1943.

*Many scholars, of course, would take issue with this depiction of Marshall, who was not only a wartime general but a postwar secretary of state who received the Nobel Peace Prize for his plan to rebuild Europe. His European Recovery Program, later dubbed the Marshall Plan, provided U.S. funds for the rebuilding of nations—both former allies and enemies—that lay in ruins as the result of the war. One scholar, Charles L. Mee, Jr., has called the Marshall Plan the "most successful piece of foreign policy conceived by any nation in the twentieth century" (Charles L. Mee, Jr., *The Marshall Plan: The Launching of Pax Americana*, New York, Simon & Schuster, 1984).

On January 27, 1943, three days after the conclusion of the conference, the U.S. air forces struck German territory for the first time in a daylight attack on the Wilhelmshaven naval base. Of 91 bombers that set out for Germany, 53 managed to hit the target. Although the German antiaircraft artillery was quite ineffective, more than 100 German fighters attacked the bombers, succeeding in destroying three.[73]

Throughout most of 1943, U.S. bombers maintained their policy of daylight, precision bombing of specific military targets in Germany and German-occupied western Europe. When they cooperated with the British, as in the combined raids against Hamburg in late July, the U.S. planes attacked only precision targets. However, as Michael Sherry has pointed out, the firestorm created by the British incendiary attack "was carefully studied by American experts, particularly with an eye to the bombing of Japan."[74]

As had been the case with the British daylight raids, however, the American daylight raids proved increasingly costly as the Germans improved their antiaircraft and fighter defenses. In July and August 1943, American casualties mounted steadily. On August 17, for example, of the 376 U.S. bombers that flew from their bases in England to hit a ball-bearings factory in Schweinfurt and a fighter-plane factory in Regensburg, 60 were destroyed, mainly by German fighters. Historian Ronald Schaffer quoted from the postraid report by a surviving American crewman:

> A shining silver object sailed past our right wing. I recognized it as a main exit door. Seconds later, a dark object came hurtling through the formation, barely missing several props. It was a man, clasping his knees to his head, revolving like a diver in a triple somersault. I didn't see his shute open.
>
> A B-17 turned gradually out of the formation to the right, maintaining altitude. In a split second, the B-17 completely disappeared in a brilliant explosion from which the only remains were four balls of fire, the fuel tanks, which were quickly consumed as they fell earthward. Our airplane was endangered by various debris. Emergency hatches, exit doors, prematurely opened parachutes, bodies, and assorted fragments of B-17s and Hun fighters breezed past us in the slipstream.[75]

U.S. losses peaked during what came to be called the "black week" of October 9–14, 1943. Several attacks incurred high losses, including another attack against the ball-bearing factories in Schweinfurt, during which 20 percent of the U.S. planes were destroyed. If sustained, such a rate of attrition would have quickly exhausted American resources and brought the offensive to a standstill.[76]

Erosion of the Commitment to Precision Bombing

In response to such intolerable losses, on November 1, 1943, the commander of the U.S. Army Air Forces, General Henry H. Arnold, ordered American bomber crews to use radar to aim bombs at the general area of specified targets when weather conditions made visual identification difficult or impossible. An added benefit of this practice of "blind bombing" was that raids could be carried out at night as well as under weather conditions that hampered German fighters.[77] In effect, this directive moved U.S. targeting policy in the direction of area bombing. Blind bombing by means of radar aids, combined with greatly increasing bomb loads and, later in the war, weakened German defenses, meant that residential areas in the vicinity of "military" targets were very frequently devastated. By October 1944, approximately 80 percent of the U.S. bomber raids over Germany were conducted by means of blind bombing. According to the official historians, such bombing "depended for effectiveness upon drenching an area with bombs."[78] According to Michael Sherry, "By 1944, the two air forces were positioned to cross paths. The RAF [British Royal Air Force] was developing techniques that gave the night bombers a precision approaching that of the AAF's [U.S. Army Air Forces] Fortresses and Liberators, while the Americans were beginning to loosen their definition of precision bombing."[79] The use of "nonvisual techniques" by U.S. bombing forces, conceded Conrad C. Crane in his study of the evolution of American airpower strategy, "did contribute to the escalation toward total war that would culminate in the Pacific."[80]

Actually, the "loosening" noted by Sherry had begun well before November 1944. Beginning in January 1944, the British and Americans initiated an air campaign against Bulgaria and Romania, Nazi allies in the Balkans, that killed thousands of civilians. Although the British bombed at night and the Americans attacked during the day, the numbers of American planes, the sheer tonnage of their bombs, and the fact that their designated targets were located in the middle of residential areas caused massive casualties. On April 4, 1944, for example, when 300 American bombers struck railroad assembly yards in Sofia, Bulgaria, "The highest concentration of bombs landed not on the rail facilities but on Sofia itself."[81] Ronald Schaffer concluded from his study of this relatively little-known campaign that "American flyers were expected to terrorize Balkan civilians without appearing to use terror tactics."[82] On June 9, 1944—just three days after the Allied landing at Normandy, France—one of the top American air force officers ordered plans drawn up for masses of American planes to drop both incendiary and high-explosive bombs on "undefended" and "virgin'" towns in Germany that were of minimal military or industrial significance. The plans also called for "maximum use of strafing fighters ... to spread the impact on the population."[83]

Not only were American air-war planners increasingly willing to accept "inadvertent" collateral damage to civilians but they were also more willing to consider explicit "morale" targeting, that is, attacks deliberately planned to hurt civilians. In late 1944, for example, the Americans initiated the so-called War-Weary Bomber Project, a plan, according to Schaffer, "to take hundreds of worn-out B-17s, fill them with 20,000 pounds of high-explosive, and aim them at enemy targets. After setting the bombers on a dead-reckoning course, their crews would bail out and automatic devices would direct the robot planes to their objectives."[84] Those "objectives" included cities. As General H. H. "Hap" Arnold, the top American air commander, wrote, "I can see very little difference between the British night area bombing and our taking a war weary airplane, launching it, say, 50 or 60 miles from Cologne and letting it fall somewhere in the city limits."[85] Despite the support of a number of top officers, the project was terminated after only a few flights, mainly because political leaders both in the United States and Great Britain feared retaliation in kind by Germany.

One explicitly anticivilian plan that was adopted by U.S. air forces at this time was Project Clarion, which was conceived in December 1944 and initiated in February 1945. Officially labeled a "General Plan for Maximum Effort Attack Against Transportation Targets," Clarion entailed American fighters and bombers roaming the largely undefended skies over rural Germany searching for small towns and villages to strafe and bomb at low altitudes. It was assumed that such raids would accelerate the erosion of public morale and, thereby, hasten the end of the war. Indeed, according to the official historians of the U.S. air offensive, Clarion was expected to have a "stupefying effect on morale."[86] Supporters of the plan felt that not only would such attacks reduce German morale but they might also teach the German citizenry a lesson for the future—not to support a government that intended to wage a war of aggression. This sentiment was expressed by President Roosevelt in August 1944, when he told his secretary of the treasury, "We have got to be tough with Germany, and I mean the German people not just the Nazis. We either have to castrate the German people or you have got to treat them in such a manner so they can't just go on reproducing people who want to continue the way they have in the past."[87]

Ostensibly, the targets for Clarion were transportation facilities, but the real victims were civilians. As one air force officer, who regarded the plan as unethical, wrote, "This is the same old baby killing plan of the get-rich quick psychological boys, dressed up in a new Kimono."[88] Although there were others who criticized the plan on a variety of pragmatic and moral grounds, in late February 1945 "thousands of American bombers and fighters" put Clarion into operation, though it never did have the decisive impact on German morale that some of its backers had predicted.[89]

The last major U.S. bombing raids in the European theater took place in February 1945. On February 3, more than 900 U.S. bombers struck Berlin with such effectiveness that as many as 25,000 people were killed.[90] Then, ten days later, U.S. bombers cooperated with the Royal Air Force in carrying out one of the most deadly and controversial raids of the war, the attack on Dresden. After night incendiary attacks by the British bombers had created vast firestorms, the bombing and strafing raids of the U.S. planes on the following day seriously handicapped fire-fighting and rescue efforts and contributed to the high death tolls.

U.S. Strategic Bombing Against Japan

Although the U.S. bombing campaign in the Pacific was guided by the same directives that governed the air war in Europe, that is, the principle of daylight, precision bombing, the first American bomber attack on Japan was originally planned

The German city of Wesel, following a devastating daylight raid by 1,000 American bombers in late March 1945.
SOURCE: Smithsonian Institution National Air and Space Museum.

to take place at night against military targets surrounded by residential areas.[91] The raid, led by General James Doolittle, occurred on April 18, 1942. It involved 16 B-25 bombers brought within striking distance of Japan on the aircraft carrier *Hornet*. The plan for night attack was disrupted when the carrier task force was sighted by a Japanese patrol vessel about 800 miles from Japan, and the planes were dispatched shortly after noon rather than under cover of darkness. The planes, dropping both high-explosive and incendiary bombs, damaged factories and military installations in several Japanese cities, but many bombs also "scattered into dense residential districts."[92] After dropping their bombs, the planes were to fly to bases in China, but several became lost and were forced to land in Japanese-occupied territory. Eight American airmen were captured by the Japanese. Three were executed and five sentenced to prison for the rest of their lives.[93] Though the actual physical damage caused by the Doolittle raid was relatively minor, the raid was a morale booster for the American military and public still smarting from the humiliation of Pearl Harbor.

Following the Doolittle raid, there was a prolonged lull in the U.S. air offensive against the Japanese home islands, both because the European theater had been assigned first priority and because the sheer distances involved posed temporarily insurmountable logistics problems. The lull continued until the United States was able to capture territory sufficiently close to Japan to serve as air bases and was able to bring into operation the massive, long-range B-29 bomber, which was originally designed in 1940 and flown for the first time in September 1942. Throughout 1943, American bombing efforts concentrated on the European theater; U.S. naval forces contained and then began to roll back the Japanese advances in the Pacific.

By 1944, however, the United States was ready to resume bombardment of the Japanese home islands. This was primarily due to two factors: the availability of large numbers of the new B-29 bombers and the acquisition of bases from which to launch them. These bases were in two quite different areas. The first was in Chengtu Province, China, which was under the control of Chinese forces friendly to the United States. The second consisted of a number of islands in the 500 mile-long Marianas chain in the South Pacific Ocean, which had to be wrested by U.S. soldiers from the Japanese in some of the bloodiest ground combat of the entire war.

Bombing from Bases in China

The United States began developing airfields in newly liberated areas of Chengtu Province, which were about 1,200 miles from targets in Japan, during spring and summer 1944. The plan called for B-29s to fly nearly 1,200 miles "over the hump" of the Himalaya Mountains from home bases in India to the newly constructed Chinese airstrips, from which they would then launch the attacks against Japan. After dropping their bombs on Japan, the planes were to fly back to the Chinese airfields. Each mission involved more than 20 hours of flying time over a distance of nearly 5,000 miles. Aviation fuel and other supplies had to be flown from India to the staging bases in China. As many as 12 gallons of fuel were consumed in order to deliver one gallon for the bombing missions.[94] One pilot interviewed by Martin Caidin stated, "It was a hell of a way to run a railroad. … For every combat mission we flew, we had to make six round-trip flights over the Hump. We were wearing out those B-29s."[95]

The first B-29 attack against Japan from the China bases took place during the night of June 15–16, 1944, when nearly 50 of the bombers targeted the massive Yawata steel plant (which produced one-fourth of Japan's steel). Later reconnaissance photos revealed that the bombs had missed their target.[96] During the next ten months, 49 more air attacks from China were launched against Japanese military and industrial targets. The results, however, were disappointing. According to an official army air forces report, the China-based bombing campaign "achieved no significant results, and whatever intangible effects were produced were obtained at too dear a price."[97]

The Bloody Struggle for Island Bases

The second basing option for the B-29s—airfields built on islands in the Marianas chain—was to prove far more successful. In March 1944, the American Joint Chiefs of Staff had given orders to the U.S. Navy to prepare to capture the Japanese-occupied Marianas, located about 1,200 miles from the Japanese home islands and well within range of the new bombers. On June 15, 1944—the very day of the first B-29 strike from the China bases—U.S. forces invaded the pivotal island of Saipan. Approximately 20,000 American soldiers stormed ashore to confront an entrenched, numerically superior enemy that was determined to defend the island at all costs. The fighting lasted for several weeks, during which the U.S. troops had to fight off suicidal "banzai charges" by the Japanese, one of which is described by Martin Caidin: "Four thousand fanatical, screaming soldiers, each man sworn to 'take seven lives to repay our country,' charged the Marine and Army troops. They carried everything from machine guns to knives and bayonets tied to the ends of long bamboo poles, and they stormed the battle-weary GI's with a howling fury."[98] On July 9, by which time the tide of battle had turned strongly against the Japanese, the Americans were horrified by mass suicides of Japanese civilians and soldiers who refused to surrender. John Dower has described the scene: "Hundreds of Japanese civilians living in the critical island outpost killed their families and themselves rather than surrender. … Whole families died in full view of the invading Allied forces by killing themselves with hand grenades provided by the Japanese military or leaping from the high cliffs into the sea or onto the rocks below."[99]

The final death toll was staggering. According to Dower, "Almost 30,000 of the emperor's men were sacrificed on Saipan (slightly less than ten times the U.S.

death count)."[100] Even before all of the Japanese defenders had been killed or captured, teams of navy engineers began constructing airstrips on which the first B-29s landed on October 12.

After securing Saipan, U.S. forces moved forward to capture other islands of strategic value for the air offensive against the Japanese home islands. The battles for these islands were every bit as deadly as was the struggle for Saipan. Iwo Jima, for example, was far closer to Japan than the Marianas, and its seven square miles of rocky surface housed a crucial radar installation that gave the Japanese advanced warning of impending B-29 raids. On February 19, 1945, the U.S. Marines landed on the beaches of Iwo Jima and began yet another bloody fight against fanatical defenders, who showered the invaders with mortars and artillery from their outpost on Mount Suribachi. In his account of the battle for Iwo Jima, William Manchester provided a vivid description of the carnage:

> The deaths on Iwo were extraordinarily violent. There seemed to be no clean wounds; just fragments of corpses. ... Often the only way to distinguish between Japanese and marine dead was by the legs: Marines wore canvas leggings and Nips khaki puttees. Otherwise identification was completely impossible. You tripped over strings of viscera fifteen feet long, over bodies which had been cut in half at the waist. Legs and arms, and heads bearing only necks, lay fifty feet from the closest torsos. As night fell the beach reeked with the stench of burning flesh.[101]

Precision Attacks from the Island Bases

B-29 raids from the hard-won Marianas airfields began in November 1944 and involved high-altitude, daylight attacks against military and military-industrial targets in accordance with earlier directives. The first raid was originally scheduled for November 16 but had to be postponed for several days because of the obscuring clouds and strong winds that were to plague many missions launched from Saipan and other bases in the region. Finally, on November 24, the first attack against Japan from Saipan was undertaken. More than 100 bombers took off for a raid against a huge aircraft-engine factory in Tokyo. A combination of bad weather over Japan and fierce Japanese fighter defenses, however, prevented most planes from hitting the target. The majority, instead, dumped their bombs on the industrial area of Tokyo, relying on radar rather than visual sighting. Subsequent missions, also aiming mainly high-explosive bombs at Japanese aircraft plants, were also hampered by the weather and increasingly desperate Japanese defenses. Not only were the Japanese islands frequently covered by dense clouds, which made precision bombing very difficult, but the jetstream winds at the high altitudes from which the bombs were dropped also compromised accuracy. If the B-29s flew with the wind, their air speed could reach 600 miles per hour, which was too fast for precision bombing. If they flew against the wind in order to aim more accurately, they become highly vulnerable to antiaircraft artillery.[102] Suicide attacks by Japanese fighter pilots were also an increasing risk.[103]

These high-altitude precision attacks continued until March 1945, but the results were unsatisfactory. Only one major aircraft factory had been destroyed and a second one slightly damaged.[104] However, a far more effective alternative to precision bombing with high-explosives would soon be developed and implemented—low-altitude bombing of urban areas with incendiary bombs.

Growing Interest in Area Incendiary Attacks

U.S. interest in the potential of area firebomb attacks against Japan predated the growing disappointment with the high-explosive precision campaign that began in November 1944 by many years. In the early 1930s, pioneer U.S. airman General Billy Mitchell called attention to the vulnerability of Japan's cities to incendiary attack. "These towns are built largely of wood and paper to resist the devastations of earthquakes and form the greatest aerial targets the world has ever seen. … Incendiary projectiles would burn the cities to the ground in short order."[105] American air commanders, although refusing to engage in explicitly identified fire attacks against urban areas in Germany, nonetheless studied the results of the British fire raids, such as the Hamburg attacks in July 1943, "with an eye to the bombing of Japan."[106]

Several organizations and committees had contributed to the growing interest in incendiary attacks against Japan. For example, in December 1942, a special panel was formed in the United States, the Committee of Operations Analysts (COA), in order to evaluate target priorities in both the European and Pacific theaters. The COA was composed of "civilians with extensive experience in dealing with complex business and industrial problems and military men well-grounded in the field of military intelligence."[107] On November 11, 1943, the COA released an important report, based on extensive analysis of the bombing campaigns in Europe, as well as potential targets in Japan, that recommended incendiary attacks against several Japanese cities. According to Ronald Schaffer, "The committee believed that a series of massive firebomb attacks on urban areas would produce a major disaster for Japan. Air raids would burn out great numbers of small subcontracting operations in homes and workshops scattered through the highly flammable cities and would damage some large plants."[108]

About a month prior to the release of the COA report, additional impetus toward firebombing was generated by another pro-incendiary study. On October 15, 1943, a report by the assistant chief of air staff for intelligence, titled "Japan, Incendiary Attack Data," also strongly urged incendiary raids against Japanese cities. The report, which came to be widely referred to as A-2, noted that more than 90 percent of Tokyo was constructed of highly flammable wooden buildings; other cities were similar. A-2 went into great detail in suggesting how to start huge fires in the Japanese cities. Military historian E. Bartlett Kerr has noted that "the report provided estimates of the bomb concentration necessary to start sweeping fires in heavily built-up urban areas. The idea was that the combustible materials in Japanese residential construction would serve as 'kindling' for conflagrations that would destroy factories and other military objectives over wide areas."[109]

Then, in June 1944, the COA recruited experts from a variety of other agencies and organizations to form the Joint Incendiary Committee, which became known as the Incendiary Subcommittee. According to Schaffer, "The central tasks of the subcommittee were to determine the forces it would take to burn down six major Japanese urban areas, all located on the island of Honshu—Tokyo, Yokohama, Kawasaki, Nagoya, Osaka, and Kobe—and to estimate the probable economic and military consequences of incinerating them."[110] The Incendiary Subcommittee reviewed an array of earlier studies, including a series begun in March 1943 by the National Defense Research Council (NDRC) that involved constructing a "village" of Japanese and German homes in Dugway, Utah, and then carefully measuring the results of various kinds of incendiary bombs dropped in different patterns. As described by Kerr, the "village"

> consisted of twelve two-story Japanese row houses and six German houses, all of which had been constructed as authentically as humanly possible. Each Japanese house, with its smooth plastered walls and sliding paper screens, was equipped with carefully placed tatami mats, low tables, sitting pillows, cupboards, charcoal braziers, even cooking utensils and chopsticks. Between the Japanese houses ran typically narrow streets—exactly 8 feet wide, as prescribed by the NDRC consultants.[111]

In September 1944, the Incendiary Subcommittee reported to the COA its recommendation that Tokyo and five other Japanese cities be attacked with massive quantities of firebombs. Such attacks, stated the report, "will produce very great economic loss, measured in man months of industrial labor—probably greater loss per ton of bombs despatched than attacks on any other target system."[112] The subcommittee report also predicted the "dehousing" of nearly 8 million workers. Moreover, noted Sherry, "The report was a rarity in that it explicitly made an estimate of probable enemy casualties, extrapolating its figures from the great Tokyo fire of 1923: some 560,000 Japanese, almost half in Tokyo, would be killed, missing, or seriously wounded."[113]

In order to assess the validity of such projections, advocates of firebombing argued that their recommended tactics should be tested in actual combat operations. There had been a few, relatively small experimental fire raids during the period of daylight precision attacks from the Marianas, but the results had been inconclusive. Accordingly, General Haywood Hansell, who commanded the U.S. air forces in the Pacific, was ordered to try an experimental fire raid against Tokyo. Although he was firmly committed to the doctrine of precision bombing, Hansell dutifully undertook such a raid against Tokyo on the evening of November 29–30, 1944. The attack, which involved only 29 bombers, was, according to Kennett, "small and inconsequential."[114] Hansell was then ordered to organize a more substantial fire raid against Nagoya, Japan. After his protests were rejected, Hansell sent out 100 B-29 bombers in a daylight raid on January 3, but once again the damage was disappointingly meager.

As a result of his reluctance to engage in area incendiary bombing, Hansell was removed from his command in early January 1945 and replaced by Curtis LeMay on January 20.[115] Troubled by none of Hansell's reservations, LeMay believed that massive fire raids on the principal Japanese cities would quickly destroy Japan's ability to carry on the war. LeMay continued the largely unproductive precision attacks for several weeks, during which he also began examining new approaches. On February 3 and 25, he launched experimental incendiary raids against Kobe and Tokyo, respectively, and was encouraged by the level of destruction.

By early March 1945, LeMay had decided on a number of radical changes from previous B-29 tactics. First, any pretense of precision bombing was eliminated when he ordered his crews to load their planes to the hilt with incendiary bombs, particularly one known as the M-69, which had been developed in early 1942 by the same National Defense Research Council that had built the imitation German and Japanese village in order to evaluate the effects of various fire bombs. The M-69 weighed just over six pounds and was stored in clusters in the bomb bays of the B-29s. When dropped from the plane, the cluster would break apart and the individual bombs would scatter as they fell to the ground. The bombs were carefully designed to start fires that would spread rapidly and be difficult to extinguish. As Bartlett E. Kerr noted in his study of the U.S. incendiary attacks against Japan,

> As the bomb passed through the roof of a house or factory, a delay fuse actuated, which, after 3 to 5 seconds, detonated an ejection-ignition charge. By this time the bomb would have come to rest, lying on its side or with its nose buried in the floor. At detonation, a TNT charge would explode, and magnesium particles would ignite the gasoline gel contained in a cloth sock. Unlike any other bomb, the explosion blew burning gel out of the tail of the casing and—like a miniature cannon—shot it as far as 100 feet. If the gel struck a combustible surface and was not extinguished it started an intense and persistent fire.[116]

LeMay's second change was that the raids would be carried out at night, which would lessen the risk posed by Japanese defenses. Since the targets would be residential areas rather than specific factories or military bases, accuracy in bomb aiming was much less important than with previous precision attacks. Third, instead of bombing from the usual 25,000 to 30,000 feet altitude in an orderly formation, the planes would strike individually from a height of only 5,000 to 7,000 feet. This would reduce the demand for fuel and allow heavier bomb loads. LeMay also believed that the low-altitude attack would confuse the Japanese air defenses, which had been developed to respond to the previous high-altitude raids.[117] Finally, defensive armaments were stripped from the planes so that more bombs could be carried.[118]

The Incineration of Tokyo

On the night of March 9–10, 1945, LeMay's new ideas were tested in a massive incendiary attack against the city of Tokyo. Although nearly 2 million people had

American B-29 bombers dropping clusters of incendiary bombs over Japan in 1945. SOURCE: Smithsonian Institution National Air and Space Museum.

evacuated Tokyo by early spring 1945, as many as 6 million still remained.[119] Tokyo was one of the most densely populated cities in the world. One section of the city had "more than 135,000 people per square mile."[120] The vast majority of the buildings were built of wood and therefore highly flammable. In his history of the air war in the Pacific, Wilbur Morrison writes that "Japan's cities were firetraps, despite some reinforced concrete buildings in Tokyo and Yokohama. Poorer sections of Tokyo were the worst, where practically all buildings were one- and two-story wood-frame houses."[121] The specific area of the city selected as the primary target zone was more than 84 percent residential.[122]

A chief rationale for an area incendiary attack against Tokyo was the fact that a substantial portion of its war production was spread out over the city in small home industries. Individual workers in their homes produced relatively small quantities of parts for various military equipment that were then collected by factories at which the finished products were assembled. As one official report stated, "These workshops are probably located in quite random fashion through the business, industrial, and residential areas. Destruction of residential areas by fire would probably account for many small-scale manufacturing enterprises."[123]

Compared with German cities, Tokyo and other Japanese cities were quite ill-prepared to cope with the fire attacks. The provisions for fire fighting and shelter-

An overview of Tokyo following a massive American incendiary bombing attack in March 1945. SOURCE: Smithsonian Institution National Air and Space Museum.

A portion of Tokyo destroyed by the American incendiary bombing attack. Note the contrast between the destroyed area and the apparently unscathed buildings in the background. SOURCE: National Archives, Military Archives Division.

ing the population were sorely inadequate, and the antiaircraft capabilities were in no way commensurate with the scale of the attack—particularly when it came at night and at low altitude.[124]

The plan of attack was to launch three streams of B-29 bombers from three air bases in the Marianas—Saipan, Guam, and Tinian. Each bomber stream was led by a special unit of "pathfinders," whose mission was to pinpoint the target area and mark it with 70-pound M-47 incendiary bombs that would quickly start fires to serve as beacons for the rest of the planes that soon followed. The bulk of the bomb load carried by the planes consisted of M-69 incendiaries. Many planes also dropped delayed-action bombs designed to interfere with fire-fighting and rescue efforts.[125] A total of 334 B-29s dropped approximately 2,000 tons of bombs at a target area within "a rectangle about three miles by four, containing a hundred thousand inhabitants per square mile, or roughly 1.25 million people."[126]

The goal of the attack was to set the target zone on fire. It was accomplished beyond anyone's expectations. The large number of planes, the sheer weight of incendiaries dropped in a concentrated area, the ineffectiveness of Tokyo's air defenses and fire-fighting efforts, and weather conditions that rendered the wooden city even more flammable than usual all contributed to create a phenomenon of fire that dwarfed even the firestorms that consumed Hamburg and Dresden—a so-called sweep conflagration. As Sherry described it, "Unlike the firestorm that sucks everything to its center, the conflagration that swept Tokyo was rapaciously expansive, a pillar of fire that was pushed over by the surface winds to touch the ground and gain new fury from the oxygen and combustibles it seized."[127] An even more vivid description is provided by Martin Caidin:

> What leaped into being in Tokyo was literally a tidal wave of flame. As the fires ignited by the initial attack flashed through the inflammable Japanese homes, they shot almost instantly high above the buildings. The spread of fire was beyond belief; it was like a great forest fire blazing in dry timber. Under these conditions fire does not simply spread, it *explodes* as it moves along. It gathers itself into great blazing spheres and like a living creature leaps from building to building, shoots across hundreds of feet, and smothers its objective in a great searing flash that in an instant transforms an entire block, or group of blocks, into an inferno. (emphasis in original)[128]

The temperature generated by the sweep conflagration exceeded 1,800 degrees Fahrenheit—hot enough to boil water in the canals that crisscrossed parts of the city.[129] According to the U.S. Strategic Bombing Survey, the wind created by the conflagration was "too strong for a man to stand up to."[130] The heat radiated from the ground endangered the bombers nearly a mile above the burning city. Caidin wrote, "The thermals that soared upward from Tokyo were too much to believe. Sixty-ton bombers were flung about like matchsticks; B-29s at five thousand feet were thrust upward in a few seconds to eight or nine thousand feet."[131]

In their planes overhead, it was possible for crew members to read charts by the light of the fires below. Because of the low altitude and the number of burning

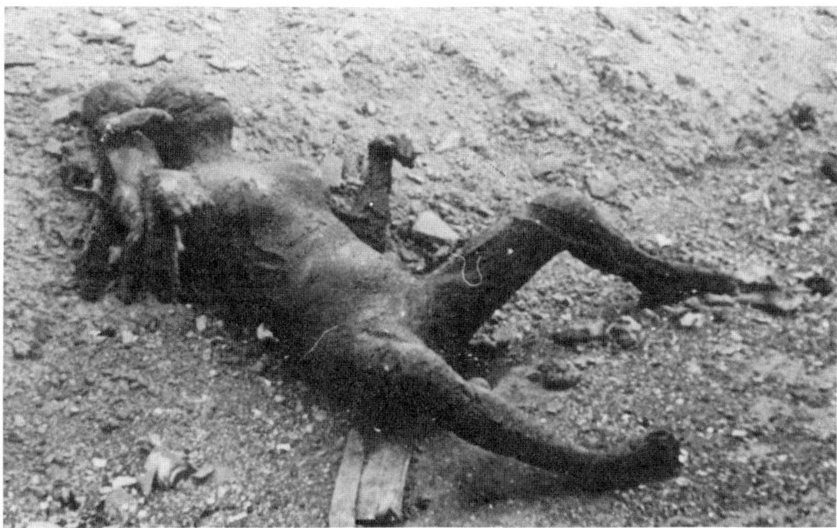

Burned corpses following an incendiary attack. SOURCE: National Archives, Military Archives Division.

bodies, some airmen were nauseated by "the overpowering, sweet-sick stench of the burning flesh that permeated the skies two miles over the tortured city."[132]

On the ground, many people who sought refuge in the canals drowned; many others were boiled to death.[133] So intense was the heat that people "burst into flame."[134] As was the case in German cities subjected to incendiary attack, bomb shelters became deathtraps for many thousands of people:

> The shelters into which thousands of people have jammed are made of wood. … The tongues of flame, the balls of fire, the great crimson sheets, exploded down the alleys and the streets, engulfing all before them. Whole families are in an instant set aflame, roasting alive in unheard paroxysms of screaming and pain as the terrible heat exploded the wooden doors and supports of the shelters into flame. It is inevitable. The shelters are of wood. The wood is dry, surrounded by heat and fire.[135]

The U.S. Strategic Bombing Survey estimated the death toll from the six-hour raid to have been 87,793, with 40,918 injuries.[136] Other estimates put the number of deaths at more than 100,000.[137] Sherry points out that "with many schoolchildren already evacuated and younger males in military service, women and old people suffered grossly disproportionate losses."[138] The removal of the dead took 25 days.[139] U.S. losses were confined to two planes shot down and 42 damaged by antiaircraft fire (none were destroyed by Japanese fighters).[140] U.S. General Thomas Power, who watched it unfold from his observation plane, called the Tokyo raid, "'the greatest single disaster incurred by any enemy in military history." He went on to state that, "There were more casualties than in any other military action in the history of the world."[141]

Within days of the Tokyo raid, similar fire attacks were conducted against other Japanese cities. LeMay knew that many of his planes were likely to be diverted to help support the invasion of Japanese-held Okinawa near the end of March, and he wanted to demonstrate the value of massive fire attacks in as convincing a manner as possible. Accordingly, on the night of March 11–12, 1945, he sent 310 B-29s on an incendiary raid against Nagoya; on March 13, 301 bombers were sent against Osaka; and on the night of 16–17, 300 planes struck the city of Kobe.[142] In April, other cities were attacked, and additional raids were sent against Tokyo in order to systematically burn areas of the city that had escaped destruction in later raids. As Kennett observed, "City burning was becoming something of a science, as LeMay's men tried various weapons and techniques."[143]

During late spring and summer 1945, LeMay's bombers continued the onslaught against Japan. Between May and August 58 cities were destroyed by firebombing.[144] By mid-June 1945, the bombers were running out of targets. Virtually every sizable city had been destroyed by firebombs, with the exception of Kyoto, which had been personally exempted from the target list by Secretary of War Henry Stimson due to its historical and religious significance, and several other cities, including Hiroshima and Nagasaki, which were being left "virgin" as potential targets for the new atomic bombs that were then being developed in the United States.[145] As the incendiary-bombing campaign continued, increasingly smaller cities were added to the target list. By July 1945, cities with populations of 100,000–200,000 were being attacked. The city of Toyama, for example, suffered 99.5 percent destruction. In August, cities with fewer than 50,000 people were struck.[146]

Atomic Attacks Against Hiroshima and Nagasaki

By early August 1945, following the successful test of an atomic bomb in the New Mexican desert on July 16, two atomic bombs were ready for use against Japan. These new weapons may have been regarded as epochal and revolutionary by the scientists who created them, but to many of the airmen who had been systematically burning the cities of Japan, they represented simply a more effective incendiary capable of hastening the end of the war and thereby precluding the need for a very costly land invasion of the Japanese home islands.* Thus, on August 6, the first atomic bomb was dropped on the city of Hiroshima. Three days after Hiroshima was destroyed, the second atomic bomb was dropped on Nagasaki.

The resulting carnage was every bit as ghastly as that caused by the earlier incendiary attacks. As one survivor, who was a six-year-old boy at the time, recalled,

*The decision to drop the atomic bombs is highly controversial. Although the official rationale was to shock the Japanese leadership into accepting the terms for unconditional surrender demanded of them by the United States and thereby end the war and save hundreds of thousands of lives, both American and Japanese, recent scholarship has called that rationale into question. We examine this issue in the following chapter, under the discussion of the healing-killing paradox in strategic bombing.

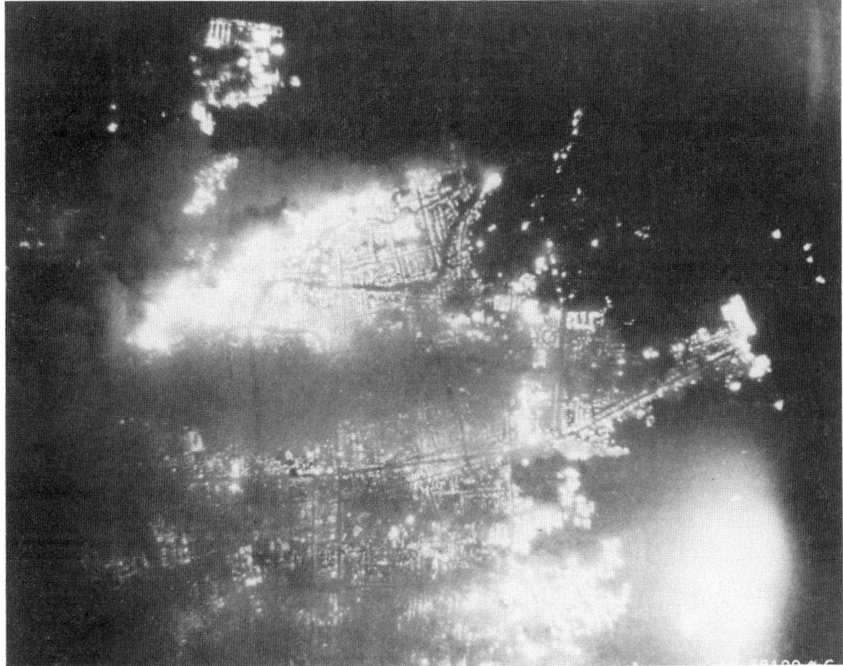

The Japanese city of Toyama, engulfed in flames following an incendiary attack by American B-29s on August 2, 1945. Ninety percent of the city was set afire. SOURCE: Smithsonian Institution National Air and Space Museum.

> Near the bridge there were a whole lot of dead people. There were some who were burned black and died, and there were others with huge burns who died with their skins bursting, and some others who died all stuck full of broken glass. There were all kinds. Sometimes there were the ones who came to us asking for a drink of water. They were bleeding from their faces and from their mouths and they had glass sticking in their bodies. And the bridge itself was burning furiously. … The details and the scenes were just like hell.[147]

Whereas the earlier incendiary raids took hours to incinerate a city, much of Hiroshima and Nagasaki were obliterated instantaneously. One moment, the city was there; the next, it had been reduced to flattened, burning desolation, populated by the dead, dying, and injured. As one survivor told psychiatrist Robert Jay Lifton,

> I climbed Hikiyama Hill and looked down. I saw that Hiroshima had disappeared. … I was shocked by the sight. … What I felt then and still feel now I just can't explain with words. Of course, I saw many dreadful scenes after that—but that experience, looking down and finding nothing left of Hiroshima—was so shocking that I simply can't express what I felt. … Hiroshima didn't exist—that was mainly what I saw—Hiroshima just didn't exist.[148]

The city of Hiroshima following the atomic attack on August 6, 1945. SOURCE: Smithsonian Institution National Air and Space Museum.

Another crucial difference between the atomic bombs and their precursors lay in the delayed effects of radiation. According to Lifton,

> Survivors began to notice in themselves and others a strange form of illness. It consisted of nausea, vomitting, and loss of appetite; diarrhea with large amounts of blood in the stools; fever and weakness; purple spots on various parts of the body from bleeding into the skin ... inflammation and ulceration of the mouth, throat and gums ... bleeding from the mouth, gums, throat, rectum, and urinary tract ... loss of hair from the scalp and other parts of the body ... extremely low white blood cell counts when those were taken ... and in many cases a progressive course until death.[149]

As many as 140,000 people were promptly killed by the Hiroshima bomb and 70,000 by the Nagasaki bomb, and additional thousands died in the months and years following the war due to the delayed effects of radiation exposure.[150]

Chapter 9

Psychological Factors in the Holocaust and Strategic Bombing

In this chapter, the Holocaust and the Allied strategic-bombing campaigns are analyzed in terms of the roles played by two psychological facilitating factors: ideological dehumanization of victims and the healing-killing paradox. The role of dehumanization in each case is examined first, followed by the role of the healing-killing paradox.

Ideological Dehumanization in the Holocaust

Dehumanization refers to the process of regarding other human beings as outsiders for whom customary moral and empathic considerations are not applicable. It can take at least two forms, ideological and technological. Ideological dehumanization, which is examined in this chapter, relies on governmental propaganda and indoctrination to portray targets of violence as subhuman and evil, thereby deserving of any degree of ruthless treatment. Technological dehumanization, which is examined in the next chapter, erases the individual identity of the victims by imposing physical distance between them and their killers.

Our review of the literature on the Holocaust disclosed evidence that dehumanization of the victims, particularly the Jews, played an important facilitating role in at least four ways: (1) dehumanizing, racist anti-Semitism formed the core of the official ideology of the German government; (2) Adolf Hitler and other top Nazi leaders espoused dehumanizing attitudes toward the Jews and other "undesirables"; (3) the media and educational institutions of Nazi Germany were skillfully exploited by government officials to disseminate dehumanizing images of the Jews and other victim groups to the general population; and (4) individuals directly involved in killing the Jews and others regarded their victims as subhuman or nonhuman. Each of these ways is discussed in turn.

Dehumanizing Racism as the Core of Nazi Ideology

In his book *A History of the Holocaust,* Yehuda Bauer noted, "In elaborating their concept of the Jews as subhuman, the Nazis described them as parasites, viruses, or loathsome creatures from the animal and insect world (rats, cockroaches). As a parasitic force, the Jews corroded, and would ultimately destroy, the culture of their host nations."[1]

Many of the dehumanizing images of Jews used by the Nazis, including associating them with animals or insects and with human excrement, had originated in earlier centuries. According to Raul Hilberg, "The picture of the Jew we encounter in Nazi propaganda and Nazi correspondence had been drawn several hundred years before. Martin Luther had drawn that portrait, and the Nazis, in their time, had little to add to it."[2] Some of the passages from Luther's 1543 diatribe "On the Jews and Their Lies" are very similar to Nazi propaganda. Luther frequently combined animal and scatological imagery, as in the following excerpt: "You [Jews] are not worthy of looking at the outside of the Bible, much less of reading it. You should read only the bible that is found under the sow's tail and eat and drink the letters that drop from there. That would be a bible for such prophets, who root about like sows and tear apart like pigs the words of the divine Majesty."[3] Later in his essay, Luther used the kind of disease analogy that the Nazis employed so often when he described the Jews as "a heavy burden, a plague, a pestilence, a sheer misfortune for our country."[4] He even cited "the judgment of Christ which declares that they [the Jews] are venomous, bitter, vindictive, tricky serpents, and children of the devil, who sting and work harm stealthily wherever they cannot do it openly."[5] Nazi propagandists were well aware of Luther's views of the Jews. Historian Lucy Dawidowicz pointed out that "Luther's protective authority was invoked by the Nazis when they came to power, and his anti-Semitic writings enjoyed a revival of popularity."[6]

To such traditionally demeaning and dehumanizing images of Jews were added, during the very decades in which Hitler developed his personal prejudices against the Jews and began his climb to political power, new and "modern" notions of the Jews as members of an alien, inferior race.[7] Nazi ideologues argued that Jews were responsible for "polluting the blood" of the Aryans. Indeed, the Nazis propounded their anti-Jewish policies as "the biological will of the German people."[8]

The new "scientific" racism meant that not even conversion to Christianity or assimilation into the mainstream of society could free them from the threat of persecution. According to Patrick Girard, "As members of a distinct race, the Jews seemed to be marked by an original stain, psychological as well as biological in nature. Conversion would not free them from this, and they continued to transmit it to their descendants, even those born of mixed marriages."[9]

Some scholars have regarded Nazi racism as an ideological glue that bound together the disparate and often contradictory ideas and demands of the Nazi party. For example, Karl Schleunes suggested:

> It was the Jew who helped hold Hitler's system together—on the practical as well as the ideological level. The Jew allowed Hitler to ignore the long list of economic and social promises he had made to the SA, the lower party apparatus, and the lower middle classes. By steering the attention of these groups away from their more genuine grievances and toward the Jew, Hitler succeeded in blunting the edge of their revolutionary wrath.[10]

Similarly, historian George L. Mosse, in his valuable history of European racism *Toward the Holocaust,* called Nazi racism a "scavenger ideology" that combined virtually all of the complaints against the Jews that had existed in the past—along with new racist accusations—into one powerful, all-embracing ideology that justified extreme measures to solve the "Jewish problem."[11]

Dehumanizing Attitudes Among Nazi Leaders

The centrality of dehumanizing anti-Semitism in the Nazi ideology reflected the attitudes of Adolf Hitler and other leaders of the government. Adolf Hitler, whom Mosse called "the key to Nazi racist policy as the true prophet of race," harbored a visceral, implacable hatred of Jews from early in his life.[12] Thus, in his earliest-known written statement about the Jews (a letter sent in September 1919), Hitler asserted: "To begin with, Jewry is unqualifiedly a racial association and not a religious association. ... Its influence will bring about the racial tuberculosis of the people."[13] More than 20 years later, during the war, Hitler told Himmler and other Nazi leaders, "Today we must conduct the same struggle that Pasteur and Koch had to fight. The cause of countless ills is a bacillus: the Jew. ... We will become healthy if we eliminate the Jew."[14] Here are seen two ideological themes that characterized the Nazi movement throughout its lethal lifespan: the theme of Jews as a separate race and the theme of the Jews as posing a threat to the biological well-being of the "Aryan" category of German people.

These themes were frequently repeated by high-level government officials during the period of actual killing operations. For example, in early October 1943, Heinrich Himmler, one of Hitler's earliest and closest associates and, as *Reichsführer* of the SS, the individual chosen by Hitler to oversee the Final Solution, used such dehumanizing biological imagery when lecturing to a group of SS officers on the dangers involved in stealing the clothing and personal possessions of murdered Jews: "Just because we have exterminated a bacterium," stated Himmler, "we do not want, in the end, to be infected by that bacterium and die by it."[15] Similarily, Hans Frank, the top Nazi administrator of the Government General area of occupied Poland in which many of the Jewish ghettos and several of the extermination camps were located, often referred to the Jews as "lice" whose elimination would restore the health of an ailing Europe.[16]

The Role of the Media and Educational Institutions

Once they had attained control of the government in 1933, the Nazis quickly exploited the mass media in order to inculcate the German populace with dehumanizing images of the Jews.[17] As Nora Levin noted, "The Nazis saturated the German mind with hate and horror of the Jew."[18] Under the direction of Joseph Goebbels, the Ministry of Information and Propaganda ensured that negative stereotypes of Jews—as Christ-killers, drinkers of Christian blood, usurious moneylenders, agents of communism, and above all as members of a degraded, inferior race that was destined to be vanquished by the superior "Aryans"—filled the newspapers, radio broadcasts, films, and other media.

Hitler's dictatorial government also utilized the educational institutions of the Third Reich in its campaign to persecute and then annihilate the Jews and other "undesirables." German schools and universities were used as propaganda tools to instill racist beliefs and attitudes espoused by Nazi leaders. In his important book *Education in the Third Reich: A Study of Race and History in Textbooks,* Gilmer Blackburn examined history textbooks to which German children and adolescents were exposed and showed that the texts were used as a means to indoctrinate Nazi ideological principles, including racism and anti-Semitism, and to ensure the persistence of those principles in future generations.[19] George Mosse has noted that instruction in racial issues was compulsory throughout the German school system: "Secondary schools were required to teach heredity, racial science, and family as well as population policies."[20]

Teaching and administrative positions in German schools were generally reserved for loyal party members who demonstrated zeal in educating students with appropriate beliefs, including racism and anti-Semitism. The exploitation of education to serve the murderous purposes of the Nazi state was not limited to the German equivalents of grade schools and high schools; universities were exploited as well. Faculties were purged of Jews and even "Aryan" individuals who were not enthusiastic members of the Nazi party. Training in professional skills became a lower priority than political indoctrination in general, and Nazi racism in particular.[21]

Dehumanization by Killers

The search for evidence of dehumanizing attitudes among actual killers in the Holocaust is hampered by the fact that relatively few killers were captured and interrogated after the war. Moreover, the focus in the war-crimes trials was less on understanding motivations than it was on simply establishing guilt for violations of international law. Also, when they did discuss their reasons for participating in the killing, the majority of captured perpetrators stressed obedience to authority, rather than trying to explain their deeper psychological motivations. Nonetheless, there are some accounts by individuals involved in the killing process that do suggest that dehumanization of the victims did in fact play at least a facilitating, if not a primary causal, role in psychologically and morally easing the task of slaughtering defenseless human beings.

Thus, Richard Breitman, in his valuable study of Heinrich Himmler's role in the Holocaust, described a meeting in which Reinhard Heydrich, Himmler's second-in-command, warned a group of SS officers about the dangers posed by Jews, whom he referred to as "the eternal subhumans." Breitman added, "This term 'subhuman' was not at all common usage in 1939, but it was to become quite common after 1941, when the Nazis had adopted what they considered to be appropriate measures to deal with subhumans."[22] The image of Jews as subhuman was expressed by a German policeman who participated in the mass shooting of Polish Jews in 1942 and wrote to a former commanding officer, "I do not know whether you too, Herr Lieutenant-General, saw such frightful Jewish types in Poland. I thank my lucky stars that I've now seen this mixed race for what it is. Then if life is kind to me I'll have something to pass on to my children. Sick with venereal disease, cripples and idiots were the norm. ... These were not human beings but ape people."[23] Animal imagery was also cited by Franz Stangl, the former commandant of the Treblinka death camp, in a prison-cell interview with British journalist Gitta Sereny. When asked by Sereny whether his participation in the killing was motivated by hate, Stangl responded: "It has nothing to do with hate. They were so weak; they allowed everything to happen—to be done to them. They were people with whom there was no common ground, no possibility of communication—that is how contempt is born. ... Quite recently I read a book about lemmings, who every five or six years just wander into the sea and die; that made me think of Treblinka."[24]

A final example is provided in a statement by a member of a police unit that had been assigned to slaughter Jews. In testimony after the war before a war-crimes tribunal, he stated:

> We police went by the phrase, "Whatever serves the state is right, whatever harms the state is wrong." I would also like to say that it never entered my head that these orders could be wrong. Although I am aware that it is the duty of the police to protect the innocent I was however at that time convinced that the Jewish people were not innocent but guilty. I believed all the propaganda that Jews were criminals and subhuman [*Untermenschen*] and that they were the cause of Germany's decline after the First World War.[25]

It should be noted that some scholars have questioned the role of dehumanizing anti-Semitism as a primary facilitator or motivator in the killers. For example, in his study of transcripts from a postwar criminal investigation of a battalion of German reserve policemen who had engaged in clearing ghettos and slaughtering Jews in Poland during an 11-month period from mid-March 1942 to mid-February 1943, Christopher R. Browning noted that "the most glaring" omission from the transcripts was "any discussion of anti-Semitism."[26] Instead, the transcripts suggested that conformity and careerism—the fear on the part of some of the men that refusal to kill would look bad on their records and possibly jeopardize their police careers after the war—were more salient considerations in motivating the men to kill and assist in killing.[27] However, near the end of his book, Browning did suggest that "pervasive racism and the resulting exclusion of the Jewish victims from any common ground with the perpetrators made it all the easier for the majority of the policemen to conform to the norms of their immediate community (the battalion) and their society at large (Nazi Germany)."[28]

The role of anti-Semitism as a predominant motivating factor for the killers has also been questioned by German historian Hans Mommsen, who noted that although some of the top Nazi leaders were in fact passionately anti-Semitic, anti-Semitism was "by no means virulent in all social strata in Germany."[29] Other motives, including enrichment at the expense of Jews who were purged from jobs and forced to sell their homes and businesses at a fraction of their worth, played important roles, suggested Mommsen.

Concluding Comments

It is clear that dehumanizing imagery of the Jews permeated German society as the result of a massive propaganda campaign ordered and organized by extremely anti-Semitic, racist Nazi leaders—above all, Adolf Hitler. There is little doubt that such ideological dehumanization of the Jews—combined with laws robbing them of their rights, livelihoods, and property and prohibiting social contacts with "Aryan" Germans—significantly increased the vulnerability of Jews to Nazi racial policies and also decreased the inclination of many Germans to empathize with or even intervene to help the Jews. Moreover, the dehumanizing anti-Jewish rhetoric of the national leaders provided legitimation and justification for those directly involved in the persecution of the Jews, regardless of other motives. Therefore, we conclude that ideological dehumanization played an important facilitating role in the Nazi genocide against the Jews of Europe.

Ideological Dehumanization in the U.S. Bombing Campaign Against Japan

Data resources on the Allied bombing campaigns—including the official histories of each campaign, the autobiographies of the two men chiefly responsible for administering them, and a variety of historical studies—disclosed no evidence of official governmental racism comparable to the anti-Semitism that formed the core of Nazi political ideology. Neither U.S. president Roosevelt nor British prime minister Churchill voiced racist statements anything like those frequently uttered by Adolf Hitler. Nor did the governments of either the United States or Great Britain undertake a racist propaganda campaign as centrally coordinated and focused as that carried out by the German Ministry of Information and Propaganda.

However, neither of the Allies was immune to racist thinking about its enemies—particularly the Japanese. The popular media in the United States did disseminate stereotyped, racist, dehumanized images of the Japanese to the general citizenry. And there is evidence that dehumanizing, racist thinking about the Japanese existed in both British and American society before and during the war. Also, a number of influential political and military leaders harbored dehumanizing attitudes toward the Japanese. Such evidence has led some scholars to conclude that dehumanization played a key role in facilitating the movement by the American leaders from a policy of precision bombing in Europe to incendiary and atomic bombing of urban areas in Japan. Evidence of dehumanization as an important facilitating factor is less clear at the level of the actual killers, for example, the crews of the bombers that torched Japanese cities. In the following sections, each of these three areas—dehumanizing cultural attitudes, racist thinking by key leaders, and dehumanizing thinking among bomber crews—is briefly examined.

Pre–World War II Racism in American and British Society

Although racist attitudes in the United States never approached the intensity, pervasiveness, and official legitimation attained by anti-Semitism in Nazi Germany, there was a historical and cultural foundation of American racial prejudice and discrimination that did provide a source of viciously dehumanizing images of the Japanese during the war. In his important book *War without Mercy: Race and Power in the Pacific War,* historian John Dower observed,

> Anti-Semitism was but one manifestation of the racism that existed at all levels in the United States and the United Kingdom. Even while denouncing Nazi theories of 'Aryan' supremacy, the U.S. government presided over a society where blacks were subjected to demeaning Jim Crow laws, segregation was imposed even in the military establishment, racial discrimination extended to the defense industries, and immigration policy was severely biased against all nonwhites.[30]

Dower went on to suggest that "the visceral hatred of Japanese" felt by the Western Allies reflected anti-Asian prejudices that had existed during the previous century and that the Japanese "were actually saddled with racial stereotypes that Europeans and Americans had applied to nonwhites for centuries."[31] Long before their sneak attack on U.S. forces at Pearl Harbor, Hawaii, on December 7, 1941, the Japanese were perceived in both the United States and Great Britain "as a race apart, even a species apart."[32] When this allegedly inferior, even subhuman, race dared to attack the United States, it "provoked a rage bordering on the genocidal among Americans."[33]

Dehumanizing Attitudes of U.S. Political and Military Leaders

Dower found, on the basis of an extensive review of American news reportage and the popular media during the war, that racist, "exterminationist" language was "familiar rhetoric in the nation's capital."[34] For example, in public testimony in 1943, General John De Witt, who was responsible for security in the western part of the United States, stated that he was not worried about German Americans or

Italian Americans but warned that Japanese Americans, being of a different race, posed a serious threat that would continue "until they are wiped off the face of the map."[35] In that same year, a member of the U.S. House of Representatives urged that Japanese be removed "even to the third and fourth generation."[36] Similarly, Michael Sherry, in his study of American bombing during the war, noted that Elliot Roosevelt, the president's son, advocated bombing Japan "until we have destroyed about half of the Japanese civilian population."[37] And Paul V. McNutt, who served as chairman of the War Manpower Commission, stated publicly that he favored "the extermination of the Japanese in toto."[38]

Allied military leaders also employed dehumanizing, racist imagery in their public pronouncements about the Japanese. According to Dower, Admiral William Halsey, who served as commander of the U.S. South Pacific Force, made many statements that "bordered on advocacy of genocide."[39] In an interview featured on the front page of the *New York Times* in January 1943, Australian general Sir Thomas Blamey stated, "Fighting Japs is not like fighting normal human beings. ... We are not dealing with humans as we know them. We are dealing with something primitive. Our troops have the right view of the Japs. They regard them as vermin."[40] According to Ronald Schaffer, U.S. Army Air Force general Haywood Hansell recalled that during the war, there was a "universal feeling" that the Japanese were "subhuman."[41]

Given such attitudes at top levels of the American political and military leadership, it is not surprising that the treatment of Japanese living in the United States during the war was far harsher than that of their German and Italian counterparts. For example, although German Americans were required (as were aliens of all national origins after 1940) to register with the Department of Justice, they were never subjected to the treatment meted out to the Japanese Americans, forced relocation from their homes on the west coast of the United States and incarceration in internment camps, despite the fact that more than 40,000 of the German-born aliens were known to be members of the "overtly pro-Nazi" German-American Bund.[42]

In the program to relocate and incarcerate the Japanese Americans, approximately 112,000 men, women, and children—the entire Japanese American populations of California, Oregon, and Washington—were evicted from their homes and transported, in some cases in crowded boxcars, to concentration camps located in blazing western deserts. In addition to having to endure degrading living conditions in the camps and the humiliation of being publicly declared threats to national security, many of the incarcerated Japanese Americans were forced by government decree to sell their homes, farms, and businesses at only a fraction of their worth. The official rationale behind this government project, carried out by the War Relocation Authority of the U.S. Department of the Interior after approval by President Roosevelt, was that the Japanese Americans could not be trusted to refrain from sabotage, divulging military secrets, and other practices intended to aid and abet Japan in its war against the United States.

However, in his study of the incarceration program, historian Roger Daniels emphasized that racist anti-Japanese attitudes and political movements had preceded the attack on Pearl Harbor and had, in fact, begun in the late 1800s and continued into the 1900s.[43] Indeed, many of the individuals and organizations on both state and national levels that had been promoting exclusionary legislation against the Japanese Americans before Pearl Harbor were instrumental in persuading the federal government to launch its "relocation" project in the early months of January 1942.

Dissemination of Dehumanizing, Racist Imagery in the Media

Dehumanizing, demonizing stereotypes of the enemy are a common feature of modern, total war. World War II was certainly no exception; governmental propaganda machines on all sides filled the media of their respective nations with degrading and demonic images of the enemy and heroic portraits of their own soldiers and citizens.

In the United States, propaganda aimed against the Japanese was conspicuously more racist and dehumanizing than that directed against Germans. Dower has asserted, on the basis of his extensive study of the wartime media, that American writers, cartoonists, songwriters, filmmakers, and other purveyers of popular culture distinguished between good and bad Germans, and between the evil Nazis and the rest of the German people, but regarded *all* Japanese as members of an alien, dangerous race. Widely read periodicals were far more likely to prominently feature accounts of Japanese atrocities than they were to report on the German persecution of the Jews and other crimes.[44] Dower's conclusion was corroborated by Roger Daniels, who argued that "any reading of the wartime Pacific Coast press ... shows clearly that, although a distinction was continually being made between 'good' and 'bad' Germans (a welcome change from World War I), few distinctions were ever made between Japanese. The evil deeds of Hitler's Germany were the deeds of bad men; the evil deeds of Tojo and Hirohito's Japan were the deeds of a bad race."[45] For example, a story in a wartime issue of the *Los Angeles Times* featured the lines: "A viper is nonetheless a viper wherever the egg is hatched—so a Japanese American, born of Japanese parents, grows up to be a Japanese not an American."[46]

The very nature of the war against Japan was described by American newspapers in far more dire terms than the war in Europe. According to Dower,

> The Hearst newspapers declared the war in Asia totally different from that in Europe, for Japan was a "racial menace" as well as a cultural and religious one, and if it proved victorious in the Pacific there would be "perpetual war between Oriental ideals and Occidental." Popular writers described the war against Japan as "a holy war, a racial war of greater significance than any the world has heretofore seen."[47]

American newspapers and magazines were filled with images of the Japanese caricatured to look like a variety of nonhuman forms, including reptiles, rats, cockroaches, rattlesnakes, and monkeys. "The simian image," observed Dower, "was ubiquitous in the American and British media, appearing in publications both conservative and liberal, popular and highbrow."[48] Although Hitler and the Nazis were occasionally portrayed as baboons or monkeys, such depictions were far less frequent than for the Japanese, and the implication was that the Nazi leaders rather than the German people were, atavistically, acting like animals.[49]

The popular columns written by war correspondent Ernie Pyle and carried by nearly 700 newspapers in the United States with a readership estimated at 14 million strongly conveyed the image of the Japanese as subhuman. In one column Pyle wrote that he "wanted a mental bath after looking at them."[50]

In view of such dehumanizing images of the Japanese, articulated publicly by government officials and widely disseminated in the popular media, it is not surprising that wartime public opinion polls found that as many as 13 percent of respondents "consistently supported the 'annihilation' or 'extermination' of the Japanese as a people" and that larger percentages supported "destroying Japan as a political entity."[51]

According to Dower, dehumanization of the Japanese was

> also part of everyday life on the home front, among civilians who in many cases had never encountered a Japanese man or woman. After Pearl Harbor, many eateries on the West Coast placed signs in their windows reading "This Restaurant Poisons Both Rats and Japs." Right-wing vigilante groups distributed pamphlets with titles like *Slap the Jap Rat,* and placed stickers with the slogan "Remember a Jap is a Jap" and the picture of a rat with a Japanese face on the windshields of their automobiles. When concrete plans were broached to evacuate the Japanese Americans to camps in other states in the interior, or to allow camp inmates to attend nearby educational institutions, the governor of Idaho opposed having any of the evacuees brought into his state and declared that "a good solution to the Jap problem would be to send them all back to Japan, then sink the island. They live like rats, breed like rats and act like rats."[52]

Dehumanizing Attitudes Among Bomber Crews?

We have seen that racism, particularly against Asians, existed in both the United States and Great Britain before and during the war, that high-ranking U.S. and British authorities publicly expressed dehumanizing attitudes about the Japanese, and that images of the Japanese as subhuman pervaded the popular media in the United States. But what of the men at lower levels in the command structure, whose responsibility was not to make policy decisions but to carry them out? Did ideological dehumanization of the people at whom the bombs were aimed facilitate the job of actually dropping them?

The data sources examined for this study revealed no evidence that ideological dehumanization of the Japanese was a conspicuous feature at the operational level of either the U.S. or British strategic-bombing campaign. Such evidence might have been found in interviews with crew members, but such interviews were not feasible. However, in several secondary sources on the bombing campaigns, whose authors did conduct interviews (e.g., the books by Martin Middlebrook, Max Hastings, and Alexander McKee cited frequently in Chapter 8), there was no indication that dehumanization played a significant role in crew members' motivations or justifications.

Nor was evidence of dehumanizing rhetoric found in issues of *Impact,* the picture magazine that was distributed to U.S. Army Air Forces pilots and support personnel during the actual bombing campaign.[53] A careful study of these magazines might, potentially, have disclosed racist imagery or language that would at least suggest that the crews were exposed to such a dehumanizing influence. However, our study disclosed no evidence of anti-Japanese or anti-German racism in the issues of *Impact.* There were no cartoons or demeaning caricatures of either Japanese or Germans. Although there was extensive use of patronizing nicknames for soldiers from both enemy nations—Germans were frequently called Jerries, and Japanese were typically referred to as Japs, such appellations as huns, Krauts, or Nips were conspicuously missing.

Thus, *Impact,* while definitely committed to building morale and esprit de corps among the aircrews, did not resort to the vilification of the enemy that has often been associated with total war. Indeed, an article in one of the last issues seemed to humanize, rather than dehumanize the Japanese. This article featured a large, two-page map of the United States on which about two dozen major and minor U.S. cities were highlighted. Paired with each American city was the name of a Japanese city of comparable population that had been attacked in the incendiary raids. The percentage of each Japanese city that had been destroyed was indicated.[54] This enabled American airmen to compare familiar cities in their own country with those they had helped to burn in Japan.

The apparent absence of dehumanizing rhetoric in that particular air force publication contrasted with printed material to which servicemen in other theaters of the war against Japan were exposed. This was particularly true for the U.S. Marines who struggled for strategically important islands in the South Pacific like Iwo Jima. In early 1945, for example, the Marine Corps magazine, *Leatherneck,* included a caricature of a Japanese depicted to look like an insect and, according to Sherry, "described the American need to combat the Japanese 'pestilence' by carrying out 'the gigantic task of extermination,' one to be finished only when 'the breeding grounds around the Tokyo area' were 'completely annihilated.' An elusive, loathsome, and fanatical foe seemed to deserve nothing less."[55]

Moreover, some Allied forces engaged in ground combat with the Japanese were, according to Dower, briefed by officers who employed a clearly dehumanizing rhetoric. He quoted an Australian general who told his troops, who were then engaged in battle with Japanese forces on the island of New Guinea, that "your enemy is a curious race—a cross between the human being and the ape. And like the ape, when he is cornered he knows how to die. But he is inferior to you, and you know it, and that knowledge will help you to victory. … You know that we have to exterminate these vermin if we and our families are to live."[56]

Did Dehumanization Facilitate the Shift to Area Incendiary Bombing Against Japan?

Some scholars have suggested that racist cultural attitudes played a role in the willingness of the American government to engage in mass firebombing of Japanese cities, in contrast to the relative restraint exercised in the U.S. bombing campaign against Germany. Thus, in his analysis of shifting American attitudes toward mass bombing during World War II, historian George Hopkins documented a growing acceptance of such bombing among American citizens as the war progressed and persisted. Moreover, Hopkins concluded from his review of newspapers and popular magazines published during the war that the American public was far more accepting, and even demanding, of obliteration bombing in the Pacific theater than in the European theater. According to Hopkins, "Public opinion played a role in the formation of the policy [of area firebombing] in Japan. There was a definite racial bias against the Japanese, and official planners had no need to worry about public reaction."[57] Likewise, Sherry cited "prevailing racial attitudes among Americans toward the Japanese" in accounting for the "ease and openness with which bombing Japan was mentioned and ethical considerations were disregarded"—particularly in comparison with decisionmaking about the bombardment of Germany.[58] Sherry also concluded that "bombing against Japan was shaped not simply by operational considerations or even by the enemy's nature and the lust for revenge it aroused, but by the lower value Americans put on Asian lives."[59]

Thus, there does appear to be evidence to suggest that dehumanizing racist attitudes toward the Japanese may have contributed to a greater willingness on the part of American authorities to openly shift from presumably precision bombing against a Caucasian enemy in Europe to deliberately indiscriminate areawide incendiary bombing against an Asian enemy in Japan.

However, such an assumption must remain guarded because other factors, besides dehumanizing racism, also created incentives to engage in area incendiary bombing in the Pacific theater. Among these factors was the steady erosion in targeting discrimination that had already taken place in Europe. Although the United States maintained a public image of a precision-bombing policy throughout the European campaign, U.S. bombers frequently engaged in what amounted to areawide attacks, though certainly not as forthrightly as in the later fire raids against Japanese cities. Also, American officials believed that precision bombing was less effective against industrial targets in Japan than had been the case in Europe because Japanese industry was assumed to be more widely dispersed in cottage industries. Another contributing factor was the fact that by the time the bloody campaign in Europe had ended, the United States was very eager to bring the Pacific war to an end and to avoid the necessity of a very costly land invasion of the Japanese home islands if at all possible. Since the proponents of strategic bombing argued that they could break the will of the Japanese without a land invasion, there were a number of policymakers willing to give them a chance to try.

Moreover, as is discussed in the following chapter, the army air force authorities responsible for the strategic bombing campaign were anxious to demonstrate that the long-range heavy bomber had a vital and unique role to play both during the war and in the postwar era, thus justifying the establishment the air force as a separate, autonomous branch of the armed forces. Finally, the behavior of the Japanese, including their humiliating sneak attack on Pearl Harbor, their fanatical defense of the South Pacific islands, and their brutal treatment of American and Allied prisoners of war, undoubtedly created a strong desire for revenge.

Notwithstanding these additional factors, however, we concur with John Dower and others that dehumanization did in fact contribute importantly to the willingness of the Allies to engage in mass bombing and that this was particularly true for the United States when it decided to torch Japanese cities crowded with civilians who had virtually no control over their government's military decisions and who, especially during the last months of the war, were left largely unprotected against the destruction from the sky. Against a background of dehumanization, other factors and motives were intensified and potential reservations reduced. As Dower concluded, "In the course of the war in Asia, racism, dehumanization, technological change, and exterminationist polices became interlocked in unprecedented ways."[60]

The Healing-Killing Paradox in the Holocaust

The essence of the concept of the healing-killing paradox is that an evil means is justified in the service of a valued, noble cause. Moral qualms that might be aroused by the evil nature of the means are assuaged or neutralized by a preoccupation with the worthiness of the goal to be attained by use of such means.

The healing-killing paradox was evident in the Holocaust in at least two ways. First, the political ideology of the Nazi Party and its top leaders clearly identified the Jews as mortal threats to Germany's vitality; their elimination was regarded as a vital service to the nation. Second, individuals involved in the Final Solution incorporated the general political ideology into their personal justifications for involvement.

Nazi Ideology

Near the end of his study of how Nazi doctors and the German medical profession contributed to the rationalization and implementation of the Holocaust, Lifton suggested that "the healing-killing paradox epitomized the overall function of the

Nazi regime."[61] In essence, killing Jews was regarded as a necessary means of restoring and protecting the vitality of "Aryan" Germany.

To the Nazis, the Jews were not merely unrepentant Christ killers, exploitative moneylenders, or members of an unassimilable minority group, identities that had been imposed upon Jews throughout the centuries. Far more ominously, the Jews were regarded as the source of pollution of the very blood of the German people. By interbreeding with Aryan Germans, the Jews allegedly threatened to undermine the racial purity upon which the future of the German "master race" depended.

Hitler, Himmler, and other leading Nazis were obsessed with the issue of racial purity and saw the campaign against the Jews as nothing less than a war for the survival of Aryans and against the danger of Jewish "pollution."[62] Thus, in *Mein Kampf* Hitler made a point of emphasizing the following passage: *"anyone who wants to cure this era, which is inwardly sick and rotten, must first of all summon up the courage to make clear the causes of this disease."*[63] Hitler regarded the Jews as the most important of these causes. In another passage he proposed what was to become a prophetic solution: "If at the beginning of the [First World] War twelve or fifteen thousand of these Hebrew corrupters of the people had been held under poison gas, as happened to hundreds of thousands of our very best German workers in the field, the sacrifice of multitudes would not have been in vain."[64] Once the war began, Hitler's designated overseer of the war against the Jews, Heinrich Himmler, echoed his master's rhetoric and rationale. In a meeting with Rudolf Höss, the commandant of the Auschwitz death camp, Himmler stated, "The Jews are the sworn enemies of the German people and must be eradicated. Every Jew that we can lay our hands on is to be destroyed now during the war without exception. If we cannot now obliterate the biological basis of Jewry, the Jews will one day destroy the German people."[65]

So central to the Nazi worldview were the notions of Aryan German racial purity and the Jewish threat to such purity that historian Karl Schleunes has termed Nazism a "theozoology," that is, a political system predicated on the assumption of different and incompatible races. According to Schleunes, "Racial purity was for the Nazis a state of paradise; the mixing of races—a Nazi equivalent of original sin—defiled this paradise and led to the confusion of good and evil, superior with inferior, and thus of the inevitable decline of civilization. In its concrete form original sin was for the Nazis the mixing of the Aryans with inferior races."[66] Other scholars of the Holocaust are in fundamental agreement. Thus, Lifton referred to the Nazi state as a "biocracy" in which "ruling authority was maintained in the name of higher biological principle."[67] And historian Karl Dietrich Bracher asserted bluntly that "the extermination grew out of the biologistic insanity of Nazi ideology."[68]

The anti-Jewish ideology of the Nazis went far beyond an ordinary, albeit radical, political campaign. In effect, it constituted a quasi-religion, complete with a deity, Adolf Hitler, and a demonic enemy, the Jew. The role of the Jew in this religion was critical. The impure, satanic, corrupting qualities of the Jew were continually cited by Nazi propagandists in contrast to the desirable qualities of the Aryan faithful.[69] As one former high-ranking Nazi, Hermann Rauschning stated, "If the Jew did not exist, we should have to invent him."[70] An important element in the Nazi "religion" was the veneration of nature.[71] This emphasis on nature both reflected and reinforced the "theozoological," "biocratic" tenets of Nazi racism and intensified the fanatical commitment to "save" and "restore" Germany by getting rid of the threat of Jewish "pollution."[72]

As noted, Propaganda Minister Joseph Goebbels made sure that dangerous, dehumanized images of the Jews pervaded the popular culture of Nazi Germany. The schools, too, were used to inculcate the healing-killing messages. An article written shortly after the war described a "widely-used" high school textbook, *Mathematics in the Service of National Political Education,* which featured, "problems stated in distorted terms of the cost of caring for and rehabilitating the chronically sick and crippled. Some of the problems asked, for example, how many new housing units could be built and how many marriage-allowance loans could be given to newly wedded couples for the amount of money it costs to care for 'the crippled, the criminal and the insane.'"[73]

The basic message of such propaganda—whether delivered by the media or in the schools—was twofold: The Jews (and other "useless outsiders") pose a threat to "our" people, and the threat must be eliminated. From these premises logically flowed a third, namely, that those who helped eliminate the Jews were contributing to the greater good of the Third Reich. Such contributions could assume a wide variety of forms, ranging from simply turning one's back on former Jewish friends all the way to driving them into the gas chambers. But the common denominator in all cases was a belief that by eliminating the Jews, one was helping to heal one's own society.

Attitudes Among Killers

As had been hoped and planned by the Nazi leaders, their racist political ideology was readily assimilated into individual efforts to justify personal involvement in the killing process. Two groups in which its influence may be observed are Nazi physicians and members of the Einsatzgruppen. The fact that these two groups are apparently so different—one a group of professional healers and the other a group of professional killers—underscores the power of the healing-killing paradox in facilitating the willingness and ability to participate in a mass killing project.

Nazi Doctors: Healers Become Killers. Given the "biocratic" nature of the Nazi political system, it is not surprising that doctors played key roles in anti-Jewish policies. Actually, their involvement in "racial purification" began years before the decision was made to exterminate the Jews. In 1933, leading German physicians were involved in drafting the so-called Sterilization Laws, which required individuals with histories of serious hereditary disease to undergo mandatory sterilization after being screened by health courts composed of physicians and eugenicists. In 1935, physicians were involved in formulating the Law for the Protection of German Blood and German Honor, which prohibited marriage or any sexual contact between Jews and Aryans. By 1939, Nazi doctors were ready and willing to contribute to more radical "biomedical" means of restoring the purity and vitality of German blood." Over time such radical procedures became politically and psychologically feasible and included the so-called "euthanasia" program, in which tens of thousands of German and Austrian mental patients and other disabled people were murdered under the supervision of physicians. When the "euthanasia" program was officially terminated by Hitler as a concession to an unprecedented (and never repeated) groundswell of popular opposition to the killing of German citizens, physicians from the program continued to practice their lethal skills by culling out inmates of concentration camps for extermination in the "euthanasia" killing centers. Later, some of the death doctors were instrumental in setting up the huge gassing facilities in the extermination camps.[74]

Lifton interviewed more than two dozen former Nazi doctors who had been involved in either the "euthanasia" program or in Nazi concentration camps, including Auschwitz (as well as 80 survivors of Auschwitz, many of whom had been inmate-physicians compelled to work closely with the Nazi doctors in the camp). At Auschwitz, physicians played several crucial roles in the killing process, including selecting which incoming prisoners were to be gassed and which were to be used as slave laborers in the camp; making selections within the camp to identify inmates no longer capable of labor (who would then be killed); observing the killing through peepholes in the doors of the gas chambers; officially declaring the victims dead; and consulting on the most efficient means of disposing of the corpses. Camp physicians also operated the "hospital" barracks, in which they performed a wide range of "medical" experiments on inmates, including attempts to develop a technique for mass sterilization of members of groups deemed racially inferior.[75]

The significance of the healing-killing paradox became quite clear in Lifton's interviews with the Nazi doctors. He found it to operate on at least two levels. First, doctors engaged in killing in order to maintain "the ecology of the camp."[76] When the camp became overcrowded, the Nazi doctors increased the proportion of those selected to die on arrival and raised standards for the physical vitality of workers in the camp so as to send more to the gas chambers. Nazi doctors argued that only by selecting those incapable of working in the camp for prompt gassing could they possibly give the other inmates a chance to survive. Thus, the killing of some inmates was defended on the grounds that it saved others.

A second healing-killing rationale emphasized the "larger biomedical vision (curing the Nordic race by ridding it of its dangerous Jewish infection)."[77] Some of the physicians appeared to have genuinely believed that the Jews posed a threat to their nation and that the elimination of the Jews was a necessary, patriotic act.

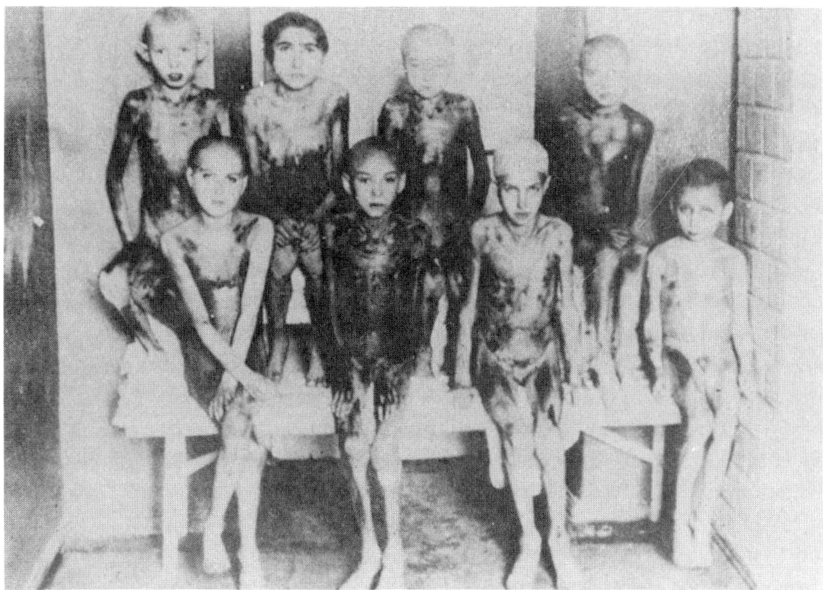

Eight Jewish children, victims of "medical" research conducted by Nazi doctors. SOURCE: Yad Vashem.

To the extent that the Jews had been officially defined as subhuman, moral qualms about murder became irrelevant: mass killing the Jews was more akin to pest extermination, or surgical excision of diseased tissue, than to killing human beings. For example, Auschwitz survivor Ella Lingens-Reiner, herself a physician, bravely asked one of the Nazi doctors in Auschwitz how he could reconcile his involvement in the mass killing with his Hippocratic oath. The SS doctor, Fritz Klein, answered: "Out of respect for human life, I would remove a purulent appendix from a diseased body. The Jew is the purulent appendix in the body of Europe."[78]

The Einsatzgruppen: Killing Justified as Healing

Although operating under very different circumstances from the Nazi doctors, soldiers in the Einsatzgruppen also manifested the healing-killing paradox. As Hilberg observed, the body-count reports sent from the killing sites to the administrative offices in Berlin typically contained descriptions of the nature of the threat that had thereby been eliminated. "Generally speaking," wrote Hilberg, "we find in the reports one overall justification for the killing: the Jewish danger. This fiction was used again and again, in many variations."[79]

Often, the murdered Jews were accused of being terrorists, or partisans, or of spreading rumors and propaganda. Other reports talked of cleansing an area of Jews to prevent the spread of epidemics allegedly caused by the Jewish living habits. The dangers posed by Jewish blood were also cited, as in the following extract from the testimony of Einsatzgruppen commander Otto Ohlendorf at his Nuremberg trial. When asked by the presiding judge why a particular group of Russians was to be killed under the orders that guided the Einsatzgruppen, Ohlendorf replied, "Because they were of Jewish origin. For you must understand the Nazi ideology, as you call it. It was the opinion of the Führer that … the carriers of this blood become especially suitable representatives of the bolshevism. That is not on account of their faith, or their religion, but because of their human make-up and character."[80] Not only in their reports but also in personal letters, killers justified their actions by citing the "danger" that they supposedly eliminated. Thus, one man wrote to a former officer that "we men of the new Germany have to be very tough with ourselves even when we are forced by circumstances to be separated from our families for quite a long time. This is the case right now. We have to settle up with the war criminals once and for all so that we can build a more beautiful and eternal Germany for our children and our children's children."[81] Another wrote to his wife:

> As I said, I am in a very gloomy mood. I must pull myself out of it. *The sight of the dead (including women and children) is not very cheering.* But we are fighting this war for the survival and non-survival of our people. You back home, thank God, do not feel the full force of that. The bomb attacks have, however, shown what the enemy has in store for us if he has enough power. You are aware of it everywhere you go along the front. My comrades are literally fighting for the existence of our people.[82]

A final expression of the healing-killing paradox is taken from a speech that Heinrich Himmler gave to a gathering of troops:

> This is an ideological battle and a struggle of races. Here in this struggle stands National Socialism: an ideology based on the value of our Germanic, Nordic blood. Here stands a world as we have conceived it: beautiful, decent, socially equal, that perhaps, in a few instances, is still burdened by shortcomings, but as a whole, a happy, beautiful world full of culture; this is what our Germany is like. On the other side stands a population of 180 million, a mixture of races, whose very names are unpronounceable, and whose physique is such that one can shoot them down without pity and compassion. These animals, that torture and ill-treat every prisoner from our side … these people have been welded by the Jews into one religion, one ideology, that is called Bolshevism.[83]

Concluding Comments

At both the political and psychological levels, the healing-killing paradox played a significant role in facilitating the Nazi killing project. Moreover, it is likely that the healing-killing paradox interacted with the dehumanization of the Jews, which was also a fundamental element in the Nazi worldview and political rhetoric. The combination of the alleged threat posed by the Jews and the fact that their otherness obviated the need for scruples created particularly potent incentives to cooperate with, or participate in, the Final Solution.

The Healing-Killing Paradox in Mass Bombing

The present study of the British and American strategic bombing campaigns disclosed evidence of a similar healing-killing paradox among three groups of people who contributed to the policy or practice of indiscriminate bombing of civilians during World War II: prewar airpower theorists who advocated the use of bombers against a wide range of targets; commanding officers during the war who helped engineer the shift from precision to areawide bombing; and scientists and others involved with the atomic bombs that were dropped on Hiroshima and Nagasaki. Each of these groups is considered in turn.

Attitudes Among Pre–World War II Airpower Theorists

The first group—the airpower theorists—includes individuals who were instrumental in developing early theories about the uses of airpower during the years between World War I and World War II. By means of their provocative writings and by virtue of their influential positions in the military policymaking hierarchy, these "prophets"—notably Italy's Guilio Douhet, Great Britain's Hugh Trenchard, and the United States' Billy Mitchell—helped shape both the nature of the air forces that were assembled in the interwar period and the uses to which those forces were put when hostilities resumed in the 1930s and 1940s.[84]

Douhet, for example, had directed the Italian air forces during 1913–1914 (although he never did learn to fly) and in 1921 wrote *Command of the Air,* a book on the role of airplanes in future wars that influenced the thinking of officers in several nations as they planned for aerial operations in the next war.[85] Like the other prophets, Douhet felt that the airplane had revolutionized warfare and that the air forces deserved to become the preeminent arm of the military in the years ahead. This view was also held by the leaders of the British and American bombing campaigns during World War II. Douhet argued that the bomber had rendered traditional distinctions between combatant and civilian obsolete and that urban areas were appropriate targets for the new weapon. In *Command of the Air,* he wrote: "Humanity and civilization may avert their eyes, but this is the way it will be, inevitably. And for that matter, the conception of belligerents and non-belligerents is outmoded. Today it is not armies but whole nations which make war; and all the citizens are belligerents and all are exposed to the hazards of war."[86]

Similar points were made by England's Hugh Trenchard, an air hero of World War I who later became marshal of the Royal Air Force. During the interwar years, Trenchard wrote, "the aim of the air force is to break down the enemy's means of resistance by attacks on objectives selected as most likely to achieve this end." Such objectives included, according to Trenchard, "centers of production, transportation, and communication."[87] Although he eschewed the idea of deliberate terroristic attacks on civilians, Trenchard recognized that attacking the aforementioned objectives would inevitably result in bombs falling on residential areas.

In the United States, General Billy Mitchell, a heroic American fighter ace during World War I whose evangelistic and often abrasive campaign for an independent strategic air force later resulted in his being court-martialed and dismissed from the service, promoted bombing attacks designed to demoralize enemy civilians. In 1924, Mitchell called the attention of American military planners to the vulnerability of Japanese cities to incendiary attack, a point apparently suggested by the earthquake-spawned fire that had killed over 100,000 Japanese in 1923.[88]

The advocacy of strategic bombing by these prophets was motivated by noble ideals. All three felt that the horror of bombing would actually bring wars to an end more rapidly than had been the case in the past. According to Trenchard, if bombs aimed at industrial targets happened to kill civilians, such "collateral damage" was a bonus that could hasten the collapse of the enemy's will to fight. Speaking of civilians, he stated, "They are not disciplined and it cannot be expected of them that they will stick stolidly to their lathes and benches under the recurring threat of air attack."[89] Mitchell, likewise, wrote that the bombing attacks against cities would be so destructive that "either a state will hesitate to go to war, or, having engaged in war, [airpower] will make the context sharper, more decisive, and more quickly finished."[90]

A closely related rationale for strategic bombing was the belief that it would make war itself more humane. Thus, both Douhet and Mitchell, according to Kennett, "argued that a war decided in the air would be a merciful substitute for the hell of the trenches" that had consumed so many young men's lives during World War I.[91] Douhet wrote that future wars fought with strategic bombers might "prove to be more humane than wars in the past in spite of all, because they may in the long run shed less blood"[92] An abhorrence of the trench warfare in the World War I has also been cited as an impetus for Britain's embracing strategic bombing. As Martin Middlebrook has stated,

> Why did the British have to resort to such an inhuman form of bombing [area bombing] in this new war? The British answer has its origins in the conditions on the Western Front between 1914 and 1918. Britain's Second World War leaders had all experienced the horrors of the Western Front. They believed, with deep passion, that such a form of land warfare, with its stalemate, its battles of attrition and their terrible casualties, must never be repeated.[93]

Thus, the very men who had clearly recognized and forthrightly pointed out the probable horrors of the new weapon also believed that this same weapon had the potential to make modern war less horrible. The infliction of unprecedented death and destruction on enemy civilians—who, during the past two and a half centuries, had been widely regarded on moral grounds as being immune from deliberate attack—was justified by the assumption that the abrogation of that earlier discrimination would ultimately prove more humane for both sides of the conflict. In other words, a means that had traditionally been regarded as evil was now regarded as noble. Ironically, a similar point was made by Adolf Hitler in *Mein Kampf*, where he wrote that "the most cruel weapons are humane if they lead to a quicker victory."[94]

Attitudes Among Wartime Military Policymakers

A second group of individuals whose statements contain indications of the healing-killing paradox were those directly involved in the actual policy and practice of bombing cities during World War II. Like the prewar airpower theorists, they argued that bombing attacks against enemy civilians would ultimately be more humane than alternative means, since bombing would bring the war to an end more quickly and would thus save not only the lives of British and American soldiers but also enemy soldiers and civilians. According to Schaffer, "The idea of shortening the war appears repeatedly in statements by air force officers, sometimes as a moral conception. The implication was that if the war could be won more quickly, fewer people would suffer."[95] This argument appears forcefully in the autobiographical writings of Arthur Harris and Curtis LeMay, the men who commanded the British and American air forces during the area-bombing campaigns of World War II. Both men saw in the bombardment of civilian areas a means by which the war could be more speedily and decisively ended and, therefore, could be more humane.

Harris's belief in the bomber as a humane alternative to ground combat was formed well before he assumed control of Bomber Command in 1942. In the 1920s, Harris had been involved in one of the first uses to which aerial bombardment had been put, the air-control campaigns against rebellious natives in Africa and elsewhere by such colonizing nations as France and Great Britain. These campaigns had been waged as early as 1911 and were resumed following the end of World War I. The French, in their air-control campaign against Moroccan rebels in 1912, not only bombed villages but also used incendiary bombs to set fire to grain fields.[96] In his autobiography, Harris described a typical air-control action against rebellious tribes in Iraq: "When a tribe started open revolt we gave warning to all its most important villages, by loud speaker from low-flying aircraft and by dropping messages, that air action would be taken after 48 hours. Then, if the rebellion continued, we destroyed the villages and by air patrols kept the insurgents away from their homes for as long as necessary until they decided to give up, which they invariably did."[97] The use of such destructive modern weaponry against virtually defenseless people was justified on the grounds that it was far less costly than ground fighting to suppress the rebellion would have been. As Harris stated of the bombing of villages, "It was, of course, a far less costly method of controlling rebellion than by military action and the casualties on both sides were infinitely less than they would have been in the pitched battle on the ground which would otherwise have been the only alternative."[98]

More than 20 years later, Harris used similar reasoning to justify the deliberate creation of mass fires in the densely populated city of Hamburg. It will be recalled that the July 1943 raid killed as many as 45,000 people in a single evening. Such casualties, believed Harris, were amply compensated for by the value of bombing for the British. "In spite of all that happened at Hamburg," Harris wrote, "bombing proved a comparatively humane method. For one thing, it saved the flower of the youth of this country and of our allies from being mown down by the military in the field, as it was in Flanders in the war of 1914–18."[99] In the Summary of his account of the bomber offensive, Harris stated:

> But without exception our bomber operations were designed to reduce the casualties of all the services or of the civilian population (as in attacks on V-weapon industries and sites) and in almost every instance our operations demonstrably had that effect. Without the intervention of Bomber Command the invasion of Europe would certainly have gone down as the bloodiest campaign in history unless, indeed, it had failed outright—as it would undoubtedly have done. … It cannot therefore be doubted that every one of the 60,000 of Bomber Command who died saved many of his fellows by his death; over and above this is to be added the contribution of all our multifarious operations to the final victory of the Allies.[100]

Thus, Harris unhesitatingly justified a practice that was regarded by many people in the closing months of the war and in the years after the war as at best questionable and at worst morally retrogessive.[101] The killing of masses of enemy civilians was a means by which his "own" people—both soldiers and civilians—could be spared. As Schaffer stated, "The Allies were killing bad people in order to save good ones, killing outlaws to spare the righteous."[102] Even Churchill, a staunch advocate of city bombing during much of the war, appeared to reverse himself and to try to politically distance himself from Harris toward the end of the war, particularly after the attack on Dresden.

Harris's counterpart in the United States Army Air Forces, Curtis LeMay, also argued forcefully in his autobiography that area bombing of civilians was justified by the lives it saved. In the following passage, LeMay recounts a wartime conversation with one of his superiors, General Lauris Norstad (chief of staff of the Twentieth Air Force), that helped embolden LeMay to make the decision to shift from high-altitude precision bombing of designated industrial targets to low-altitude incendiary attacks against large areas of Japanese cities:

> General Arnold [the overall commander of the U.S. Army Air Forces] needed results. Larry Norstad had made that very plain. In effect he had said: "You go ahead and get results with the B-29. If you don't get results you'll be fired. If you don't get results, also, there'll never be any Strategic Air Forces of the Pacific. … If you don't get results it will mean eventually a mass amphibious invasion of Japan, to cost probably half a million more American lives."[103]

LeMay returned to the presumed sparing of American lives as justification for mass killing of Japanese civilians in a stream-of-consciousness-like passage a few pages later in his autobiography (the ellipses are in the original):

> How many types do we employ? We use the E-46 [incendiary] clusters, but we don't load entirely with that stuff. We've got to use some other types as well. Also mix in some high explosive bombs, especially in the 314th [squadron] if I have Tommy [Powers] lead. Those HE's [high explosives] will make the Japs stay under cover, and not come rushing out to extinguish the first fires. … Each type of weapon has some good points as well as some bad points; but if I now had my choice, and had available an overwheming quantity of any type of fire bomb which could be employed, I wouldn't stick to one particular type. No. Of course, magnesium makes the hottest fire, and it'll get things going where probably the napalm might not. But the napalm will splatter farther, cover a greater area. We've got to mix it up. We're not only going to run against those inflammable wooden structures. We're going to run against masonry too. That's where the magnesium comes in handy. … No matter how you slice it, you're going to kill an awful lot of civilians. Thousands and thousands. But, if you don't destroy the Japanese industry, we're going to have to invade Japan. And how many Americans will be killed in an invasion of Japan? Five hundred thousand seems to be the lowest estimate. Some say a million. … We're at war with Japan. We were attacked by Japan. Do you want to kill Japanese, or would you rather have Americans killed?[104]

For LeMay, the presumed saving of American lives entirely justified resorting to a practice that many have regarded as immoral, and some, such as Leo Kuper and Vahakan Dadrian, have regarded as genocidal. The healing-killing paradox renders traditional morality quite irrelevant. As LeMay wrote, "But to worry about the *morality* of what we are doing—Nuts. A soldier has to fight. We fought. If we accomplished the job in any given battle without exterminating too many of our own folks, we considered that we'd had a pretty good day" (emphasis in original).[105]

The Atomic Bombs

The third group that manifested the healing-killing paradox were those involved with the atomic bombs. These individuals were physically distant from the war itself but nonetheless contributed decisively to the practice of mass bombing of large areas of cities, of which the atomic bomb was undoubtedly the apotheosis. The healing-killing paradox motivated the U.S. effort to build the atomic bombs as well as the decision to use them against Japanese civilians.

Albert Einstein and Leo Szilard, the two scientists who in October 1939 convinced Franklin Roosevelt to support an investigation into the feasibility of an atomic bomb (a decision that later led to the establishment of the so-called Manhattan Project to actually create atomic bombs), were refugees from the Nazi Reich who feared that German physicists might deliver such a weapon to Hitler, who would have no qualms about using it ruthlessly against his enemies. Although Einstein and Szilard fully appreciated the grave dangers entailed in bringing such a revolutionary weapon into existence, they felt that the danger of Hitler obtaining it first outweighed any other considerations and drafted a letter to that effect that would be given to Roosevelt.[106]

When the letter written by Einstein and Szilard was delivered to President Roosevelt by Alexander Sachs, Sachs chose to introduce his verbal presentation of the need for the new weapon by emphasizing the potential peaceful uses of nuclear fission. Only after stressing the "healing" applications of the technology—generation of power and medical uses—did Sachs discuss "bombs of hitherto unenvisaged potency and scope," which Germany might obtain and use against the United States and its allies.[107]

Throughout the early years of the Manhattan Project, many scientists submerged doubts about the long-range moral and political implications of the new weapon in their more immediate fears of the Nazi menace. Then, in summer 1944, they learned from a special team of scientists that accompanied the Allied troops on the D-Day invasion of the European continent that the Nazis had never been even close to developing an atomic bomb of their own.[108] At this point, one scientist, Josef Rotblat, felt that since the original rationale for trying to unleash the power of the atom in a new weapon was no longer applicable, continued development of the bomb should be reconsidered. He left the bomb project.[109]

Many others, however, felt that a new rationale for the atomic bomb had emerged, namely, using its unprecedented destructiveness to shock Japanese leaders into unconditional surrender and thereby eliminate the need for the planned invasion of the Japanese home islands, to which LeMay referred. As General Leslie Groves, the military commander of the Manhattan Project, wrote after the war, "We were trying to perfect a weapon that, however repugnant to us as human beings, could nevertheless save untold numbers of American lives."[110] In his diary, President Truman wrote, after the successful test of an atomic bomb but before the attacks against Hiroshima and Nagasaki, "The target will be a purely military one and we will issue a warning statement asking the Japs to surrender and save lives. ... It seems to be the most terrible thing ever discovered, but it can be made the most useful."[111] After the war, Truman said, in response to a question about the decision to drop the bomb, "I wanted to save a half million boys on our side. ... I never lost any sleep over my decision."[112]

Taking some lives in order to save others was also emphasized by Secretary of War Henry Stimson. Robert Jay Lifton notes that Stimson fully appreciated the terrible potential of the new weapon. "In his diaries," writes Lifton, "Stimson referred to the weapon as 'most secret,' 'the dreadful,' 'the terrible,' 'the dire,' 'the awful,' 'the diabolical,' and 'the most terrible weapon ever known in human history, one bomb of which could destroy a whole city.'"[113] Yet despite such reservations, Stimson went ahead and recommended that the bombs be dropped on Japanese cities. At least two psychological processes may have facilitated Stimson's painful decision. One of these, suggests Lifton, was a form of psychological numbing: "Stimson had to shut down his moral imagination—his considerable sensitivity to imagery of holocaust—and impose on himself a rather absolute form of numbing, in order to make a decision he felt needed making."[114] The other psychological process, which also may have helped Stimson "shut down his moral imagination," involved the healing-killing paradox. Like Harris and LeMay, Stimson justified the mass killing of enemy civilians by the savings in American lives that such an action would presumably make possible. Killing Japanese was a lesser evil than engaging in an operation that would have killed many Americans. Thus, shortly after the war, Stimson wrote: "My chief purpose [in recommending the use of the atomic bombs] was to end the war in victory with the least possible cost in the lives of the men in the armies which I had helped to raise."[115]

The "healing" properties of the new weapon were also stressed by Winston Churchill in his postwar memoirs. After reminding readers of the terrible casualties suffered by American forces in their struggles for Okinawa and suggesting that an invasion of the Japanese home islands "might well" have required "the loss of a million American lives and half that number of British," Churchill wrote that with the availability of the atomic bomb,

> now all that nightmare picture had vanished. In its place was the vision—fair and bright indeed it seemed—of the end of the whole war in one or two violent shocks. ... To avert a vast, indefinite butchery, to bring the war to an end, to give peace to the world, to lay healing hands upon its tortured peoples by a manifestation of overwhelming power at the cost of a few explosions, seemed, after all our toils and perils, a miracle of deliverance.[116]

However, in a provocative article, "Hiroshima: The Strange Myth of Half a Million American Lives Saved," Rufus E. Miles took issue with the assumption—defended publicly by Stimson, Churchill, and American president Harry S. Truman—that the primary justification for the use of the atomic bombs against Japan was that it constituted the only feasible alternative to a land invasion that would have resulted in the deaths of hundreds of thousands of Americans. Miles suggested that there were a number of alternative approaches to ending the war, including diplomacy, a naval blockade, and continuation of the nonnuclear bombing campaign. Moreover, he cited recently declassified documents that showed that even during the war, the top military officers responsible for planning the anticipated invasion of Japan never expected casualties of such magnitude. Miles concluded from such documents that the "number of American deaths prevented by the two bombs would almost certainly not have exceeded 20,000 and would probably have been much lower, perhaps even zero."[117] His purpose was not to second-guess the decision but rather to expose a myth that has dominated postwar interpretations of the decision to drop the atomic bombs on Japanese cities. In doing so, however, he provided an insight into how the healing-killing paradox can distort thinking and memory. He suggested that such inflated casualty estimates by Churchill, Truman, and others "can be explained by a subconscious compulsion to persuade themselves and the American public that, horrible as the atomic bombs were, their use was actually humane inasmuch as it saved a huge number of lives. The larger the estimate of deaths averted, the more self-evidently justified the action seemed."[118]

Miles's conclusions have been supported by other scholars. In an important article in 1990 on the historiography of the decision to use the bomb, making use of source materials that had recently become available, J. Samuel Walker concluded, "The consensus among scholars is that the bomb was not needed to avoid an invasion of Japan and to end the war within a relatively short time" and that "an invasion [of Japan] was a remote possibility."[119] Similarly, Barton Bernstein, also making use of heretofore unavailable sources, pointed out many omissions and distortions in Henry Stimson's famous essay, quoted earlier, defending the decision to bomb Hiroshima and Nagasaki.[120] Gar Alperovitz has gone so far as to assert that some historians "now believe that the atomic bomb probably even prolonged the war and cost American lives rather than saved them" by reducing American incentive to modify the terms for unconditional surrender that delayed formal capitulation by the already-defeated Japanese.[121]

Concluding Comments

Our examination of three groups of people involved in the theory, policy, and practice of mass bombing of civilians suggests that the healing-killing paradox may facilitate a difficult, controversial decision by making actions that would ordinarily be regarded as unacceptable, or at least highly questionable, more morally and emotionally palatable. This is not to suggest that the healing-killing paradox is by itself both a necessary and sufficient cause for such a decision to be made. Such decisions invariably involve weighing a number of factors in a complex, shifting, often confusing calculus. However, the healing-killing paradox may enter into the decisionmaking process by creating or augmenting the tendency to either eliminate some considerations as irrelevant or else to fail to devote sufficient attention to possible alternatives, particularly when there may be other, less noble motivations for choosing a debatable action.

For example, Curtis LeMay was told that failure to demonstrate the decisive value of the B-29s in the bombing campaign against Japan would cost him his job and the army air forces their status in the postwar era, as well as necessitate a costly land invasion. His preoccupation with the potential of area incendiary bombing to reduce American losses, an undeniably noble goal, may have obscured powerful incentives created by the other goals, which were of a more selfish nature. In such a case, where both noble and selfish goals are sought, the healing-killing paradox may increase the likelihood that evil or questionable means will be used to obtain these goals.

Similarily, there is little doubt that the noble goal of saving lives was a primary motive for dropping the atomic bombs on Japan, but there is also evidence to suggest that other motives and interests also entered into the decision. A number of alternative reasons for dropping the atomic bombs have been suggested, including a desire on the part of Truman and his top advisers to end the war before the Soviet Union invaded Japan and the belief that American demonstration of the bomb would make the Soviets more tractable in postwar negotiations over the boundaries and political systems in eastern Europe.[122] More mundane factors involved the self-interests of the various organizations, and their individual members, that were involved in the complex decisionmaking process. Leon Sigal, in a provocative book, examined such organizational interests in various branches of the military, the Manhattan Project, and various committees convened to decide on targets and other issues involving operational use of the new bombs. He concluded that "organizational interests rather than national purpose dominated the planning and execution, if not the decision, to use the atomic bomb" and that such interorganizational politicking for preferred options "helps explain why Truman was never exposed to a detailed presentation of the alternatives."[123] He even suggested that "to Groves and the scientific administrators of the MED [the Manhattan Engineering District, or Manhattan Project], only successful wartime use of the bomb would justify both past appropriations and continued support for research into the atom."[124]

The subtle yet powerful healing-killing paradox has the potential to seriously erode moral differences between adversaries or enemies, in this case the armed forces of democratic nations fighting in a total war against the armed forces of totalitarian regimes. As Lewis Mumford wrote after the war, "By taking over this method [area bombing] as a cheap substitute for conventional warfare—cheap in soldiers' lives, costly in its expenditures of other human lives and in the irreplaceable historic accumulation of countless lifetimes—these democratic governments sanctioned the dehumanized techniques of fascism. This was Nazidom's firmest victory and democracy's most servile surrender."[125]

Chapter 10

Organizational and Scientific-Technological Factors in the Holocaust and Strategic Bombing

In this chapter, the Holocaust and the strategic-bombing campaigns are first analyzed in terms of two organizational facilitating factors, compartmentalization of knowledge and tasks and organizational loyalty. Then the role of two scientific-technological factors—scientific rationalization and technical distancing—is examined in each case.

Compartmentalization

Compartmentalization refers to the tendency of bureaucratic organizations to divide complex tasks into specialized subtasks. This tends to render the end product of the tasks less visible and salient to many of the functionaries who help produce it. In turn, the tendency toward invisibilty of the end product has the potential to reduce the sense of personal responsibility for that end product, thus reducing potential moral and empathic inhibitions against involvement in the project—particularly in projects that involve hurting and killing other human beings.

The Holocaust

Numerous analysts of the Holocaust have recognized the significance of bureaucratization and its concomitant compartmentalization in facilitating the Nazi killing project. The early years of Nazi persecution of the Jews, particularly during the prekilling stage of the Holocaust from 1933 through 1938, were characterized by vacillations among alternative policies and by many unplanned, spontaneous outbreaks of vandalism and violence. However, once the anti-Jewish measures were bureaucratically organized under the direction of key figures in the party hierarchy, the efficiency and scale of anti-Jewish actions increased dramatically. As Nora Levin has written,

> Bureaucrats, with the air of confident specialists, would now deplore "crude" anti-Jewish prejudice and "old-fashioned" excesses and put into motion drastic murderous actions by muffled language. Anti-Semitism became professionalized and mass murder became an administrative process. Later, a whole language camouflaging murder created a distance-machinery between the murderous specialist-policy maker and the murderers.[1]

Richard Rubenstein arrived at a similar conclusion from his study of the Holocaust: "It was only possible to overcome the moral barrier that had in the past prevented the systematic riddance of surplus populations when the project was taken out of the hands of bullies and hoodlums and delegated to bureaucrats."[2] Finally, Zygmunt Bauman, in his provocative book *Modernity and the Holocaust,* emphasized that

> the bureaucratic mode of action left its indelible imprint of the Holocaust process. Its fingerprints are all over the Holocaust history, for everyone to see. True, bureaucracy did not hatch the fear of racial contamination and the obsession with racial hygiene. For that it needed visionaries, as bureaucracy picks up where visionaries stop. But bureaucracy made the Holocaust. And it made it in its own image.[3]

As is typical of bureaucratically organized enterprises of vast scale, the Holocaust was characterized by extensive division of labor, which led to compartmentalization of knowledge and responsibilities. The complexity and myriad levels of the Nazi bureaucracy have been explicated in great detail by Raul Hilberg in his masterpiece, *The Destruction of the European Jews.* Therein, he identified four key groups that dominated the administration of German society in general and the genocide against the Jews in particular: the ministerial bureaucracy with its civil servants, the armed forces, business and industry, and the Nazi Party organization. According to Hilberg,

> The civil service infused the other hierarchies with its sure-footed planning and bureaucratic thoroughness. From the army the machinery of destruction acquired its military precision, discipline, and callousness. Industry's influence was felt in the great emphasis upon accounting, penny saving, and salvage, as well as in the factorylike efficiency of the killing centers. Finally, the party contributed to the entire apparatus an "idealism," a sense of "mission," and a notion of "history making."[4]

Individuals in many sectors of society contributed to the various stages of the genocide, beginning with the early legalistic persecution of the Jews and culminating in the death camps. Similarly, many areas of knowledge and skill were required for a killing process that consumed millions and spanned many nations over a period of more than six years. A suggestive, yet still very incomplete, listing has been provided by Richard Rubenstein:

> The destruction process required the cooperation of every sector of German society. The bureaucrats drew up the definitions and decrees; the churches gave evidence of Aryan descent; the postal authorities carried the messages of definition, expropriation, denaturalization, and deportation; businesses dismissed their Jewish employees and took over "Aryanized" properties; the railroads carried the victims to their place of execution, a place made available to the Gestapo and the SS by the *Wehrmacht*.[5]

Not only do many sectors of society contribute to genocide but individual involvement can assume many forms and degrees of complicity. For example, one form of complicity is passive accommodation and acquiescence to the escalating persecution and violence. The German teaching profession provides an important case in point. In April 1933, barely three months after Hitler and the Nazis took power in Germany, the Law to Prevent Overcrowding of German Schools and Universities was passed. This law dictated that Jewish teachers, from the primary grades through the universities, were to be summarily dismissed from their positions. German historian Karl Dietrich Bracher noted, "In 1933–34 alone, more than 1600 scholars, including more than 1000 professors and lecturers (approximately 15 percent of the entire teaching body) became the victims of mass firings." In the cities of Berlin and Frankfurt, 32 percent of the university faculty was purged.[6] For every academic and teaching position vacated by a Jew, an "Aryan" German was able to gain a job or promotion. Other professors, who in no way personally benefited from the campaign against the Jews, tacitly condoned the discriminatory policies by their conspicuous silence. In her study of the German universities during the Nazi period, Alice Gallin indicated that many professors, adhering to a tradition that university faculty were above politics, refused to take a stand against the antidemocratic, proracist political rhetoric of the Nazis.[7]

In addition to benefiting from the passivity of bystanders, genocidal projects also require the participation of many accomplices, who never "get their hands dirty" or even witness the actual killing but who nonetheless make indispensable contributions. For example, the articulation, rationalization, and promulgation of a victimizing ideology is a central feature of all genocides. Also, accomplices are needed to formulate and administer policies and practices that persecute a targeted group.

German academics played an integral role in the ideological rationalization of anti-Jewish measures during all stages of the Holocaust. Among specific academic disciplines, a number of anthropologists helped to promulgate "scientific racism," which asserted that Jews were genetically inferior, and even dangerous, to the "Aryan" Germans.[8] The field of eugenics, likewise, contributed to the public acceptance of measures designed to segregate Jews from contact with non-Jewish Germans by providing what appeared to be a scientific rationale for such treatment.[9]

Educators served as important accomplices to the Nazi ideological campaign against the Jews. Many university professors, through their lectures and publications, lent direct public support to Hitler's unbridled racism and to the Nazi movement.[10] As noted in the preceding chapter, schools became important propaganda instruments, relentlessly inculcating students of all ages with the Nazi ideological principles of unquestioning obedience to authority and anti-Semitism.

As was also discussed previously, the German medical profession lent its prestige and expertise both to racist Nazi ideology and to policies designed to guarantee "racial purity." And members of the legal profession drafted law after law that robbed the Jews of their jobs, their businesses, and their homes.[11] Similarly, the German business community served as an important accomplice by taking over enterprises that Jews were forced, by law, to relinquish.[12]

Yet another way in which accomplices can aid and abet genocidal projects is by serving the support system for direct killing. For example, the Final Solution depended upon the identification, capture, and shipment of victims from throughout Europe to the sites of their execution. Historian Christopher Browning has described the variety of individuals who participated in the early stages of this process:

> Even a single transport of German Jews required the involvement of many municipal authorities other than the local police. An assembly and loading area, usually in the cargo depot, had to be made available by the local railway authorities. Officials from the Finance Office collected property inventories from the deportees, liquidated the property, and turned the proceeds over to the Tax Office. Personnel from the Labor Office collected work books, and the Housing Office disposed of vacant apartments. On a wider scale, officials of the *Reichsbahn* [German railroad system] provided transport for deportations from all over Europe. The Foreign Office, anxious to preserve its dwindling influence within the Nazi regime, intensified its activity on behalf of Nazi Jewish policy by pressuring their allied and satellite countries to cooperate and by smoothing out complications involving Jews with foreign citizenship.[13]

Accomplices also served the killing project by designing, creating, and servicing the technology needed to carry out the actual killing. Thus, trained architects drafted the detailed blueprints for the huge gas chamber–crematoria complexes at the Auschwitz-Birkenau death camp. A German firm, Topf and Sons, designed and built the cremation furnaces and the ventilation system for the gas chambers.[14] Zyklon B, the gas used at Auschwitz, was manufactured and distributed by several companies that made up what Hilberg has called "the extermination industry."[15]

These groups have in common the fact that their contributions to the mass-killing project never required them to dirty their hands with the blood of the murdered victims. Thus, for every man and woman directly involved in the actual killing process, there were many others who contributed to that end result in settings far removed from the mass-shooting sites and death camps. As Hilberg has written, "Most bureaucrats composed memoranda, drew up blueprints, signed correspondence, talked on the telephone, and participated in conferences. They could destroy a whole people by sitting at their desks."[16]

A case in point is provided by the infamous Wannsee Conference, held in January 1942, at which representatives from the major German government agencies met to plan the final solution to the "Jewish problem." Adolf Eichmann, who recorded the minutes of that planning session, was later brought to trial in Israel for his participation in the Holocaust. When accused of crimes against humanity for his key role in administering the roundups and transport of millions of Jews to the extermination camps, Eichmann pled not guilty on the grounds that he had never personally killed even a single Jew.[17]

We suggest that bureaucratic compartmentalization played an important facilitating role in enabling a wide range of ordinary men and women to serve the genocidal project of the Nazis. Hilberg has emphasized that "the bureaucrats who were drawn into the destruction process were not different in their moral makeup from the rest of the population. The German perpetrator was not a special kind of German."[18] According to Hilberg, the most important problems faced by perpetrators and accomplices of the destruction process were psychological. He identified two main components in an "arsenal" of psychological defenses that enabled "the German bureaucrat to cope with his moral inhibitions." The first was a "mechanism of repressions" that included careful control of information to prevent most involved parties from realizing the ultimate result of their contributions. Also involved was an elaborate language of euphemisms to conceal the reality of what was being done to the Jews. For example, gas chambers were routinely termed "special installations"; shipment to the death camps was termed "evacuation."[19] The second component was a "system of rationalizations" that included the belief that although others may have engaged in criminal conduct, one's own contribution was not criminal. Hilberg gave the example of how an official "who was signing orders could console himself with the thought that he did not do the shooting."[20]

A similar observation was made by Christopher Browning. In *Ordinary Men: Reserve Police Battalion 101 and the Final Solution in Poland,* Browning reported on his detailed study of a battalion of largely middle-aged German policemen from Hamburg, many of whom became cold-blooded ghetto clearers and mass killers of Polish Jews during an 11-month period between mid-March 1942 and mid-February 1943. Although most of them had come of age in the pre-Nazi years and had grown up without the barrage of anti-Jewish propaganda with which the Nazis inundated Germany, and even though their commanding officer gave them, at the beginning at least, the option of not participating in the shooting of defenseless Jews, the majority of them went ahead and killed. However, Browning observed that those men who were assigned to duties other than direct killing, such as rounding up the Jews and forcing them into trucks or trains for transport to their deaths, had far less psychological difficulty than when they were personally responsible for the shooting. He concluded that "the policemen's detachment, their sense of not really participating or being responsible ... is stark testimony to the desensitizing effects of division of labor."[21]

The Strategic-Bombing Campaigns

Our examination of the British and American bombing campaigns disclosed evidence of compartmentalization in three specific groups: high-level decisionmakers, who were often far removed from the end results of their policies; crews of the bombers, who at times were deceived about the true nature of their missions; and the men who designed and decided to drop the atomic bombs on Hiroshima and Nagasaki. Each of these is considered in turn.

High-Level Decisionmakers. Key decisions concerning the strategic-bombing campaigns in both the European and Pacific theaters of operation were made in complex organizational networks by a variety of actors, including political and military leaders, who were frequently far removed, both geographically and bureaucratically, from the cities that were blown up and burned and the people who were killed, injured, and rendered homeless. For example, Michael Sherry noted that the American Twentieth Air Force, which was responsible for bombing operations against Japan, "waged war by assembly-line procedures that divided tasks and fractioned responsibilities." He went on to observe, "The end product of its efforts—the target folder, and then the destruction—emerged from a long planning process in which the designers rarely saw their creation, and the operators had little to do with the design."[22]

The policy decisions that emerged from the bargaining and compromises among the top-level actors then filtered down through numerous levels of the command structure, finally reaching the men who had the responsibility of carrying them out in the skies over Europe and Japan. Military officers below the very top political decisionmaking levels felt that they were merely enacting their particular roles in following directives that descended from far above them in the organizational hierarchy. Ronald Schaffer suggested that both Generals Curtis LeMay and Carl Spaatz, who played key administrative roles in both the firebombing of Japanese cities and the atomic attacks against Hiroshima and Nagasaki, "felt that the system of command absolved air force leaders from moral responsibility for the effects of nuclear bombing." As evidence, he quoted Spaatz's statement after the war: "The military man carries out the orders of his political bosses. ... So that didn't bother me at all."[23]

Compartmentalization of decisionmaking and implementation also characterized the British mass-bombing campaign. According to physicist Freeman Dyson, who served during the war as a scientific adviser to British Bomber Command,

> Bomber Command was an early example of the new evil that science and technology have added to the old evils of soldiering. Technology has made evil anonymous.

> Through science and technology, evil is organized bureaucratically so that no individual is responsible for what happens. Neither the boy in the Lancaster aiming his bombs at an ill-defined splodge on his radar screen, nor the operations officer shuffling papers at squadron headquarters, nor I sitting in my own little office in the Operational Research Section and calculating probabilities, had any feeling of personal responsibility. None of us ever saw the people we killed. None of us particularly cared.[24]

The importance of contributions from individuals organizationally removed from the end results of their work was also noted by Rev. John Collins, who served as chaplain at High Wycombe, the headquarters for Bomber Command in England. Collins wrote after the war that

> Bomber Command Headquarters was perhaps the most soul-destroying, the most depressing of the ... places in which I had to serve. For there, in contrast with the natural beauty of the surroundings the evil ... policy of the carpet bombing of German cities was planned. ... The majority of the personnel were simply clerks in uniform, for most of whom any interest or glamour in being attached to Bomber Command had long since gone.[25]

Finally, the facilitating role of compartmentalizaton was suggested by no less an authority on the British bombing campaign than Air Marshal Sir Robert Saundby, who served as Arthur Harris's second-in-command during the outright area-bombing period of British operations. In his preface to David Irving's book, *The Destruction of Dresden,* Saundby wrote that the destruction of that city, swollen with refugees late in the war, was "one of those terrible things that sometimes happen in wartime, brought about by an unfortunate combination of circumstances. Those who approved it were neither wicked nor cruel, though it may well be that they were too remote from the harsh realities of war to understand fully the appalling destructive power of air bombardment in the Spring of 1945."[26]

The Bomber Crews. Historians of the bombing campaigns have noted that bomber crews were at times deliberately misled about the nature of the targets they had been ordered to attack. As is discussed later in this chapter, the physical realities of bombing (darkness, clouds, high altitudes) tended to shield crews from awareness of the results of their actions. Such shielding was augmented by the practice of withholding potentially disturbing details about their targets from preraid briefings. As Martin Middlebrook discovered in his study of the fire raids against Hamburg and other German cities,

> Whatever else may be said about the aircrew of Bomber Command, their original motives for volunteering for the R.A.F. were based on the highest of ideals. Not one in a hundred would ever have thought that he would become part of a force that would deliberately and regularly rain down high explosive and fire on to the homes of ordinary German families. ... The aircrew were subject to the same type of Press influence and conditioning as the general public and what they were told at the briefings about

> the targets they were to attack was often as limited and selective as what the British public were told by the Air Ministry. The industrial importance and the strength of the target's defenses were always stressed. Thereafter, it was mostly a question of what coloured Target Indicators the Pathfinders were using and of other operational details.[27]

Similarly, several veterans of the Dresden fire raid indicated in interviews with Alexander McKee that their preraid briefings were misleading with respect to the nature of the target. As one crew member told McKee, "I'm pretty sure, we were told at the briefing that there were many thousands of Panzer troops in the streets, either going to or coming back from the Russian Front. My personal feeling is, that if we'd been told the truth at the briefing [that Dresden had very little military significance and was crowded with civilian refugees fleeing from the advancing Russian army], some of us wouldn't have gone."[28] Another crew member told McKee: "We went to Dresden with the usual sinking feeling of personal fear, suppressed by busying ourselves with our technical tasks, in the usual ignorance of why our masters chose the target and briefed on the matter only so far as was relevant to destroying what they wanted to destroy."[29]

The Atomic Bombs. The American project to build and drop the atomic bombs was characterized by extensive compartmentalization of knowledge. Under the direction of General Leslie Groves, the various programs of the Manhattan Project were shrouded in rigid secrecy, not only from outsiders but from insiders as well. Information was provided to individual workers on a strictly need-to-know basis.[30] Schaffer has suggested that "lack of information hindered scientists and others from exploring moral issues."[31]

Many scientists and engineers were recruited without being told the ultimate goal of the project. The end result of the highly specialized tasks to which they were assigned was known only to a handful of top administrators. Many had surmised that they were working on an important new weapon, but few appreciated just how new it really was until the first atomic bomb was tested in the Alamogordo desert on July 16, 1945. Even when the nature of the new weapon was known among the personnel of the Manhattan Project, few had the basis for imagining its impact on a highly flammable, crowded city. Veterans of the Manhattan Project recalled that when the first photographs from Hiroshima and Nagasaki were circulated among the personnel, some among them were surprised and horrified as the actual results of their efforts became evident for the first time.

Not only the scientists and engineers who designed and built the bombs but also the aircrews who dropped them were kept in ignorance of the actual nature of their assignments until the very last moment. As Curtis LeMay has written,

> Let's affirm once more that this atomic business went from start to finish in perfect security—a magnificently kept secret. I had been told what it was about, yet still I didn't actually know what the bomb would do. Nobody else knew either. ... In the 509th [the squadron assigned to drop the bombs], each man knew his own job; yet he

didn't know anything about The Bomb. They were aware only that it was large in size, and required special training for the people who would handle it.[32]

Concluding Comments

In both the Holocaust and the mass-bombing campaigns we found evidence of organizationally imposed compartmentalization of knowledge and tasks. People involved in each killing project undoubtedly had a multiplicity of motives and incentives for participating in the project, including feelings of patriotism, a desire for career advancement, and superior orders. However, the very nature of the Nazi genocide and the incendiary and atomic bombing of population centers—the intentional slaughtering of large numbers of civilians—thereby also entailed the repudiation of moral and ethical principles that were central to the German, British, and American cultural heritages. We suggest that the organizational compartmentalization of knowledge and tasks psychologically facilitated participation by minimizing awareness of, and reflection on, the humane and moral implications of the policy and practice of mass bombing. Put differently, it was one of a number of factors that helped ordinary, if not "good," people perform the dirty work of their respective nations during a total war.[33]

Organizational Loyalty

Organizational loyalty refers to the tendency of members of organizations to become preoccupied with the maintenance or expansion of their particular organization and to evaluate policy options and moral issues in terms of their potential impact on parochial organizational interests rather than from a nonpartisan, objective perspective. Advancement of the organization itself and individual advancement within the organization may become ends in themselves. Threats to the organization often mean threats to livelihood and self-esteem. Contributions to the security and expansion of the organization are often rewarded with promotions and other incentives. Thus, competition among or within organizations may lead individual functionaries to put career mobility above humane or ethical considerations as they consider involvement in particular projects or activities.

The Holocaust

Although Nazi Germany was a dictatorship dominated by Adolf Hitler, and despite the fact that Hitler deeply hated the Jews and craved their extirpation from German territory, the actual policies that were developed to solve "the Jewish question" came not from Hitler but from many individuals and organizations who competed among each other for predominance in this crucial realm of national security. According to historian Karl Schleunes, "The effect of Hitler's aloof stance was the exact opposite of what the *Führerprinzip* [the notion that Hitler was in absolute control of all important Nazi policies] would lead one to expect. Instead of authority clearly established at the top, there was no authority at all. A decision-making vacuum rather than a decision-making authority existed at the level from which decisions had to come."[34]

Many organizations and individuals within them had much to gain from the war against the Jews. Individuals and agencies saw the persecution of the Jews as a means by which they could establish themselves in advantageous positions in Nazi society. According to Leon Poliakov, "The [Nazi] regime gave full license to the repressed desires and lust for power that played a leading role in the genocidal system and the martyrdom of the Jews. Countless officials in all kinds of positions competed with one another to 'solve the Jewish question.'"[35] Schleunes, noting that many agencies struggled for predominance in the anti-Jewish campaign, has written that "these struggles to carve out areas of influence in the making of Jewish policy encouraged the building of personal empires or power bases from which to wage the struggle."[36]

One example of the factionalism and competition that contributed to the momentum of the Holocaust was the rivalry between the SA, the brown-shirted party radicals who favored economic boycotts against the Jews as well as physical violence, and the SS, the elite party organization that had originated as a branch of the SA, that favored forcing the Jews to emigrate from German territory after stripping them of most of their wealth, and that eventually became the predominant agency in organizing first the expulsion and then the extermination of the Jews.

Another Nazi rivalry that resulted in worsening conditions for the Jews took place between Heinrich Himmler, the supreme leader of the SS, and Hans Frank, who commanded the Government General area of Nazi-occupied Poland. As they tried to outdo each other in measures against the Jews, the two rivals contributed to escalating persecution and radicalization of anti-Jewish policies. According to Hilberg, "It is characteristic that, as enemies and rivals, Himmler and Frank competed only in ruthlessness. The competition did not benefit the Jews; it helped to destroy them."[37]

There was intense rivalry and competition even within the SS, as the Reich Security Main Office (RSHA), which was responsible for exterminating the Jews, struggled with the Economic-Administrative Main Office (WVHA), which wanted to keep hundreds of thousands of Jews alive as slave laborers in industries owned by the SS.[38]

Within these and other empires, cadres of personnel evolved with strong incentives to loyally and creatively serve their particular agency or branch. Thus, dedicated young men and women within competing empires struggled to invent more effective approaches to eliminating the Jewish presence in German society and, later, once the decision to annihilate the Jews had been made, to develop more effective killing techniques. A number of historians, for example, have noted the intense competition between Christian Wirth, who used carbon monoxide gas in the Polish death camps, and Rudolf Höss, who favored Zyklon B in his Auschwitz-Birkenau facility.[39]

Amidst such a welter of competing organizations, a sense of organizational loyalty was bound to develop, that is, a sense that advancing one's organization was tantamount to one's personal advancement. Thus, in her study of Adolf Eichmann, Hannah Arendt emphasized, "It must be remembered that all these organs, wielding enormous power, were in fierce competition with one another—which was no help to their victims, since their ambition was always the same: to kill as many Jews as possible. This competitive spirit ... inspired in each man a great loyalty to his own outfit."[40] A similar point was made by Albert Breton and Ronald Wintrobe in their analysis of the "bureaucracy of murder" in Nazi Germany. Rejecting the simplistic notion that subordinates in large bureaucracies simply follow orders from superiors in the organizational hierarchy, Breton and Wintrobe emphasized the role of "entrepreneurship" among individual functionaries in "coming up with new ideas, new initiatives, new policies."[41] They also stressed the importance of loyalty to the organization. Nazi Germany was no exception. In their concluding comments, the authors wrote, "We have sought to show that the bureaucratic structure of Nazi Germany was extremely competitive, that the bureaucrats ... active in the bureaucracy were energetic, entrepreneurial, and competitive and that, except at the end, subordinates were intensely loyal to their superiors."[42]

The career of Adolf Eichmann, who ascended within the SS as an expert on Jewish matters and who eventually coordinated the shipments of Jews from all over Europe to the Auschwitz-Birkenau death camp, provides a case in point. At his trial in Jerusalem in 1961, Eichmann claimed that he, personally, bore no ill will toward the millions of Jews to whose deaths he contributed but that, instead, he was merely striving to ensure for himself a respectable status within his organization.[43] In their analysis of the Nazi bureaucracy, Breton and Wintrobe noted that "Eichmann—like innumerable other Nazi subordinates—was a competitive entrepreneurial bureaucrat in a very competitive bureaucracy." They went on to assert, "It is the fact that there were thousands of Eichmanns, all entrepreneurial and competitive and all fiercely loyal to their superiors that explains the terrible efficiency of the Nazi bureaucracy of murder."[44]

Loyalty to the organization, in addition to focusing the attention of functionaries on parochial organizational interests rather than ethical values, can also help ensure career advancement. A fascinating, and chilling, glimpse into the role of careerism in facilitating the involvement of ordinary individuals in mass killing is provided by Christopher Browning's study, mentioned earlier, of a battalion of German reserve policemen who slaughtered Polish Jews and assisted in the clearing of ghettos. In searching for explanations of how these ordinary men could become ruthless killers, Browning examined and discarded a number of possible factors, including ideological motivation and special indoctrination, as well as fear that refusal to kill would incur dire sanctions by their superiors. He noted also that they were not so-called desk murderers, who contributed to the project as bureaucratic paper-shufflers far away from the actual killing. What, then, could account for their willingness and ability to do what they did? Browning emphasized the role of careerism—the fear on the part of some of the men that refusal to kill would look bad on their records and possibly jeopardize their police careers after the war.[45]

The Strategic Bombing Campaigns

Our study discovered strong indications of organizational loyalty in both the British and American mass-bombing campaigns. In each case, there was a powerful yearning for autonomy and preeminence of the air forces both during and after the war, as well as resentment of efforts by the land and sea branches of the military to thwart such goals. There was also the belief, on the part of both British and American air officers, that a conspicuously successful mass-bombing campaign would contribute importantly to the postwar fortunes of the air forces. Finally, there was a willingness to deceive the public regarding the actual nature of bombing practices in order to avoid image tarnishing and negative public relations.

The British Bombing Campaign. Even though the British air force entered World War II as an independent branch of the military, its leaders were concerned with demonstrating its unique value during the war, as well as with setting the stage for its status in the postwar era. The Royal Air Force (RAF) had been established in spring 1918, when the Royal Navy Flying Service and the Royal Flying Corps were merged in an effort to give the air arm of the military greater centralization and autonomy. The principal reason for this consolidation was to more effectively counter the German aerial offensive against London during World War I. In 1917, for example, more than 27 raids by Gotha bombers had killed hundreds of people and spread panic throughout the city.[46]

Hugh Trenchard was placed in command of the new, independent RAF and promptly set about to demonstrate the value of strategic bombing. Under Trenchard, the RAF launched a series of retaliatory bombing raids against German industrial targets. However, the war ended before the British bomber offensive was able to demonstrate that the RAF had made a decisive contribution to the victory. Therefore, during the years between World Wars I and II, Trenchard was preoccupied with trying to convince politicians, the British public, and leaders of the army and navy that the newest branch of the service promised to revolutionize future warfare and that it deserved even greater independence and resources than it currently enjoyed.

However, although there was general consensus that the airplane would play an important role in the next war, there was also a range of opinion regarding just what that role should be. The army and navy tended toward the view that the air forces should provide tactical support for ground and sea operations, a role the air force officers accurately perceived as subservient to the older services. The RAF officers' preference, not surprisingly, was for the air force to undertake an independent strategic bombing campaign against the enemy nation. Some of the most influential airpower advocates argued that if given proper freedom and sufficient funding, the air force had the potential to compel the enemy to surrender without the need for the kind of bloody land invasion and ghastly trench warfare that had horrified soldier, sailor, and airman alike in the previous war.

Trenchard's successors, most notably Arthur Harris, continued the struggle to maximize the resources and responsibilities accorded to the Royal Air Force. Harris's autobiography contains numerous bitter passages on the obstacles to this struggle erected by the rival services. "At the conferences of the Chiefs of Staff," Harris observed, "the Chief of the Air Staff . . . has to hold his own against the very natural demands of the other services, whose heads were just as anxious to prove that their own weapons would be decisive."[47] After suggesting that the RAF, as the newest service, had an "inferiority complex" during the early stages of World War II, Harris commented that that "attitude of the Air Ministry led the R.A.F. to give up far more than it should have on several occasions. Very soon after the war started it should have been obvious that the weapon the R.A.F. had—air power—made the air force by its possession, if for this war only, the senior service."[48]

Yet even after the strategic-bombing offensive was well under way in World War II, the RAF continued to encounter resistance to its own agenda from the army and navy. According to Harris, such interservice rivalry actually prevented Bomber Command from being far more successful than it was. He wrote,

> We were only prevented from having that force [needed to defeat Germany by bombing in 1944] by the fact that the Allied war leaders did not have enough faith in strategic bombing. As a result, the two older services were able to employ a large part of the nation's war effort and industrial capacity in the production and use of their older weapons, and were also able, when the older weapons failed, to get what amounted to more than half our existing bomber force used for their own purposes.[49]

In the final chapter of his autobiography, Harris gave vent to his resentment toward the rival services and to his gratitude for the efforts of Hugh Trenchard to defend the status of the air force: "For nearly twenty years, I watched the army and navy, both singly and in concert, engineer one deliberate attempt after another to destroy the Royal Air Force. Time after time they were within a hairbreadth of success; time after time Trenchard, and Trenchard alone, saved us."[50]

The yearning for organizational autonomy and prestige, combined with the pressures of interservice rivalry, led the airmen, and the bomber enthusiasts in particular, on a quest to prove the unique value of their service. According to R. J. Overy, "Inter-service rivalry encouraged air force leaders to search for strategies peculiar to the air force in defence of its independence and operational integrity, even when their military value was questionable."[51] A similar conclusion was reached by Max Hastings:

> The Royal Air Force had entered the Second World War committed to demonstrating that the air-dropped bomb was a weapon of unique potential. Political, social, and professional pressure on the infant service had driven the airmen to a passionate level of belief. ...The airmen, desperately jealous of their freedom, became obsessed with their need for an independent function, and only a strategic-bomber offensive seemed able to provide it.[52]

The obsession to which Hastings referred led Harris to advocate one form of warfare that only the Royal Air Force Bomber Command could undertake—mass bombing of German population centers. Shortly after assuming command of Bomber Command in February 1942 (after the disastrous year, 1941, in which the fortunes of Bomber Command had reached their nadir), Harris felt compelled to quickly and dramatically put Bomber Command back on the map. As he wrote in his autobiography,

> So during 1942 Bomber Command remained the smallest and weakest of the Commands and was likely to remain so unless something was done about it and done quickly. ... I had to regard the operations of the next few months not only as training or trial runs from which, and only from which, we could learn many essential lessons, but also as commercial travellers' samples which I could show to the War Cabinet.[53]

The first of Harris's "travellers' samples" was the German town of Lübeck, chosen for its readily located position on the bank of a large river and the flammability of its crowded, wooden buildings. "It was not," wrote Harris, "a vital target, but it seemed to me better to destroy an industrial town of moderate importance than to fail to destroy a large industrial town."[54] On the evening of March 28–29, 1942, a total of 234 bombers carrying 160 tons of high explosive bombs and 140 tons of incendiaries succeeded in burning down nearly half the town.[55]

The success of the attack, combined with tolerably low losses of British planes and crews, helped revive morale within Bomber Command as well as restore its status in the eyes of the War Cabinet and the British public. No sooner had Lübeck and several other cities been successfully attacked than Harris began planning another "traveller's sample"—the thousand-plane raid against Cologne, Germany, which took place on May 30. Again, interservice rivalry appears to have played an important role in Harris's reasoning, at least retrospectively: "Such a demonstration was, in fact, the only argument I could see which was at all likely to prevent our squadrons from being snatched away and our effort diverted to subsidiary targets, or to extract the equipment we so desperately needed, the radar navigational aids and the target indicators, from the torpid departments which withheld them for so long."[56]

At the same time that British bombing policy was moving in the direction of outright mass bombing of civilians, efforts were made to conceal this trend from the public. Press releases gave the impression that only selected precision targets were struck, and governmental censorship ensured that the true extent of damage would be concealed. As Martin Middlebrook stated quite bluntly,

> In some ways, Area Bombing was a three-year period of deceit practised upon the British public and on world opinion. It was felt to be necessary that the exact nature of R.A.F. bombing should not be revealed. It could not be concealed that German cities were being hit hard and that residential areas in those cities were receiving many of the bombs, but the impression was usually given that industry was the main target and that any bombing of workers' housing areas was an unavoidable necessity.[57]

Similarly, in his study of the fire raid on Dresden in the final months of the European war, Alexander McKee found strong evidence of efforts by both England and the United States to withhold information about the nature and extent of the damage from their respective publics. However, "only in Britain," noted McKee, "was it possible to keep the massacres from becoming public knowledge, and then for a time only."[58] A principal means by which British authorities carried out their deception involved the Air Ministry's control of information released to the press. According to Middlebrook, "The actual method used was the Air Ministry Official Communique that was issued after the raid and the press briefings given to aviation journalists by Air Ministry or Bomber Command press officers. The news published never contained outright lies but was a skillful selection of material designed to produce the desired effect."[59] Such methods were quite effective. In his analysis of the evolution of British bombing policy, Stephen Garrett noted that a public opinion poll conducted in England in 1944 "revealed that 75 percent of those questioned assumed that Bomber Command was being directed solely at military targets." Only 10 percent of the respondents were aware that city centers in Germany were being targeted by British planes.[60]

The U.S. Bombing Campaign. Similar indications of organizational loyalty were also found in our examination of the American mass-bombing campaign. Indeed, the quest for organizational autonomy and preeminence may have been even stronger in the case of the U.S. Army Air Forces, since they lacked the degree of independence enjoyed by the Royal Air Force during World War II and were not established as a separate service until 1947.[61] After World War I, all branches of the military in the United States experienced reductions in budget allocations. According to Schaffer, since the air force "was a new service which in the early years had only a small constituency among military suppliers, Congress, and the general public, the airmen had to work especially hard for a share of the small military budgets of the 1920s and 1930s."[62] Also, Sherry noted that many Air Corps officers "had endured wholesale reduction in rank after the war's end and a glacial pace of promotion thereafter. So had most other army officers. ... Infantry or artillery officers also worried about dead-end careers, but at least their branches of service were not suspect in the eyes of high command. For airmen alone, personal ambition meshed precisely with professional progress."[63]

Interservice rivalry was every bit as much of a problem for the American airpower advocates as it was for their British counterparts. As Arthur Harris wrote, "There was just as intense a struggle in America as in England between those in the air force who were anxious to develop a strategic bombing force, and the army and navy who made every effort to restrict the development and use of the new weapon."[64]

So intense was the concern among U.S. Air Corps officers for the wartime and postwar status of their service that some scholars have suggested that organizational interests played an important role in the evolution of bombing policy in general, and the embrace of urban, incendiary attacks in particular. In his analysis of the formation of American air strategy, for example, Sherry suggested that "personal and organizational anxiety provided one spurt to escalation of the air war."[65] One example is provided by the plan proposed by General Ira Eaker to attack German submarines by targeting their coastal bases rather than by directly targeting the submarines at sea, which would have entailed a degree of control over the bombers by the navy, even though the latter approach was found to be more effective. As Sherry noted, "To admit that the submarine war was better won that way [i.e., "direct aerial operations against subs at sea"] would have undercut long-standing claims for the air forces as an independent strategic weapon. In that sense, organizational goals were perhaps foremost in the Eaker plan."[66]

Another example of organizational loyalty is provided by General Curtis LeMay. Like his British counterpart, Arthur Harris, LeMay expressed vehement resentment toward the rival services in his autobiography, where, for example, he decried the treatment accorded General Billy Mitchell for his efforts to attain the independence of the air forces from the army. "When the Army punished Billy Mitchell," wrote LeMay, "they were in effect trying to punish the entire then-existent Air Service. When the Army sought to force an iron gag into Billy Mitchell's mouth, they were trying to gag all proponents of air power under their command." LeMay then proceeded to describe the lowly status of American air forces in the years before World War II in vivid terms, "In 1930, and during successive seasons through which we would have to skimp and save and Do Without, our Corps was treated like the bereaved orphan in fairy tales. We had a pallet of straw in a cold garret; and the cook threw us some scraps only after everyone else in the household staff had been fed."[67]

As was the case with British proponents of airpower, strategic bombing was regarded by the Americans as the means by which the new service could demonstrate its special value. Writing of the American air commanders in the aftermath of Pearl Harbor, Schaffer suggested that "not only did they want to contribute as much as possible to the winning of the war, but they hoped that by making a massive display of effective strategic bombing, they would ensure their preeminence in the postwar military establishment as an independent air force."[68] Schaffer is echoed by Conrad C. Crane, who alludes in his study of U.S. bombing strategy during World War II to U.S. Army Air Forces chief of staff General Henry "Hap" Arnold's "consuming desire to justify an independent air service [that] put pressure on AAF combat leaders to produce decisive bombing results."[69]

As we have seen, the Americans initially favored a precision-bombing policy but gradually moved in the direction of area bombing, culminating in the deliberate creation of firestorms in Japanese cities. One important motive for this shift may well have been the hope that the more dramatic results of the area-bombing campaigns would help to serve their postwar interests. According to Conrad Crane, "Advocates for an independent air force saw their last chance to prove its value against Japan."[70] And Sherry concluded that "the imperatives of invasion were not the foremost considerations leading the AAF to firebombing; it made that choice in March [of 1945] because incendiary bombing was easy and because doing it rescued the AAF's flagging fortunes."[71] In his autobiography, Curtis LeMay acknowledged that his decision to shift from high-altitude precision bombing to low-altitude incendiary bombing was motivated in part by a desire to demonstrate the importance of the long-range bombers. He recalled that he had been told by his commanding officer, "If you don't get results, also, there'll never be any Strategic Air Forces of the Pacific—after the battle is finally over in Europe.'"[72]

Another parallel to the British case may be found in efforts by American airpower advocates to prevent the American public from perceiving the actual nature of the area-bombing campaign. As Ronald Schaffer has noted, "[USAAF General Ira] Eaker was so concerned about public perceptions of the AAF that he sought to control the way its history would be written."[73] Sherry reached a similar conclusion, asserting, "Public relations remained the art of balancing deception and truth, depending on which enhanced that benefit. ... The long-range goal was still to cultivate an image favorable to securing autonomy and maximum resources for the postwar air force."[74]

Toward the end of the European war, when the United States had already begun area bombing of population centers, top air force leaders tried to suppress accounts of the American role in the devastating raid on Dresden. Their principal goal was to persuade the American public that the prevailing policy was still precision bombing of military targets. According to Schaffer,

> That image, so essential to the AAF in its wartime struggle for resources, so crucial to its leaders' vision of a postwar independent air arm, continued to preoccupy AAF officials. Around the world they worked closely with filmmakers, publishers, and journalists, arranging to have the story of air power told so that after the war, as General Arnold explained, the United States would not tear down what "cost us so much blood and sweat to build up." The picture the AAF presented to the men and women who served in its ranks and to the American public was of precision bombing—destroying railroad installations, oil tanks, ammunition dumps, and factories—not indiscriminate burning or blowing up of German homes.[75]

Concluding Comments

An examination of both the Holocaust and the British and American bombing campaigns revealed intense competition among organizations and factions within the respective governments. In the context of the bureaucratic organization that pervaded all three societies, such competition created conditions conducive to the development of intense organizational loyalty, which in turn facilitated the escalation of violence.

Scientific Rationalization

Scientific rationalization refers to the political exploitation of scientists and scientific research to promote desired policies and practices. This can assume a number of forms. Evidence of questionable validity may be willingly embraced with little or no provision for independent outside scientific assessment. Alternatively, valid data may be misinterpreted with a bias toward supporting an already firm position on an issue or option.

The Holocaust

A number of analysts of the Holocaust have concluded that scientists and other scholars made crucial contributions to policies and practices that culminated in the Final Solution. Writing of the role of science and scientists in the Nazi era, George L. Mosse stated, "Science was absorbed by Nazi culture, and in turn helped to give this culture an air of intellectual respectability."[76] In an early study of the roles of German academics and scientists in contributing to the Holocaust, Max Weinreich concluded that at each stage in the escalating campaign against the Jews,

> the German rulers had theorists at hand who praised their achievements in reducing the Jews and supplied the academic formulae and the scholarly backing for each further step in German policies, until the "extinguishment" of the "eternally hostile forces" was accomplished to the best of the murderers' abilities. Nor did this last step lack theoretical backing. ... No discipline of science that could be of use to the regime failed. The hundreds of names we have dealt with range from physical and cultural anthropologists to philosophers, historians, jurists, economists, geographers, and demographers, to theologians, linguists, and medical men.[77]

Since Weinreich's pioneering study, a number of analysts have explored the contributions of scientists to the Nazi regime in general and the Holocaust in particular. For example, Alan Beyerchen traced the development of so-called Aryan physics, a movement promoted by two Nobel prizewinners, Phillip Leonard and Johannes Stark, that was dedicated to purging the discipline of physics of "Jewish influence." Such an effort obviously required gross distortion of the historical development and current status of the field, since many of the major contributions had been made by such Jews as Albert Einstein, just as it obviously played into the hands of the Nazi ideologues. Although the majority of German physicists did not join this pseudoscientific movement, neither did they forthrightly resist or denounce it, any more than they protested the summary dismissals of their Jewish colleagues. As Beyerchen stated, "There was practically no political opposition to National Socialism by physics community leaders."[78] In other words, the discipline of physics as a whole tended to passively condone the scientism of a radical racist minority.

The German medical profession contributed both prestige and expertise to Nazi racial ideology as well as policies intended to ensure "racial purity." In 1933, for example, prominent doctors played an important role in creating a law that mandated compulsory sterilization of all Germans suspected of having hereditary sicknesses. "Hereditary-health" courts, with at least two physicians presiding, were established to screen hundreds of thousands of people with a variety of allegedly hereditary ailments ranging from mental retardation to alcoholism.[79] In 1935, just two years after the imposition of the Sterilization Laws, German physicians provided significant impetus for the passage of the so-called 'Nuremberg Laws, which were directed specifically at the Jews. One of them, the Law for the Protection of German Blood and German Honor, made it illegal for Jews to marry or to have any sexual relations with non-Jews. According to historian Lucy Dawidowicz, this law "legitimated racist anti-Semitism and turned the 'purity of blood' into a legal category."[80] These laws both reflected and reinforced what Robert Jay Lifton has aptly called the Nazi "ideology of biological renewal."[81] That ideological vision eventually led to the direct murder of mentally disabled patients and, later, to the Final Solution, which sought to murder every Jewish man, woman, and child in Nazi-controlled Europe.

The Strategic-Bombing Campaigns

Historians of strategic bombing have provided evidence that scientific rationalization played an important role in facilitating the deliberate targeting of population centers. In the British case, evidence of the political manipulation of scientific data may be found in the reactions of strategic-bombing advocates to three reports on bombing by committees of scientists commissioned by the government.

The first of these—the so-called Lloyd Report—was released in December 1940. It evaluated the early results of the bombing campaign and concluded that it was already highly effective. The drafters of the report, as were all scientists endeavoring to assess the value of particular targeting schemes, were greatly hampered by limitations in their data. However, when the Lloyd Report claimed that the bombers had aleady destroyed as much as 15 percent of German oil resources, many bombing policymakers enthusiastically and uncritically accepted the findings as vindication of their current policy, despite the fact that even Churchill, an acknowledged supporter of the bomber offensive, was very skeptical, believing that it greatly overestimated the actual damage that had been caused. As Max Hastings has suggested, the eagerness of the airmen to accept the report stemmed from the fact that "they were simply desperate for good news of bombing, and when it came they received it uncritically. To have allowed themselves to believe the truth [i.e., that the report was unrealistically optimistic] would have been the negation of scores of careers dedicated to the fulfillment of the Trenchard doctrine."[82]

The opposite reaction was elicited by the Butt Report, which in August 1941 disclosed the gross inaccuracies and ineffectiveness of night "precision" bombing. Whereas both aircrews and the leaders of Bomber Command had assumed that many, if not most, of the bombers were finding and hitting their targets, the committee of scientists headed by D. M. Butt found that fewer than one-third of the planes claiming to have hit their assigned targets had actually come within five miles of their aiming points. The optimism that had been engendered earlier by the Lloyd Report was directly threatened. However, as Hastings noted, "The Royal Air Force was not disposed to make much of the Butt Report. … The chronic lack of clear thinking that had dogged bombing policy since the end of the First World War persisted even in the face of the most convincing evidence."[83] Similarly, R. J. Overy observed that it was "very easy to ignore much intelligence that did not confirm what the air forces wanted."[84] Although the leaders of Bomber Command were willing to dismiss these disturbing findings, Winston Churchill was not, particularly in view of the fact that losses of bomber crews over Germany had been steadily mounting. The combination of such intolerable losses and the fact that the men and planes were being sacrificed for such meager results led to an order in November 1941 to drastically curtail British bomber sorties over Germany.

One response to the Butt Report was a growing momentum toward targeting large areas of cities in order to weaken the morale of the enemy population. This form of strategic bombing did not depend upon high levels of accuracy. As Hastings noted, the findings of the Butt Report, despite resistance, meant that "a new policy had become inevitable."[85] An important feature of the new policy was the employment of incendiary bombs against highly flammable cities such as Lübeck, Cologne, and Hamburg.[86]

In March 1942, yet another scientific report gave powerful support to the advocates of area bombing and ultimately contributed to its official adoption by the British government. This report was released by Frederick A. Lindemann, Churchill's chief science adviser and close personal friend. Lindemann argued that a campaign aimed at "dehousing" German workers would quickly result in the inability of Germany to continue the war. Furthermore, Lindemann maintained that such results could be obtained by relatively few planes.

In the Lindemann memo, the advocates of area bombing had what they believed to be credible scientific justification for their targeting policy. The fact that precision bombing had been found to be both infeasible and ineffective, combined with the new scientific evidence for area bombing, provided, according to Hastings, the "final rationalization" for area bombing.[87]

However, many scientists, including Henry Tizard, one of England's most prestigous scientists and defense advisers, questioned Lindemann's figures and conclusions on a number of grounds. The efforts of the critics to subject the memo to careful review were resisted successfully by both Lindemann and the top policymakers in Bomber Command. As C. P. Snow has written,

> I do not think that … I have ever seen a minority view [that of Tizard and the other skeptics] so unpopular. Bombing had become a matter of faith. … The Air Ministry fell in behind the Lindemann paper. The minority view was not only defeated, but squashed. The atmosphere was more hysterical than is usual in English official life; it had the faint but just perceptible smell of a witch hunt. Tizard was actually called a defeatist. Strategic bombing, according to the Lindemann policy, was put into action with every effort the country could make.[88]

In each of these three cases, it appears that scientific evidence was either accepted or dismissed on the basis of whether it confirmed the biases and preferences of decisionmakers concerned with strategic-bombing policy in Great Britain. Thus, in the debate over area bombing, science was used not to dispassionately and objectively evaluate alternative targeting policies but instead to justify policies that individuals and organizations had already come to believe in and support.

Scientists also contributed to the American strategic-bombing campaign. Like their British counterparts, they played key roles in analyzing targeting options, designing the actual bombs, and evaluating the effectiveness of bombing.[89]

They also helped rationalize the policy of bombing population centers, especially in Japan. Both Sherry and Dower found that social science data was used by advocates of strategic bombing to support their claims that the "primitive" Japanese would quickly succumb to the demoralizing effects of incendiary bombing of urban areas. According to Sherry,

> The social scientists' characterization of the Japanese as a culturally and psychologically immature and childish people victimized by repressive toilet training—the "Scott Tissue interpretation of history," as one anthropologist snidely described this line of argument—dovetailed with more vicious popular stereotypes of a simian race arrested in its development. Similarly, the language of individual and social pathology gave sophisticated expression to popular notions of a mad people driven by a lust to torture and conquer. More specifically, the impression they conveyed of a psychologically brittle people provided sanction, if unwitting, to the terror bombing of Japanese cities—a kind of scientific gloss on the widely held (if also disputed) notion that the Japanese would crack under the strain of bombing.[90]

Concluding Comments

There are important differences between the role of science in the two cases examined. The racism that helped rationalize the segregation, persecution, and, eventually, extermination of the Jews was clearly pseudoscientific. It was the product of scholarly ideologues and opportunists who expropriated legitimate science for blatantly political purposes. Science and technology did, however, make many important contributions to the overall Allied war efforts in general and to the strategic-bombing campaigns in partiçular. The development of radar, the steady improvement in bomb-aiming technology, and the careful emprical work by the United States Strategic Bombing Survey are just a few examples of the useful application of legitimate science to the war. However, it would be a mistake to assume that science was always applied in an objective, unbiased manner. We have seen, in the British case, that "scientific" data could be accepted or rejected depending on the biases of the policymakers.

Technical Distancing

Scholars of both war and genocide have commented on the tendency for technology to increase the physical distance between killers and victims. By eliminating the individual identity of the victims and by lumping them together into an anonymous mass, such technical distancing may reduce psychological barriers, such as empathy and moral inhibitions, against killing them.

The Holocaust

The dehumanization of the Jewish victims of the Holocaust, as discussed in the preceeding chapter, was not limited to racist ideology. The evolution of the killing technology itself made it progressively easier for the killers to carry out their duties in an impersonal manner.

The initial killing method of choice for the Nazis was mass shooting by the Einsatzgruppen who followed the German army forces into Russia and rounded up and killed all the Jews they could find. Of the approximately 3,000 men involved in the mass shootings, the majority had not volunteered for that specific duty but had been selected more or less at random from various police and other government agencies. Before being sent into the field, many were subjected to an intense ideological indoctrination. Although many quickly adapted to the job, which eventually became routinized, and a few sadists delighted in the opportunity to engage in mass murder in the service of their nation, some began to experience severe emotional difficulties. Among the former Nazi doctors interviewed by Lifton was a former Luftwaffe neuropsychiatrist who during the war had treated a number of Einsatzgruppen soldiers for such problems as insomnia, nightmares, and anxiety attacks. Lifton's informant estimated that a substantial minority (as many as 20 percent) of the soldiers in the killing units experienced such forms of mental or emotional disturbance as the result of shooting people, often at point-blank range, day after day, week after week.[91]

The psychological stresses involved in such work could even find expression in the killers' bathetic self-pity. For example, at his postwar Nuremberg trial, former Einsatzgruppen officer Paul Blobel testified, "The nervous strain was far heavier in the case of our men who carried out the executions than in that of their victims. From the psychological point of view they had a terrible time."[92] In response to the prevalence of such emotional problems among the killers, it became standard procedure in some units to keep the men well-supplied with alcohol in an effort to prevent guilt and anxiety from interfering with their work.[93]

The emphasis on mass shooting began to shift after Himmler went into the field to personally observe a killing action. After nearly fainting into the body pit after pieces of brain from one of the victims splattered his boots, Himmler ordered his officers to seek a "more humane" means of killing the Jews that would reduce the stress on the killers. In response to this order, gas vans were brought into operation, but the soldiers found them little better. Although the killers were spared the necessity of aiming the gun and pulling the trigger, they loathed the task of prying the tangled corpses out of the back of the gas van.[94]

It was neither mass shooting nor mobile gas vans but huge stationary gas chambers that became the preferred killing technology for the Final Solution. The combination of such gas chambers and nearby crematoria made possible an assembly-line killing process that was at the same time more efficient and less personal. As Hannah Arendt suggested, the very size of the gas chambers (the largest ones at Auschwitz-Birkenau could each hold 2,000 people at one time) made the act of killing completely impersonal.[95] Likewise, the sheer masses of victims—anonymously packed together in the boxcars used to transport them to the death camps, herded en masse into the undressing rooms, and crammed naked into the gas chambers—tended to depersonalize the killing process.

Thus, in his prison-cell interviews with Gitta Sereny, Franz Stangl, the former commandant of the Treblinka death camp, was asked if he ever regarded the hundreds of thousands of people gassed at Treblinka as human beings. Although he had been bothered at first, Stangl replied, he soon came to regard the victims as "cargo." When asked by Sereny when this change took place, Stangl stated: "I think it started the day I first saw the *Totenlager* [storage area for corpses] in Treblinka. I remember Wirth [an SS officer] standing there, next to the pits full of blue-black corpses. It had nothing to do with humanity—it couldn't have; it was a mass—a mass of rotting flesh." Sereny then asked Stangl whether the killing of children ever evoked any special response in him or made him think of his own children, to whom he was deeply devoted. He said no, that he "rarely saw them as individuals. It was always a huge mass. I sometimes stood on the wall and saw them in the tube [the fenced-in corridor between the undressing sheds and the gas chambers]. But—how can I explain it—they were naked, packed together, running, being driven with whips."[96]

The mass-gassing process itself proved to be less stressful for the killers than the face-to-face mass-shooting method. The technician who climbed up on the roof of the gas chamber and poured cansful of gas crystals through special openings into the darkened, packed chamber below was considerably more physically and, therefore, psychologically detached from the victims than the soldier aiming at

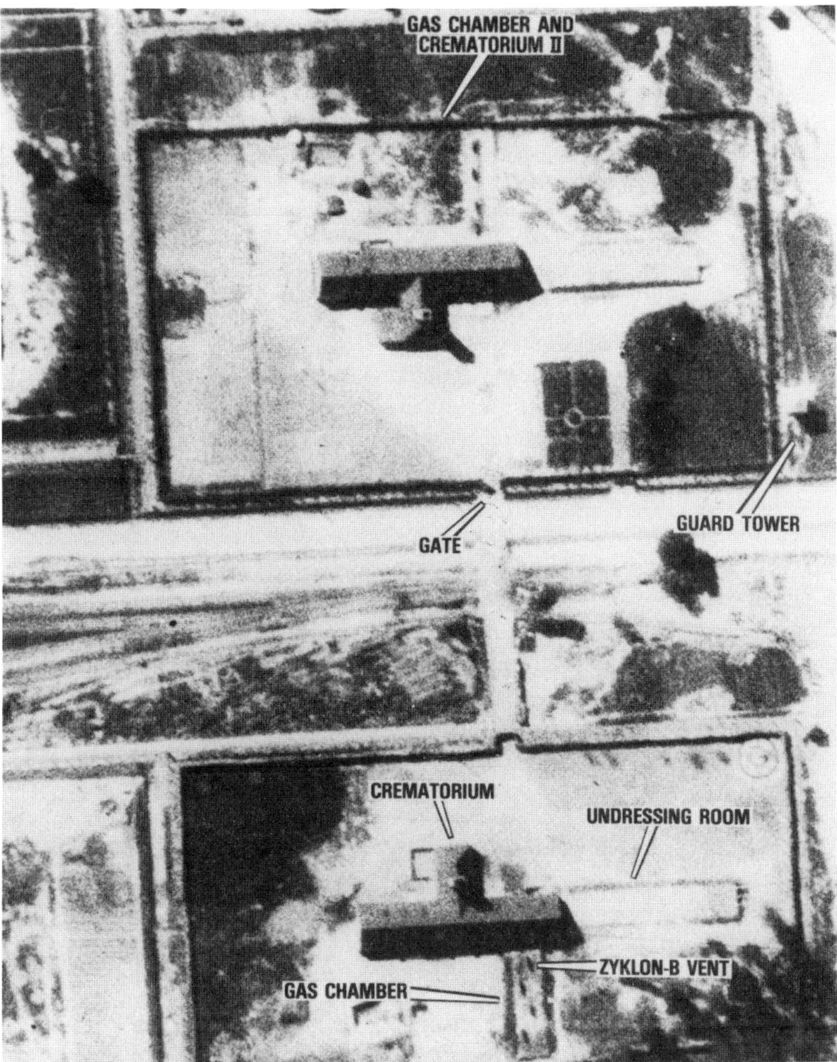

An aerial close-up of two gas chamber–crematoria buildings at Auschwitz-Birkenau. In order to slaughter as many as 2,000 people at one time, all the killers had to do was walk on the roof of the underground gas chamber, take the lids off the vents for the Zyklon B, and pour gas crystals down the holes into the chamber. As noted in the text, Auschwitz commandant Rudolf Höss found gassing far more "calming" than shooting., SOURCE: U.S. Holocaust Memorial Museum.

and shooting person after person marching before him in a seemingly interminable line. In his autobiography, written in his prison cell after the war, Rudolf Höss, the former commandant of Auschwitz, wrote,

> I must admit openly that the gassings had a calming effect on me, since in the near future the mass annihilation of the Jews was to begin. … I was always horrified of death by firing squads, especially when I thought of the huge numbers of women and children who would have to be killed. I had had enough of hostage executions, and the mass killings by firing squad ordered by Himmler and Heydrich. Now I was at ease. We were all saved from these bloodbaths.[97]

The Strategic-Bombing Campaigns

The altitude from which bombs were dropped, which steadily increased as the war progressed, may have eased the psychological burden on aircrews engaged in mass bombing of civilians.[98] The primary impetus for increased altitude was to outdistance the range of enemy flak, and each new generation of bombers was designed to fly higher than the preceding one. This development had the side effect of further increasing the distance between the bomber crews and their targets. Hence, the combination of high altitude, frequent cloud cover during day raids, and the darkness at night meant that many crews did not see the people or even buildings at which they were aiming. According to Kennett, "Photographs taken at thirty thousand feet gave no clue to the human effects of a raid, nor did other sources. In this vacuum, imagination and extrapolation could picture the population of an enemy town deprived of its homes but not of life and limb."[99] Alexander McKee, who interviewed numerous British veterans of the fire raid on Dresden, commented, "Normally, everything was very remote, even when there were colossal fires burning down below."[100] As one of the men McKee interviewed described it,

> In general, you saw a light on the ground, which was the fires—but mainly you saw a glowing light in the smoke. Then searchlights above and ack-ack around you. There was always a weird feeling of unreality in Bomber Command. You were living in, say, Cambridgeshire or Norfolk; you were thinking of friends, pubs, girls, even intellectual pursuits. Then you were launched for eight hours into a different world at 20,000 feet over Germany.[101]

A similar picture emerged from Martin Middlebrook's interviews with men who participated in the devastating fire raid over Hamburg:

> Aircrews were rarely told that the Aiming Point and the ensuing bombing areas had been selected in order to wipe out residential areas. A few hours later, when they were flying over the target, the ground seemed very remote 20,000 feet below. Theirs was a very detached and impersonal form of war. The aircrew knew that many of their bombs must be hitting residential districts but this was all thought to be a necessary part of the main task.[102]

And in his memoirs of the war, American bomber pilot Philip Ardery wrote, "The brutality of heavy bombardment is highly impersonal. I was used to carrying out my mission four miles above the point of impact. It is difficult under those circumstances to get any feeling of injuring the enemy at all."[103]

When the bombing altitude was dramatically reduced, however, the numbing psychological effects of distance were also reduced. For example, during the fire raids over Japan under the direction of Curtis LeMay, when American B-29 bombers switched from high-altitude attacks to very low-level bombing runs, crews were brought very close to the infernos that they had created. There were times when the nauseating stench of burning flesh was trapped in the bomb bays and carried over a thousand miles back to their air bases in the Marianas. Wilbur Morrison recorded that after the incendiary attack on Tokyo, "when the crews returned to their bases, they handed in their reports with hands that shook, with shock and horror still reflected in their eyes from what they had witnessed just a few hours before."[104]

A second group of individuals for whom physical distance from the actual killing may have facilitated involvement in the killing project includes analysts and planners who helped rationalize and organize the bombing campaign. Writing of them, Schaffer suggested, "The routines of their work and the physical detachment of conducting war from offices far from the target area made it less difficult to inflict pain that might have been agonizing to administer face to face, and enabled them to avoid the combat fatigue that develops in people who think too much about those they are killing."[105] Such physical distance from the actual violence was reinforced psychologically by the "scientific" objectivity of their analyses. According to Sherry,

> The rhetoric and methodology of civilian expertise also defined goals by the distance they interposed between the designers and victims of destruction. The more sophisticated the methods of destruction became, the less language and methods of measurement allowed men to acknowledge the nature of that destruction. A dehumanized rhetoric of technique reduced the enemy to quantifiable abstractions. Statistics of man-hours lost and workers dehoused objectified many of the enemy's experiences and banished almost altogether one category, his death.[106]

Concluding Comments

It is likely that the physical distance between killers and victims exercised a facilitating effect on the willingness and ability of functionaries of both the German genocide and the Allied mass-bombing programs to engage in the slaughter of innocent, often defenseless, civilians. However, any such technological dehumanization was but one among a constellation of powerful factors—including the obligation to obey orders from superiors and a conviction that the killing projects were in the service of national security and survival—that psychologically facilitated participation in the killing project. An important difference, however, between

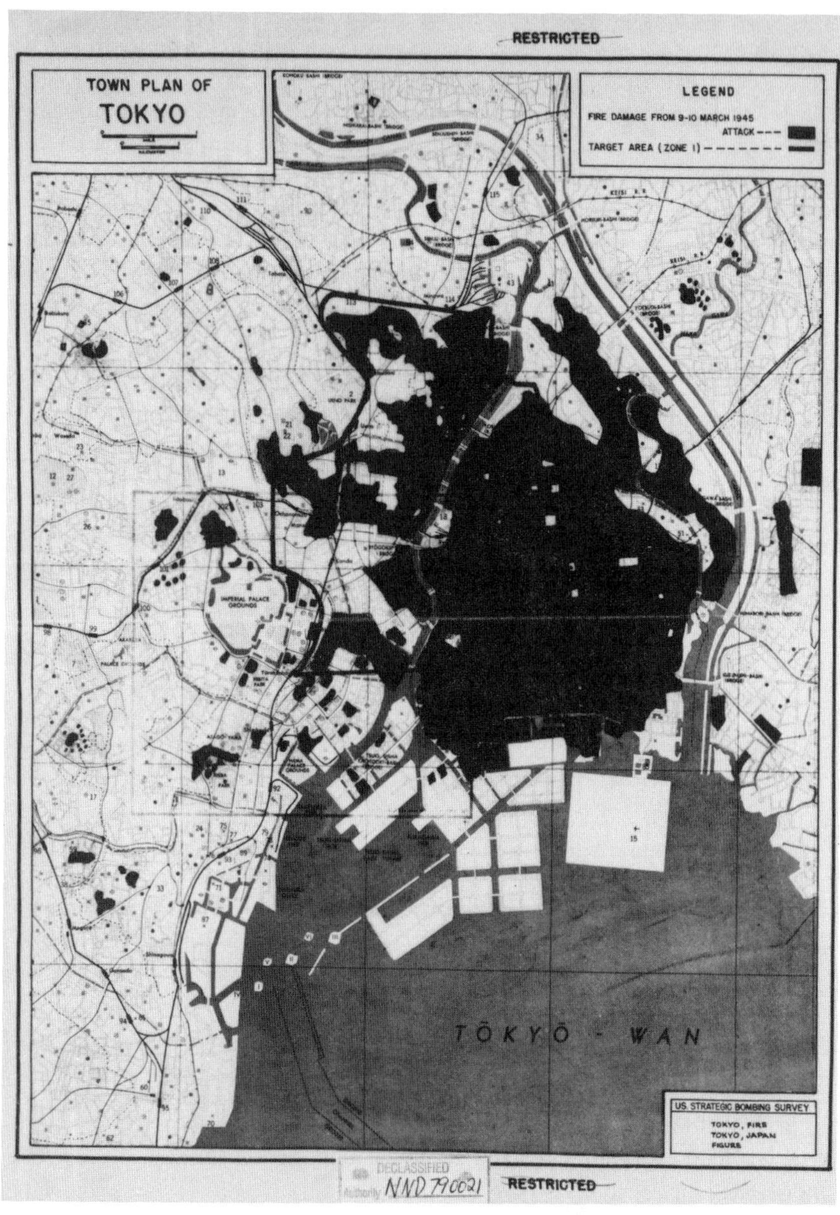

A map of the city of Tokyo, with the area destroyed by firebombs marked in black. Later raids would be routed to fill in the gaps. SOURCE: National Archives, Military Archives Division.

the two cases is that the bomber crews were additionally distracted by preoccupation with sheer survival in the lethal skies and an understandable desire to wreak vengeance against the enemy for its aggression and atrocities.

In this chapter and in the one that preceded it, we have seen that despite important differences between the Holocaust and the strategic-bombing campaigns, the two killing projects were in fact facilitated by some of the same psychological, organizational, and scientific-technological processes. This finding in no way diminishes the uniqueness of each case, nor does it render the differences between them irrelevant. It does, however, alert us to the fact that genocide and total war may not be as distinct and different as many people have assumed them to be.

Part 3

Lessons, Legacies, and Prospects

Chapter 11

What We Have Learned From This Study

> Whoever fights monsters should see to it that in the process he does not become a monster. And when you look into an abyss, the abyss also looks into you.
>
> —*Friedrich Nietzsche (1886)*[1]

This chapter is divided into two sections. In the first, we provide answers to several of the questions that were posed at the beginning of the book. We do so by summarizing points made earlier. Then, in the second section, we discuss what we have learned from the comparative analysis of the Holocaust and strategic bombing presented in Chapters 9 and 10, with particular attention to the question, Was strategic bombing genocidal?

With this comparative study of genocide and total war, and of the Holocaust and strategic bombing, we hoped to provide answers to the questions posed in Chapter 1. We repeat some of them here:

> Is the twentieth century indeed the most murderous in history? If so, why? How have bureaucratic organization and advances in science and technology contributed to the scale of mass killing during this century? How can the willingness of apparently normal men and women to contribute to mass killing projects be explained? What psychological and social processes facilitate involvement in policies and programs that entail slaughtering masses of innocent, defenseless human beings? Why has the problem of mass killing not received the degree of attention that its scale and momentum warrant? What is the relationship between warfare and genocide? Should they be regarded as distinct, unrelated phenomena, or do they have important commonalities? Is it ever appropriate to define war as "genocidal"?

For present purposes, we have grouped these questions into three basic ones, which we now attempt to answer.

Has the Twentieth Century Been the Most Murderous?

Our basic answer to this question is yes. In Chapter 2, we reviewed the work of Pitirim Sorokin, Gil Elliot, and William Eckhardt, all of whom undertook detailed study of the toll of collective violence during the twentieth century in comparison with prior centuries and concluded that the twentieth has been the worst.

With respect to questions concerning *why* this century has been so violent, we suggest that a combination of ancient psychological capacities, combined with modern bureaucratic and technological developments, helps account for the fact that organized killing has been so common and massive during the past 90 or so years. The phenomenon of dehumanization, promoted by religious and political ideologies and facilitated by rhetoric and dogma, undoubtedly operated throughout history as a means by which killing of others was justified and made psychologically easier. Likewise, the healing-killing paradox is by no means a modern development. Killing others in order to save one's own group, and having such killing justified by religious and political leaders, are as old as civilization.

Although bureaucracy did not originate during the twentieth century, it certainly did become the predominant form of large-scale social organization. Most, indeed virtually all, of the wars and genocides during this century relied heavily upon bureaucracy in order to plan and implement policies and operations, including deliberate slaughter of enemies. We saw in Chapters 5 and 10 how such features of bureaucracy as hierarchical structure, division of labor, organizational loyalty, and amoral rationality all have made it easier for the large numbers of people needed for mass-killing projects to make their contributions, whether as accomplices or as perpetrators. Early in the book, we also noted Israel W. Charny's conclusion, based on a careful study of many cases of genocidal killing, that the vast majority of men and women who contribute to such killing are psychologically normal rather than being sadists or psychopaths. Charny's conclusion, we emphasize, has been corroborated by other scholars.[2] We suggest that bureaucracy plays an important role in enabling such "normal" individuals to participate in mass-killing projects by routinizing obedience, diminishing the sense of personal responsibility, and impeding concerns with moral and human implications.

Like bureaucracy, science and technology did not originate during the present century, but in no prior century have they possessed such prestige and influence. As shown in Chapter 2, one of the most striking features of the twentieth century has been the increased capacity for destruction and killing. And as discussed in Chapters 2, 5, and 10, another crucial feature has been the ability to kill large numbers of people from ever-greater distances, a development that significantly enhances the ability to dehumanize the victims. Both features are direct results of advances in science and the application of technology. Moreover, in our age of science and technology, scientific (and pseudoscientific) rationalization of governmental policies is a ubiquitous practice. Policies involving mass killing are no exception.

Why Has the Subject of Genocidal Killing Been So Neglected?

Several reasons were cited in Chapter 1 for the fact that the scholarly attention focused specifically on the subjects of genocide and genocidal killing has been so grossly inadequate relative to the urgency and scale of the problem. We noted that this subject does pose formidable challenges to the student and scholar, ranging from linguistic and conceptual ambiguities and controversies to difficulties in obtaining valid data. We also discussed the intrinsic repulsiveness of the subject and how it can engender psychological numbing, despair, and fatalism. Yet another disincentive may be created by the inescapably political nature of this realm of study. Confronting the problem of state-sanctioned mass killing is often tantamount to facing the fact that one's own nation has engaged in it. It also generates the question of when detached scholarship is no longer sufficient and potentially risky political activism may become a moral imperative. Finally, we examined some of the intellectual and political challenges posed by the act of looking at governmental mass killing in comparative perspective, a practice likely to offend some who feel that their particular experience is incomparably unique and others who resent having an action they supported or in which they participated examined in the same context with genocides that are widely seen as unforgivably evil. One potential disincentive that we did not discuss earlier but that merits at least a passing mention is the fact that genocide studies, by falling outside the mainstream of academic disciplines and acceptable areas of specialization and substantive research within them, are not as readily fundable as many other subjects that have larger constituencies in both academia and in the funding community.

What Is the Relationship Between Genocide and Total War?

In Chapter 4, we examined several important connections and commonalities between genocide and total war. One connection on which there is considerable consensus is that war in general, and total war in particular, create psychological, social, and political conditions conducive to genocidal killing. They do so in a number of ways: by exacerbating fears and anxieties that can be directed against a scapegoat group either within the society or in an enemy society; by reducing democratic checks and balances or reinforcing totalitarian tendencies; by utilizing trained and often brutal professional killers in the military to hunt down and slaughter internal and external enemies; by increasing the vulnerability of the victims in a variety of ways; and by creating a climate of psychological numbing and desensitization among members of the society that is engaged in the genocidal killing.

Moreover, a fundamental similarity stems from the fact that both genocide and total war employ the massacre of large numbers of innocent, helpless noncombatants as a means of obtaining their objectives. In Chapter 1, we noted the growing trend toward increased vulnerability of civilians in modern war, pointing out that civilian deaths constituted only about 5 percent of the total death toll in World War I but as much as 66 percent in World War II and 70–80 percent in wars of the 1970s and 1980s. In Chapter 4, we argued that the crime of genocide, as defined by the United Nations Genocide Convention, is not necessarily excluded from the categories of war crimes and crimes against humanity. International law prohibits, under all three categories of crime, the indiscriminate slaughter of civilians.

Yet another commonality between genocide and total war is the fact that most modern genocides and wars are conducted by nation-states (or collectivities aspiring to become nation-states) and are rationalized as being necessary for the enhancement, protection, or restoration of national security. The implications of this were examined in Chapter 4. Also, both genocide and total war thrive in a totalitarian political environment. Put conversely, both forms of governmental mass killing are less likely to be employed by democracies than by totalitarian regimes. We return to this point later in this chapter. Finally, in Chapter 5, we showed how a number of psychological, organizational, and scientific-technical processes and factors facilitate both genocide and total war.

Was Strategic Bombing Genocidal?

> Stench everywhere: piles of human bone remnants at the furnace. Here is the antidote to qualms about strategic bombing.
>
> —*Bruce Hopper (after visiting Buchenwald in 1945)*[3]

> In principle, the extermination camps where the Nazis incinerated over six million helpless Jews were no different from the urban crematoriums our air force improvised in its attacks by napalm bombs on Tokyo. ... Our aims were different, but our methods were those of mankind's worst enemy.
>
> —*Lewis Mumford (1959)*[4]

In Chapter 4, we observed that Leo Kuper, one of the world's foremost genocide scholars, has asserted that the term "genocide" should "be applied to the atomic bombing of the Japanese cities of Hiroshima and Nagasaki by the U.S.A. and to the pattern bombing by the Allies of such cities as Hamburg and Dresden."[5] More recently, Kuper wrote, "I should have added the firebombing of Tokyo."[6] Kuper is not the only scholar to label strategic bombing, of which the atomic bombings of Hiroshima and Nagasaki were the apotheosis, as genocidal. In an article accusing both Japan and the United States of committing war crimes during World War II, Shigetoshi Iwamatsu called the atomic bombs "genocide weapons" and claimed that "the devastation [they caused] might be termed genocide."[7] Even Jack Nusan Porter, whose catalog of misapplications of the term "genocide" was cited earlier in this book, labeled the atomic bombings an example of "questionable genocide" in the same article in which he decried inappropriate application of the term.[8]

As we showed in Chapter 4, other scholars—including Irving Louis Horowitz, Israel W. Charny, and R. J. Rummel—have demonstrated inconsistency in their writings on the question of whether genocide and warfare in general should be regarded as convergent or as mutually exclusive and, by extension, whether acts of war like strategic bombing may fit within definitions of "genocide" and "genocidal."

Still other scholars have strongly disagreed with the premise that war and genocide may overlap and that strategic bombing was genocidal. Thus, in their important textbook on genocide, Chalk and Jonassohn wrote, "Our definition of genocide also excludes civilians of aerial bombardment in belligerent states."[9] And Helen Fein, who is among the handful of leading genocide scholars in world, has clearly stated her disagreement with those "genocide-labelers" who regard the atomic bombings as genocidal: "To equate Hiroshima and Auschwitz belies the distinctive ends and design of each plan and their distinctive effects."[10]*

In order to answer the question of whether strategic bombing was genocidal, we employ two approaches. First, we summarize differences and similarities between the two cases of mass killing. Since there is widespread consensus that the Holocaust did in fact constitute an extreme case of genocide, finding that strategic bombing had important features in common with the Holocaust would lend support to those who argue, as has Kuper, that strategic bombing was in fact genocidal.† The second approach assesses the extent to which strategic bombing meets the criteria for genocide as specified by the closest approximation to a universally accepted definition—that in the United Nations Genocide Convention. For this purpose, we will once again rely on the criteria derived from the Genocide Convention by Helen Fein for her comparative study of the U.S. war in Vietnam and the Soviet war in Afghanistan. (As we saw in Chapter 4, Fein concluded that the war in Vietnam was not genocidal but that the war in Afghanistan was.)

The Holocaust and Strategic Bombing: Differences and Similarities

In this subsection, we first recapitulate a number of important differences and similarities between the Holocaust and strategic bombing that were identified in

*Fein's wording is rather peculiar. We know of no one who has *equated* strategic bombing with the Holocaust. As we discussed in the first chapter, the comparative approach we have utilized in this study involves identifying differences, as well as similarities, between cases or phenomena. For two cases of mass killing to fit within the concept of "genocide," or "genocidal," they need not be equal, but they would need to have crucial features in common.

†The consensus on the Holocaust as an extreme example of genocide unfortunately is not universal, as evidenced by the current prominence of scholars who deny that there was a Holocaust and by public opinion polls indicating that as many as one in five Americans express doubt that it actually occurred. For an excellent discussion of Holocaust deniers, see Deborah Lipstadt, *Denying the Holocaust: The Growing Assault on Truth and Memory*, New York, Free Press, 1993. On the Roper poll results, see Anonymous, "1 out of 5 in New Survey Express Some Doubt About the Holocaust," *New York Times*, April 20, 1993, p. A8.

the first chapter. Then we discuss several other differences and similarities that emerged from our comparative analysis. In the next subsection, we evaluate whether strategic bombing met Fein's criteria for designating actions as genocide. In the third and final subsection, we state our answer to the question, Was strategic bombing genocidal?

One very important difference between the two cases concerns the degree of risk to which the implementers were exposed. As noted in Chapter 1, the SS and auxiliary troops that staffed the Einsatzgruppen and the death camps incurred very little personal risk. They were heavily armed, and their victims, with very few exceptions, were completely defenseless. Compared with service on either the eastern or western fronts, where soldiers engaged in armed combat with the enemy, the death camps were an oasis of security for the Nazis stationed at them. In strong contrast, the Allied bomber crews were frequently at extreme personal risk due to German and Japanese antiaircraft artillery and planes. As also noted in Chapter 1, the casualty rates for British and American heavy-bomber crews were extremely high. Even the very process of taking off and flying complex machines loaded with tons of incendiary and high-explosive bombs was inherently risky. Accidents on takeoff, in flight, and on landing claimed hundreds of Allied lives.

A second difference involves the goal of the mass killing. Thus, in the case of bombing, mass killing is widely seen as a means to an end, that is, surrender, rather than an end in itself, as many regard the Nazi attempt to exterminate the Jews of Europe. (Although we largely agree with this assessment, we suggest that closer analysis may narrow the difference somewhat. We return to this point further on).

A third difference identified at the outset of this study concerned the nature of the victims. We noted that the Jews and other victims of Nazi genocide were almost entirely unarmed civilian members of minority groups who had done nothing to threaten German national interests and warrant reprisals, much less being slaughtered. In contrast, the majority of the victims of Allied strategic bombing were civilian citizens of enemy nations that had committed acts of aggression against Great Britian and the United States. Unlike the Jews, the German and Japanese citizens had heavily armed protectors manning antiaircraft and other defenses and governmentally organized rescue and relief operations designed to reduce their risk and suffering as much as possible.

Three important similarities between the Holocaust and strategic bombing were also identified in the first chapter. Perhaps the most important for the purposes of this study is the fact that both projects entailed the slaughter of masses of helpless, innocent civilians. Few, if any, would contest the assertion that the victims of the Holocaust were innocent and, in virtually all cases, helpless. Many were killed abruptly and by complete surprise, with no chance to escape or resist. Others were forced into ghettos where extended periods of hunger and disease weakened them physically and mentally prior to their being rounded up and transported to death camps. Some who managed to escape found themselves in a harsh environment of anti-Semitism and were at constant risk of being turned over to authorities by local people motivated by fear, greed, or hatred. The victims of strategic bombing were not nearly as defenseless as were the victims of the Holocaust, but as we noted in Chapter 8, even flak, fighter planes, and fire departments were unable to spare tens of thousands of inhabitants of cities like Hamburg, Dresden, and Tokyo from airborne destruction. A family cowering in its basement in a German or Japanese city under massive incendiary attack was no more able to escape or defend itself than its counterpart confined in a Polish ghetto. By the same token, just as most of the victims of the Holocaust were killed indiscriminantly because they were members of a group deemed undesirable or threatening to the Nazis rather than for what they had done or not done as individuals, so were many of the victims of strategic bombing. Large numbers of these victims were disabled or elderly; many were women and children—all killed anonymously and indiscriminantly simply because they happened to live in areas targeted for annihilation.

Two other similarities were noted in Chapter 1. First, both killing projects were authorized by the highest national leaders, rationalized as being in the service of vital national interests, and implemented by duly authorized agents of their respective governments. Second, neither project would have been possible without the contributions of psychologically normal individuals, many of whom were highly educated, scientifically accomplished, and culturally refined.

These points do not exhaust relevant differences and similarities between the Holocaust and strategic bombing. Another important difference involves the nature of the political systems of the nations involved. Germany, of course, was a totalitarian nation with a dictatorial leader, a secret-police network dedicated to ruthlessly suppressing any dissent within the Reich, and a Ministry of Propaganda that tightly controlled the information to which Germans and others under German domination were exposed. Great Britain, the United States, and other nations that contributed to the strategic-bombing campaigns were, in contrast to Nazi Germany, democracies with freely elected leaders, civil liberties, and a free press. It is important to note, however, that under the pressures of total war, those elected leaders and their delegates made important decisions in secret, many civil liberties were curtailed, and censorship and propaganda permeated the media.[11]

Also, the postwar fate of key policymakers in the Holocaust differed greatly from that of comparable figures in the British and American bombing campaigns. The Nazis were appropriately vilified after the war by world opinion, and several dozen of their leaders were brought to trial as perpetrators of terrible war crimes and crimes against humanity. In contrast, the men responsible for strategic bombing, particularly in the United States, fared much better. The postwar fate of Curtis LeMay, under whose leadership much of the destruction of Japan had taken place, provides a good example. LeMay went from World War II to become chief of staff of the United States Air Force and an early commander in chief of the Strategic Air Command, the branch of the U.S. Air Force equipped with nuclear weapons.*

Rather than expressing doubt or shame over the atomic bombings, President Harry Truman proudly proclaimed to a group of sailors shortly after Hiroshima and Nagasaki had been destroyed, "This is the greatest thing in history."[12] In contrast to many ordinary Germans who felt a profound sense of shame for what their nation had done to so many millions of innocent people, the American public expressed little shame for what the United States had done when it dropped the atomic bombs on Japan. At the time of the bombings, according to historian Paul Boyer, the American public was "overwhelmingly favorable" in its response to news of the Hiroshima attack. Indeed, Boyer has pointed out that public opinion polls at the time indicated that 85 percent of respondents approved of the atomic attacks.[13]†

Other similarities between the Holocaust and strategic bombing include the incremental nature of each project; the fact, shown in Chapters 9 and 10, that both were facilitated by similar psychological, organizational, and scientific-technological processes; and the fact that both represented gross violations of international law. Each of these points is addressed in turn.

As was discussed in Chapter 7, the Holocaust began not as an outright extermination program but instead as a campaign of random violence, social and economic harassment, and legal discrimination designed to coerce the Jews into emigrating from the German Reich. Only after this policy proved unfeasible, and only after ad hoc, trial and error development of mass-killing techniques had occurred, did the goal evolve to become genocide. Chapter 8 showed that both the United States and Great Britain began the war with a firm commitment to avoid bombing population centers and killing civilians but that during the war this resolve progressively eroded until the point was reached where both nations carefully designed their aerial attacks to inflict maximal damage on enemy cities and their inhabitants.

Our comparative analysis also disclosed that the six facilitating factors identified in Chapter 5 operated in both cases of mass killing, though the specific manifestations and the relative contributions varied in each case. Thus, in the Holo-

*Ironically, in 1964 LeMay was awarded the highest honor that a foreigner can receive from the Japanese government—the First Class Order of the Grand Cordon of the Rising Sun. Unfortunately, the Japanese writer who mentioned this in his book did not explain the rationale behind the award. (See Hoito Edoin, *The Night Tokyo Burned*, New York, St. Martin's Press, 1987, p. 238.)

†The passage of time has not appreciably weakened the approval, as shown by a poll conducted in late 1991 indicating that only 16 percent of Americans felt that their government should make an apology to Japan for the bombings. (Steven Weisman, "Japanese Think They Owe Apology and Are Owed One on War, Poll Shows," *New York Times*, December 8, 1991, Section A, p. 26.)

caust, ideological dehumanization of victims played a crucial role in contributing to the willingness and ability of the German nation to engage in the mass killing of Jews. The official government ideology declared the Jews to be members of an inferior race to whom customary moral and empathic concerns did not apply. In the American bombing campaign, ideological dehumanization of the Asiatic Japanese was far more extensive than of the European Germans, and a number of scholars have argued that this difference played an important, though not exclusive, role in the willingness to engage in area incendiary bombing in Japan—but not in Germany, as was discussed in Chapter 9.

The healing-killing paradox was found to play an important role in the Holocaust in a number of ways. At the political level, the official ideology identified the Jews as mortal threats to the "Aryan" Germans and declared the elimination of the Jews to be an important contribution to the vitality of the Reich. This political legitimation of the Final Solution was incorporated into the mentalities of the Nazi perpetrators and their accomplices, thus making it psychologically easier to engage in behavior that their Christian heritage and cultural tradition regarded as atrocious.

The importance of the healing-killing paradox in facilitating the Holocaust calls into question the conventional notion, alluded to previously in the discussion of differences between the Holocaust and strategic bombing, that unlike the mass-bombing campaigns, in which slaughter was a means to the end of unconditional surrender that would end the war, the Nazi killing was purely and simply an end in itself. A closer examination suggests that for some Nazis and their accomplices, exterminating Jews was regarded as being in the service of a greater good, for example, eliminating the risk of race pollution; destroying the threat of communism, which the Jews were alleged to promote; or reducing the danger of partisan resistance (which, as noted in Chapter 7, was a rationale for involving the Wehrmacht in anti-Jewish actions in Russia). In all of these cases, killing functioned as a means to an end. To say that killing Jews was a means to an end, however, does not presume that the end was valid or justified, but it does remind us that relatively few of the perpetrators and accomplices of the Holocaust were sadists who killed simply for the sake of killing and that the majority were "ordinary" men and women who regarded themselves as "good" people doing the necessary "dirty work" in the service of their nation.[14]

With respect to strategic bombing, the healing-killing paradox was found to operate among three groups of people who contributed to the mass-bombing campaigns: prewar airpower theorists, wartime-bombing policymakers, and scientists involved with the atomic bomb project. It did so by making a difficult, controversial decision—the slaughter of enemy civilians—more emotionally and morally palatable.

Both organizational facilitating factors examined in this study—bureaucratic compartmentalization and organizational loyalty—played important roles in the

Holocaust. In the Holocaust, many so-called desk murderers were needed to locate, collect, and transport the millions of victims to the hidden sites where the actual killing took place. Compartmentalization enabled them to make their contributions by muting their awareness of the end results of their labors. Likewise, loyalty to organizations with interests in the killing project was also found to play a role in key individuals such as Adolf Eichmann, as well as in many others whose career advancement was promoted by their service to the Final Solution.

Evidence of both bureaucratic compartmentalization of knowledge and tasks and organizational loyalty was also found in the mass-bombing campaigns. With respect to the former factor, top-level decisionmakers were found to be organizationally and geographically removed from the results of their decisions, and crew members were at times deliberately misled regarding the actual nature of their targets. With respect to the latter factor, an intense interservice rivalry between the air forces and the older branches of the military was noted in both the British and the American cases. The autobiographies of Harris and LeMay are replete with statements of their need to prove the unique worth of their service against the competing claims of rivals in the army and navy. In both the British and the American cases, mass bombing during the war was seen by the airmen as a means by which the postwar preeminence of their service might be ensured. Not only did this yearning for organizational advancement facilitate the dismissal or distortion of moral concerns but it also led the air leaders of both nations to engage in deliberate deceit about the true nature of the bombing war.

In both the Holocaust and strategic bombing, scientific rationalization helped legitimate the adoption of policies that entailed mass killing. Thus, members of several academic disciplines in Nazi Germany, including physics and medicine, provided allegedly scientific justification for racist anti-Jewish measures. Scientific rationalization also played an important role in promoting the adoption of mass bombing. Policymakers tended to ignore scientific findings with which they disagreed and to uncritically accept those that supported their preferences. Again, science was manipulated for the purpose of rationalizing a controversial policy. Finally, technical distancing eased the psychological burdens on both Nazi killers and bomber crews both by imposing physical distance between killer and victim and by rendering the victims anonymous.

A final, and crucial, similarity to be discussed here is that both the Holocaust and strategic bombing violated international law. Specifically, both projects featured actions that constituted war crimes (which include "murder, ill-treatment or deportation to slave labor or for any other purpose of civilian population of or in occupied territory") and crimes against humanity (which include "murder, extermination, enslavement, deportation and other inhumane acts committed against any civilian population, before or during the war").[15]*

*Both war crimes and crimes against humanity also constitute violations of what Michael Walzer has called "the war convention," that is, "the set of articulated norms, customs, professional codes, legal precepts, religious and philosophical principles, and reciprocal arrangements that shape our judge-

That the Holocaust violated such laws is well known and was extensively and indisputably documented during the Nuremberg trials. However, our allegation that the Allies did so in their mass bombardment of German and Japanese cities, which appear on face value to clearly fit within the definitions given previously, needs further discussion. Why, it might be asked, was not strategic bombing included among the offenses for which German leaders were charged at Nuremberg? After all, as we have seen in Chapter 8, the Germans killed thousands of civilians with their bombardment of Coventry, Rotterdam, and London and with their indiscriminate attacks with V-1 buzz bombs and V-2 ballistic missiles. Nor was strategic bombing cited at the International Military Tribunal–Far East, in which Japanese military and political leaders were charged with war crimes and crimes against humanity—despite the fact, as shown in Chapter 6, that the Japanese employed aerial bombardment against crowded cities in their aggressions against China.

The reason for such apparent illogic is given quite bluntly by Telford Taylor, who served as an American prosecutor at the first trial in Nuremberg and then as chief prosecutor at the 12 subsequent war-crimes trials. In a book on the relevance of the Nuremberg principles to the U.S. war in Vietnam, Taylor wrote that "aerial bombardment had been used so extensively and ruthlessly on the Allies as well as the Axis side that neither at Nuremberg nor at Tokyo was the issue made a part of the trials."[16] More recently, in his memoirs of the trials, Taylor wrote that the German bombing "paled by comparison" to that conducted by Great Britain and the United States against Germany and Japan.[17] In other words, the victorious Allies chose not to focus on the criminal nature of aerial bombardment of civilians because to have done so would have probably aided the attorneys for the German and Japanese defendants, to say nothing of directing attention to the fact that they, themselves, had wrought vastly greater aerial carnage than their fascist enemies.

Before we leave this issue, it is important to note that some authorities have acknowledged the atrocious and criminal nature of strategic bombing, particularly by means of atomic bombs. For example, President Truman's wartime chief of staff, Admiral William Leahy, wrote in his postwar memoirs: "In being the first to use it [the atomic bomb], we had adopted an ethical standard common to the barbarians of the Dark Ages."[18] Similarily, in the postwar Tokyo war-crimes trial, in which the United States and ten other nations found Japanese political and military leaders guilty of war crimes and crimes against humanity, one of the justices, in a dissenting opinion, called the dropping of the atomic bombs "the only near approach to the directives ... of the Nazi leaders during the second world war."[19] Michael Walzer, in his widely cited book on ethics and warfare, asserted that had

---

ments of military conduct." An important tenet of the war convention, and of the religious tradition of "just war," is the principle of "noncombatant immunity"; in other words, adversaries must make all possible efforts to discriminate between soldiers and civilians and to spare the latter from direct attack (Michael Walzer, *Just and Unjust Wars: A Moral Argument with Historical Illustrations*, New York, Basic Books, 1977, p. 44).

the Japanese destroyed an American city with an atomic bomb, "the action would clearly have been a crime, one more for Truman's list" in the war-crimes trials.[20] Finally, Helen Fein, in a discussion of why she does not accept the label of "genocide" for the atomic bombings, acknowledges that on the basis of her reading of relevant international law, she does view them as constituting a war crime.[21]

Did Strategic Bombing Meet the Criteria for Genocide?

Our second approach to answering the question of whether strategic bombing was genocidal is to apply the criteria derived by Fein in order to discriminate between the crime of genocide and other international crimes to the case of strategic bombing. In Chapter 4, we summarized Fein's comparative analysis of the U.S. war in Vietnam and the Soviet war in Afghanistan, in which she used those criteria to assess allegations that both wars constituted genocides. Let us now restate her criteria and apply them to strategic bombing.

On the basis of the United Nations Genocide Convention, Fein identified the following five criteria that spell out "necessary and sufficient conditions to impute genocide."[22] To quote from her paper:

1. There is a sustained attack, or continuity of attacks, by the perpetrator to physically destroy group members.
2. The perpetrator is a collective or organized actor or a commander of organized actors.
3. Victims are selected because they are members of a collectivity.
4. The victims are defenseless or are killed regardless of whether they surrendered or resisted.
5. The destruction of group members is undertaken with intent to kill and murder is sanctioned by the perpetrators.[23]

With respect to the first criterion, there can be little doubt that the strategic-bombing campaigns, particularly during their incendiary phases, constituted a series of sustained, continuous attacks that physically destroyed hundreds of thousands of members of the German and Japanese national groups. It has been estimated that "over 500,000 German civilians lost their lives to Allied bombing."[24] In Japan, American bombers "burned out 180 square miles of sixty-seven cities, killed more than 300,000 people, and wounded another 400,000."[25]* The atomic bombs, as was noted in Chapter 1, had the additional dimension of killing people years after their direct exposure, due in large part to the delayed effects of radiation. Psychiatrist Robert Jay Lifton, who conducted the first in-depth interview study of Hiroshima survivors, observed that the bomb evoked for them "a special terror, *an image of a weapon which not only instantly kills and destroys on a*

*Though Conrad Crane does not say so explicity, presumably this figure excludes the victims of the atomic bombs.

colossal scale but also leaves behind in the bodies of those exposed to it deadly influences which may emerge at any time and strike down their victims" (emphasis in original).[26] Thus, the initial death toll from the atomic bombing of Nagasaki was approximately 70,000; within five years an additional 70,000 had died, many, no doubt, due to radiation.[27]

It should be noted that Fein's criterion does not require that the entire group be destroyed or that there be specific intent to destroy it in entirety. Indeed, the Genocide Convention specifically included intent to destroy designated groups "in whole *or in part*" under its jurisdiction (emphasis added).[28] Thus, genocide scholar Uriel Tal has written, "According to the Genocide Convention an act of annihilation is termed genocide even if it is not directed at or carried out on an entire group; the concept of genocide can apply also to the intention of exterminating parts of a group, because of their membership in it."[29]

Fein's second criterion specifies that the prepetrator be "a collective or organized actor or a commander of organized actors." Like the Holocaust and most other cases of genocide in the modern era, the bombing raids were authorized by national governments and carried out by officials of the governments—in other words, by "collective," "organized" actors. The fact that the killing policies, in both cases, were legitimated at the highest levels of government helped secure the cooperation of the large numbers of ordinary citizens and soldiers who were needed to actually implement them.

Her third criterion stipulates that the "victims are selected because they were members of a collectivity." Although, as noted in Chapter 4, the Genocide Convention excludes political groups from among those, such as racial and ethnic groups, under its protection, many scholars have criticized this provision and in their own definitions have included political groups. It is noteworthy that Fein, who is well known for her commitment to very careful use of the term "genocide," does not limit the coverage of this criterion only to the groups originally specified in the Genocide Convention. Moreover, the Genocide Convention does, according to some scholars, permit some latitude in interpretation in its listing of protected groups by stating that "genocide means any of the following acts committed with intent to destroy, in whole or in part, a national, ethnical, racial or religious group, *as such*" emphasis added).[30] Regarding this rather ambiguous phrase, Leo Kuper has written, "I prefer to interpret the phrase to mean 'using the national or racial origin, or religious belief, as the criterion for selecting the individuals killed.'"[31]

The collectivity to which the victims of bombing belonged was an enemy nation rather than a religious or racial group, as was the case with the majority of victims of Nazi genocide. As members of a national group, the vast majority of Germans and Japanese who died in the incendiary and atomic attacks were targeted in an anonymous, impersonal manner. They were killed not because of what they had done as individuals but simply because of their national origin and the fact that they lived and worked in target zones. By its very nature, mass bombing, particularly by incendiary and atomic bombs, is indiscriminate. As R. J. Rummel, who in Chapter 4 was cited as a scholar who shifted from an initial conviction that genocide and war are mutually exclusive categories to the belief that certain kinds of mass killing during war do constitute a form of genocidal violence, has written, "Deliberately targeting civilians with explosive and incendiary bombs simply because they happen to be under the command and control of an enemy Power is no better than lining them up and machine gunning them, a clear atrocity."[32]

The fourth criterion requires that the victims are either defenseless "or are killed regardless of whether they surrendered or resisted." Clearly, the vast majority of the civilian victims of strategic bombing were personally defenseless. It is true that efforts were made by their governments to provide protection in the form of active defenses and bomb shelters, but the high death tolls attest to the inadequacy of those defenses. Indeed, as noted in Chapter 8, the Allies deliberately tried to degrade rescue and recovery efforts in a variety of ways, including the use of delayed-action bombs. Moreover, in certain bombing attacks, such as the combined British and American attack against Dresden and the American atomic bombings of Japan, enemy defenses were very inadequate. The individual civilian cowering in a shelter was completely powerless. Most civilian victims, furthermore, were indeed "killed regardless of whether they surrendered or resisted." Their national leaders did have the capacity to surrender and thereby end the bombing, but the individual citizens of the totalitarian states had virtually no influence over their leaders. Nor could they, as individuals, surrender to or resist their killers, who attacked from high in the air.

Fein's final criterion requires that the destruction was done "with intent to kill" and that the killing was "sanctioned by the perpetrators." As noted in Chapter 4, the issue of intent is complex and problematic. As Leo Kuper has observed, the Genocide Convention did not specify objective criteria for determining intent, and the resulting ambiguity has created "a ready basis for the denial of guilt."[33] However, Fein has provided valuable guidance in her discussion of the intent issue, where she emphasizes that the essence of intent is "evidence of repetition of destruction either in design or as a foreseeable outcome."[34]

We suggest that strategic bombing—particularly the incendiary bombing of large areas of cities crowded with defenseless civilians—manifested a clear intent to destroy masses of human beings and, by doing so, demoralize the survivors into reducing their contributions to the war effort and perhaps even pressing their leaders to surrender. Euphemistic expressions such as "dehousing" notwithstanding, the fire raids were carefully planned to take advantage of weather conditions, highly flammable buildings, and calculated disruption of rescue efforts to wreak maximal damage by deliberately creating firestorms in densely populated residential and industrial areas of cities. To use Fein's words, the firebombing "manifested repetition of destrucion" as a "foreseeable outcome" designed to produce "foreseeable results," namely, vast areas of densely populated cities turned into ash. After each raid, the results were carefully photographed and the areas that had been incinerated marked on maps to help plan future raids to fill in the gaps.*

The second component of this criterion, that the "murder" must be "sanctioned by the perpetrators," is also met by the strategic-bombing campaigns. For this criterion to be met, the destruction must not be an aberration or an exception but an integral element of official policy. Nor must the actual implementers of the policy be punished for their roles. In her comparative analysis of the U.S. war in Vietnam and the Soviet war in Afghanistan, Fein found the fact that American soldiers who participated in the My Lai massacre were brought to trial and Soviet perpetrators of massacres were not to be an important factor in her conclusion that the U.S. war was not genocidal but the Soviet war was.[35] As noted both in Chapter 8 and previously in this chapter, the decisions to engage in area bombing were made by legitimate authorities and approved by government leaders in both the United States and Greata Britain, which is to say they were "sanctioned" at high levels. The military officers and enlisted men in the European and Pacific theaters who did the operational planning for the incendiary attacks on cities and who serviced and flew the planes were in no way punished during or after the war for their contributions. On the contrary, many, particularly on the American side, were promoted into higher rank and greater responsibility in the postwar U.S. Air Force.

Our Answer to the Question

Having reviewed important differences and similarities between the Holocaust, as a quintessential example of genocide, and strategic bombing, we now have reached the point where we must state our answer to the question, Was strategic bombing genocidal? Put bluntly, our answer is yes, it was. Before discussing our rationale for reaching that answer, however, we would like to address several points that bear upon the question itself.

A first point is why the question is even worth asking. Why do we regard it as an important question? We realize that even posing it will offend many people who believe in the moral rightness of the World War II bombing campaigns, particularly those veterans who still carry scars, both physical and mental, and who cher-

*In his valuable critique of the British bombing of German cities, Stephen Garrett notes that apologists for the area offensive often defend it by citing the "principle of double effect," which states, in essence, that under certain circumstances it is morally acceptable to violate the war convention and deliberately attack noncombatants. One of the criteria for the principle of double effect to apply is that the destruction of civilians must be a reluctantly tolerated side effect rather than a deliberate goal, that is, must be a means to an end. Garrett concludes that "the principle of double effect hardly can be offered as a defense of the area offensive simply because the evil side-effect in this case (the random killing of noncombatants) was not an unintended or regrettable consequence of a legitimate military action but was instead one of the main points of the strategy" (Stephen Garrett, *Ethics and Airpower in World War II*, New York, St. Martin's Press, 1993, p. 21). The same could be said for the U.S. area offensive against Japan.

ish the memories of compatriots who gave their lives to a cause in which they deeply believed. And as we also noted in Chapter 1, even suggesting that another case of mass killing may have something in common with the Holocaust will offend those who believe that the Holocaust was a singular, sui generis event in history. We are acutely aware that we ask this question and give our answer from the sheltered ivory tower of academia, looking back with hindsight on decisions and events made decades ago under conditions of threat and uncertainty.

Possible reasons for investigating whether the term "genocide" is applicable to strategic bombing, or any other case of mass killing, for that matter, include a desire to lay a basis for legal proceedings against the perpetrators or to make a case that the surviving victims deserve some form of compensation or reparation. These, however, are not our reasons.*

We feel the question is worth asking for a number of other reasons. The first and most fundamental reason is simply that governmental mass killing has been and continues to be a threat to the survival of millions of human beings. Yet our understanding of this threat is still rudimentary, and our efforts—as individual scholars, as citizens of powerful nations, and as a world community—to contain, prevent, and resist it are grossly inadequate. In view of the magnitude of the problem and the inadequacy of our understanding of it, we feel strongly that a wide spectrum of inquiries and analyses, no matter how iconoclastic or provocative, is not only justifed but urgently needed. The fact, as documented in the following chapter, that some of the leading nations of the world continue to base their national security on what has appropriately been described as a policy of retaliatory genocide with nuclear weapons and that other dangerous trends portend future outbreaks of genocidal killing, makes creative study of collective violence even more necessary.[36] Our primary reason and goal, in short, is to learn from the past in order to understand and prevent genocidal killing in the future.

Another reason for posing the question of whether strategic bombing was genocidal is that the question bears directly on the ongoing controversy over the relationship between genocide and war, on both the conceptual and operational levels. A positive answer would lend support to those, such as Leo Kuper, who have argued that strategic bombing, and the atomic bombings in particular, were genocidal. It would also lend support to the arguments that war and genocide are not necessarily mutually exclusive, that the line between war and genocide may be narrow and blurred, and that warfare itself can be genocidal. A related implication of a positive finding is that the popular conception of genocide, which for a number of reasons is closely associated with the specific case of the Holocaust, might be broadened to encompass a wider range of events, thereby raising awareness of the magnitude and seriousness of the problem of genocidal killing. A finding that there were no important parallels and commonalities between the Holocaust and the atomic bombings—or that differences between them were more

*The authors thank Daniel Ellsberg for suggesting these points in a personal communication.

significant than any similarities—would reinforce the alternative viewpoint, that war and genocide are indeed distinct, discrete, separate phenomena.

There are risks involved in answering this question. We have already mentioned the probability of offending many people by staining the memory of the courageous aircrews and by insulting the feelings of Holocaust survivors and scholars. Another risk, and one that we have not taken lightly, is that the term "genocide" itself may become weakened by broadening its scope to include additional cases of deliberate mass killing. As Helen Fein has written, "We study, work, and act in a public arena in which the term 'genocide' has been so debased by semantic stretch that its use stirs suspicion."[37] And we agree with Hugo Adam Bedau that "genocide is not just another crime, not even another 'war crime' or 'crime against humanity.' For many it is the ultimate crime."[38] However, it is necessary to acknowledge and understand the extent to which practices of war, both in the past and potentially in the future, fit within what Charny has called "the universe of genocide."[39]

Having made these points, we turn now to our rationale for claiming that the strategic-bombing campaigns deserve to be labeled "genocidal." Our first reason is that, as we sifted through the welter of definitions and controveries over just what genocide is, we reached the conclusion that its essence lies in the deliberate, calculated slaughter of masses of defenseless, innocent human beings on the basis of their membership in a group rather than because of what they as individuals did or did not do. As Fein has correctly pointed out, the motives for genocidal killing vary widely from case to case, as do the methods of killing and the proportion of the victim group that is extirpated. But one thing that all cases of genocide and genocidal killing have in common is that large numbers of people are destroyed in a purposeful manner. We would add that genocide is usually a crime committed by and for governments and that the killing can be either direct and immediate, as was the case with gas chambers and mass shooting, or indirect and delayed, as is the case with socially created famine. With these features in mind, and in view of the realities of strategic bombing—particularly incendiary and atomic bombing—we suggest that strategic bombing was genocidal.

Our second reason for reaching this decision is that strategic bombing, in our opinion, clearly fits the criteria specified by Fein for discriminating between war crimes and the crime of genocide. In other words, the same criteria that led her to conclude that the U.S. war in Vietnam was not genocidal and that the Soviet war in Afghanistan was genocidal have led us to conclude that Allied strategic bombing was genocidal.

In closing this chapter, we make the following points. If, in fact, strategic bombing warrants being labeled "genocidal," then thinking about genocide, both by the general public and the scholarly community, needs to be expanded to include a wider range of cases than many have been willing to consider. Such expanded thinking must contend with the premise that the capacity for genocidal killing is not limited to obvious monsters like Joseph Stalin, Adolf Hitler, Idi Amin, and Pol

Pot but is widely shared. We must also face the fact that religious conviction, advanced education, and scientific expertise do not automatically confer immunity from the capacity to become implicated in a genocidal project; nor does the fact that one is a loving spouse and parent. Psychologically normal, "good" people can and have participated in demonic projects. Not only totalitarian regimes but also democracies have been willing to directly engage in genocidal killing, to support client states that engage in it, and to make the preparations for it.

Chapter 12

Changing the Future

> **Given the temptation of despair, our need can be simply stated: We must confront the image that haunts us, making use of whatever models we can locate. Only then can we imagine the changes in consciousness that must accompany (if not precede) changes in public policy on behalf of a human future. We must look into the abyss in order to see beyond it.**
>
> —*Robert Jay Lifton (1986)*[1]

In this concluding chapter, we examine an important legacy of strategic bombing and then consider prospects for the future, in terms of both the probability of more outbreaks of genocidal killing and the potential to resist and prevent such outbreaks.

In the first section, we examine the nuclear arms race between the United States and the Soviet Union during the Cold War as an important legacy of World War II in general, and of strategic bombing in particular. We make three main points about the preparations for nuclear war. First, we identify significant continuities between strategic bombing and early postwar nuclear weapons policies, particularly in the United States, which was the first nation to possess and use nuclear weapons. Second, we assert that had the preparations for nuclear war by both superpowers been transformed into actual nuclear conflict, the result would have been genocidal. Put differently, and more strongly, the Cold War nuclear national security policies of the United States and the Soviet Union entailed the willingness to perpetrate genocide.* Our third point concerning the nuclear threat is that the same facilitating factors found to operate in the Holocaust and strategic bombing also operated in the preparations for nuclear war.

In the second section, we identify and very briefly survey three dangerous trends in the post–Cold War world that portend future outbreaks of genocidal violence. First, we discuss recent work on the synergistically interacting impacts of

*The same point can be made about the other nations that relied upon the possession and threatened use of nuclear weapons during the Cold War (and that continue to do so). They include Great Britain, France, China, and Israel. On proliferation, see, for example, John M. Deutch, "The New Nuclear Threat," *Foreign Affairs*, Fall 1992, pp. 120–134. See also Martin van Crevald, *Nuclear Proliferation and the Future of Conflict*, New York, Free Press, 1993.

The mushroom cloud from a British atomic bomb test in Australia in June 1956. This test was part of a British project to develop thermonuclear weapons. SOURCE: Crown Copyright.

persistent structural violence, overpopulation, environmental pollution, and resource depletion. Second, we note the rising tide of refugees in the contemporary world. Finally, we address the dangers posed by the spread of nuclear, chemical, and biological weapons of mass destruction.

In the third and final section we attempt to answer the question, posed at the beginning of the book, of what might be done in order to reduce the problem of genocidal killing. First, we review the work of several scholars who have proposed concrete actions for anticipating, preventing, and punishing genocide. Then we look back on the psychological, organizational, and scientific-technological factors that were found to facilitate genocide and total war in general—and the Holocaust, strategic bombing, and the preparations for nuclear war in particular—and make preliminary suggestions for resisting them. The book concludes with reflections on the role of education in preventing genocide.

The Preparations for Nuclear Omnicide

> **A vicious spiral has been created that gives the arms race a "mad momentum" of its own and drives it forward blindly.**
>
> —*Herbert York (1970)*[2]

No consideration of governmental mass killing in general, and genocide and modern war in particular, can be complete without reference to the preparations by a diverse group of nations for a war waged with nuclear weapons.* For more than 30 years, the United States and the Soviet Union held the world under the threat of nuclear annihilation with their policies of deterrence through the capacity for mutually assured destruction. As we suggest later in this chapter, even with the recent end of the Cold War and disintegration of the Soviet Union, the threat posed by nuclear weapons remains both real and substantial.

In the following discussion, we focus on the nuclear weapons policies of the United States and do so for several reasons. The first reason is that the United States was the initiator of the nuclear arms race and is therefore the logical starting point for understanding the genocidal nature of nuclear weapons. By engaging in strategic bombing of urban areas, first with incendiary bombs and then with the atomic bombs, the United States helped legitimate the premise that slaughtering civilians is an acceptable practice in war and that atomic weapons are acceptable tools for actual implementation of the slaughter. Until 1949, the United States was the only nation in the world that possessed nuclear weapons, and in the early years after World War II, our government decided to make them the foundation of its national security and defense policy. In later years, after the Soviet Union had acquired its own nuclear weapons capability, the United States continued to lead and set the pace for subsequent developments and escalations. As Herbert York, a distinguished nuclear physicist and defense policymaker, wrote in his 1970 book *Race to Oblivion: A Participant's View of the Arms Race,* "I have emphasized American actions partly because I shared responsibility for some of them, partly because I know the details involved in most of the rest and hence understand them far better that I do Russian actions, but most importantly because of a fact that many people sense but do not quite grasp: *In the vast majority of cases the initiative has been ours*" (emphasis added).[3]

A second reason for focusing on the United States is that information on the realm of U.S. nuclear weapons and policies is more readily obtained than is information on other nuclear-armed nations, particularly Russia.† Finally, as citizens of the United States, we feel a particular responsibility to examine the nuclear pol-

*In view of the unprecedented destructiveness of nuclear weapons, some scholars have questioned the appropriateness of the term "war" when used in connection with the word "nuclear." As an alternative to the misleading concept of "nuclear war," philosopher John Somerville has proposed the term "nuclear omnicide" (which he has derived from the Latin word *omni,* meaning "all," and the Greek word *cide,* meaning "to kill") to convey the probability that a war fought with nuclear weapons would constitute a categorically new dimension of mass killing. See John Somerville, "Nuclear 'War' Is Omnicide," in Michael Allen Fox and Leo Groarke, Editors, *Nuclear War: Philosophical Perspectives,* New York, Peter Lang, 1985, p. 4.

†One of the results of the end of the Cold War, fortunately, is much greater access to Soviet archives; the opportunites to learn about Soviet nuclear polices are greater now than ever before. A case in point is the recent disclosure that the Soviet Union, for many years, had a "doomsday" arrangement to launch massive numbers of its nuclear weapons under certain conditions. Bruce G. Blair, "Russia's Doomsday Machine," *New York Times,* Vol. 143, October 8, 1993, p. A23.

icies of our own nation from the perspective gained from our study of genocide and total war and of the Holocaust and strategic bombing.

Continuities Between Strategic Bombing and Nuclear Weapons Policy

For present purposes, we will discuss three ways in which postwar American nuclear weapons policy evolved directly from the policy and practice of strategic bombing. Before proceeding, however, we want to emphasize that this discussion does not purport to be either exhaustive or definitive. There may well be other continuities between the two policies. If so, we earnestly hope that other scholars will identify and examine them. Also, the evidence we have presented to document these continuities is meant to be suggestive rather than conclusive. We believe that the understanding of strategic bombing, both in its own right and as a form of genocidal killing in a "century of genocide," is still woefully inadequate for many otherwise "educated" people, including many who regard themselves as knowledgeable about military history. Therefore, more research—and education—on such issues as those we examine herein is needed.

The first continuity between wartime strategic bombing and postwar nuclear weapons policy was suggested by John Dower in his discussion of the racist imagery that permeated American attitudes toward the Japanese. As World War II drew to a close, and as the military alliance between the United States and the Soviet Union began to be undermined by American concerns about the dangers posed by Soviet (and Chinese) communism in Europe and Asia after the war, some of the dehumanizing, racist hatred that had been directed against the Japanese began to be transferred to the Soviets, who, according to one writer at the time, were also "Asiatic."[4] As that same writer, H. C. McGinnis, writing in *Catholic World,* warned,

> With Russia's expert mechanized forces spearheading an invasion of Europe and, according to current Red tactics, with stupendous concentrations of *Red artillery blasting holes in white defenses through which literally scores of millions of hate-infuriated colored warriors will pour* to wreak vengeance for the thousands of injustices heaped upon their people, Europe would probably become a veritable shambles. (emphasis added)[5]

In other words, Dower suggested that Americans, who had grown accustomed to identifying the Japanese in racial terms (in contrast, as shown in Chapter 9, to the attitude toward Germans), were susceptible to extending the same kind of thinking to Russians. As Dower wrote, "So, as World War Two built to its ferocious climax, the vision of a Yellow Peril and a Red Peril began, at least for some observers, to fuse in an absolutely overpowering way."[6]

Dower's suggestion is supported indirectly by the work of fellow historian Paul Boyer. In his valuable study of American thought and culture in the early postwar years, Boyer emphasized that his review of the popular literature of the time revealed that fears engendered by the atomic bombs helped to create "a time of cultural crisis," involving "a new and threatening reality of almost unfathomable proportions" to which "the dominant … response was confusion and disorientation."[7] As the Soviet Union, with its ideology of revolutionary communism, began to aggressively occupy eastern Europe and as Mao Tse-tung's communist cadres took over China, the world's most populous nation, in 1949, any fears that may have been harbored about either the Red or Yellow Peril were likely to be exacerbated. We saw in Chapter 9 that dehumanizing images of the Japanese may well have facilitated the American resort to incendiary bombing attacks against their crowded cities. If, after the war, Russians and Chinese were also widely perceived not only as political opponents and military threats but also as members of an alien, dangerous race, it is possible that such a dehumanizing perception may have reduced reluctance to contain whatever threat they allegedly posed with policies involving nuclear slaughter.

The extent to which racist anti-Russian and -Chinese thinking after the war was reinforced by the precedent of racist anti-Japanese thinking during the war and the possibility that such dehumanizing attitudes may have facilitated the American embrace of nuclear weapons to contain the communist threat are, in our opinion, still speculative but certainly worthy of further study.

A second and considerably less speculative continuity between strategic-bombing and nuclear war plans stems from the fact that key individuals and groups who played important roles in making and implementing policies on strategic bombing also played important roles in the early preparations for nuclear war. Space constraints allow us to examine, and briefly, only three of them, but we emphasize again that the present discussion can and needs to be extended by other scholars in order to more fully expose the process by which the United States and several other nations became willing to rely upon weapons of mass destruction as the cornerstone of national security.

The first group to be considered includes the scientists in the Manhattan Project. Needless to say, without the contributions of many of the world's leading physicists and other scientists and engineers, there never would have been an atomic bomb developed before the end of the war, and it is possible that the creation of such a weapon might have been postponed for a considerable period after the war. However, it is less widely appreciated that the Manhattan Project not only invented the first atomic bombs but also discovered the possibility of creating a vastly more powerful weapon, which came to be known as the "superbomb" and also as the hydrogen bomb.[8] Some of the Manhattan Project scientists, including J. Robert Oppenheimer, argued against developing such a weapon after the war; others, such as Edward Teller, lobbied aggressively and successfully for the opposite course.[9]

A second group that played important roles in both strategic bombing and the formulation of early nuclear war plans were economists, mathematicians, and other academics who had served during the war as operational analysts using quantitative skills to promote the Allied war effort, and then after the war as analysts and consultants called upon by the U.S. government to help integrate nuclear weapons into our defense plans as "rationally" as possible. Many served as employees of the Rand corporation, a think tank formed shortly after the war to conduct research for the U.S. Air Force.

According to Fred Kaplan, who has closely studied the evolution of nuclear strategy, during World War II, operational researchers (as they were known in Britain) and operational analysts (as they were known in the United States) "carefully examined data on the most recent military operations to determine the facts, elaborated theories to explain the facts, then used the theories to make predictions about operations of the future."[10] By doing so, they made many important contributions to the Allied victory in the war, including recommending bomb loads and targets, identifying the most effective formations for attacking bombers, and increasing the efficiency of efforts to seek and destroy German submarines.[11] According to Gregg Herken, another historian of nuclear strategy, operational research was also used during World War II to help "bring about the terrible firestorms that consumed cities in Germany and Japan."[12]

After the war, a number of operational analysts-researchers joined Rand, which, according to Kaplan, "had its origins in the military planning rooms of World War II."[13] Rand played a key role in making concrete decisions about what kinds and how many nuclear weapons the air force felt it needed in order to fulfill its mission of deterring war in the postwar period. According to Kaplan, the scientists at Rand were "rational analysts, and they would attempt to impose a rational order on something that many thought inherently irrational—nuclear war. They would invent a whole new language and vocabulary in their quest for rationality, and would thus condition an entire generation of political and military leaders to thinking about the bomb the way that the intellectual leaders at Rand thought about it."[14]

The third group that we will examine here is the Strategic Air Command (SAC), the branch of the U.S. Air Force that, in the first years after World War II, was the only military unit equipped with nuclear weapons. In the years following the war, SAC strove to retain its "ownership" of the bomb and, along with that ownership, its claim to the lion's share of the available defense spending. As Kaplan noted, "In 1946, the Strategic Air Command was created as guardian over the new weapon, and shortly thereafter the Air Force was made an independent service. In the early years of postwar demobilization, the Air Force was the only service of the armed forces to get practically as much money from the President and Congress as it wanted."[15]

Some of the key air force leaders who had been responsible for planning the strategic-bombing campaigns during the war, such as Curtis LeMay and others, continued their service to the nation after the war by serving in, and in LeMay's case, commanding, SAC. In essence, the U.S. plans to wage nuclear war between 1945 and 1961 were significantly influenced by men who had been responsible for formulating and implementing the policy of obliteration bombing of German and Japanese cities during World War II. SAC leaders felt that the atomic bombs could be used in essentially the same ways that high-explosive bombs and firebombs were used during the war. Although there were some differences among them regarding specifc targeting priorities, most favored nuclear attack against enemy cities, just as had been done with incendiary and atomic bombs during World War II.[16]

Not surprisingly, other offices in the nuclear-armed air force, staffed, like SAC, by many veterans from the strategic-bombing campaigns, also promoted a continuation of World War II targeting policies with postwar nuclear weapons. Writing of nuclear strategy in the late 1940s and early 1950s, Kaplan noted: "The Air Target Division, of which Target Programs was a part, was filled with military targeteers busily applying to the atomic age the principles that they had pursued in the strategic bombing campaigns of World War II. It was these officers who came up with such atomic targeting concepts as 'the Sunday punch' and 'killing a nation.'"[17]

By the early 1950s, according to David Alan Rosenberg, one of the leading scholars of U.S. operational nuclear war planning, SAC had effectively "seized" control of such planning.[18] An indication of just how powerful SAC actually was has been provided by William Arkin and Peter Pringle in their book *SIOP: The Secret U.S. Plan for Nuclear War.* SAC's power was embodied in General Curtis LeMay, who became its second commander in 1948. "SAC was," wrote Arkin and Pringle,

> supposed to submit the [atomic war] plans directly to the JCS [Joint Chiefs of Staff] for review and approval, although LeMay became so independent that from 1951 until 1955 the JCS never received a copy of the plans: LeMay considered the details of operational planning a closely guarded secret and simply refused to let anyone know what they were. He could have been ordered to produce them, of course, and eventually he was, but for six crucial years America's nuclear war planning was unregulated.[19]

Not only did SAC plan to carry out atomic attacks against enemy cities in retaliation for unspecified aggressive acts but it also seriously entertained the notion of using its atomic arsenal against the Soviet Union even before any overt aggression had occurred. According to Herken, "The topic of preventive war—meaning an unprovoked attack by the United States on the Soviet Union—had been discreetly discussed in some government and military circles since the advent of the atomic bomb."[20] LeMay's successor as commander of the Strategic Air Command, Thomas Power, wrote in his memoirs of that era that he thought it "evident that we may have to take military actions of various types which, with certain qualifications, might fall under the public's broad concept of 'preventive war.'"[21] Notwithstanding these and other suggestions favorable to the idea, Eisenhower formally rejected the notion of preventive war in fall 1954.

There was, however, as Herken has pointed out, a "nether region" between preventive war and preemptive attack.[22] Whereas preventive war referred to the use of U.S. atomic weapons against the Soviet Union in the absence of any provocation, simply as a means of preventing the enemy from ever acquiring the capacity for serious aggression with its own atomic weapons, preemption involved attacking the Soviet Union when it was thought to be in the process of preparing to attack the United States and before it could carry out such an attack.

Thus, the "nether region" between prevention and preemption left a good deal of room for American first use of nuclear weapons against the Soviet Union. Under the direction of leaders such as Curtis LeMay, SAC strove to exploit that room as far as possible. According to Herken, at a secret briefing in 1954, LeMay asserted that "the idea of striking second was 'not in keeping with United States history.' 'I want to make it clear that I am not advocating a preventive war,' LeMay explained at the briefing. But, he said, 'I believe that if the U.S. is pushed in the corner far enough we would not hesitate to strike first.'"[23] On another occasion, LeMay told Robert Sprague, who had been sent by Eisenhower to visit SAC headquarters in order to find out just how the secretive LeMay intended to use "his" nuclear weapons: "If I see that the Russians are amassing their planes for an attack, I'm going to knock the shit out of them before they take off the ground."[24]

The Genocidal Nature of Nuclear War

At the beginning of this chapter, we made the assertion that the plans to wage nuclear war were, and are, plans for genocidal killing. Had deterrence failed and had the deployed nuclear weapons been launched according to the plans for their use, the result would have been unequivocally genocidal. Indeed, we have suggested that the concept of genocide, as repulsive as it is and should be, is inadequate for conveying the scale of slaughter and the depth of evil that nuclear war would have wrought—and still could. In this section, we provide reasons and evidence for our assertion.

We have seen that there were strong continuities between the wartime policy of strategic bombing of cities and the early postwar plans to target nuclear weapons against enemy cities.* These plans entailed the willingness to inflict death and destruction on a scale that dwarfed Dresden, Tokyo, and Hiroshima and Nagasaki. And as the size of the American nuclear arsenal increased, so did the scale of megadeath that our planners were willing to cause.

According to Rosenberg, the first nuclear war plan, code-named Broiler, in 1947, called for dropping 34 atomic bombs on 24 cities.[25] By December 1948, Op-

*As Gregg Herken has pointed out, even though both the British and American postwar assessments of the strategic-bombing campaigns questioned the efficacy of striking population centers as opposed to specific industrial targets, "the postwar debate that should have arisen over the effects of strategic bombing was preempted by the atomic raids on Hiroshima and Nagasaki" (Greg Herken, *Counsels of War*, New York, Alfred A. Knopf, 1985, p. 76).

eration Trojan called for dropping 113 atomic bombs on 70 Soviet cities. Such an attack would have caused tens of millions of immediate deaths and many more delayed fatalities. U.S. war plans in the early 1950s were designed to leave the Soviet Union "nothing but a smoking, radiating ruin at the end of two hours."[26] Thus, the official war plan for 1955 would have obliterated 118 of the 134 major Soviet cities. According to official estimates, these attacks would have caused approximately 77 million prompt casualties, of which 60 million would have been deaths. Cities in China were also targeted, as were capital cities in nations allied with the Soviet Union and China.[27]* By 1961, the U.S. war plan—by then known as the Single Integrated Operation Plan, or SIOP—was officially expected to cause mass death on a scale beyond comprehension. According to Thomas Powers, "The [U.S.] Joint Chiefs of Staff officially estimated that the first SIOP would kill somewhere between 360 million and 425 million people under Communist control. The SIOP provided for no middle ground, no breathing space, no time to reconsider. When ordinary diplomacy came to an end, we were going to do our damndest to exterminate a fifth of the globe."[28]

In the context of such staggering projected death tolls, we would point out that our comparative study suggested several disturbing parallels between the Holocaust and nuclear war planning in general and between the Nazi SS and nuclear SAC in particular. Briefly, both emerged as very powerful organizations that were responsible for the national security. Second, both organizations, for various reasons, were willing to consider genocidal means (extermination of Jews in the case of the Nazis and atomic bombing of cities in the case of the United States) in order to fulfill their missions of safeguarding their nations' security. Third, these genocidal national security policies were made more feasible by the efforts of intellectuals who were hired to help rationalize, popularize, and implement the resort to mass killing. Fourth, both organizations operated in important ways behind a cloak of secrecy. Finally, both organizations were staffed primarily by psychologically normal, patriotic men and some women who felt that they were making vital contributions to the security of their nation.[29]

As the vastly more powerful hydrogen bombs began to be developed and integrated into the U.S. and Soviet arsenals, nuclear war plans entailed even greater levels of death and destruction. The destructive power of the hydrogen bomb was as revolutionary in comparison with the atomic bomb as was the latter relative to conventional weaponry. Even Robert Oppenheimer, who had served as director of the wartime Manhattan Project to develop the first atomic bombs, resisted efforts to develop the hydrogen bomb. A key advisory committee, which he chaired, emphasized that the new weapon would be "in a totally different category from an atomic bomb" with "no inherent limit in the destructive power that may be at-

*From our perspective, it is imperative to emphasize that millions of completely innocent people who happened to live in neutral nations in the paths of radioactive fallout would have been slaughtered had such a plan been put into operation.

tained." Its report even asserted that such a bomb "might become a weapon of genocide."[30]

Although both superpowers justified their accumulating stockpiles of hydrogen bombs as being necessary to deter each from attacking the other, the danger of their actual use was never absent. Thus, in 1962, when the United States discovered that the Soviet Union had managed to sneak a number of intermediate-range nuclear-armed missiles into Cuba, the so-called Cuban missile crisis brought the world to the brink of actual nuclear war, a war that could have caused hundreds of millions of deaths. During the 13 days of the crisis, President Kennedy and his advisers considered a range of options to compel the Soviets to remove the missiles. The options ranged from behind-the-scenes diplomatic negotiations to a naval blockade around Cuba to an air strike against the missile base followed by an invasion of the island. The pressure on Kennedy and his advisers was intense. As one of them later wrote: "Each one of us was being asked to make a recommendation which would affect the future of all mankind, a recommendation which, if wrong and if accepted, could mean the destruction of the human race."[31] Even though the vote among Kennedy's top advisers was nine to seven for the air strike and invasion, Kennedy chose the blockade instead. Much to everyone's relief, shortly after the blockade had commenced, the Soviets agreed to remove the missiles, bringing the crisis to a close.

How great was the risk of nuclear war during the 13 days of the Cuban missile crisis? There is, of course, no way to know for certain; President Kennedy is reported to have thought at the time that the odds of nuclear war were as great as one in three.[32] Nearly 30 years later, in 1992, Robert McNamara, one of Kennedy's top advisers during the crisis, stated that "had a U.S. invasion been carried out, if the missiles had not been pulled out, *there was a 99 percent probability that nuclear war would have been initiated*" (emphasis added).[33] However great the danger, the fact remains that the leaders of the United States were willing to consider nuclear omnicide as a real option for resolving a political-military crisis. They—and their Soviet counterparts—were, as Lifton and Markusen have argued, "willing to take risks that could result in crossing the threshold into genocide or provoking the adversary to do the crossing."[34]

The Cuban missile crisis was neither the first nor the last time the United States threatened to use its nuclear weapons. Former nuclear war planner Daniel Ellsberg has pointed out that since Hiroshima and Nagasaki, "every president from Truman to Reagan, with the possible exception of Ford, has felt compelled to consider or direct serious preparations for possible imminent U.S. initiation of tactical or strategic nuclear warfare, in the midst of an ongoing, intense, non-nuclear conflict or crisis."[35]

A more recent "refinement" of American nuclear war plans is known as "ethnic targeting," that is, using highly accurate nuclear weapons to strike specific ethnic groups in the Soviet Union.[36] This doctrine, which emerged during the Carter administration, is best illustrated by a series of questions posed to Zbiginew

Brzezinski, Carter's national security adviser, while he was receiving a briefing on U.S. nuclear weapons policy. To Brzezinski's question, "Where are the criteria for kiling Russians?" the briefer responded that the plan under discussion would kill about 113 million Russians. Whereupon Brzezinski retorted, "No, no, I mean *Russian* Russians." Brzezinski's point was that the ethnic Russians, who occupied the principal positions of power in the Soviet military and government, were the main group that had to be "deterred," and, if deterrence failed, eliminated. Brzezinski also argued that such ethnically focused targeting could "speed the breakup of the Russian empire."[37]

Ethnic targeting has been called "genocide as a substitute for massive retaliation" that "would strike Europeans as behavior more typical of the defendants than the prosecutors at Nuremberg."[38] Put bluntly, ethnic targeting meets the precise definition of genocide because it singles out for destruction a specific group on the basis of its ethnic background.

Even with the end of the Cold War, tens of thousands of nuclear weapons remain in the arsenals of the United States, Russia, Ukraine (at this writing in early 1994), Great Britain, France, China, and Israel. Ambitious plans to reduce these arsenals could founder if economic chaos in Russia provokes the overthrow of the democratically elected government and its replacement by militaristic hard-liners. Russian president Boris Yeltsin, in a January 1992 meeting with President Bush, warned that the Cold War could return if improvements in the lives of Russians and other former Soviets are not made soon. Yeltsin was quoted by the *Wall Street Journal* as saying, "If reform in Russia goes under, that means there will be a cold war—the cold war will turn into a hot war—this is again going to be an arms race."[39]

As yet, these nuclear arsenals pose only a potential threat to humankind; those nations that possess nuclear weapons do so in order to deter the use of nuclear (and, in some cases, nonnuclear) weapons against them. However, in order for such deterrence to be credible, the nuclear-armed nations must be ready and willing to actually use the weapons.

If even a fraction of the existing nuclear arsenals was used in combat, it is likely that more people would die than in any genocide or war in history. A 1984 study by the World Health Organization calculated that a war fought with approximately one-half of the Soviet and American nuclear arsenals (as they existed in the mid-1980s) could have promptly killed as many as 1 billion people and that another 1 billion could die within the first year as a result of radiation exposure, untreated burns and other injuries, the lack of food and water, and so on.[40] In addition to directly causing deaths and injuries, nuclear war would inflict great damage to the global environment. For example, the smoke and soot from fires started by nuclear detonations are likely to drift into the higher levels of the earth's atmosphere and reduce the amount of sunlight and heat that reaches the surface. Some scientists have hypothesized that such consequences would create what has been called a nuclear winter and would drastically reduce the survival chances for anyone who escaped the initial effects of the war.[41] Reputable scientists have even warned that the possibility of human extinction cannot be ruled out as a consequence of nuclear war and nuclear winter.[42]*

As noted, some scholars have questioned the appropriateness of the term "war" when used in connection with nuclear weapons. In recognition of the uniquely destructive nature of nuclear weapons and the fact that they are deeply embedded in the national security arrangements of several nations, Lifton and Markusen suggested the concept of a nuclear "genocidal system." "A genocidal system," they wrote, "is not a matter of a particular weapons structure or strategic concept so much as an overall constellation of men, weapons, and war-ighting plans which, if implemented, could end human civilization in minutes and the greater part of human life on the planet within hours."[43]

Factors Facilitating the Preparations for Nuclear Omnicide

The lessons of this study for the problem of the nuclear threat are disturbing. As the following discussion makes clear, the same facilitating factors that expedite genocide and total war also characterize the preparations for nuclear omnicide.

Ideological Dehumanization. During the decades of the Cold War, both the United States and the Soviet Union engaged in vilification of each other in speeches by leaders and in government propaganda. Indeed, John Dower makes the provocative case in terms of the United States that the dehumanizing racist rhetoric aimed against the Japanese was transferred to the new enemy, the Soviet Union. According to Dower,

> The war hates and race hates of World War Two, that is, proved very adaptable to the cold war. Traits which the Americans and English had associated with the Japanese, with great empirical sobriety, were suddenly perceived to be really more relevant to the Communists (deviousness and cunning, bestial and atrocious behavior, homogeneity and monolithic control, fanaticism divorced from any legitimate goals or realistic perceptions of the world, megalomania bent on world conquest). ... Enemies changed, with wrenching suddenness, but the concept of "the enemy" remained impressively impervious to drastic alteration.[44]

George Kennan, whose February 1946 analysis of Soviet expansionism played a key role in the U.S. policy of attempting to "contain" such expansion during the Cold War, complained in 1982 about the U.S. tendency to engage in an "endless series of distortions and over-simplifications, this systematic dehumanization of the leadership of another great nation."[45]

*Other scientists, citing more recent data, question whether extinction of the human race is a real possibility. Richard Turco, one of the discoverers of the nuclear-winter phenomenon, told a newspaper reporter in early 1990: "My personal opinion is that the human race wouldn't become extinct, but civilization as we know it would" (Malcolm W. Browne, "Nuclear Winter Theorists Pull Back: Scientists Say They Overestimated Warfare's Effect on Climate," *New York Times*, January 23, 1990, p. B5)."

The vilification went in both directions, as Robert Reiber and Robert Kelly observed:

> The rhetoric of the Cold War confrontation was soon awash with the themes of barbarism. In Soviet political demonology, the United States was caricatured as a greedy beast intent upon seizing control of the world by bankrupting it and by plundering the meager resources of the weak and poor. Similarly, American propaganda churned up images of the Soviet Union trampling and crushing its weaker neighbors under its military juggernaut, while fostering international subversion.[46]

This official portrayal of the targets of nuclear weapons as evil and inhuman could and did mute moral or empathic qualms among personnel responsible for selecting those targets. As former air force target planner Henry Nash has written, "The unsavory aspects of such ruminations [on the 'human consequences' of the use of nuclear weapons] were blunted by the reminder that America's victims deserved their fate. . . . Describing the Soviet leadership as evil, corrupt, immoral, sadistic, and inhumane—plus being communists—provided at least a partial justification for their elimination."[47]

Dehumanization is also promoted by the highly technical context of nuclear weapons policymaking and implementation. Those engaged in planning for nuclear omnicide tend to be preoccupied by the technical, rather than human, dimensions of nuclear "war" and its potential consequences. To quote nuclear target planner Nash again, "The strong technological and quantitative orientation of these tasks held the attention of analysts and the relationship of weapons to human life was an incidental consideration."[48] Political scientist Roman Kolkowitz has described the realm of nuclear strategy as one of "overabstraction, scientism, numerology, and technical jargon."[49] A similar point was made by former nuclear weapons designer Theodore Taylor. Long after repudiating his earlier work and becoming an antinuclear advocate, Taylor told an interviewer:

> And never that I can remember [did I have] a daydream about those people [who were targeted by the weapons Taylor had designed] . . . as individuals, what they might look like, how many of them one would see slammed up against the walls of the nearest building and splattered all over the place. You don't think about that. . . . If you start thinking about that too much, you are not going to be able to think . . . very creatively about new ways of making bombs.[50]

Special mention needs to be made of the important role of language in promoting the dehumanization process. Indeed, killing projects in general tend to rely on what Hannah Arendt aptly termed "language rules," which enable people to talk about their grisly tasks without focusing on their true nature.[51] As Herbert Kelman has observed, "Moral inhibitions are less easily subdued if the functionaries, in their own thinking and in their communication with each other, have to face the fact that they are engaged in organized murder. Such moral constraints are augmented by prudential ones when it comes to the writing of memoranda and the issuing of communiques. The difficulty is handled by the well-known bureaucratic inventiveness in the use of language."[52]

People involved with nuclear weapons employ a special vocabulary of euphemistic jargon. Lifton referred to this as "the anesthetizing quality of the language of nuclear weapons." "What are we to make," he wrote, "of terms like 'nuclear exchange,' 'escalation,' 'nuclear yield,' 'counterforce,' 'megatons,' or of 'window of opportunity?' *Quite simply, these words provide a way of talking about nuclear weapons without really talking about them*" (emphasis in original).[53] Similarly, Carol Cohn, after spending several months in the company of nuclear strategists, found that nuclear language was not only euphemistic but also, as she put it, "racy, sexy, snappy."[54] She noted that "you can get so good at manipulating the words that it almost feels like the whole thing is under control. ... The more I stayed, the more conversations I participated in, the less frightened I was of nuclear war."[55] The jargon helped deflect awareness from the human dimensions of nuclear weapons: "I *couldn't* stay connected, couldn't keep human lives as my reference points" (emphasis in original).[56] Cohn's experience is corroborated by Henry Nash, who wrote, "Beyond its usual function in facilitating communication, language in Defense, and in the intelligence community in general, helps to obscure the reality of what the work was all about—to distract attention from the homicidal reality and give a brighter hue to the ominous."[57]

The Healing-Killing Paradox. The very invention of nuclear weapons by the United States was motivated by the fear that Hitler might acquire them first and, if he did, use them with ruthless impunity against his enemies. The scientists in the Manhattan Project, among whom were a number of Jewish refugees from Nazi-dominated Europe, felt that their work was a sort of holy crusade against a greater evil. Later, when it became evident that Germany would not acquire a nuclear capability, the theme of the crusade shifted for many of the personnel to that of bringing the war in the Pacific to an end by inducing Japan to surrender. As noted, Secretary of War Henry Stimson, despite his clear awareness of the horrific nature of the new weapon, chose to focus on its value in ending the war and promoting the peace in the postwar era.

Maintaining the capacity for nuclear omnicide is justified on the grounds that it is necessary in order to deter conflict from breaking out. By focusing on the alleged deterrent value of nuclear weapons, those responsible for them can avoid thinking about their inherently genocidal nature as well as the implications of their use should deterrence fail. As physicist and former defense scientist Herbert York stated, the "fixation on deterrence provides the hooker" that enables humane, decent people to "produce ... the most hideous and destructive kinds of weapons."[58] Indeed, the focus on the "healing" function of deterrence tends to push aside recognition that the very preparations for nuclear "war," which create a state of "permanent war threat," run the risk of precipitating the very catastrophe the weapons are designed to prevent.[59]

Compartmentalization. Compartmentalization is a prominent feature of the preparations for nuclear omnicide. Indeed, the sophistication and complexity of technologies involved necessitate contributions from a wide variety of specialists, many of whom have little knowledge or understanding of the others' jobs. Thus, as we saw in Chapter 10, compartmentalization of knowledge characterized the American project to build and drop the first atomic bombs. Under the direction of General Leslie Groves, the various programs and departments of the Manhattan Project were cloaked in rigid secrecy, not only from outsiders but from insiders as well. Information was provided to individual specialists on a strictly need-to-know basis, with the result that many scientists and engineers were recruited without being told what the ultimate goal of the project was. Not only the individuals who designed and built the bombs but also the aircrews who dropped them were kept in ignorance of the actual nature of their assignments until the very last moment.

For another example, this time during the Cold War period, Henry Nash's unusually candid reflections of his career as a nuclear target planner are once again instructive. "What was it about work with Air Targets that made me insensitive to its homicidal implications?" he asks. He continues, "Our office behavior was no different from that of men and women who might work for a bank or insurance company. What enabled us to calmly plan to incinerate vast numbers of unknown human beings without any sense of moral revulsion?"[60] According to Nash, compartmentalization played a crucial role:

> Because of the size of the Defense bureaucracy, managerial efficiency called for the compartmentalization of work and, within our intelligence operation, one basis for compartmentalization was the "need to know." This meant that analysts were permitted to know something only if it were needed to complete an assigned task. ... Need to know, initially designed to help reduce intelligence leaks, restricted each analyst's appreciation of the larger context of which his job was a small part. Obscuring the "big picture" helped promote peace of mind.[61]

Organizational Loyalty. Organizational loyalty has contributed importantly to the continued reliance on nuclear weapons as the foundation of American and, presumably, other nations' defense policies, as well as to the overall momentum of the nuclear arms race. For example, in the early years of the Cold War, rivalry among the three branches of the U.S. armed forces led to distorted estimates of the size and quality of the Soviet nuclear arsenal (with important implications for the size and quality of the U.S. nuclear arsenal allegedly needed for deterrence). The air force, in particular, which was the first branch to be equipped with nuclear weapons, tended to exaggerate Soviet nuclear capabilities, first by warning of a "bomber gap" and then by claiming the existence of a "missile gap," both of which were decidedly unfavorable to the United States. Such exaggerations served to justify the air force's arguments for large increases in its own bomber and missile forces.[62] The navy, for its part, had vested interests in interpreting the available data in a way that diminished the Soviet military threat. As Kaplan observed, during the early 1960s, "the Army and the Navy competed against the Air Force for scarce budgetary resources; if the Soviets had only a few ICBM's in the works, that would deny the Air Force its chief rationale for building several thousand ICBMs and would, thus, leave more for the non-nuclear forces of the Army and the Navy."[63]

There have been cases in which one branch of the military lobbied for a particular nuclear weapons system when it saw a chance to improve its own position relative to the other branches. For example, during the 1950s, the U.S. Army strongly advocated the development of small, battlefield nuclear weapons, known as tactical nuclear weapons, in part because of their inability to acquire other kinds. According to Herken, "The idea of tactical nuclear warfare as an alternative to the atomic blitz had found a ready sponsor in the Army. That service—after continually losing out to the Air Force and its air-atomic emphasis in budget battles—retaliated in the summer of 1951 by pursuing a Cal Tech study of tactical nuclear weapons and warfare."[64] Predictably, the air force strongly resisted such a move.

Similar motives influenced the navy's embrace of the so-called neutron bomb (a special type of hydrogen bomb) in 1959.[65] Herken recounted the story of how Samuel Cohen,

> the self-professed "father of the neutron bomb," found allies among those in the military who resented the Air Force's dominance in the military budget. ... "The Navy fell in love with it," Cohen remembered. Locked in its annual struggle with the Air Force over the defense budget, and in search of a justification for its politically imperiled fleet of aircraft carriers, the Navy had seized upon the neutron bomb as one nuclear weapon that could be uniquely its own preserve.[66]

Organizational loyalty also influenced the military's thinking about the moral dimensions of nuclear weapons. In 1949, when only the air force possessed an atomic capability, navy leaders argued that such weapons were immoral. One rear admiral testified before Congress that the air force's atomic-bomb-based strategy was "ruthless and barbaric ... random mass slaughter of men, women, and children ... morally wrong ... contrary to our fundamental ideas."[67] However, just a few years later, when the navy had its own nuclear weapons, it strongly advocated deterrence based on the threat of destroying enemy cities and lobbied Congress for increased appropriations in order to build up its own nuclear capability.[68]

Scientific Rationalization. The enterprise of justifying more and better nuclear weapons and devising plans for their use has the appearance of scientific empiricism and precision. From the dawn of the nuclear age, individuals responsible for nuclear strategy have aspired and claimed to operate according to careful scientific standards. Thus, the Rand corporation, which was established by the air force shortly after World War II to provide "scientific" analysis to guide policy for atomic weapons, had a strong penchant for quantitative analysis rather than for the "softer" data of political and social science. According to Kaplan,

> Quantitative analysis had triumphed at RAND, through the spread of systems analysis and game theory and ... through the domination over the rest of RAND by the mathematics division. These sorts of studies were scientific, so it was thought; there were numbers, calculations, rigorously checked, sometimes figured on a computer. Maybe the numbers were questionable, but they were tangible, unlike the theorizing, the Kremlinology, the academic historical research and interpretation produced by social science.[69]

Many important decisions about U.S. nuclear weapons policy were made on the basis of ostensibly rigorous Rand studies and comparable analysis by other think tanks. Elaborate "scenarios" of "nuclear exchanges," complete with precise estimates of fatalities, were spun forth. Vast sums of money were invested in many types of new weapons systems. However, these eventful decisions, not just in the United States but in all the nuclear powers, were based on a chimera, a veneer. As James Fallows observed, "On the basis of theories, billions of dollars have been spent, and tens of thousands of men have been trained and deployed. Each of these decisions has been an act of faith, for the doctrines and theories are pure theology."[70]

Technical Distancing. As was the case with both the Holocaust and strategic bombing, the planning for nuclear omnicide is done, to a great extent, by individuals far removed from the reality of the damage their inventions and plans could cause. For those who would do the actual killing, the physical and psychological distance from the victims is far greater than in the case of the Nazi gas chambers or even the bomber crews miles above their targets. The nuclear weapons would be launched by young men and women buried in underground missile silos, submerged beneath the ocean in submarines, or flying high above the ground in airplanes—all hundreds or even thousands of miles from the targets. Most of those who will be responsible for actually using the weapons do not even know their precise destination.

We have seen that the nuclear threat has been engendered and perpetuated by some of the same psychological and social factors that have made our present era an age of genocide and a century of total war. Whether the human species will ultimately free itself of this self-created threat to survival remains to be seen. At best, the nuclear era will be looked back on by our more enlightened descendants as an unfortunate and disgraceful chapter in our history—very much as the history of slavery is regarded today. At worst, the United States, the former Soviet Union, and other nuclear-armed nations—whose embrace of nuclear weapons and the threat of nuclear omnicide has provided legitimation, incentive, and means for other nations and terrorists to do the same—may find themselves consumed in

Two French air force officers in an underground missile launch control center. If given the order, they would launch missiles with thermonuclear warheads with a yield equivalent to one million tons of high explosive. SOURCE: SIRPA "AIR."

future conflagrations. This dismal scenario is rendered plausible by an array of dangerous trends that are likely to worsen in coming years and that are discussed in the following section.

Dangerous Trends

In this section we briefly examine three trends that create a grave potential for the outbreak of genocidal violence in the near future: first, structural violence—a form of violence that, unlike genocide and war, is not overt and direct but nonetheless causes millions of deaths each year; second, the growing tide of refugees in many regions of the world; third, the increasing danger that nuclear, chemical, and biological weapons of mass destruction will spread into politically and militarily volatile nations and regions.

Structural Violence

The literature on collective violence focuses predominantly on warfare and genocide; however, it is important to note that there are other ways by which governmental decision and indecision may cause massive loss of life. For example, the creation or tolerance of harmful social conditions is an important—though insufficiently appreciated—means by which governmental policies result in large numbers of deaths. The concept of structural violence addresses this fact.[71]

Structural violence, according to William Eckhardt and Gernot Köhler, "is the violence created by social, political, and economic institutions and structures which may lead to as much death and harm to persons as does armed violence."[72] A closely related concept, benign neglect, was mentioned in 1982 by Horowitz in his important essay "Functional and Existential Visions of Genocide," where he alluded to "one shadowy area of genocide that permits the state to take lives by indirection, for example by virtue of benign neglect, or death due to demographic causes."[73]

Estimates of structural violence are calculated by comparing the life expectancies of people in poor countries with those in wealthier countries.[74] For example, Haiti has an average life expectancy of 56 years, compared with the United States, which has an average life expectancy of 75 years.[75] The main reason for such a gap lies in impoverished living conditions that are not inevitable but instead reflect policy choices within the respective countries and in the international community as well. Extreme poverty is seen, at least in the modern era, more as the result of inequitable distribution of resources than of purely "natural" conditions such as drought and pestilence.

Many of the deaths associated with structural violence, Eckhardt suggested, are "largely caused by hunger and hunger-related diseases that can be prevented by good food and safe water better distributed than they are today."[76] In an analysis of worldwide malnutrition and starvation, Phillips Foster reported that about one-tenth of the world's approximately 5 billion people—that is, 500 million—are chronically hungry or malnourished. Other analysts, he noted, put the estimate considerably higher. Of the hundreds of millions of underfed people throughout the world, more than 1 million, during an average year, die from starvation and hunger-related disease.[77]

Moreover, despite important advances in agricultural productivity, a rising global population is likely to create even higher levels of hunger deaths in the future. In 1991, Lester Brown warned that the global population is projected to add at least 960 million people during the decade of the 1990s. "The record population growth projected for the nineties," he wrote, "means the per capita availability of key resources such as land, water, and wood will also shrink at an unprecedented rate."[78]

Exacerbating the problem of overpopulation is the continuing depletion of vital natural resources and the degredation of the planetary ecosystem. Such trends as desertification (the erosion or exhaustion of the topsoil needed for productive agriculture); deforestation (the burning and cutting of vast areas of forests); acid rain (which has destroyed tens of thousands of lakes in Scandinavia, North America, and Europe); and the extinction of as many as 10,000 plant and animal species each year mean that more people are going to have to compete for fewer resources.[79] The pace at which the environment is being degraded is accelerating. In a prescient article, "Environmental Change and Violent Conflict," Canadian peace researcher Thomas F. Homer-Dixon and his colleagues point out that "renewable-resource scarcities of the next 50 years will probably occur with a speed, complexity and magnitude unprecedented in history. Entire countries can now be deforested in a few decades, most of a region's topsoil can disappear in a generation, and acute ozone depletion may take place in as few as 20 years."[80] Homer-Dixon is echoed by Robert D. Kaplan, who writes, "It is time to understand 'the environment' for what it is: *the* national-security issue of the early twenty-first century" (emphasis in original).[81]

Structural violence requires urgent attention not only because of the scale of the death tolls but also because it is directly related to armed violence in at least two ways. First, structural violence, by causing suffering and death as the result of institutionalized social inequality, creates conditions conducive for the outbreak of overt violence, particularly in the form of revolution and civil war. According to Kaplan,

> The intense savagery of the fighting in such diverse cultural settings as Liberia, Bosnia, the Caucasus, and Sri Lanka—to say nothing of what obtains in American inner cities—indicates something very troubling that those of us inside the stretch limo,* concerned with issues like middle-class entitlements and the future of interactive cable television, lack the stomach to contemplate. It is this: a large number of people on this planet, to whom the comfort and stability of a middle-class life is utterly unknown, find war and a barracks existence a step up rather than a step down.[82]

Second, by diverting societal resources from programs to meet human needs and by destroying portions of the economic infrastructure, armed violence tends to aggravate economic and social conditions that cause structural violence.

The Rising Tide of Refugees

Another dangerous trend is the startling increase in refugees and displaced persons at the end of the twentieth century. Millions of people fled armed confict in order to save their lives and millions more sought to escape political repression and economic impoverishment in their own countries. According to one estimate, there were over 18 million refugees in the world in 1991; many had illegally entered other countries and many more existed in crowded refugee camps far from their home countries. By early 1994, the total number of refugees had grown to 19 mil-

*The "stretch limo" image was given to Kaplan by Homer-Dixon, who suggested to him: "Think of a stretch limo in the potholed streets of New York City, where the homeless beggars live. Inside the limo are the air-conditioned, post-industrial regions of North America, Europe, the emerging Pacific Rim, and a few other isolated places, with their trade summitry and computer-information highways. Outside is the rest of mankind, going in a completely different direction" (Robert D. Kaplan, "The Coming Anarchy," *Atlantic Monthly*, February 1994, p. 58).

lion, compared with "only" an estimated 2.8 million in 1976.[83] Writing in May 1992, Judy Mayotte estimated that there were more than 23 million people "internally displaced within their own countries."[84]

A single war—the Persian Gulf War of 1991—displaced as many as 5 million people from Iraq, Kuwait, and other Gulf nations.[85] Many of them had worked in Kuwait in order to send part of their earnings back to their families in impoverished countries like Bangladesh, Sri Lanka, Pakistan, and the Philippines.

The breakup of the Soviet bloc spurred a massive exodus of refugees from eastern European nations to wealthier neighbors to the west. After the failed coup in Russia in August 1992, 25 million Russians living outside the Russian Federation became, according to Lidia Grafova, "refugees in countries that used to be their homes."[86]

In late 1991 and early 1992, thousands of Haitians risked their lives in overcrowded boats to reach haven from a military dictatorship and abject poverty, only to be held at a huge refugee encampment at the U.S. naval base in Guantánamo Bay, Cuba, before being forcibly repatriated to Haiti.[87]

The wars in former Yugoslavia have also spawned hundreds of thousands of refugees. According to the Commissariat of Refugees of the Republic of Serbia in Belgrade, there were approximately 460,000 refugees living in Serbia in 1993, most of whom were Serbs who had fled from Croatia and Bosnia and Herzegovina. Children under the age of 18 constituted 42 percent of the refugees, and nearly 85 percent of the adults were women.[88] Comparably large numbers of Muslims and Croats have also been displaced from their former homes in Serb-controlled regions of former Yugoslavia.

As political and economic conditions continue to deteriorate in many nations of the world, it is likely that the flow of refugees will continue. An influx of foreigners into a situation with preexisting tensions and, in many cases, festering ethnic rivalries and hatreds can lead to the resurgence of racism and overt conflict.[89] In this context, it is important to recall, from Chapter 3, Richard Rubenstein's warning that stateless people are often particularly susceptible to being targeted for mass killing.[90]

Proliferation of Weapons of Mass Destruction

Into the disturbing context of ongoing structural violence—exacerbated by overpopulation, resource depletion, and political and economic turmoil—are pouring increasing numbers of extremely deadly weapons. In addition to the tens of thousands of nuclear weapons still deployed by the United States and Russia (as of mid-1993, the two nations still possessed approximately 26,000 nuclear weapons between them), a nuclear weapons capability has been attained by several other nations, including China, France, Great Britain, India, Israel, Pakistan, and South Africa.[91] Ominously, other nations, such as Libya, North Korea, and Iraq, have striven to obtain nuclear weapons. Indeed, one of the reasons given by the United States for the use of military force against Iraq in the Persian Gulf War of 1991 was the fear that the Iraqis would soon possess nuclear weapons.[92] In a sobering analysis of the risks of nuclear weapons proliferation in coming years, John Deutch concluded that "the world will almost certainly confront additional nations that either overtly or covertly possess a nuclear capability. This altered balance of power will influence political and military events in unpredictable and dangerous ways."[93]

In addition to being concerned about the risk of nuclear weapons proliferation, many analysts are worried by the growing number of nations that have acquired, or may soon acquire, chemical and biological weapons, which have been aptly called the poor man's [or nation's] atom bombs. Chemical weapons come in a variety of forms and kill by a variety of means, ranging from choking to burning the skin to disruption of nerve transmissions. Symptoms of the latter include "sweating, nausea, vomiting, staggering coma, and convulsion, followed by cessation of breathing and death."[94] Biological weapons come in two varieties: "toxins (toxic chemicals produced by living organisms) and pathogens (living organisms that produce disease)."[95]

Besides the United States, the former Soviet Union, and Iraq, all of whom openly acknowledge possessing chemical weapons, other nations "strongly suspected of stockpiling or producing chemical weapons" include Egypt, India, Iran, Israel, North and South Korea, Libya, Pakistan, Syria, and Taiwan. All of these nations also currently possess ballistic missiles potentially capable of being used to deliver chemical warheads to their targets.[96]

Fewer nations have a biological warfare capability. The United States, Great Britain, and Japan once had biological weapons but have since dismantled their stockpiles. Iraq and Syria, however, are "strongly suspected of stockpiling such weapons today."[97]

Money spent on such weaponry and military readiness is diverted from money used to meet basic human needs, thus aggravating the problem of structural violence. As Ruth Leger Sivard wrote in 1993, "In a world spending over $600 billion a year on military programs, over 1 billion people lack basic health care, one adult in four is unable to read and write, one-fifth of the world population goes hungry every day."[98]

Prospects for Reducing Genocidal Killing

The scholar who researches the subject of genocidal killing should do so not merely to satisfy an academic curiosity but also to express a deep concern about human survival. Greater understanding of the phenomenon of genocide and related forms of collective violence is urgently needed, but so are concrete efforts to anticipate, prevent, and punish it. In this concluding section, we survey the work of several scholars who have addressed the question of how genocidal killing might be prevented.

Raphael Lemkin and Leo Kuper on the Role of the United Nations

We saw in Chapter 3 how a Polish jurist named Raphael Lemkin lobbied the United Nations to declare certain genocidal acts as crimes under international law. Lemkin's concept of genocide was embodied in the Convention on the Prevention and Punishment of the Crime of Genocide adopted formally by the United Nations in 1951. It was earnestly hoped by many that in the years following World War II the United Nations would prevent anything as catastrophic as the Holocaust from ever happening again.

Unfortunately, it is necessary to conclude that in the 40-plus years since the United Nations adopted Lemkin's idea as the basis of its convention on genocide, that international organization has not been able to prevent a single case of genocide. Since the end of World War II, the epidemic of genocidal killing has raged in such places as Tibet, East Timor, Sudan, the former Yugoslavia, Kurdistan, Iraq, and Rwanda. Nor has the United Nations been able to punish the perpetrators of genocide. Indeed, it has actually rewarded a perpetrator: Although Pol Pot and his Khmer Rouge were responsible for murdering millions of people in Cambodia between 1975 and 1979, they nonetheless were seated in the United Nations as that country's official representatives.

No one among the concerned scholars of genocide studies has been more troubled by this state of affairs than Leo Kuper. We noted earlier how zealously he has worked to carry on Lemkin's goal of preventing genocides. It was Kuper who helped extend awareness of the range of episodes of state-induced mass murder to include the Third World—especially those in Africa in the 1960s and 1970s. Having been born and largely raised in South Africa, Kuper developed his intellectual interest in genocide at the very time former multiethnic and multitribal colonies were seeking to integrate their plural societies in the process of forming new nation-states. Kuper was immediately convinced that the atmosphere of decolonization would prove a fertile ground for genocides. Subsequent events proved him all too right.

In 1985, Kuper published *The Prevention of Genocide.* In it, he explained why he devoted his career to genocide studies. He asserted that every individual on this earth has the right to life, but he also acknowledged that although the United Nations had guaranteed this right to life, it had been largely unable to translate words and lofty sentiments into actions. Mllions have been slaughtered while the United Nations remained helpless to intervene.

In the concluding portion of the book, which addressed the question of punishment and prevention, Kuper analyzed the reasons the United Nations has been so impotent in its declared purpose of preventing genocides.[99] Kuper's main point is that the United Nations represents not only the nation-states of the world but the cultural groups dominant in each of them. As Kuper wrote, "the UN Charter makes no specific provision for the protection of minorities." He continued: "The Universal Declaration of Human Rights also fails to deal with the protection of minorities."[100] The vulnerability of minorities in plural societies exacerbates the growing world problem of proliferating potential genocidal situations.

It follows that because so many atrocities occur in poorly integrated plural societies, much effort is needed from institutions of one sort or another to abolish the inequality between groups by protecting the rights of the vulnerable minorities. However, according to Kuper, the United Nations' main method of coping with the oppression of minorities is to issue "a plethora ... of standard-setting declarations, resolutions, and convenants for the regulation of human rights ... and the continuous mounting of new resolutions, new declarations, new covenants."[101]

For example, among the minority groups throughout the world especially vulnerable to genocide are indigenous peoples "inhabiting areas with exploitable resources."[102] By "indigenous," Kuper referred to hunting and gathering communities such as the "Indians" of North and South America. Important efforts to help these people have come from organizations outside the United Nations, such as the International Labour Committee on Indigenous Peoples and Their Land. In 1981, the Conference of Specialists on Ethnocide and Ethnodevelopment in Latin America was convened, which was effective in promoting the rights of native peoples.

One of the most hopeful developments in the process of preventing future genocides is the rapid increase of nongovernmental organizations whose very purpose is the "promotion and protection of internationally recognized human rights."[103] At the time Kuper published his book, at least 2,000 such groups had been identified. The model movement has been and continues to be Amnesty International, which has been monitoring violations of human rights since 1961. The importance of such organizations cannot be overstated. They represent, in part, what may be called "an early warning system based on the impartial gathering of information about potential genocidal situations."[104]

Kuper also believes in unofficial contacts with representatives of friendly governments in the UN who can exert pressures on offending nations. This proved to be a major factor in limiting the Iranian persecution of Baha'is in 1982. Governments can also be made to see the long-term dangers of a genocidal policy pursued by a neighboring state and may be prodded into cutting off economic or other contacts in order to stop the massacres. As a last resort, there is the possibility of what Kuper calls "forceful humanitarian intervention."[105] According to Kuper, this has happened in three major cases since World War II:

1. The invasion of East Pakistan by India in 1971 to stop the genocidal killing of Bengalis.
2. The invasion of Cambodia (Kampuchea) by Vietnam in 1979 to stop the Khmer Rouge–imposed genocide of their own people.
3. The invasion of Uganda by Tanzania in 1979 to stop Idi Amin from the mass murder of his and other peoples in the country.

Although Kuper has rightly criticized the United Nations for its inability to play a greater role in the prevention and punishment of genocide, it would be a mistake to dismiss its potential. As this book goes to press, United Nations Protection Forces are making a major contribution to reducing bloodshed and providing humanitarian relief to citizens in the war-ravaged former Yugoslavia. Moreover, the United Nations Security Council has sought to establish a war-crimes tribunal that would evaluate evidence of war crimes and crimes against humanity in former Yugoslavia and, potentially, prosecute perpetrators.[106]

Israel W. Charny on a Genocide Early-Warning System

Israel Charny is another scholar who has successfully combined an intellectual interest in genocide with an activist concern for its prevention and elimination. Though Charny has a more psychological approach to the causes of genocide than does Kuper, both share a common practical approach on how it can be countered internationally. Kuper, in fact, has praised Charny for having established the Institute of the Holocaust and Genocide at Tel Aviv University, which functions as a repository for data on both genocidal situations and "violations of human rights that fall short of genocide."[107] In 1982, Charny held a conference in Israel on genocide in comparative perspective and now publishes a journal with articles on Holocaust and genocide studies. The data compiled by his institute on atrocities throughout the world are freely transmitted to the media.[108]

Charny is also worried about the threat of "even greater mass extinction" posed by nuclear and other modern weapons of mass destruction.[109] He finds absolutely no moral justification for using these weapons that aim to annihilate "a helpless target people."[110] Since his basic tenet in pursuing genocide studies is to defend "the concept that lives of human beings are inviolate and sacred," he has also focused on the dangerous impact of overpopulation and pollution on the ecology of earth.[111] His institute has collected an immense fund of information on potential cases of genocide. "It remains to be determined," Charny concludes, "if we can develop sufficient human will to act to prevent these terrible occurrences of mass death."[112]

Among Charny's most important concrete proposals is the one calling for the establishment of a "world genocide early warning system" that would monitor information on human rights violations throughout the world and identify cases that appear to be moving in the direction of genocide or genocidal killing. Charny has identified a number of signs and symptoms of evolving genocide, which he calls "early warning processes." Early recognition and exposure of these processes in specific situations may stimulate efforts by the United Nations, by nongovernmental organizations, or by nations to intervene *before* the killing starts. This is not the place for a full treatment of Charny's valuable ideas, but readers are urged to consult his article "Early Warning, Intervention, and Prevention of Genocide," which is followed by an excellent annotated bibliography.[113]

Recognition and Reduction of Factors that Facilitate Genocidal Killing

Another approach to thinking about preventing future outbreaks of genocidal killing is to return to the six faciliating factors that were examined earlier in this book and to briefly consider how each might be confronted and resisted.

Thus, *dehumanization* and *technical distancing,* both of which make it easier to kill others by reducing the capacity for empathy and by excluding victims from moral considerations that might otherwise constrain violence, may be resisted by simply learning more about the "enemy," "the despised minority," or "others" who are being targeted for violence. The more one knows about other human beings, the less able one is to stereotype them in a narrow, inaccurate manner. In his valuable study of genocidal killing *The Roots of Evil,* psychologist Ervin Staub suggested that "crosscutting relations" between potential or former adversary groups can overcome the dehumanizing tendency. According to Staub, "To reduce prejudice requires positive contact. … To evolve an appreciation of alikeness and a feeling of connectedness, members of subgroups of society must live together, work together, play together; their children must go to school together."[114] Staub also emphasized that when subgroups come together in pursuit of shared goals, for example, to reduce a problem that threatens them all, previous differences become much less salient and common interests much more so.

The recognition that all human beings are members of a single species and that all are threatened by certain problems that transcend racial, ethnic, religious, and national lines—for example, the threat of nuclear war and the growing deterioration of the global ecosystem—led Lifton and Markusen to advocate the development of a "species consciousness" or "species mentality" as an antidote to the "genocidal mentality." They defined species mentality as "an expansion of collective awareness, an altered sense of self, that embraces our reality as members of a single species and thereby opens up a new psychological, ethical, and political terrain."[115]

Reducing the tendency toward dehumanization would also help expose the *healing-killing paradox* for what it is—a psychological rationalization for using immoral, illegal means to solve a problem that confronts one's "own" group. If the "others" whose death or elimination is presumably necessary to benefit one's own group are seen as fellow human beings rather than as anonymous numbers or subhuman forms of life, it will be more difficult to justify killing them. However, seeing potential victims as fully human, and having a greater capacity to empathize with them, is not enough to neutralize the healing-killing paradox. It is also essential that values and norms against wanton killing become more solidly integrated into the socialization and education of children and that sanctions against such killing be more meaningfully incorporated into national and international law. One means by which such values and norms can be promoted is through codes of ethics in which students of professions are schooled and to which members of professions are expected to adhere. Although the existence of a code of ethics does not guarantee adherence, it at least increases the incentives to avoid certain kinds of behavior, such as the slaughter of innocents, that are ethically proscribed. Moreover, codes of ethics can facilitate whistle-blowing by insiders who perceive that their organization is engaging in behavior or promoting policies that violate basic ethical principles.[116]

Emphasis on professional codes of ethics could also help in resisting the temptation toward *scientific rationalization,* which has been found to contribute importantly to modern genocides. Again, there is no guarantee that clear awareness of ethical principles will deter scientists from allowing themselves to be exploited by political interests or from willingly contributing to genocidal projects, but careful education of students may at least help deter such scientism. Another approach to resisting the exploitation of science for immoral purposes is the continued support of what Joel Primack and Frank von Hippel have called "public interest science," that is, science that operates beyond the confines of government and big business, independently evaluates evidence and policies, and, when appropriate, blows the whistle on shoddy research or other abuses of science.[117]

Finally, the pitfalls of bureaucracy, in the forms of *compartmentalization* and *organizational loyalty,* may be resisted in a number of ways. Again, codes of ethics, although not sufficient by themselves, can at least contribute to resistance against policies that entail harm to innocents. Moreover, some of the work done by Rosabeth Moss Kanter on "humanizing bureacuracy" by promoting social inclusiveness and shared responsibilities may help bureaucrats retain a sense of the human impacts of their jobs and a greater sense of personal responsibility for what their organization produces.[118] Finally, to the extent that sheer economic concerns may blind employees of large bureaucratic organizations to the immoral implications of their work, alternative forms of employment will be needed, as will further study on the economic conversion of industries involved in the business of weapons design and manufacture to the production of other goods.[119]

This cursory listing of antitheses to the six facilitating factors is certainly not intended to constitute a thorough program for preventing genocidal killing. Instead, it is intended to stimulate awareness of valuable work that has already been done and to encourage further work. Genocide and genocidal killing are complex, multicausal phenomena, and no single approach can hope to effectively comprehend or prevent them.

A Plea for Education About Genocide

Finally, we end this book with a plea for vastly increased efforts to disseminate information about the problem of genocidal killing, both to students and to the general citizenry. Further scholarly study of the problem is essential, as are ongoing efforts to strengthen international legal sanctions against the slaughter of innocents. However, in order for such sanctions to be successfully and meaningfully integrated into the international political arena, new generations of students and citizens must appreciate just how serious the epidemic of genocidal killing has become. Moreover, in addition to recognizing the scale and urgency of the problem, they must learn about how it might be reduced and eventually eliminated. We suggest that a necessary, though not sufficient, condition is the development of college and university courses on genocide as a subject in its own right and in comparative perspective.

Such education, although certainly no panacea, would generate at least two salutary effects. First, a growing number of college- and university-educated men and women would acquire what Robert Jay Lifton has called a "formed awareness" of the problem. By "formed," as opposed to partial or "fragmentary," awareness, Lifton refers to "awareness that *in*forms our sense of self and world, that affects our actions and our lives and is part of an evolving pattern of illumination and commitment"(emphasis in original).[120] As citizens of democracies, individuals with such an awareness of genocide are in a position to support political candidates and policies that address the problem in useful ways and that can thereby contribute to concrete political and legal steps to anticipate and prevent future outbreaks of genocidal violence—and that can, when prevention fails, intervene and punish the perpetrators. Second, out of such courses will come future scholars who will make important contributions to our understanding of the problem of governmental mass killing, as well as future diplomats and jurists and human rights advocates who will become directly engaged in the struggle to transcend it.

Notes

CHAPTER 1

1. Gil Elliot, *Twentieth Century Book of the Dead,* New York, Charles Scribner's Sons, 1972, p. 6. For a concise discussion of man-made death, see also Richard Rhodes, "Man-Made Death: A Neglected Mortality," *Journal of the American Medical Association,* Vol. 260, 1988, pp. 686–687.

2. For wars in 1992, see Ruth Leger Sivard, *World Military and Social Expenditures 1993,* Washington, DC, World Priorities, 1993, p. 20. For civilian death tolls, see Eric Markusen, "Genocide and Modern War," in M. Dobkowski and I. Walliman, Editors, *Genocide in Our Time,* Ann Arbor, MI, Pierian Press, 1992, p. 123.

3. For an alarming survey of nuclear proliferation dangers, see John M. Deutch, "The New Nuclear Threat," *Foreign Affairs,* Fall 1992, pp. 120–134. See also Martin van Crevald, *Nuclear Proliferation and the Future of Conflict,* New York, Free Press, 1993. We return to this problem in Chapter 12.

4. Elliot, *Twentieth Century Book of the Dead,* p. 1.

5. Israel W. Charny, "Genocide and Mass Destruction: Doing Harm to Others as a Missing Dimension in Psychopathology," *Psychiatry,* Vol. 49, May 1986, pp. 144–157.

6. Everett C. Hughes, "Good People and Dirty Work," *Social Problems,* Vol. 10, Summer 1962, pp. 3–11.

7. Helen Fein, *Accounting for Genocide: National Responses and Jewish Victimization During the Holocaust,* New York, Free Press, 1979.

8. Helen Fein, "Is Sociology Aware of Genocide?: Recognition of Genocide in Introductory Sociology Texts in the United States, 1947–1977," *Humanity and Society,* Vol. 3, 1977, p. 187. A recently reported follow-up study of introductory sociology textbooks found that 39 percent of the texts that Fein examined mentioned genocide as a subject—generally in a very cursory fashion. Genocide was mentioned in only 42 percent of the texts published between 1977 and 1990. See Christy B. Buchanan, "Introductory Sociology Texts Revisited: Recognition of Genocide in Texts, 1977–1990," as summarized in *Sociological Abstracts,* December 1992, Conference Abstracts Supplement, p. 42.

9. Zygmunt Bauman, *Modernity and the Holocaust,* Ithaca, NY, Cornell University Press, 1989, p. 3.

10. Ronald C. Kramer and Sam Marullo, "Toward a Sociology of Nuclear Weapons," *Sociological Quarterly,* Vol. 26, No. 3, 1985, p. 283.

11. Frank Chalk and Kurt Jonassohn, *The History and Sociology of Genocide: Analyses and Case Studies,* New Haven, CT, Yale University Press, 1990.

12. William H. McNeill, *The Rise of the West: A History of the Human Community,* Chicago, University of Chicago Press, 1963.

13. For a valuable discussion of the debate over the comprehensibility of the Holocaust, see Dan Magurshak, "The Incomprehensibility of the Holocaust: Tightening Up Some Loose Usage," in Alan Rosenberg and Gerald Meyers, Editors, *Echoes from the Holocaust:*

Philosophical Reflections on a Dark Time, Philadelphia: Temple University Press, 1988, pp. 421–431. See also the review essay by Eric Markusen on the 1991 book *Lessons and Legacies: The Meaning of the Holocaust in a Changing World* (Evanston, IL: Northwestern University Press), edited by Peter Hayes, in *Holocaust and Genocide Studies,* Vol. 7, No. 2, Fall 1993, pp. 263–273.

14. William Eckhardt, "Civilian Deaths in Wartime," *Bulletin of Peace Proposals,* Vol. 20, No. 1, 1989, 89–98.

15. On the Holocaust, see Raul Hilberg, "Notation on Sources," in *The Destruction of the European Jews, Vol. III,* Revised and Definitive Edition, New York and London, Holmes & Meier, 1985, pp. 1223–1228; on the Cambodian genocide see David Hawk, "Tuol Sleng Extermination Centre," *Index on Censorship,* Vol. 15, No. 1, 1986, pp. 25–31.

16. On the Armenian genocide, see Roger W. Smith, "Denial of the Armenian Genocide," in Israel W. Charny, Editor, *Genocide: A Critical Bibliographic Review, Vol. II,* New York, Facts on File, 1991, pp. 63–85; on the genocidal crimes of Stalin, see R. J. Rummel, *Lethal Politics: Soviet Genocide and Mass Murder Since 1917,* New Brunswick, NJ, and London, Transaction Books, 1990.

17. Rummel, *Lethal Politics,* p. 236.

18. Alexander McKee, *Dresden 1945: The Devil's Tinderbox,* New York, E. P. Dutton, 1984, p. 321.

19. The low figure of 25,000 is given by Conrad C. Crane, *Bombs, Cities, and Civilians: American Airpower Strategy in World War II,* Lawrence, University Press of Kansas, 1993, p. 114; the figure of 70,000 is given by McKee, *Dresden 1945,* p. 322.

20. Richard Rhodes, *The Making of the Atomic Bomb,* New York, Simon & Schuster, 1986, pp. 734, 740.

21. Patrick Tyler, "Health Crisis Said to Grip Iraq in Wake of War's Destruction," *New York Times,* May 22, 1991, p. A6. Considerable controversy surrounds estimates of the Iraqi death toll. See, for example, John G. Heinrich, "The Gulf War: How Many Iraqis Died?" *Foreign Policy,* No. 90, Spring 1993, pp. 108–125, for a relatively low estimate. Higher figures are argued by William H. Arkin and several others in letters to the editor in the following volume of the journal.

22. Bruno Bettleheim, "The Ultimate Limit," in *Surviving and Other Essays,* New York, Vintage Books, 1980, p. 7.

23. Stalin quote in John Bartlett, *Familiar Quotations,* Fourteenth Edition, Boston, Little, Brown, 1968, p. 954.

24. Elliot, *Twentieth Century Book of the Dead,* p. 5.

25. Bauman, *Modernity and the Holocaust,* p. 103.

26. Chalk and Jonassohn, *The History and Sociology of Genocide,* pp. 173–203

27. Henry Huttenbach, "Locating the Holocaust on the Genocide Spectrum: Toward a Methodology of Definition and Categorization," *Holocaust and Genocide Studies,* Vol. 3, No. 3, 1988, p. 297.

28. Jack Nusan Porter, "What Is Genocide? Notes Toward a Definition," in J. N. Porter, Editor, *Genocide and Human Rights: A Global Anthology,* Washington, DC, University Press of America, 1982, pp. 9–10.

29. Helen Fein, "Genocide: A Sociological Perspective," *Current Sociology,* Vol. 38, No. 1, 1990, p. 55.

30. Alan Rosenberg and Evelyn Silverman, "The Issue of the Holocaust as a Unique Event," in Dobkowski and Walliman, *Genocide in Our Time,* pp. 47–65.

31. David Vital, "After the Catastrophe: Aspects of Contemporary Jewry," in Hayes, *Lessons and Legacies,* p. 137.

32. Wiesel quote in Rosenberg and Silverman, "The Issue of the Holocaust as a Unique Event," p. 51.

33. Steven Katz, "Ideology, State Power, and Mass Murder/Genocide," in Hayes, *Lessons and Legacies* p. 89; see also S. Katz, "Essay: Quantity and Interpretation—Issues in the Comparative Historical Analysis of the Holocaust," *Holocaust and Genocide Studies,* Vol. 4, No. 2, 1989, pp. 127–148. See also *The Holocaust and Mass Death Before the Modern Age,* Oxford, Oxford University Press, 1994, which is the first in a projected three-volume series of books on the singularity of the Holocaust by Katz. For an argument that certain groups of Gypsies in German-occupied Europe were targeted by the Nazis for total extermination, see, for example, Ian Hancock, "Introduction," in David Crowe and John Kolsti, Editors, *The Gypsies in Eastern Europe,* New York, M. E. Sharpe, 1990, pp. 1–10.

34. Ernst Nolte, "A Past That Will Not Pass Away (A Speech It Was Possible to Write, but Not to Present)," *Yad Vashem Studies,* Vol. 19, 1998, p. 71.

35. For a valuable examination of the *Historikerstreit,* see Peter Baldwin, Editor, *Reworking the Past: Hitler, the Holocaust, and the Historian's Debate,* Boston, Beacon Press, 1990. See also the excellent annotated bibliography in Rosenberg and Silverman, "The Issue of the Holocaust as a Unique Event," pp. 55–65.

36. Yehuda Bauer, "Holocaust and Genocide: Some Comparisons," in Hayes, *Lessons and Legacies,* p. 37.

37. Bauer distinguishes between "genocides," in which masses of people are slaughtered, and "holocausts," in which the *entire* victim group is targeted for elimination. Bauer includes the Armenian genocide in the latter category. See Y. Bauer, *A History of the Holocaust,* New York and London, Franklin Watts, 1982, pp. 331–332.

38. Franklin H. Littell, "Early Warning: Detecting Potentially Genocidal Movements," in Hayes, *Lessons and Legacies,* p. 306.

39. Charles S. Maier, *The Unmasterable Past: History, Holocaust, and German National Identity,* Cambridge, MA, Harvard University Press, 1988, pp. 69–70.

40. Michael Sherry, *The Rise of American Air Power: The Creation of Armageddon,* New York and London, Yale University Press, 1987, p. 204.

41. Quoted in Crane, *Bombs, Cities, and Civilians,* p. 51.

42. Stephen A. Garrett, *Ethics and Airpower in World War II: The British Bombing of German Cities,* New York, St. Martin's Press, 1993, p. 51

43. Alvin H. Rosenfeld, "Popularization and Memory: The Case of Anne Frank," in Hayes, *Lessons and Legacies,* p. 243.

44. John Ford, "The Morality of Obliteration Bombing," Richard Wasserstrom, Editor, *War and Morality,* Belmont, CA, Wadsworth, 1970, pp. 21–23.

45. The Committee for the Compilation of Materials on Damage Caused by the Atomic Bombs in Hiroshima and Nagasaki, *Hiroshima and Nagasaki: The Physical, Medical, and Social Effects of the Atomic Bombings,* New York, Basic Books, 1981 [1977], p. 367.

46. Littell, "Early Warning: Detecting Potentially Genocidal Movements," p. 307; see also Eric Markusen, "Professions, Professionals, and Genocide," in Charny, *Genocide: A Critical Bibliographical Review, Vol. II,* pp. 264–298.

CHAPTER 2

1. William James, "The Moral Equivalent of War," in Richard Wasserstrom, Editor, *War and Morality,* Belmont, CA, Wadsworth, 1970 [1910], pp. 4–14.

2. Lord Montgomery of Alamein, *A History of Warfare,* Cleveland, OH, and New York, World Publishing, 1968, p. 29.

3. Frank Chalk and Kurt Jonassohn, *The History and Sociology of Genocide: Analyses and Case Studies,* New Haven, Yale University Press, 1990, pp. 7, 64.

4. For general information on Assyria, see Georges Contenau, *Everyday Life in Babylon and Assyria,* New York, Norton Library, 1966, pp. 142–157; H.W.F. Saggs, *The Greatness That Was Babylon,* New York, Hawthorne Books, 1962, pp. 83–140.

5. Quoted in C. J. Dunn et al., *The Last Two Million Years,* Pleasantville, NY, Reader's Digest Association, 1979, p. 56.

6. Stanley Chodorow, et al., *A History of the World,* New York, Harcourt Brace Jovanovich, 1986, p. 42.

7. Chalk and Jonassohn, *The History and Sociology of Genocide,* p. 74.

8. Our information on the history of Carthage is taken from B. H. Warmington, *Carthage,* Baltimore, Pelican Paperbacks, 1960.

9. Chalk and Jonassohn, *The History and Sociology of Genocide,* pp. 74–93.

10. Quoted in Gwynne Dyer, *War,* New York, Crown, 1985, p. 31.

11. On the Mongols from the perspective of medieval world history, see John L. LaMonte, *The World of the Middle Ages,* New York, Appleton-Crofts, 1949, pp. 536–537; see also T. W. Arnold, *The Caliphate,* Oxford, Oxford University Press, 1965, pp. 81–82; and M. Prawdin, *The Mongol Empire: Its Rise and Legacy,* New York, Free Press, 1961.

12. Quoted in Kuper, *Genocide: Its Political Use in the Twentieth Century,* New Haven, CT, Yale University Press, 1981, p. 12.

13. Joseph R. Strayer and Hans W. Gatzke, *The Mainstream of Civilization,* Third Edition, New York, Harcourt Brace Jovanovich, 1979, pp. 433–434.

14. Dyer, *War,* p. 60; Montgomery, *A History of Warfare,* p. 279.

15. Dyer, *War,* p. 60.

16. Dyer, *War,* p. 70.

17. J.F.C. Fuller, *The Conduct of War, 1789–1961,* New Brunswick, NJ, Rutgers University Press, 1961, p. 35.

18. Fuller, *The Conduct of War,* p. 36.

19. Fuller, *The Conduct of War,* p. 36.

20. Pitirim Sorokin, *Social and Cultural Dynamics, Vol. III,* New York, Bedminister Press, 1962 [1937], p. 356.

21. Dyer, *War,* p. 77.

22. Fuller, *The Conduct of War,* p. 99.

23. Richard Preston and Sydney Wise, *Men in Arms: A History of Warfare and Its Interrelationships with Western Society,* Fourth Edition, New York, Holt, Rinehart, and Winston, 1979, p. 247.

24. Bernard Brodie and Fawn Brodie, *From Crossbow to H-Bomb,* Bloomington and London, Indiana University Press, 1973, p. 133.

25. Dyer, *War,* p. 85.

26. Quoted in Robert O'Connell, *Of Arms and Men: A History of War, Weapons, and Aggression,* New York, Oxford University Press, 1989, p. 197.

27. Dyer, *War,* p. 77.

28. Quoted in Raymond Aron, *The Century of Total War,* New York, Doubleday, 1954, pp. 108–109.

29. Barbara Tuchman, "Historical Clues to Present Discontents," in *Practicing History,* New York, Knopf, 1981, p. 267.

30. Gil Elliot, *Twentieth Century Book of the Dead,* New York, Charles Scribner's Sons, 1972, p. 1.

31. Roger W. Smith, "Human Destructiveness and Politics: The Twentieth Century as an Age of Genocide," in Isidor Wallimann and Michael Dobkowski, Editors, *Genocide and the Modern Age: Etiology and Case Studies of Mass Death,* New York, Greenwood Press, 1987, p. 21.

32. Barbara Harff, "The Etiology of Genocides," in Wallimann and Dobkowski, *Genocide and the Modern Age,* p. 46.

33. Barbara Harff and Ted Robert Gurr, "Toward Empirical Theory of Genocides and Politicides: Identification and Measurement of Cases Since 1945," *International Studies Quarterly,* Vol. 32, 1988, p. 359.

34. Aron, *The Century of Total War.*

35. O'Connell, *Of Arms and Men,* p. 280.

36. William Eckhardt, "Civilian Deaths in Wartime," *Bulletin of Peace Proposals,* Vol. 20, No. 1, 1989, p. 89.

37. Eckhardt's data cited in Ruth Leger Sivard, *World Military and Social Expenditures, 1987–88,* Washington, DC, World Priorities, 1988, p. 28.

38. Sivard, *World Military and Social Expenditures, 1987–88,* p. 28.

39. Dyer, *War,* p. 82.

40. Quincy Wright, *A Study of War,* Chicago, University of Chicago Press, 1942, p. 305. Wright was echoed by sociologist Raymond Aron, who wrote, "The army industrializes itself, industry militarizes itself; the army absorbs the nation: the nation models itself on the army" (*The Century of Total War,* p. 88).

41. Hornell Hart, "Acceleration in Social Change," in Francis Allen et al., Editors, *Technology and Social Change,* New York, Appleton-Century-Crofts, 1957, pp. 41–43.

42. Hart, "Acceleration in Social Change," p. 43.

43. Richard Rhodes, *The Making of the Atomic Bomb,* New York, Simon & Schuster, 1986, p. 101.

44. Aron, *The Century of Total War,* p. 86.

45. Dyer, *War,* p. 83.

46. Preston and Wise, *Men in Arms,* p. 301.

47. Rhodes, *The Making of the Atomic Bomb,* p. 91.

48. Richard Rubenstein, *The Age of Triage: Fear and Hope in an Overcrowded World,* Boston, MA, Beacon Press, 1983, p. 161.

49. Dyer, *War,* p. 82.

50. Lee Kennett, *A History of Strategic Bombing,* New York, Charles Scribner's Sons, 1982, p. 33.

51. Yehuda Bauer, *A History of the Holocaust,* New York, Franklin Watts, 1982, pp. 58–59.

52. Richard Gabriel, *The Painful Field: The Psychiatric Dimension of Modern War,* New York, Greenwood Press, 1988, p. 50. The phrase "machines of destruction" is on p. 48.

53. Gabriel, *The Painful Field,* pp. 51–63.

54. Anthony H. Cordesman and Abraham R. Wagner, *The Lessons of Modern War, Volume II: The Iran-Iraq War,* Boulder and San Francisco, Westview Press, 1990, p. 2.

55. Cordesman and Wagner, *The Lessons of Modern War*, p. 2.

56. Gabriel, *The Painful Field*, p. 7.

57. Paul Walker and Eric Stambler, "... and the Dirty Little Weapons," *Bulletin of the Atomic Scientists*, Vol. 47, No. 4, 1991.

58. Anonymous, "The Damage Was Not Collateral," *New York Times*, March 24, 1991, Op-Ed page.

59. George Lopez, "The Gulf War: Not So Clean," *Bulletin of the Atomic Scientists*, Vol. 47, No. 4, 1991, p. 32.

60. Walker and Stambler, "... and the Dirty Little Weapons," p. 22.

61. Patrick Tyler, "Health Crisis Said to Grip Iraq in Wake of War's Destruction," *New York Times*, May 22, 1991, p. A6. (As noted in note 21 for Chapter 1, there is controversy over such estimates.)

62. Elliot, *Twentieth Century Book of the Dead*, p. 1.

63. Sorokin, *Social and Cultural Dynamics*.

64. Sorokin data summarized by Wright, *A Study of War*, p. 656.

65. Sorokin, *Social and Cultural Dynamics*, p. 342.

66. Pitirim Sorokin, *The Crisis of Our Age: Its Social and Cultural Outlook*, New York, E. P. Dutton, 1954, p. 203.

67. William Eckhardt, "War-Related Deaths Since 3000 BC," Paper presented to the 1991 annual meeting of the International Society for the Comparative Study of Civilizations, Santo Domingo, Dominican Republic, p. 2.

68. Eckhardt, "Civilian Deaths in Wartime," p. 90.

69. R. J. Rummel, "War Isn't This Century's Biggest Killer," *Wall Street Journal*, July 7, 1986, Op-Ed page.

70. Helen Fein, "Genocide: A Sociological Perspective," *Current Sociology*, Vol. 38, No. 1, 1990, p. 83.

CHAPTER 3

1. Berenice A. Carroll, *Design for Total War: Arms and Economics in the Third Reich*, The Hague, Mouton, 1968, p. 9.

2. Ward Churchill, "Genocide: Toward a Functional Definition," *Alternatives*, Vol. 11, 1986, p. 403.

3. Carl von Clausewitz, *On War*, Edited and Translated by Michael Howard and Peter Paret, Princeton, NJ, Princeton University Press, 1976 [1832], pp. 75–76.

4. von Clausewitz, *On War*, p. 592.

5. von Clausewitz, *On War*, pp. 75, 77, 75, respectively.

6. Richard Preston and Sydney Wise, *Men in Arms: A History of Warfare and Its Interrelationships with Western Society*, Fourth Edition, New York, Holt, Rinehart, and Winston, 1979, p. 238.

7. Hans Speier, "The Social Types of War," in *Social Order and the Risks of War*, Cambridge, MA, MIT Press, 1971 [1941], p. 223.

8. Carroll, *Design for Total War*, p. 23.

9. Hans Speier, "Ludendorf: The German Concept of Total War," in *Social Order and the Risks of War*, [1993], p. 288.

10. von Clausewitz, *On War*, p. 87.

11. Carroll, *Design for Total War*, p. 21.

12. Quoted in Carroll, *Design for Total War*, p. 33.

13. Quoted in Carroll, *Design for Total War,* p. 32.
14. Quoted in Carroll, *Design for Total War,* p. 32.
15. Gil Elliot, *Twentieth Century Book of the Dead,* New York, Charles Scribner's Sons, 1972, pp. 45–46.
16. Arthur Marwick et al., *War and Change in Twentieth-Century Europe, Book V,* Buckingham, England, Open University Press, 1990, p. 13.
17. Hans Speier, "Class Structure and Total War," in *Social Order and the Risks of War,* p. 254. (Essay originally published in 1939.)
18. Ian F. W. Beckett, "Total War," in Colin McInnes and G. D. Sheffield, Editors, *Warfare in the Twentieth Century: Theory and Practice,* London, Unwin Hyman, 1988, p. 8.
19. Edward Luttwak, *A Dictionary of Modern War,* New York, Harper and Row, 1971, p. 203.
20. Richard Hobbs, "The Growth of the Idea of Total War," in *The Myth of Victory: What Is Victory in War?* Boulder, CO, Westview Press, 1979, p. 59.
21. Raymond Aron, *The Century of Total War,* New York, Doubleday, 1954, p. 88.
22. See, for example, Beckett, "Total War," p. 12.
23. Carroll, *Design for Total War,* pp. 11–12.
24. Marjorie Farrar, "World War II as Total War," in L. L. Farrar, Editor, *War: A Historical, Political, and Social Study,* Santa Barbara, CA, ABC-Clio, 1978, p. 171.
25. Frederick Sallagar, *The Road to Total War,* New York, Von Nostrand Reinhold, 1969, p. 2.
26. Robert Harris and Jeremy Paxman, *A Higher Form of Killing: The Secret Story of Chemical and Biological Warfare,* New York, Hill and Wang, 1982, pp. 107–136.
27. J.F.P. Veale, *Advance to Barbarism: The Development of Total Warfare from Sarajevo to Hiroshima,* London, Mitre Press, 1953.
28. Raphael Lemkin, *Axis Rule in Occupied Europe,* Washington, DC, Carnegie Endowment for International Peace, 1944, p. 80.
29. Lemkin, *Axis Rule in Occupied Europe,* p. 79.
30. Lemkin, *Axis Rule in Occupied Europe,* p. 81.
31. Lemkin, *Axis Rule in Occupied Europe,* pp. 82, 90.
32. Lemkin, *Axis Rule in Occupied Europe,* p. 79. For an excellent article and annotated bibliography on ethnocide, see Alison Palmer, "Ethnocide," in Michael N. Dobkowski and Isidor Wallimann, Editors, *Genocide in Our Age,* Ann Arbor, MI, Pierian Press, 1992, pp. 1–21.
33. Lemkin, *Axis Rule in Occupied Europe,* pp. 82–89, 89.
34. Lemkin, *Axis Rule in Occupied Europe,* p. 80.
35. Lemkin, *Axis Rule in Occupied Europe,* p. xiii.
36. See James E. Mace et al., *Commission on the Ukrainian Famine: Report to Congress,* Washington, DC, U.S. Government Printing Office, 1988.
37. Leo Kuper, *Genocide: Its Political Use in the Twentieth Century,* New Haven, CT, Yale University Press, 1981, p. 29.
38. Leo Kuper, *The Prevention of Genocide,* New Haven, CT, Yale University Press, 1985.
39. Elliot, *Twentieth Century Book of the Dead.*
40. Elliot, *Twentieth Century Book of the Dead,* p. 23.
41. Richard L. Rubenstein, *The Cunning of History: The Holocaust and the American Future,* New York, Harper Colophon Books, 1978 [1975], p. 7.
42. Rubenstein, *The Cunning of History,* p. 8.

43. Rubenstein, *The Cunning of History,* p. 11.

44. Rubenstein, *The Cunning of History,* p. 44.

45. Rubenstein, *The Cunning of History,* p. 14.

46. Rubenstein, *The Cunning of History,* p. 12.

47. Rubenstein, *The Cunning of History,* p. 12.

48. Richard L. Rubenstein, *The Age of Triage: Fear and Hope in an Overcrowded World,* Boston, MA, Beacon Press, 1983.

49. Rubenstein, *The Age of Triage,* p. 8.

50. Quoted in Rubenstein, *The Age of Triage,* p. 50.

51. Quoted in Rubenstein, *The Age of Triage,* p. 50.

52. Rubenstein, *The Age of Triage,* p. 110.

53. Rubenstein, *The Age of Triage,* p. 98.

54. Rubenstein, *The Age of Triage,* p. 114.

55. Rubenstein, *The Age of Triage,* p. 113.

56. Irving Louis Horowitz, *Taking Lives: Genocide and State Power,* Third Edition (augmented), New Brunswick, NJ, Transaction Books, 1982 [1976], p. 4.

57. Horowitz, *Taking Lives,* pp. 3–4.

58. Horowitz, *Taking Lives,* pp. 43–65.

59. Irving Louis Horowitz, "Genocide and the Reconstruction of Social Theory: Observations on the Exclusivity of Collective Death," in Isidor Wallimann and Michael N. Dobkowski, Editors, *Genocide and the Modern Age: Etiology and Case Studies of Mass Death,* New York, Greenwood Press, 1987, pp. 61–63.

60. Horowitz, "Genocide and the Reconstruction of Social Theory," p. 61.

61. Horowitz, "Genocide and the Reconstruction of Social Theory," p. 62.

62. Helen Fein, *Accounting for Genocide: National Responses and Jewish Victimization During the Holocaust,* New York, Free Press, 1979.

63. Helen Fein, "Genocide: A Sociological Perspective," *Current Sociology,* Vol. 38, No. 1, 1990.

64. Fein, *Accounting for Genocide,* p. 7.

65. Fein, *Accounting for Genocide,* p. 4.

66. Fein, *Accounting for Genocide,* p. 7.

67. On the Bulgarian treatment of Jews during the Nazi period, see Lucy S. Dawidowicz, *The War Against the Jews,* New York, Bantam Books, pp. 522–527. On more recent treatment of Turks in Bulgaria, see *Bulgaria: Imprisonment of Ethnic Turks,* London, Amnesty International, 1988.

68. Fein, *Accounting for Genocide,* p. 84.

69. Fein, *Accounting for Genocide,* p. 92.

70. Fein, *Accounting for Genocide,* p. 9.

71. Fein, *Accounting for Genocide,* p. 9.

72. Kuper, *Genocide.*

73. Kuper, *Genocide,* p. 9.

74. Kuper, *Genocide,* p. 14.

75. Kuper, *Genocide,* p. 14.

76. Kuper, *Genocide,* p. 10.

77. Kuper, *Genocide,* pp. 161–185.

78. Kuper, *Genocide,* p. 183.

79. Kuper, *Genocide,* p. 183.

80. Israel W. Charny, *How Can We Commit the Unthinkable? Genocide: The Human Cancer,* Boulder, CO, Westview Press, 1982, p. 2.

81. Charny, *How Can We Commit the Unthinkable?* p. 2.

82. Charny, *How Can We Commit the Unthinkable?* p. 4.

83. Charny, *How Can We Commit the Unthinkable?* p. 17.

84. Charny, *How Can We Commit the Unthinkable?* p. 33.

85. Charny, *How Can We Commit the Unthinkable?* p. 41.

86. Charny, *How Can We Commit the Unthinkable?* p. 44.

87. Israel W. Charny, Editor, *Genocide: A Critical Bibliographic Review, Vols. I and II,* New York, Facts on File, 1988 and 1991, respectively. See also I. W. Charny, Editor, *The Widening Circle of Genocide: Genocide: A Critical Bibliographic Review, Vol III,* New Brunswick, NJ, Transaction Press, 1994.

88. Robert Jay Lifton, "Preface," in Lifton and Markusen, *The Genocidal Mentality: Nazi Holocaust and Nuclear Threat,* New York, Basic Books, 1992, pp. xi–xii. See also Robert Jay Lifton and Eric Olson, Editors, *Explorations in Psychohistory: The Wellfleet Papers,* New York, Simon & Schuster, 1974.

89. Robert Jay Lifton, *Thought Reform and the Psychology of Totalism: A Study of "Brainwashing" in China.* Chapel Hill and London, University of North Carolina Press, 1989 [1961].

90. Robert Jay Lifton, *Death in Life: Survivors of Hiroshima,* New York, Random House, 1967; Lifton, *Revolutionary Immortality: Mao Tse-tung and the Chinese Cultural Revolution,* New York, Random House, 1968; Lifton, *Home from the War: Vietnam Veterans—Neither Victims nor Executioners,* New York, Simon & Schuster, 1973; Lifton, *The Nazi Doctors: Medical Killing and the Psychology of Genocide,* New York, Basic Books, 1986.

91. Lifton and Markusen, *The Genocidal Mentality,* p. xii.

92. For an exposition of Lifton's theoretical model of genocide applied to the Cambodian genocide of 1975–1979, see Eric Markusen, "Comprehending the Cambodian Genocide: An Application of Lifton's Model of Genocidal Killing," *Psychohistory Review,* Vol. 20, No. 2, 1992, pp. 145–169.

93. Lifton and Markusen, *The Genocidal Mentality.*

94. Lifton and Markusen, *The Genocidal Mentality,* p. 3.

95. Frank Chalk and Kurt Jonassohn, *The History and Sociology of Genocide: Analyses and Case Studies,* New Haven, CT, Yale University Press, 1990, p. 4.

96. Chalk and Jonassohn, *The History and Sociology of Genocide,* p. 23.

97. Chalk and Jonassohn, *The History and Sociology of Genocide,* p. 23.

98. Quoted in Chalk and Jonassohn, *The History and Sociology of Genocide,* p. 58.

99. Chalk and Jonassohn, *The History and Sociology of Genocide,* p. 29.

100. Chalk and Jonassohn, *The History and Sociology of Genocide,* p. 35.

101. Chalk and Jonassohn, *The History and Sociology of Genocide,* p. 416.

CHAPTER 4

1. Irving Louis Horowitz, *Taking Lives: Genocide and State Power, Third Edition,* New Brunswick, NJ, Transaction Books, 1982 [1976], p. 32.

2. R. J. Rummel, "Dimensions of Foreign and Domestic Conflict Behavior: A Review of Empirical Findings," in Dean G. Pruitt and Richard C. Snyder, Editors, *Theory and Research on the Causes of War,* Englewood Cliffs, NJ, Prentice-Hall, 1969, p. 227.

3. Kurt Jonassohn, "What Is Genocide?" in Helen Fein, Editor, *Genocide Watch,* New Haven, CT, Yale University Press, 1992, p. 22.

4. Leo Kuper, *Genocide: Its Political Use in the Twentieth Century,* New Haven, CT, Yale University Press, 1981, p. 46.

5. Leo Kuper, "Genocide and the Technological Tiger," *Internet on the Holocaust and Genocide,* No. 32, 1992, p. 1.

6. Kuper, *Genocide,* pp. 40, 101.

7. On the genocide of the Guayaki (Aché), see Richard Arens, *Genocide in Paraguay,* Philadelphia, Temple University Press, 1976; on the genocide of the European Jews, see, for example, Raul Hilberg, *The Destruction of the European Jews, Vol. III,* Revised and Definitive Edition, New York, Holmes & Meier, 1985.

8. Frank Chalk and Kurt Jonassohn, *The History and Sociology of Genocide: Analyses and Case Studies,* New Haven, Yale University Press, 1990, pp. 29–40.

9. Leo Kuper, "The Genocidal State: An Overview," in Pierre van den Berghe, Editor, *State Violence and Ethnicity,* Boulder, University Press of Colorado, 1990, p. 38.

10. Israel W. Charny, "Toward a Generic Definition of Genocide," in George L. Andreopolous, Editor, *Genocide: Conceptual and Historial Dimensions,* Philadelphia, University of Pennsylvania Press, 1994, p. 68. (This is the published version of Charny's paper, which was titled, "A Proposal of a New Encompassing Definition of Genocide: Including New Legal Categories of Accomplices to Genocide, and Genocide as a Result of Ecological Destruction and Abuse.")

11. Leo Kuper, *The Prevention of Genocide,* New Haven, CT, Yale University Press, 1985, p. 105.

12. Charny, "Toward a Generic Definition of Genocide," p. 69.

13. Helen Fein, "Genocide: A Sociological Perspective," *Current Sociology,* Vol. 38, No. 1, 1990, p. 22.

14. Ward Churchill, "Genocide: Toward a Functional Definition," *Alternatives* Vol. 11, 1986, p. 403.

15. Kuper, "The Genocidal State," p. 19.

16. Charny, "Toward a Generic Definition of Genocide," p. 91.

17. Vahakn N. Dadrian,"A Typology of Genocide," *International Review of Modern Sociology,* Vol. 15, 1975, p. 206.

18. Hans Speier, "The Social Types of War," in *Social Order and the Risks of War,* Cambridge, MA, MIT Press, 1971 [1941], p. 223.

19. Anatol Rapoport, "Introduction," in Carl von Clausewitz, *On War,* Edited by A. Rapoport, London, Penguin Books, 1968, p. 62.

20. Horowitz, *Taking Lives,* p. 32.

21. Horowitz, *Taking Lives,* p. 56.

22. Horowitz, *Taking Lives,* p. 56.

23. Israel W. Charny, "Genocide: The Ultimate Human Rights Problem," *Social Education* (Special Issue on Human Rights), Vol. 49, No. 6., 1985, p. 448.

24. Charny, "Toward a Generic Definition of Genocide," p. 85.

25. Charny, "Toward a Generic Definition of Genocide," p. 81.

26. Charny, "Toward a Generic Definition of Genocide," pp. 81–82.

27. Rummel, "Dimensions of Foreign and Domestic Conflict Behavior," pp. 226–227.

28. R. J. Rummel, *Lethal Politics: Soviet Genocide and Mass Murder Since 1917,* New Brunswick, NJ, and London, Transaction Books, 1990, p. 241.

29. Rummel, *Lethal Politics*, p. 241.
30. R. J. Rummel, *Democide: Nazi Genocide and Mass Murder*, New Brunswick and London, Transaction Books, 1992, p. 94.
31. R. J. Rummel, "Power Kills; Absolute Power Kills Absolutely," *Internet on the Holocaust and Genocide*, No. 38, June 1992, p. 11.
32. Robert Jay Lifton and Eric Markusen, *The Genocidal Mentality: Nazi Holocaust and Nuclear Threat*, New York, Basic Books, 1990.
33. Kuper, *Genocide*, p. 26.
34. Kuper, *Genocide*, p. 60.
35. Kuper, *Genocide*, p. 66.
36. Helen Fein, "Genocide: A Sociological Perspective," pp. 18–19.
37. Helen Fein, "Discriminating Genocide from War Crimes: Vietnam and Afghanistan Reexamined," *Denver Journal of International Law and Policy*, Vol. 22, No. 1, Fall 1993, p. 33.
38. Kuper, *The Prevention of Genocide*, p. 157.
39. Kuper, *The Prevention of Genocide*, pp. 157–160.
40. Vahakn N. Dadrian, "A Typology of Genocide," *International Review of Modern Sociology*, Vol. 15, 1975, p. 206.
41. Henry R. Huttenbach, "Locating the Holocaust on the Genocide Spectrum: Toward a Methodology of Definition and Categorization," *Holocaust and Genocide Studies*, Vol. 3, No. 3, 1988, p. 297.
42. Dadrian, "A Typology of Genocide," p. 206.
43. Marjorie Farrar, "World War II as Total War," in L. L. Farrar, Editor, *War: A Historical, Political, and Social Study*, Santa Barbara, CA, ABC-Clio, 1978, p. 173; Quincy Wright, *A Study of War*, Chicago, University of Chicago Press, 1942, p. 402.
44. James J. Reid, "The Concept of War and Genocidal Impulses in the Ottoman Empire, 1821–1918," *Holocaust and Genocide Studies*, Vol. 4, No. 2, 1988, pp. 175–191.
45. Barbara Harff, "The Etiology of Genocides," in Isidor Wallimann and Michael Dobkowski, Editors, *Genocide and the Modern Age: Etiology and Case Studies of Mass Death*, New York, Greenwood Press, 1987, p. 46.
46. Vahakn N. Dadrian, "The Structural-Functional Components of Genocide: A Victimological Approach to the Armenian Case," in Israel Drapkin and Emilio Viano, Editors, *Victimology*, Vol. 4, Lexington, MA, Lexington Books, 1974, p. 129.
47. Reid, "The Concept of War and Genocidal Impulses in the Ottoman Empire, 1821–1918," p. 184.
48. C. T. Onions, Editor, *The Oxford University Dictionary*, Oxford, Clarendon Press, 1955, p. 1213.
49. Roman Hrabar et al., *The Fate of Polish Children During the Last War*, Warsaw, Interpress, 1981.
50. Raul Hilberg, "Opening Remarks: The Discovery of the Holocaust," in Peter Hayes, Editor, *Lessons and Legacies: The Meaning of the Holocaust in a Changing World*, Evanston, IL, Northwestern University Press, 1991, p. 15.
51. Barbara Harff, "Recognizing Genocides and Politicides," in Helen Fein, Editor, *Genocide Watch*, New Haven, CT, Yale University Press, 1992, p. 39.
52. Harff, "Recognizing Genocides and Politicides," p. 39.
53. Fein, "Discriminating Genocide from War Crimes," p. 31.
54. Fein, "Discriminating Genocide from War Crimes," p. 36.
55. Chalk and Jonassohn, *The History and Sociology of Genocide*, pp. 23–24.

56. Kuper, "Genocide and the Technological Tiger," p. 1.

57. Sydney Goldenberg, "Crimes Against Humanity 1945–1970," *Western Ontario Law Review*, Vol. 10, 1971, p. 5.

58. Quoted in Goldenberg, "Crimes Against Humanity 1945–1970," p. 2.

59. Quoted in Goldenberg, "Crimes Against Humanity 1945–1970," p. 3.

60. Quoted in Goldenberg, "Crimes Against Humanity 1945–1970," p. 3.

61. Churchill, "Genocide: Toward a Functional Definition," p. 408.

62. Quoted in Kuper, *Genocide*, p. 19.

63. Lawrence J. LeBlanc, *The United States and the Genocide Convention*, Durham and London, Duke University Press, 1991.

64. Kuper, *Genocide*, pp. 26–27.

65. Uriel Tal, "On the Study of the Holocaust and Genocide," *Yad Vashem Studies*, Vol. 13, 1979, p. 18.

66. Kuper, *Genocide*, pp. 24–30.

67. Quoted in Kuper, *The Prevention of Genocide*, p. 12.

68. See Kuper, *The Prevention of Genocide*, for a thorough critical analysis of this issue.

69. Hugo Adam Bedau, "Genocide in Vietnam?" in Virginia Held et al., Editors, *Philosophy, Morality, and International Affairs*, New York, Oxford University Press, 1974, p. 45.

70. Fein, "Discriminating Genocide from War Crimes," p. 36.

71. Fein, "Discriminating Genocide from War Crimes," p. 29.

72. Fein, "Discriminating Genocide from War Crimes," pp. 37–38.

73. Fein, "Discriminating Genocide from War Crimes," p. 39.

74. Fein, "Discriminating Genocide from War Crimes," pp. 43–44.

75. Fein, "Discriminating Genocide from War Crimes," p. 56.

76. Fein, "Discriminating Genocide from War Crimes," p. 56.

77. Fein, "Discriminating Genocide from War Crimes," p. 55.

78. Fein, "Discriminating Genocide from War Crimes," p. 55.

79. Fein, "Discriminating Genocide from War Crimes," p. 41.

80. Fein, "Discriminating Genocide from War Crimes," p. 60.

81. Gaines Post, "Medieval and Renaissance Ideas of Nation," in Philip P. Wiener, Editor in Chief, *Dictionary of the History of Ideas, Vol III*, New York, Charles Scribner's Sons, 1973, p. 318. Though references to the literature on the nation-state and nationalism are scattered about in a variety of monographic and other textual sources, we are familiar with only one attempt to bring together every major approach to these concepts and to critique the ways in which they have been analyzed and categorized. Anthony Smith's *Theories of Nationalism* (New York, Holmes & Meier, 1983) is an ambitious and comprehensive work that reviews, among other relevant topics, most aspects of nationalism and the nation-state in terms of European origins and development, anticolonialism, militarism in Europe and the Third World, and modernization and the problem of identity in multicultural nation-states. The only serious limitation of Smith's book is that it covers the world only through the 1970s and needs to be updated.

82. Morton H. Fried, "State: The Institution," in David L. Sills, Editor, *International Encyclopedia of the Social Sciences, Vol. 15*, New York, Macmillan and Free Press, 1968, p. 145.

83. Anthony Giddens, *The Nation-State and Violence: A Contemporary Critique of Historical Materialism, Vol. 2*, Berkeley and Los Angeles, University of California Press, 1985, p. 20.

84. Pierre van den Berghe, Editor, *State Violence and Ethnicity*, Boulder, University Press of Colorado, 1990, p. 1.

85. Fried, "State: The Institution," pp. 145–146.

86. van den Berghe, *State Violence and Ethnicity,* p. 10.

87. Chalk and Jonassohn, *The History and Sociology of Genocide,* p. 26.

88. Joseph Amato, "Freedom, Fatalism, the State," *Phoenix,* Vol. 9, Nos. 1, 2, 1983, p. 25.

89. Hans Kohn, *Nationalism: Its Meaning and History,* Princeton, NJ, D. Van Nostrand, 1955, p. 9.

90. van den Berghe, *State Violence and Ethnicity,* p. 4.

91. Arnold Toynbee, "Death in War," in *Man's Concern with Death,* St. Louis, MO, McGraw-Hill, 1968, p. 148.

92. Horowitz, *Taking Lives,* p. 179.

93. Toynbee, "Death in War," p. 148.

94. Helen Fein, *Accounting for Genocide: National Responses and Jewish Victimization During the Holocaust,* New York, Free Press, 1979, p. 9.

95. Herbert Kelman, "Violence Without Moral Restraint: Reflections on the Dehumanization of Victims and Victimiziers," *Journal of Social Issues,* Vol. 29, 1973, p. 39.

96. Rummel, "Power Kills; Absolute Power Kills Absolutely," pp. 5, 2. Fein also notes that "recent research on genocide since 1945 confirms that the perpetrators are much more likely to be revolutionary and authoritarian states than democratic states." (Fein, "Discriminating Genocide from War Crimes," p. 78.)

97. Fein, "Discriminating Genocide from War Crimes," pp. 61–62.

98. On Native Americans, see Chalk and Jonassohn, *The History and Sociology of Genocide,* pp. 195–204; on aborigines in Australia, see Tony Barta, "Relations of Genocide: Colonization of Australia," in Isidor Wallimann and Michael N. Dobkowski, Editors, *Genocide and the Modern Age,* New York, Greenwood Press, 1987, pp. 237–251; for other cases, see van den Berghe, *State Violence and Ethnicity,* p. 11.

99. Farrar, "World War II as Total War," p. 173.

100. Wright, *A Study of War,* p. 302.

101. Quoted in J.F.C. Fuller, *The Conduct of War, 1789–1961,* New Brunswick, NJ, Rutgers University Press, 1961, p. 180.

102. Rummel, "Power Kills; Absolute Power Kills Absolutely," p. 5.

CHAPTER 5

1. Robert Jay Lifton, *The Nazi Doctors: Medical Killing and the Psychology of Genocide,* New York, Basic Books, 1986, p. 456.

2. Leo Kuper, *Genocide: Its Political Use in the Twentieth Century,* New Haven, CT, Yale University Press, 1981, p. 86.

3. Herbert Kelman, "Violence Without Moral Restraint: Reflections on the Dehumanization of Victims and Victimizers," *Journal of Social Issues,* Vol. 29, 1973, p. 51.

4. Erik H. Erikson, "Evolutionary and Developmental Considerations," in Lester Grinspoon, Editor, *The Long Darkness: Psychological and Moral Perspectives on Nuclear Winter,* New Haven and London, Yale University Press, 1986, pp. 65–66. See also Viola W. Bernard et al., "Dehumanization," in Nevitt Sanford and Craig Comstock, Editors, *Sanctions for Evil,* San Francisco, Jossey-Bass, 1971, pp. 102–104. (The entire book is an invaluable resource for anyone concerned about genocidal killing.)

5. See, for examples, Kuper, *Genocide,* pp. 85–92; Israel W. Charny, *How Can We Commit the Unthinkable? Genocide: The Human Cancer,* Boulder, CO, Westview Press, 1982, pp.

206–209; Ervin Staub, *The Roots of Evil: The Origins of Genocide and Other Group Violence,* Cambridge, Cambridge University Press, 1989, p. 61.

6. Kelman, "Violence Without Moral Restraint," p. 49. Helen Fein has pointed out that victims of genocide tend to be excluded from the "sanctified universe of obligation—that circle of people with reciprocal obligations to protect each other whose bonds arose from their relation to a deity or sacred source of authority." *Accounting for Genocide: National Responses and Jewish Victimization During the Holocaust,* New York, Free Press, 1979, p. 4. See also "Moral Exclusion and Injustice," a special issue of *Journal of Social Issues,* Vol. 46, No. 1, 1990, Susan Opotow, Editor.

7. William Barry Gault, "Some Remarks on Slaughter," *American Journal of Psychiatry,* Vol. 128, October 1971, p. 452.

8. Herbert Hirsch and Roger W. Smith, "The Language of Extermination in Genocide," in Israel W. Charny, Editor, *Genocide: A Critical Bibliographic Review, Vol. II,* New York, Facts on File, 1991, pp. 386–403.

9. Kelman, "Violence Without Moral Restraint, p. 48.

10. Lifton, *The Nazi Doctors,* p. 445.

11. Max Hastings, *Bomber Command,* London, Michael Joseph, 1979, pp. 122–140.

12. Jeremy Iggers, "Euphemisms Can Impair Clear Thinking About War," *Minneapolis Tribune,* February 6, 1991, pp. 1E–2E.

13. Lifton, *The Nazi Doctors,* p. 456.

14. Robert Payne, *Massacre,* New York, Macmillan, 1973, p. 63.

15. Charny, *How Can We Commit the Unthinkable?* p. 113

16. "Whatever the nature of the economic system," notes Irving Louis Horowitz, "our epoch bears witness to a constant expansion in state power, growth in bureaucratic norms, and an increase in administrative domination and disposition of people." *Taking Lives: Genocide and State Power,* Third Edition, New Brunswick, NJ, Transaction Books, 1982 [1976], p. 137. In their discussion of Max Weber's theory of bureaucracy, sociologists Blau and Scott state, "Almost all modern administrative organizations (as well as some ancient ones) are bureaucratically organized." Peter M. Blau and W. Richard Scott, *Formal Organizations,* San Francisco, Chandler, 1962, p. 32.

17. Richard L. Rubenstein, *The Cunning of History: The Holocaust and the American Future,* New York, Harper Colophon Books, 1978, p. 22. Rubenstein is echoed by sociologist Randall Collins. In his study of the evolution of human cruelty, Collins found bureaucracy to be an important reason for the "ferocious" face-to-face cruelty of the past having been extensively replaced by a new kind of cruelty: callousness, or "cruelty without passion." Although he recognizes that callous cruelty has existed throughout history, he suggests that it is "especially characteristic of large-scale, bureaucratic organizations" and that "the structural of bureaucracy seems uniquely suited for the perpetration of callous violence." Randall Collins, "Three Faces of Evil: Towards a Comparative Sociology of Evil," *Theory and Society,* Vol. 1, 1974, p. 432.

18. Fein, *Accounting for Genocide,* p. 22.

19. Vahakn N. Dadrian, "The Common Features of the Armenian and Jewish Cases of Genocide: A Comparative Victimological Perspective," in Israel Drapkin and Emilio Viano, Editors, *Victimology, Vol. V,* Lexington, MA, D. C. Heath, 1975, p. 107. Writing of the same genocide, Arnold Toynbee also referred to the important role played by the bureaucratic organizational efficiency achieved by its administrators. Arnold Toynbee, *Experiences,* Oxford, Oxford University Press, 1969, pp. 241–242.

20. Karl D. Jackson, "The Ideology of Total Revolution," in K. D. Jackson, Editor, *Cambodia 1975–1978: Rendezvous with Death,* Princeton, Princeton University Press, 1989, p. 37.

21. David Hawk, "The Photographic Record," in *Cambodia 1975–1978,* p. 209. Bureaucratic organization in the Cambodian genocide was epitomized by Tuol Sleng, a torture and execution facility in the capital city of Phnom Penh that had its own "Interrogator's Manual." In another publication, Hawk called it "a unique contribution to the modern annals of torture. Along with mundane admonitions about using sharpened pencils, not smudging reports, not lying down while questioning prisoners, and praise for the wisdom and glory of the Party, is an enumeration of 'soft' interrogation techniques and an extraordinarily frank exposition of the philosophy and practice of systematic torture." David Hawk, "Tuol Sleng Extermination Centre," *Index on Censorship,* Vol. 15, No. 1, 1986, p. 26.

22. In his discussion of total war, Raymond Aron stated, "The supreme laws of the nation at war may be summed up in two words, both of importance in the industrial order: 'organization' and 'rationalization.'" Raymond Aron, *The Century of Total War,* New York, Doubleday, 1954, p. 87.

23. Peter M. Blau and Marshall W. Meyer, *Bureaucracy in Modern Society,* Third Edition, New York, McGraw-Hill, 1987, pp. 19–20.

24. Robert Michels, "Assimilation of the Discontented into State Bureaucracy," in Robert Merton et al., Editors, *Reader in Bureaucracy,* Glencoe, IL, Free Press, 1952, p. 142.

25. Don Martindale, *Institutions, Organizations, and Mass Society,* Boston, Houghton Mifflin, 1966, p. 144.

26. Fred Katz, "A Sociological Perspective to the Holocaust," *Modern Judaism,* Vol. 2, 1982, p. 274.

27. Max Weber, "Bureaucracy," in H. H. Gerth and C. W. Mills, Editors and Translators, *From Max Weber: Essays in Sociology,* New York, Oxford University Press, 1958, pp. 228–229. Likewise, in his analysis of organizational commitments, Philip Selznick observed, "an organizational system, whatever the need or intent which called it into being, generates imperatives derived from the need to maintain the system. … Further, the tendency of established relations and procedures to persist and extend themselves, will create the unintended consequence of committing the organization to greater involvement than provided for in the initial decision to act." Phillip Selznick, "A Theory of Organizational Commitments," in Merton et al., *Reader in Bureaucracy,* pp. 199–200.

28. Morton Halperin, et al., *Bureaucratic Politics and Foreign Policy,* Washington, DC, Brookings Institution, 1974, especially pages 26–63.

29. Weber, "Bureaucracy," pp. 215–216.

30. See Robert Jay Lifton and Eric Markusen, *The Genocidal Mentality: Nazi Holocaust and Nuclear Threat,* New York, Basic Books, 1990, pp. 78–81, for a brief overview of the role of science and technology in modern society.

31. Don Martindale, *Sociological Theory and the Problem of Values,* Columbus, OH, Charles E. Merrill, 1974, p. 211.

32. Francis Allen, "Influence of Technology on War," in Francis Allen et al., Editors, *Technology and Social Change,* New York, Appleton-Century-Crofts, 1957, p. 353.

33. Similarly, John Nef, in *War and Human Progress,* observes that "hand-to-hand fighting became less frequent with the general use of gunpowder during the sixteenth century. It retained some importance nevertheless, especially when decisive battles were fought during and after the Napoleonic wars. But hand-to-hand fighting now seldom plays any serious part in deciding a battle; it plays still less part in deciding a war." John Nef, *War and Human*

Progress: An Essay on the Rise of Industrial Civilization, New York, W. W. Norton, 1968 [1950], p. 373; see also John Keegan, *The Face of Battle,* New York, Viking Press, 1976, pp. 325–333.

34. Irving Louis Horowitz, *Taking Lives: Genocide and State Power,* Third Edition, New Brunswick, NJ, Transaction Books, 1982, p. 87.

35. Kurt Jonassohn, "What Is Genocide?" in Helen Fein, Editor, *Genocide Watch,* New Haven, CT, Yale University Press, 1992, p. 22.

36. Lewis Coser, "The Visibility of Evil," *Journal of Social Issues,* Vol. 25, 1969, p. 105.

37. Steven Katz, "Technology and Genocide: Technology as a 'Form of Life,'" in Alan Rosenberg and Gerald Meyers, Editors, *Echoes from the Holocaust: Philosophical Reflections on a Dark Time,* Philadelphia, Temple University Press, 1989, p. 268.

38. Helen Fein, "Genocide: A Sociological Perspective," *Current Sociology,* Vol. 38, No. 1, 1990, p. 102.

CHAPTER 6

1. Emperor Meiji quoted in Edward Behr, *Hirohito Behind the Myth,* New York, Vantage Books, 1990, p. 223.

2. Ancient Japanese poem quoted in Behr, *Hirohito Behind the Myth,* p. 124.

3. Behr, *Hirohito Behind the Myth,* p. 92.

4. John K. Fairbank et al., *East Asia: The Modern Transformation,* Boston, Houghton Mifflin, 1965, p. 707.

5. Behr, *Hirohito Behind the Myth,* p. 77.

6. Paul Johnson, *Modern Times: The World from the Twenties to the Eighties,* New York, Harper Colophon, 1991, p. 319.

7. Ronald Spector, *Eagle Against the Sun: The American War with Japan,* New York, Free Press, 1985, p. 35.

8. John W. Dower, *War Without Mercy: Race and Power in the Pacific War,* New York, Pantheon Books, 1986, p. 206.

9. Behr, *Hirohito Behind the Myth,* p. 103.

10. Behr, *Hirohito Behind the Myth,* p. 107.

11. Behr, *Hirohito Behind the Myth,* p. 111.

12. Behr, *Hirohito Behind the Myth,* p. 115.

13. R. J. Rummel, *China's Bloody Century: Genocide and Mass Murder Since 1900,* New Brunswick, NJ, and London, Transaction Books, 1991, p. 106.

14. Dower, *War Without Mercy,* pp. 210, 288.

15. Phillip R. Piccigallo, *The Japanese on Trial: Allied War Crimes Operations in the East, 1945–51,* Austin, University of Texas Press, 1979, p. xii.

16. Piccigallo, *The Japanese on Trial,* p. 162.

17. Piccigallo, *The Japanese on Trial,* p. 137.

18. H. J. Timperley, *Japanese Terror in China,* New York, Modern Age Books, 1938, p. 71.

19. Tom Moser, *China, Burma, India,* Alexandria, Virginia, Time Life Books, 1978, p. 11.

20. Dower, *War Without Mercy,* p. 38.

21. Dower, *War Without Mercy,* p. 38.

22. Behr, *Hirohito Behind the Myth,* p. 160.

23. Mark A. Ryan, "The Rape of Nanking: The Genesis of an Atrocity," Minneapolis, University of Minnesota, MA Thesis, Department of History, Summer 1990, p. 4.

24. Ryan, "The Rape of Nanking," p. 7.

25. Rummel, *China's Bloody Century,* pp. 145–146.
26. Behr, *Hirohito Behind the Myth,* p. 160.
27. Ryan, "The Rape of Nanking," p. 5.
28. Piccigallo, *The Japanese on Trial,* p. 163.
29. Behr, *Hirohito Behind the Myth,* p. 161.
30. Behr, *Hirohito Behind the Myth,* p. 164.
31. Behr, *Hirohito Behind the Myth,* p. 351.
32. Behr, *Hirohito Behind the Myth,* p. 164.
33. Peter Williams and David Wallace, *Unit 731: Japan's Secret Biological Warfare in World War II,* New York, Free Press, 1989, p. 16.
34. Behr, *Hirohito Behind The Myth,* p. 165.
35. Williams and Wallace, *Unit 731,* pp. 50–51.
36. Williams and Wallace, *Unit 731,* p. 21.
37. Behr, *Hirohito Behind the Myth,* p. 165.
38. Williams and Wallace, *Unit 731,* p. 24.
39. Williams and Wallace, *Unit 731,* p. 25.
40. Rummel, *China's Bloody Century,* p. 140.
41. Williams and Wallace, *Unit 731,* pp. 140–141.
42. Williams and Wallace, *Unit 731,* p. 37.
43. Williams and Wallace, *Unit 731,* p. 41.
44. Williams and Wallace, *Unit 731,* p. 48.
45. Gil Elliot, *Twentieth Century Book of the Dead,* New York, Charles Scribner's Sons, 1972, p. 65.
46. Elliot, *Twentieth Century Book of the Dead,* p. 65.
47. Rummel, *China's Bloody Century,* p. 139.
48. Spector, *Eagle Against the Sun,* p. 1.
49. Donald Knox, *Death March: The Survivors of Bataan,* Harcourt Brace Jovanovich, 1981, p. 23.
50. Dower, *War Without Mercy,* p. 104.
51. Knox, *Death March,* p. xi.
52. Knox, *Death March,* p. 36.
53. Quoted in Knox, *Death March,* p. 138.
54. Knox, *Death March,* p. 128.
55. Knox, *Death March,* p. 130.
56. Knox, *Death March,,* p. 133.
57. Knox, *Death March,* p. 151.
58. Knox, *Death March,* p. 221.
59. Dower, *War Without Mercy,* p. 48.
60. Dower, *War Without Mercy,* p. 165.
61. Frank A. Reel, *The Case of General Yamashita,* Chicago, University of Chicago Press, 1949, pp. 53–54.
62. A. G. Allbury, *Bamboo and Bushido,* London, Robert Hale, Limited, 1955, p. 14.
63. Dower, *War Without Mercy,* p. 43.
64. Allbury, *Bamboo and Bushido,* p. 88.
65. Allbury, *Bamboo and Bushido,* pp. 25–38.
66. Allbury, *Bamboo and Bushido,* p. 22.
67. Allbury, *Bamboo and Bushido,* p. 43.

68. Allbury, *Bamboo and Bushido,* p. 41.
69. Allbury, *Bamboo and Bushido,* p. 53.
70. Allbury, *Bamboo and Bushido,* p. 67.
71. Allbury, *Bamboo and Bushido,* pp. 80–81.
72. Gwen Drew, *Prisoner of the Japs,* New York, Alfred A. Knopf, 1943, p. 4.
73. Wenzell Brown, *Hong Kong Aftermath,* New York, Smith and Durrell, n.d., pp. 111–112.
74. Rummel, *China's Bloody Century,* p. 154.
75. Rummel, *China's Bloody Century,* p. 23.
76. Rummel, *China's Bloody Century,* p. 24.
77. Rummel, *China's Bloody Century,* p. 91.
78. Rummel, *China's Bloody Century,* p. 94.
79. Rummel, *China's Bloody Century,* p. 103.
80. Dower, *War Without Mercy,* p. 45.
81. Dower, *War Without Mercy,* p. 45.
82. General Rudolfo Graziani quoted in A. J. Barker, *Rape of Ethiopia 1936*, New York, Ballantine Books, 1971, p. 69.
83. Barker, *Rape of Ethiopia,* p. 71.
84. Barker, *Rape of Ethiopia,* pp. 20–29.
85. Barker, *Rape of Ethiopia,* p. 56.
86. Barker, *Rape of Ethiopia,* p. 69.
87. Barker, *Rape of Ethiopia,* p. 77.
88. Barker, *Rape of Ethiopia,* p. 91.
89. Barker, *Rape of Ethiopia,* p. 105.
90. Johnson, *Modern Times,* p. 323.
91. Johnson, *Modern Times,* p. 329.
92. Johnson, *Modern Times,* p. 328.
93. Johnson, *Modern Times,* p. 328.
94. Johnson, *Modern Times,* p. 329.
95. Johnson, *Modern Times,* p. 329.
96. Johnson, *Modern Times,* p. 330.
97. Johnson, *Modern Times,* p. 334.
98. Johnson, *Modern Times,* p. 334.
99. Johnson, *Modern Times,* p. 339.
100. Johnson, *Modern Times,* p. 339.
101. Johnson, *Modern Times,* p. 339.
102. Johnson, *Modern Times,* p. 338.
103. M. S. Venkataramani, *Bengal Famine of 1943: The American Response,* Bombay, Vikas, 1973, p. 6.
104. Tarakchandra Das, *Bengal Famine of 1943*, Calcutta, University of Calcutta, 1949, p. 101.
105. Famine Inquiry Commission, *Report on Bengal,* Calcutta, Superintendent Government Press, 1945, p. 25.
106. Famine Inquiry Commission, *Report on Bengal,* p. 27.
107. Quoted in Venkataramani, *Bengal Famine of 1943*, p. 5.
108. Venkataramani, *Bengal Famine of 1943*, p. 8.
109. Quoted in Venkataramani, *Bengal Famine of 1943*, p. 17.
110. Quoted in Venkataramani, *Bengal Famine of 1943*, p. 8.

111. Venkataramani, *Bengal Famine of 1943*, p. 27.
112. Das, *Bengal Famine 1943*, p. 31.
113. Venkataramani, *Bengal Famine of 1943*, p. 33.
114. Wallace quoted in Venkataramani, *Bengal Famine of 1943*, p. 34.
115. Venkataramani, *Bengal Famine of 1943*, pp. 47–55.
116. Venkataramani, *Bengal Famine of 1943*, p. 65.
117. Quoted in Venkataramani, *Bengal Famine of 1943*, p. 66.
118. Venkataramani, *Bengal Famine of 1943*, p. 66.
119. William Eckhardt, "War-Related Deaths Since 3000 BC," Paper presented to the 1991 annual meeting of the International Society for the Comparative Study of Civilizations, Santo Domingo, Dominican Republic, 1991, p. 23.
120. Elliot, *Twentieth Century Book of the Dead*, p. 54.
121. Elliot, *Twentieth Century Book of the Dead*, pp. 55–56.
122. Bohdan Wytwycky, *The Other Holocaust: Many Circles of Hell*, Washington, DC, Novak Project, 1980, p. 52.
123. Wytwycky, *The Other Holocaust*, pp. 55–56.
124. Wytwycky, *The Other Holocaust*, p. 72.
125. Wytwycky, *The Other Holocaust*, p. 74.
126. Wytwycky, *The Other Holocaust*, p. 74.
127. Wytwycky, *The Other Holocaust*, p. 75.
128. Wytwycky, *The Other Holocaust*, p. 75.
129. Wytwycky, *The Other Holocaust*, p. 75.
130. Hans Frank quoted in Wytwycky, *The Other Holocaust*, p. 19.
131. Quoted in Wytwycky, *The Other Holocaust*, p. 41.
132. Wytwycky, *The Other Holocaust*, p. 42.
133. Wytwycky, *The Other Holocaust*, p. 43.
134. Wytwycky, *The Other Holocaust*, p. 77. See also Richard C. Lukas, "The Polish Experience During the Holocaust," in Michael Berenbaum, Editor, *A Mosaic of Victims: Non-Jews Persecuted and Murdered by the Nazis*, New York, New York University Press, 1990, pp. 88–95.
135. Wytwycky, *The Other Holocaust*, p. 50.
136. Wytwycky, *The Other Holocaust*, p. 51.
137. Wytwycky, *The Other Holocaust*, p. 51.
138. Wytwycky, *The Other Holocaust*, p. 53.
139. Wytwycky, *The Other Holocaust*, p. 38. See also Jiri Lipa, "The Fate of Gypsies in Czechoslovakia Under Nazi Domination," in Berenbaum, *A Mosaic of Victims*, pp. 200–206.
140. Quoted in Edmund Paris, *Genocide in Satellite Croatia*, Chicago, American Institute for Balkan Affairs, 1961, pp. 132–133.
141. Paris, *Genocide in Satellite Croatia*, p. 14.
142. Paris, *Genocide in Satellite Croatia*, p. 5.
143. Paris, *Genocide in Satellite Croatia*, p. 59.
144. Paris, *Genocide in Satellite Croatia*, p. 62.
145. Paris, *Genocide in Satellite Croatia*, pp. 103–104.
146. Paris, *Genocide in Satellite Croatia*, pp. 101–102.
147. Paris, *Genocide in Satellite Croatia*, p. 102.
148. Paris, *Genocide in Satellite Croatia*, p. 103.
149. Paris, *Genocide in Satellite Croatia*, p. 9.

150. Danubian Research and Information Center, Budapest, 1985, p. 14.

151. Danubian Research and Information Center, 1985, p. 14.

152. Danubian Research and Information Center, 1985, p. 14.

153. Danubian Research and Information Center, 1985, p. 23.

154. Danubian Research and Information Center, 1985, p. 23.

155. Danubian Research and Information Center, 1985, p. 23.

156. Lucy Dawidowicz, *The War Against the Jews,* New York, Holt, Rinehart and Winston, 1975, p. 522.

157. R. J. Rummel, *Lethal Politics: Soviet Genocide and Mass Murder Since 1917,* New Brunswick, NJ, and London, Transaction Books, 1990, p. xiii.

158. Rummel, *Lethal Politics,* p. 152.

159. Quoted in Rummel, *Lethal Politics,* pp. 154–155.

160. Rummel, *Lethal Politics,* p. 157.

161. Quoted in Rummel, *Lethal Politics,* p. 163.

162. Rummel, *Lethal Politics,* p. 163.

163. Ann Sheehy and Bohdan Nahaylo, *The Crimean Tatars, the Volga Germans, and the Meskhetians: Soviet Treatment of National Minorities,* London, Minority Rights Group, 1980, p. 5.

164. Sheehy and Nahaylo, *The Crimean Tatars, the Volga Germans, and the Meskhetians,* p. 8.

165. Sheehy and Nahaylo, *The Crimean Tatars, the Volga Germans, and the Meskhetians,* p. 8.

166. Sheehy and Nahaylo, *The Crimean Tatars, the Volga Germans, and the Meskhetians,* p. 8.

167. Rummel, *Lethal Politics,* p. 158.

168. Rummel, *Lethal Politics,* p. 166.

169. Rummel, *Lethal Politics,* p. 161.

CHAPTER 7

1. Richard Rubenstein, *The Cunning of History: The Holocaust and the American Future,* New York, Harper Colophon Books, 1978, p. 2.

2. R. J. Rummel, *Democide: Nazi Genocide and Mass Murder,* New Brunswick and London, Transaction Books, 1992, p. 13.

3. Yehuda Bauer, *A History of the Holocaust,* New York, Franklin Watts, 1982, p. 85.

4. Bauer, *A History of the Holocaust,* p. 93.

5. Gunter W. Remmling, "Discrimination, Persecution, Theft, and Murder Under Color of Law: The Totalitarian Corruption of the German Legal System, 1933–1945," in Isidor Wallimann and Michael N. Dobkowski, Editors, *Genocide and the Modern Age: Etiology and Case Studies of Mass Death,* New York, Greenwood Press, 1987, pp. 185–201.

6. Bauer, *A History of the Holocaust,* p. 123.

7. Heinz Höhne, *Order of the Death's Head: The Story of Hitler's SS,* New York, Ballantine Books, Fifth Printing, 1984, p. 145.

8. Lucy Dawidowicz, *The War Against the Jews,* New York, Holt, Rinehart and Winston, 1975, pp. 70–87.

9. Ian Hancock, "'Uniqueness' of the Victims: Gypsies, Jews, and the Holocaust," *Without Prejudice. The EAFORD International Review of Racial Discrimination,* Vol. 1, No. 2, 1988, p. 59.

10. Leni Yahil, *The Holocaust: The Fate of European Jewry, 1932–1945*, Translated by Ina Friedman and Haya Galai, New York, Oxford University Press, 1990, p. 111.

11. Karl Schleunes, *The Twisted Road to Auschwitz: Nazi Policy Toward German Jews, 1933–1939*, Chicago, University of Illinois Press, 1970, p. 160.

12. Quoted in Leon Poliakov, *Harvest of Hate: The Nazi Program for the Destruction of the Jews in Europe*, New York, Holocaust Library, 1979, p. 30.

13. Nora Levin, *The Holocaust: The Destruction of European Jewry, 1933–1945*, New York, Schocken Books, [1968], 1973, p. 138.

14. Bialer quoted in Martin Gilbert, *The Holocaust: A History of the Jews During the Second World War*, New York, Holt, Rinehart and Winston, 1985, pp. 129–130.

15. Arno Mayer, *Why Did the Heavens Not Darken? The "Final Solution" in History*, New York, Pantheon, 1988, p. 178.

16. Emilia Borecka, *Warszawa 1945*, Warsaw, Panstwowe Wydawnictwo Naukowe, 1985, p. 306.

17. Bauer, *A History of the Holocaust*, p. 140.

18. Levin, *The Holocaust*, pp. 164–184.

19. Yahil, *The Holocaust*, p. 137.

20. Bohdan Wytwycky, *The Other Holocaust: Many Circles of Hell*, Washington, DC, Novak Project, 1980, pp. 32–33.

21. Levin, *The Holocaust*, p. 160.

22. Raul Hilberg, *The Destruction of the European Jews, Vol. I*, Revised and Definitive Edition, New York, Holmes & Meier, 1985, pp. 259–266.

23. Bauer, *A History of the Holocaust*, p. 170.

24. Levin, *The Holocaust*, p. 216.

25. Robert Jay Lifton, *The Nazi Doctors: Medical Killing and the Psychology of Genocide*, New York, Basic Books, 1986, p. 46.

26. Lifton, *The Nazi Doctors*, pp. 149, 254.

27. Michael Tregenza, "Belzec Death Camp," *Wiener Library Bulletin*, Vol. 30, 1977, p. 13.

28. Christopher R. Browning, *Fateful Months: Essays on the Emergence of the Final Solution*, Revised Edition, New York, Holmes & Meier, p. 59.

29. Uwe Dietrich Adam, "The Gas Chambers," in François Furet, Editor, *Unanswered Questions: Nazi Germany and the Genocide of the Jews*, New York, Schocken Books, 1989, p. 138.

30. Rummel, *Democide*, p. 13.

31. Lifton, *The Nazi Doctors*, p. 139.

32. Quoted in Yahil, *The Holocaust*, p. 249.

33. Quoted in Mayer, *Why Did the Heavens Not Darken?* p. 209.

34. Jürgen Förster, "The German Army and the Ideological War Against the Soviet Union," in Gerhard Hirshfield, Editor, *The Policies of Genocide: Jews and Soviet Prisoners of War in Nazi Germany*, London, Allen & Unwin, 1986, p. 17.

35. Quoted in Förster, "The German Army and the Ideological War Against the Soviet Union," p. 20.

36. Höhne, *Order of the Death's Head*, p. 405.

37. Mayer, *Why Did the Heavens Not Darken?* p. 238.

38. Mayer, *Why Did the Heavens Not Darken?* p. 255.

39. Quoted in Förster, "The German Army and the Ideological War Against the Soviet Union," p. 24.

40. Förster, "The German Army and the Ideological War Against the Soviet Union," p. 20.

41. Omer Bartov, *The Eastern Front, 1941–45: German Troops and the Barbarisation of Warfare,* New York, St. Martin's Press, 1986, p. 121.

42. Mayer, *Why Did the Heavens Not Darken?* p. 265.

43. Poliakov, *Harvest of Hate,* p. 123.

44. Gilbert, *The Holocaust,* p. 218.

45. Mayer, *Why Did the Heavens Not Darken?* p. 268.

46. Gilbert, *The Holocaust,* p. 175.

47. Hilberg, *The Destruction of the European Jews, Vol. I,* p. 332.

48. Browning, *Fateful Months,* p. 60.

49. Browning, *Fateful Months,* p. 64.

50. Hilberg, *The Destruction of the European Jews, Vol. I,* p. 341.

51. Mayer, *Why Did the Heavens Not Darken?* p. 252.

52. Bartov, *The Eastern Front, 1941–45,* pp. 111–112.

53. Hilberg, *The Destruction of the European Jews, Vol. I,* p. 301.

54. Mayer, *Why Did the Heavens Not Darken?* pp. 244–245.

55. Mayer, *Why Did the Heavens Not Darken?* p. 205.

56. Mayer, *Why Did the Heavens Not Darken?* p. 252.

57. Bartov, *The Eastern Front, 1941–45,* pp. 107–111.

58. Wladyslaw T. Bartoszewski, Editor, *Surviving Treblinka: Samuel Willenberg,* Oxford, Blackwell, 1989, p. 9.

59. Danuta Czech, *Auschwitz Chronicle 1939–1945,* New York, Henry Holt, 1990, pp. 85–86.

60. Quoted in Poliakov, *Harvest of Hate,* p. 199.

61. Browning, *Fateful Months,* pp. 8–38; particularly pp. 32, 38.

62. Quoted in Bauer, *A History of the Holocaust,* p. 205

63. Bauer, *A History of the Holocaust,* p. 206.

64. Hilberg, *The Destruction of the European Jews, Vol. I,* p. 369.

65. Leon Wells, *The Janowska Road,* New York, Macmillan, 1963, p. 175.

66. Bauer, *A History of the Holocaust,* p. 200.

67. Bartoszewski, *Surviving Treblinka,* p. 9.

68. Bartoszewski, *Surviving Treblinka,* p. 9.

69. Yankiel Wiernik, "A Year in Treblinka," in Alexander Donat, Editor, *The Death Camp Treblinka,* New York, Holocaust Library, 1979, pp. 158–159.

70. Hilberg, *The Destruction of the European Jews, Vol. III,* p. 1219.

71. Bartoszewski, *Surviving Treblinka,* p. 9.

72. Jozef Marszalek, *Majdanek: The Concentration Camp in Lublin,* Warsaw, Interpress, 1986.

73. Konnilyn Feig, *Hitler's Death Camps: The Sanity of Madness,* New York, Holmes & Meier, 1983, p. 318.

74. Hannah Arendt, *The Origins of Totalitarianism,* New York, Harcourt Brace, 1951, p. 449. For a detailed examination of the gas chambers at Auschwitz-Birkenau, see Jean-Claude Pressac, *Auschwitz: Technique and Operation of the Gas Chambers,* New York, Beate Klarsfeld Foundation, 1989.

75. Filip Friedman, *This Was Oswiecim: The Story of a Murder Camp,* London, United Jewish Relief Appeal, 1946, p. 19.

76. Filip Müller, *Eyewitness Auschwitz: Three Years in the Gas Chambers*, New York, Stein and Day, 1981, pp. 37–38.

77. Müller, *Eyewitness Auschwitz*, p. 61.

78. Müller, *Eyewitness Auschwitz*, p. 117.

79. Gilbert, *The Holocaust*, p. 728.

80. Müller, *Eyewitness Auschwitz*, p. 139.

81. Jane Perlez, "Decay of a Twentieth Century Relic: What's the Future of Auschwitz?" *New York Times*, January 4, 1994, p. A4.

82. Alan Berger, "The Holocaust: The Ultimate and Archetypal Genocide," in Israel W. Charny, Editor, *Genocide: A Critical Bibliographic Review, Vol. I*, New York, Facts on File, 1988, p. 59.

83. Bauer, *A History of the Holocaust*, p. 336.

CHAPTER 8

1. Quoted in Daniel Ellsberg, "The Responsibility of Officials in a Criminal War," in *Papers on the War*, New York, Simon & Schuster, 1972, p. 277. The book from which the Nietzsche quote was taken, *Beyond Good and Evil: Prelude to a Philosophy of the Future*, was originally published in 1886 and reissued by Vintage Books in 1966. The passage quoted is on p. 89 of the Vintage edition.

2. Quoted in Richard Rhodes, *The Making of the Atomic Bomb*, New York, Simon & Schuster, 1986, p. 310.

3. Quoted in Martin Middlebrook, *The Battle of Hamburg: Allied Bomber Forces Against a German City in 1943*, New York, Charles Scribner's Sons, 1981, pp. 19–20.

4. Lee Kennett, *A History of Strategic Bombing*, New York, Charles Scribner's Sons, 1982, p. 106–110.

5. Noble Frankland, *Bomber Offensive: The Devastation of Europe*, New York, Ballantine Books, 1970, p. 21.

6. Anthony Verrier, *The Bomber Offensive*, New York, Macmillan, 1969, p. 110.

7. Kennett, *A History of Strategic Bombing*, p. 111.

8. George Quester, "Bargaining and Bombing During World War II in Europe," *World Politics*, April 1963, pp. 417–422.

9. Kennett, *A History of Strategic Bombing*, p. 108.

10. R. Ernest Dupuy and Trevor N. Dupuy, *The Encyclopedia of Military History*, New York, Harper and Row, 1977, pp. 1050–1051.

11. Kennett, *A History of Strategic Bombing*, p. 109.

12. Kennett, *A History of Strategic Bombing*, pp. 112–113.

13. Quester, "Bargaining and Bombing During World War II in Europe," p. 424.

14. R. J. Overy, *The Air War, 1939–1945*, New York, Stein and Day, 1980, p. 38.

15. Frederick Sallagar, *The Road to Total War*, New York, Von Nostrand Reinhold, 1969, p. 66.

16. Quester, "Bargaining and Bombing During World War II in Europe," p. 427.

17. Quoted in Sallagar, *The Road to Total War*, p. 70.

18. Quester, "Bargaining and Bombing During World War II in Europe," p. 428.

19. Sallagar, *The Road to Total War*, p. 67.

20. Rhodes, *The Making of the Atomic Bomb*,

21. James L. Stokesbury, *A Short History of Air Power*, New York, William Morrow, 1986, p. 179.

22. Sallagar, *The Road to Total War,* p. 90.

23. Quoted in Charles Webster and Noble Frankland, *The Strategic Air Offensive Against Germany, Vol. I,* London, Her Majesty's Stationery Office, 1961, p. 157.

24. Webster and Frankland, *The Strategic Air Offensive Against Germany, Vol. I,* p. 157.

25. Max Hastings, *Bomber Command,* London, Michael Joseph, 1979, p. 100.

26. Sallagar, *The Road to Total War,* p. 94.

27. Quoted in Webster and Frankland, *The Strategic Air Offensive Against Germany, Vol. I,* p. 144.

28. Kennett, *A History of Strategic Bombing,* p. 75–76.

29. Arthur Harris, *Bomber Offensive,* London, Collins Press, 1947, p. 277.

30. Quoted in Hastings, *Bomber Command,* p. 141.

31. Kennett, *A History of Strategic Bombing,* p. 130.

32. David Irving, *The Destruction of Dresden,* New York, Ballantine Books, 1965, p. 96.

33. Webster and Frankland, *The Strategic Air Offensive Against Germany, Vol. I,* p. 392.

34. Kennett, *A History of Strategic Bombing,* pp. 131–132.

35. Ralph Barker, *The Thousand Plane Raid,* New York, Ballantine Books, 1966, p. 220.

36. George Quester, *Deterrence Before Hiroshima: The Air Power Background of Modern Strategy,* New York, John Wiley, 1966, p. 145; see also Overy, *The Air War, 1939–1945,* pp. 73–75.

37. Quoted in Michael Sherry, *The Rise of American Air Power: The Creation of Armageddon,* New York and London, Yale University Press, 1987, p. 154.

38. Middlebrook, *The Battle of Hamburg,* p. 328.

39. Sherry, *The Rise of American Air Power,* p. 153.

40. Quoted in Gordon Musgrove, *Operation Gomorrah: The Hamburg Firestorm Raids,* New York and London, Jane's Publishing, 1981, p. 109.

41. Horatio Bond, *Fire and the Air War,* Boston, National Fire Protection Association International, 1946, pp. 117–118.

42. Quoted in Middlebrook, *The Battle of Hamburg,* p. 244.

43. Martin Caidin, *A Torch to the Enemy,* New York, Ballantine Books, 1979 [1960], p. 93.

44. Musgrove, *Operation Gomorrah,* p. 98.

45. Quoted in Middlebrook, *The Battle of Hamburg,* p. 276.

46. Caidin, *A Torch to the Enemy,* p. 98.

47. Quoted in Musgrove, *Operation Gomorrah,* p. 109.

48. Kennett, *A History of Strategic Bombing,* pp. 146–148.

49. Middlebrook, *The Battle of Hamburg,* p. 328.

50. Earl R. Beck, *Under the Bombs: The German Home Front, 1942–1945,* Lexington, University Press of Kentucky, 1986, p. 76.

51. Kennett, *A History of Strategic Bombing,* p. 155.

52. Kennett, *A History of Strategic Bombing,*, p. 122.

53. Kennett, *A History of Strategic Bombing,*, p. 160.

54. Irving, *The Destruction of Dresden,* p. 76.

55. Robert Saundby, "Introduction," in Irving, *The Destruction of Dresden,* p. 9; for a more recent, concurring assessment, see Alexander McKee, *Dresden 1945: The Devil's Tinderbox,* New York, E. P. Dutton, 1984, p. 70.

56. Quoted in McKee, *Dresden 1945,* p. 102.

57. Rhodes, *The Making of the Atomic Bomb,* p. 592.

58. McKee, *Dresden 1945,* pp. 113, 160, 225–227.

59. Irving, *The Destruction of Dresden*, p. 196.
60. Quoted in Irving, *The Destruction of Dresden*, pp. 155–156.
61. Quoted in McKee, *Dresden 1945*, p. 182.
62. McKee, *Dresden 1945*, p. 321.
63. Irving, *The Destruction of Dresden*, pp. 8–9.
64. Hastings, *Bomber Command*, p. 404; see also Michael Walzer, *Just and Unjust Wars*, New York, Basic Books, 1977, pp. 323–325.
65. Quoted in Sherry, *The Rise of American Air Power*, p. 91.
66. Overy, *The Air War, 1939–1945*, p. 63.
67. Quoted in Sherry, *The Rise of American Air Power*, p. 99.
68. Quoted in Wesley F. Craven and James Lea Cate, *The Army Air Forces in World War II, Vol. I*, Chicago and London, University of Chicago Press, 1948, p. 149.
69. Craven and Cate, *The Army Air Forces in World War II, Vol. I*, p. 597.
70. George E. Hopkins, "Bombing and American Conscience During World War II," *Historian*, Vol. 28, 1968, p. 460.
71. Quoted in Sherry, *The Rise of American Air Power*, p. 109.
72. Kennett, *A History of Strategic Bombing*, p. 136.
73. Craven and Cate, *The Army Air Forces in World War II, Vol. II*, 1949, p. 323.
74. Sherry, *The Rise of American Air Power*, p. 156.
75. Quoted in Ronald Schaffer, *Wings of Judgment: American Bombing in World War II*, New York and Oxford, Oxford University Press, 1985, pp. 65–66.
76. Kennett, *A History of Strategic Bombing*, p. 153.
77. Schaffer, *Wings of Judgment*, p. 67.
78. Craven and Cate, *The Army Air Forces in World War II, Vol. III*, 1951, p. 723.
79. Sherry, *The Rise of American Air Power*, p. 162.
80. Conrad C. Crane, *Bombs, Cities, and Civilians: American Airpower in World War II*, Lawrence, KS, University Press of Kansas, p. 76.
81. Schaffer, *Wings of Judgment*, p. 56.
82. Schaffer, *Wings of Judgment*, p. 56; for a different opinion, see Crane, *Bombs, Cities, and Civilians*, p. 98.
83. Quoted in Schaffer, *Wings of Judgment*, p. 73.
84. Schaffer, *Wings of Judgment*, p. 85.
85. Quoted in Schaffer, *Wings of Judgment*, p. 85.
86. Craven and Cate, *The Army Air Forces in World War II, Vol. III*, p. 732.
87. Quoted in Schaffer, *Wings of Judgment*, p. 88.
88. Quoted in Schaffer, *Wings of Judgment*, p. 92.
89. Schaffer, *Wings of Judgment*, p. 94.
90. Schaffer, *Wings of Judgment*, p. 97.
91. Quester, *Deterrence Before Hiroshima*, p. 162.
92. Sherry, *The Rise of American Air Power*, p. 123.
93. Kennett, *A History of Strategic Bombing*, p. 163.
94. Kennett, *A History of Strategic Bombing*, p. 166.
95. Quoted in Caidin, *A Torch to the Enemy*, p. 35.
96. Kennett, *A History of Strategic Bombing*, p. 167.
97. Quoted in Caidin, *A Torch to the Enemy*, p. 41
98. Caidin, *A Torch to the Enemy*, p. 44.

99. John W. Dower, *War Without Mercy: Race and Power in the Pacific War,* New York, Pantheon Books, 1986, p. 45.

100. Dower, *War Without Mercy,* p. 45.

101. William Manchester, *Goodbye Darkness,* New York, Little, Brown, 1980, p. 340.

102. Schaffer, *Wings of Judgment,* p. 124.

103. Caidin, *A Torch to the Enemy,* p. 62.

104. Hoito Edoin, *The Night Tokyo Burned,* New York, St. Martin's Press, 1987, p. 34.

105. Quoted in Sherry, *The Rise of American Air Power,* p. 58.

106. Sherry, *The Rise of American Air Power,* p. 156.

107. Bartlett E. Kerr, *Flames over Tokyo: The U.S. Army Air Force's Incendiary Campaign Against Japan,* New York, D. I. Fine, 1991, p. 22.

108. Schaffer, *Wings of Judgment,* pp. 111–112.

109. Kerr, *Flames over Tokyo,* p. 42.

110. Schaffer, *Wings of Judgment,* p. 113.

111. Kerr, *Flames over Tokyo,* p. 31.

112. Quoted in Sherry, *The Rise of American Air Power,* p. 229.

113. Sherry, *The Rise of American Air Power,* p. 229.

114. Kennett, *A History of Strategic Bombing,* p. 169.

115. Kennett, *A History of Strategic Bombing,* p. 169.

116. Kerr, *Flames over Tokyo,* p. 14.

117. Schaffer, *Wings of Judgment,* p. 126.

118. Kennett, *A History of Strategic Bombing,* p. 170.

119. Sherry, *The Rise of American Air Power,* p. 274.

120. Crane, *Bombs, Cities, and Civilians,* p. 132.

121. Wilbur H. Morrison, *Point of No Return: The Story of the Twentieth Air Force,* New York, Times Books, 1979, p. 197.

122. Rhodes, *The Making of the Atomic Bomb,* p. 596.

123. Quoted in Kerr, *Flames over Tokyo,* p. 72.

124. Caidin, *A Torch to the Enemy,* pp. 86, 99.

125. Edoin, *The Night Tokyo Burned,* p. 206.

126. Kennett, *A History of Strategic Bombing,* p. 171.

127. Sherry, *The Rise of American Air Power,* p. 276.

128. Caidin, *A Torch to the Enemy,* pp. 117–118.

129. Sherry, *The Rise of American Air Power,* p. 276.

130. David MacIsaac, Editor, *U.S. Strategic Bombing Survey, Vol. X,* New York, Garland, 1976 [1946], p. 94.

131. Caidin, *A Torch to the Enemy,* p. 119.

132. Caidin, *A Torch to the Enemy,* p. 121.

133. Schaffer, *Wings of Judgment,* p. 134.

134. Edoin, *The Night Tokyo Burned,* p. 64.

135. Caidin, *A Torch to the Enemy,* pp. 131–132.

136. Schaffer, *Wings of Judgment,* p. 132.

137. Rhodes, *The Making of the Atomic Bomb,* p. 599.

138. Sherry, *The Rise of American Air Power,* p. 277.

139. Dower, *War Without Mercy,* p. 41.

140. Schaffer, *Wings of Judgment,* p. 132.

141. Quoted in Schaffer, *Wings of Judgment,* p. 132.

142. Kerr, *Flames over Tokyo,* pp. 214–217.

143. Kennett, *A History of Strategic Bombing,* p. 171.

144. Overy, *The Air War,* p. 100.

145. Otis Cary, "The Sparing of Kyoto, Mr. Stimson's 'Pet City,'" *Japan Quarterly,* Vol. 22, 1975, pp. 337–347.

146. Kennett, *A History of Strategic Bombing,* p. 175.

147. Quoted in Rhodes, *The Making of the Atomic Bomb,* pp. 724–725.

148. Quoted in Rhodes, *The Making of the Atomic Bomb,* p. 728.

149. Robert Jay Lifton, *Death in Life: Survivors of Hiroshima,* New York, Random House, 1967, p. 57.

150. Rhodes, *The Making of the Atomic Bomb,* pp. 734, 740.

CHAPTER 9

1. Yehuda Bauer, *A History of the Holocaust,* New York, Franklin Watts, 1982, pp. 90–91.

2. Raul Hilberg, *The Destruction of the European Jews, Vol. I,* Revised and Definitive Edition, New York, Holmes & Meier, 1985, p. 15.

3. Martin Luther, "The Jews and Their Lies," in Franklin Sherman, Editor, *Luther's Works, Vol. 47,* Philadelphia, Fortress Press, 1971 [1543], p. 212.

4. Luther, "The Jews and Their Lies," p. 265.

5. Luther, "The Jews and Their Lies," p. 277.

6. Lucy Dawidowicz, *The War Against the Jews,* New York, Holt, Rinehart and Winston, 1975, p. 23.

7. Helmut Krausnick, "The Persecution of the Jews," in Helmut Krausnick et al., Editors, *The Anatomy of the SS State,* New York, Walker, 1968, p. 6.

8. Krausnick, *The Anatomy of the SS State,* p. 7.

9. Patrick Girard, "Historical Foundations of Anti-Semitism," in Joel E. Dimsdale, Editor, *Survivors, Victims, and Perpetrators,* Washington, DC, Hemisphere, 1980, p. 69.

10. Karl Schleunes, *The Twisted Road to Auschwitz: Nazi Policy Toward German Jews, 1933–1939,* Chicago, University of Illinois Press, 1970, p. 261.

11. George L. Mosse, *Toward the Final Solution: A History of European Racism,* New York, Harper and Row, 1978, p. 234.

12. Mosse, *Toward the Final Solution,* p. 204.

13. Quoted in Lucy Dawidowicz, *A Holocaust Reader,* New York, Behrman House, 1976, p. 30.

14. Quoted in Richard Breitman, *The Architect of Genocide: Himmler and the Final Solution,* New York, Knopf, 1991, p. 234.

15. Quoted in Hilberg, *The Destruction of the European Jews, Vol. I,* p. 20.

16. Hilberg, *The Destruction of the European Jews, Vol. I,* p. 20.

17. Mosse, *Nazi Culture: Intellectual, Cultural, and Social Life in the Third Reich,* New York, Grosset and Dunlap, 1966, p. 66.

18. Nora Levin, *The Holocaust: the Destruction of European Jewry, 1933–1945,* New York, Schocken Books, 1973, p. 11.

19. Gilmer Blackburn, *Education in the Third Reich: A Study of Race and History in Textbooks,* Albany, State University of New York, 1985, especially pp. 24–33, 139–149.

20. Mosse, *Nazi Culture,* p. 66.

21. Karl Dietrich Bracher, *The German Dictatorship: The Origins, Structure, and Effects of National Socialism,* New York, Praeger, 1970, pp. 259–272.

22. Breitman, *The Architect of Genocide,* p. 59.

23. Quoted in Ernst Klee et al., Editors, *The Good Old Days: The Holocaust as Seen by Its Perpetrators and Bystanders,* New York, Free Press, 1991, pp. 158–159.

24. Quoted in Gitta Sereny, *Into That Darkness: An Examination of Conscience,* New York, Vintage Books, 1983, pp. 232–233.

25. Quoted in Klee et al., *The Good Old Days,* pp. 220–221.

26. Christopher R. Browning, *Ordinary Men: Reserve Police Battalion 101 and the Final Solution in Poland,* New York, HarperCollins, 1992, p. 73.

27. Browning, *Ordinary Men,* pp. 159–189.

28. Browning, *Ordinary Men,* p. 186.

29. Hans Mommsen, "The Reaction of the German Population to the Anti-Jewish Persecution and the Holocaust," in Peter Hayes, Editor, *Lessons and Legacies: The Meaning of the Holocaust in a Changing World,* Evanston, IL, Northwestern University Press, 1991, p. 144.

30. John W. Dower, *War Without Mercy: Race and Power in the Pacific War,* New York, Pantheon Books, 1986, p. 5.

31. Dower, *War Without Mercy,* p. 10.

32. Dower, *War Without Mercy,* p. 8.

33. Dower, *War Without Mercy,* p. 36.

34. Dower, *War Without Mercy,* p. 81.

35. Quoted in Dower, *War Without Mercy,* p. 51.

36. Quoted in Dower, *War Without Mercy,* p. 51.

37. Quoted in Michael Sherry, *The Rise of American Air Power: The Creation of Armageddon,* New York and London, Yale University Press, 1987, p. 245.

38. Quoted in Sherry, *The Rise of American Air Power,* p. 245.

39. Dower, *War Without Mercy,* p. 85.

40. Quoted in Dower, *War Without Mercy,* p. 71.

41. Quoted in Ronald Schaffer, *Wings of Judgment: American Bombing in World War II,* New York and Oxford, Oxford University Press, 1985, p. 153.

42. Gordon Daniels, *Concentration Camps USA: Japanese Americans and World War II,* Hinsdale, IL, Dryden Press, 1971, p. 27.

43. Daniels, *Concentration Camps USA,* pp. 1–25.

44. Dower, *War Without Mercy,* p. 35.

45. Daniels, *Concentration Camps USA,* p. 34.

46. Quoted in Dower, *War Without Mercy,* p. 80.

47. Dower, *War Without Mercy,* p. 7.

48. Dower, *War Without Mercy,* p. 87.

49. Dower, *War Without Mercy,* p. 87.

50. Quoted in Dower, *War Without Mercy,* p. 78.

51. Dower, *War Without Mercy,* pp. 53–54.

52. Dower, *War Without Mercy,* p. 92.

53. Air Force Historical Foundation, *Impact: The Army Air Forces; Confidential Picture History of World War II, Vol. 8,* New York, James Parton, 1982.

54. *Impact,* Vol. 8, pp. 92–93.

55. Sherry, *The Rise of American Air Power,* p. 246.

56. Quoted in Dower, *War Without Mercy,* p. 71.

57. George L. Hopkins, "Bombing and American Conscience During World War II," *Historian,* Vol. 28, 1968, p. 470.

58. Sherry, *The Rise of American Air Power*, p. 60.

59. Sherry, *The Rise of American Air Power*, p. 285.

60. Dower, *War Without Mercy*, p. 93.

61. Robert Jay Lifton, *The Nazi Doctors: Medical Killing and the Psychology of Genocide*, New York, Basic Books, 1986, p. 431.

62. Lucy Dawidowicz, *The Holocaust and the Historians*, Cambridge, MA, Harvard University Press, 1981, pp. 9, 20.

63. Quoted in Lifton, *The Nazi Doctors*, p. 1.

64. Quoted in Dawidowicz, *The War Against the Jews*, p. 3.

65. Quoted in Breitman, *Architect of Genocide*, p. 189.

66. Schleunes, *The Twisted Road to Auschwitz*, p. 51.

67. Lifton, *The Nazi Doctors*, p. 17.

68. Bracher, *The German Dictatorship*, p. 430.

69. Leon Poliakov, *Harvest of Hate: The Nazi Program for the Destruction of the Jews in Europe*, New York, Holocaust Library, 1979, p. 5.

70. Quoted in Poliakov, *Harvest of Hate*, p. 6.

71. Robert Pois, "Jewish Treason Against the Laws of Life: Nazi Religiosity and Bourgeois Fantasy," in Michael Dobkowski and Isidor Wallimann, Editors, *Towards the Holocaust: The Social and Economic Collapse of the Weimar Republic*, Westport, CT, Greenwood Press, 1983, p. 385.

72. Mosse, *Toward the Final Solution*, p. 206.

73. Leo Alexander, "Medical Science Under Dictatorship," *New England Journal of Medicine*, Vol. 241, July 14, 1949, p. 39.

74. Lifton, *The Nazi Doctors*, pp. 96–151.

75. Lifton, *The Nazi Doctors*, pp. 271–277.

76. Lifton, *The Nazi Doctors*, p. 151.

77. Lifton, *The Nazi Doctors*, p. 151.

78. Quoted in Ella Lingens-Reiner, *Prisoners of Fear*, London, Gollancz, 1948, pp. 1–2.

79. Hilberg, *The Destruction of the European Jews, Vol. I*, p. 329.

80. Quoted in International Military Tribunal, *Trials of War Criminals Before the Nürnberg Military Tribunals, Vol IV*, Washington, DC, U.S. Government Printing Office, 1949, p. 275.

81. Quoted in Klee et al., *The Good Old Days*, p. 158.

82. Quoted in Klee et al., *The Good Old Days*, p. 163; emphasis was added by Klee.

83. Quoted in Breitman, *Architect of Genocide*, p. 177.

84. Lee Kennett, *A History of Strategic Bombing*, New York, Charles Scribner's Sons, 1982, pp. 39–57.

85. Noble Frankland, *Bomber Offensive: The Devastation of Europe*, New York, Ballantine Books, 1970, p. 14.

86. Quoted in Kennett, *A History of Strategic Bombing*, p. 55–56.

87. Quoted in Kennett, *A History of Strategic Bombing*, p. 75–76.

88. Kennett, *A History of Strategic Bombing*, p. 164.

89. Quoted in Kennett, *A History of Strategic Bombing*, p. 76.

90. Quoted in Sherry, *The Rise of American Air Power*, p. 30.

91. Kennett, *A History of Strategic Bombing*, p. 179.

92. Quoted in Stephen Garrett, *Ethics and Airpower in World War II: The British Bombing of German Cities*, New York, St. Martin's Press, 1993, p. 6.

93. Martin Middlebrook, *The Battle of Hamburg: Allied Bomber Forces Against a German City in 1943*, New York, Charles Scribner's Sons, 1981, p. 341.

94. Quoted in Breitman, *Architect of Genocide*, p. 63.

95. Schaffer, *Wings of Judgment*, p. 152.

96. Kennett, *A History of Strategic Bombing*, p. 15.

97. Arthur Harris, *Bomber Offensive*, London, Collins Press, 1947, pp. 22–23.

98. Harris, *Bomber Offensive*, p. 23.

99. Harris, *Bomber Offensive*, p. 176.

100. Harris, *Bomber Offensive*, pp. 268–269.

101. John Ford, "The Morality of Obliteration Bombing," in Richard Wasserstrom, Editor, *War and Morality*, Belmont, CA, Wadsworth, 1970, pp. 15–41; see also Lewis Mumford, "The Morals of Extermination," *Atlantic*, Vol. 204, October 1959, pp. 37–49.

102. Schaffer, *Wings of Judgment*, p. 62.

103. Curtis LeMay, with McKinley Kantor, *Mission with LeMay*, New York, Doubleday, 1965, p. 347.

104. LeMay, *Mission with LeMay*, pp. 351–352.

105. LeMay, *Mission with LeMay*, p. 383.

106. For the definitive story of the U.S. atomic bomb project, see Richard Rhodes, *The Making of the Atomic Bomb*, New York, Simon & Schuster, 1986. For the American scientists' intense fears of the German atomic bomb project, see Thomas Powers, *Heisenberg's War: The Secret History of the German Bomb*, New York, Knopf, 1993.

107. Quoted in Rhodes, *The Making of the Atomic Bomb*, p. 314.

108. Powers, *Heisenberg's War*, pp. 269–372.

109. Josef Rotblat, "Leaving the Bomb Project," *Bulletin of the Atomic Scientists*, August 1985, pp. 16–18.

110. Quoted in Schaffer, *Wings of Judgment*, p. 175.

111. Quoted in Rhodes, *The Making of the Atomic Bomb*, p. 691.

112. Quoted in Barton J. Bernstein, "A Postwar Myth: 500,000 U.S. Lives Saved," *Bulletin of the Atomic Scientists*, June-July 1986, p. 38.

113. Robert Jay Lifton, *The Broken Connection: On Death and the Continuity of Life*, New York, Simon & Schuster, 1979, p. 377.

114. Lifton, *The Broken Connection*, p. 377.

115. Henry Stimson, "The Decision to Use the Atomic Bomb," *Harper's Magazine*, Vol. 194, February 1947, pp. 100, 105.

116. Quoted in Rufus E. Miles, Jr., "Hiroshima: The Strange Myth of Half a Million American Lives Saved," *International Security*, Vol. 10, No. 2, Fall 1985, p. 123.

117. Miles, "Hiroshima," p. 121.

118. Miles, "Hiroshima," p. 138.

119. J. Samuel Walker, "The Decision to Use the Bomb: A Historiographical Update," *Diplomatic History*, Vol. 14, No. 1, Winter 1990, p. 110.

120. Barton J. Bernstein, "Seizing the Contested Terrain of Early Nuclear History: Stimson, Conant, and Their Allies Explain the Decision to Use the Atomic Bomb," *Diplomatic History*, Vol. 17, No. 1, 1993, pp. 35–72.

121. Gar Alperovitz, "Why the United States Dropped the Bomb," *Technology Review*, August-September 1990, p. 33.

122. Barton J. Bernstein, *The Atomic Bomb: The Critical Issues*, Boston, Little, Brown, 1976, pp. vii–xix, 69–79.

123. Leon V. Sigal, *Fighting to a Finish: The Politics of War Termination in the United States and Japan, 1945*, Ithaca and London, Cornell University Press, 1988, pp. 218–219, 181.

124. Sigal, *Fighting to a Finish*, p. 221.

125. Lewis Mumford, "The Morals of Extermination," p. 39.

CHAPTER 10

1. Nora Levin, *The Holocaust: The Destruction of European Jewry, 1933–1945*, New York, Schocken Books, 1973, p. 91.

2. Richard L. Rubenstein, *The Cunning of History: The Holocaust and the American Future*, New York, Harper Colophon Books, 1978, p. 27. (This passage was emphasized in the original.)

3. Zygmunt Bauman, *Modernity and the Holocaust*, Ithaca, NY, Cornell University Press, 1989, p. 105.

4. Raul Hilberg, *The Destruction of the European Jews, Vol. I*, Revised and Definitive Edition, New York, Holmes & Meier, 1985, p. 62.

5. Rubenstein, *The Cunning of History*, pp. 4–5.

6. Karl Dietrich Bracher, *The German Dictatorship: The Origins, Structure, and Effects of National Socialism*, New York, Praeger, 1970, p. 269.

7. Alice Gallin, *Midwives to Nazism: University Professors in Weimar Germany, 1925–1933*, Macon, GA, Mercer University Press, 1986.

8. George L. Mosse, *Toward the Holocaust: A History of European Racism*, New York, Harper and Row, 1978, p. 73.

9. Robert Proctor, *Racial Hygiene: Medicine Under the Nazis*, Cambridge, MA, Harvard University Press, 1988; Benno Müller-Hill, *Murderous Science: Elimination by Scientific Selection of Jews, Gypsies, and Others, Germany 1933–1945*, Translated by George R. Fraser, Oxford and New York, Oxford University Press, 1989.

10. Gallin, *Midwives to Nazism*.

11. See Gunter Remmling, "Discrimination, Persecution, Theft, and Murder Under Color of Law: The Totalitarian Corruption of the German Legal System, 1933–1945," in Isidor Wallimann and Michael N. Dobkowski, Editors, *Genocide and the Modern Age: Etiology and Case Studies of Mass Death*, New York, Greenwood Press, 1987, pp. 185–201, for a detailed account of the complicity of the German legal profession in enacting and enforcing anti-Jewish laws.

12. Hilberg, *The Destruction of the European Jews, Vol. I*, pp. 94–134.

13. Christopher R. Browning, "The Germany Bureaucracy and the Holocaust," in Alex L. Grobman et al., Editors, *Genocide: Critical Issues of the Holocaust*, Chappaqua, NY, Rossel Books, 1983, pp. 147–148.

14. Jean-Claude Pressac, *Auschwitz: Technique and Operation of the Gas Chambers*, New York, Beate Klarsfeld Foundation, pp. 93–121.

15. Hilberg, *The Destruction of the European Jews, Vol. III*, p. 887.

16. Hilberg, *The Destruction of the European Jews, Vol. III*, p. 1024.

17. Hannah Arendt, *Eichmann in Jerusalem: A Report on the Banality of Evil*, Revised and Enlarged Edition, New York, Penguin Books, 1976, p. 244. Eichmann was found guilty and hanged.

18. Hilberg, *The Destruction of the European Jews, Vol. III*, p. 1011.

19. Hilberg, *The Destruction of the European Jews, Vol. III*, pp. 1012–1016.

20. Hilberg, *The Destruction of the European Jews, Vol. III*, p. 1027.

21. Christopher R. Browning, *Ordinary Men: Reserve Police Battalion 101 and the Final Solution in Poland,* New York, HarperCollins, 1992, p. 163.

22. Michael Sherry, *The Rise of American Air Power: The Creation of Armageddon,* New York and London, Yale University Press, 1987, p. 224.

23. Ronald Schaffer, *Wings of Judgment: American Bombing in World War II,* New York and Oxford, Oxford University Press, 1985, p. 152

24. Freeman H. Dyson, *Disturbing the Universe,* New York, Harper and Row, 1979, p. 30.

25. Quoted in Max Hastings, *Bomber Command,* London, Michael Joseph, 1979, p. 250. (Ellipses in original.)

26. Robert Saundby, "Introduction," in David Irving, *The Destruction of Dresden,* New York, Balllantine Books, 1965, p. 9.

27. Martin Middlebrook, *The Battle of Hamburg: Allied Bomber Forces Against a German City in 1943,* New York, Charles Scribner's Sons, 1981, p. 347.

28. Quoted in Alexander McKee, *Dresden 1945: The Devil's Tinderbox,* New York, E. P. Dutton, 1984, p. 66.

29. Quoted in McKee, *Dresden 1945,* p. 165. See also Stephen A. Garrett, *Ethics and Airpower in World War II,* New York, St. Martin's Press, 1993, p. 81, for a discussion of deceiving British aircrews regarding the nature of their targets.

30. Richard Rhodes, *The Making of the Atomic Bomb,* New York, Simon & Schuster, 1986, pp. 378, 460, 502.

31. Schaffer, *Wings of Judgment,* p. 179.

32. Curtis LeMay with McKinley Kantor, *Mission with LeMay,* New York, Doubleday, 1965, p. 385.

33. Everett C. Hughes, "Good People and Dirty Work," *Social Problems,* Vol. 10, Summer 1962, pp. 3–11.

34. Karl Schleunes, *The Twisted Road to Auschwitz: Nazi Policy Toward German Jews, 1933–1939,* Chicago, University of Ilinois Press, 1970, p. 170.

35. Leon Poliakov, *Harvest of Hate: The Nazi Program for the Destruction of the Jews in Europe,* New York, Holocaust Library, 1979, pp. 32–33.

36. Karl Schleunes, *The Twisted Road to Auschwitz,* p. 170.

37. Hilberg, *The Destruction of the European Jews, Vol. I,* p. 205.

38. Heinz Höhne, *The Order of the Death's Head: The Story of Hitler's SS,* New York, Ballantine Books, 1984, pp. 440–444.

39. See, for examples, Höhne, *The Order of the Death's Head,* 1984, pp. 422–426; Gerald Reitlinger, *The Final Solution,* New York, A. S. Barnes, 1961, pp. 145–150.

40. Arendt, *Eichmann in Jerusalem,* p. 71.

41. Albert Breton and Ronald Wintrobe, "The Bureaucracy of Murder Revisited," *Journal of Political Economy,* Vol. 94, No. 5, 1986, p. 909.

42. Breton and Wintrobe, "The Bureaucracy of Murder Revisited," p. 909.

43. Arendt, *Eichmann in Jerusalem,* pp. 135–150.

44. Breton and Wintrobe, "The Bureaucracy of Murder Revisited," p. 909.

45. Browning, *Ordinary Men,* p. 75.

46. Lee Kennett, *A History of Strategic Bombing,*, New York, Charles Scribner's Sons, 1982, pp. 22–28.

47. Arthur Harris, *Bomber Offensive,* London, Collins Press, 1947, p. 57.

48. Harris, *Bomber Offensive,* p. 57.

49. Harris, *Bomber Offensive,* p. 263.

50. Harris, *Bomber Offensive,* p. 277.
51. R. J. Overy, *The Air War, 1939–1945,* New York, Stein and Day, 1980, p. 17.
52. Hastings, *Bomber Command,* p. 348.
53. Harris, *Bomber Offensive,* p. 104.
54. Harris, *Bomber Offensive,* p. 105.
55. Charles Webster and Noble Franklin, *The Strategic Air Offensive Against Germany, Vol. I,* London, Her Majesty's Stationery Office, 1961, pp. 391–393.
56. Harris, *Bomber Offensive,* p. 109.
57. Middlebrook, *The Battle of Hamburg,* p. 343.
58. McKee, *Dresden 1945,* p. 265.
59. Middlebrook, *The Battle of Hamburg,* p. 344.
60. Garrett, *Ethics and Airpower in World War II,* p. 89.
61. Kennett, *A History of Strategic Bombing,* p. 87.
62. Schaffer, *Wings of Judgment,* p. 11.
63. Sherry, *The Rise of American Air Power,* p. 50.
64. Harris, *Bomber Offensive,* p. 264.
65. Sherry, *The Rise of American Air Power,* p. 151.
66. Sherry, *The Rise of American Air Power,* p. 151.
67. LeMay, *Mission with LeMay,* p. 77.
68. Schaffer, "American Military Ethics in World War II: The Bombing of German Civilians," *Journal of American History,* Vol. 67, September 1980, p. 324.
69. Conrad C. Crane, *Bombs, Cities, and Civilians: American Airpower Strategy in World War II,* Lawrence, KS, University Press of Kansas, 1993, p. 6.
70. Crane, *Bombs, Cities, and Civilians,* p. 118
71. Sherry, *The Rise of American Air Power,* p. 309.
72. LeMay, *Mission with LeMay,* p. 347.
73. Schaffer, "American Military Ethics in World War II," p. 324.
74. Sherry, *The Rise of American Air Power,* p. 18.
75. Schaffer, *Wings of Judgment,* pp. 69–70.
76. George L. Mosse, *Nazi Culture: Intellectual, Cultural, and Social Life in the Third Reich,* New York, Grosset & Dunlap, 1966, p. 200.
77. Max Weinreich, *Hitler's Professors: The Part of Scholarship in Germany's Crimes Against the Jewish People,* New York, Yiddish Scientific Institute (YIVO,) 1946, pp. 239–240.
78. Alan Beyerchen, "The Physical Sciences," in Henry Friedlander and Sybil Milton, Editors, *The Holocaust: Ideology, Bureaucracy, and Genocide,* Millwood, NY, Kraus International Publications, 1980, p. 157.
79. Robert Jay Lifton, *The Nazi Doctors: Medical Killing and the Psychology of Genocide,* New York, Basic Books, 1986, p. 25.
80. Lucy S. Dawidowicz, *The War Against the Jews,* New York, Holt, Rinehart and Winston, 1975, p. 63.
81. Lifton, *The Nazi Doctors,* pp. 437–438.
82. Hastings, *Bomber Command,* p. 99.
83. Hastings, *Bomber Command,* pp. 108–109.
84. Overy, *The Air War,* p. 112.
85. Hastings, *Bomber Command,* p. 134.
86. Kennett, *A History of Strategic Bombing,* pp. 128–131.
87. Hastings, *Bomber Command,* p. 157.

88. C. P. Snow, *Science and Government*, Cambridge, MA, Harvard University Press, 1961, pp. 50–51.

89. Gordon Daniels, Editor, *A Guide to the Reports of the United States Strategic Bombing Survey*, London, Royal Historical Society, 1981, pp. xvi–xxvi.

90. Sherry, *The Rise of American Air Power*, p. 250; see also John Dower, *War Without Mercy: Race and Power in the Pacific War*, New York, Pantheon Books, 1986, pp. 114–146.

91. Lifton, *The Nazi Doctors*, p. 15.

92. Quoted in Höhne, *The Order of the Death's Head*, pp. 412–413.

93. Reitlinger, *The Final Solution*, p. 217; see also Browning, *Ordinary Men*, pp. 82–83.

94. Christopher R. Browning, *Fateful Months: Essays on the Emergence of the Final Solution*, Revised Edition, New York, Holmes & Meier, 1991, pp. 64–65.

95. Hannah Arendt, *The Origins of Totalitarianism*, New York, Harcourt Brace, 1951, p. 449.

96. Gitta Sereny, *Into That Darkness: An Examination of Conscience*, New York, Vintage Books, 1983, p. 201.

97. Quoted in Steven Paskuly, Editor, *Death Dealer: The Memoirs of the SS Kommandant at Auschwitz*, Buffalo, NY, Prometheus Books, 1992, pp. 156–157. Höss's memoirs were originally written between October 1946 and April 1947 while he was imprisoned in Poland. He was later hanged at Auschwitz.

98. Kennett, *A History of Strategic Bombing*, p. 140.

99. Kennett, *A History of Strategic Bombing*, p. 187.

100. McKee, *Dresden 1945*, p. 164.

101. McKee, *Dresden 1945*, p. 164.

102. Middlebrook, *The Battle of Hamburg*, pp. 347–348.

103. Philip Ardery, *Bomber Pilot: A Memoir of World War II*, Lexington, KY, University Press of Kentucky, 1978, p. 107.

104. Wilbur H. Morrison, *Point of No Return: The Story of the Twentieth Air Force*, New York, Times Books, 1979, p. 229.

105. Schaffer, *Wings of Judgment*, p. 182.

106. Sherry, *The Rise of American Air Power*, pp. 234–235.

CHAPTER 11

1. Quoted in Daniel Ellsberg, "The Responsibility of Officials in a Criminal War," in *Papers on the War*, New York, Simon & Schuster, 1972, p. 277. (The book from which the Nietzsche quote was taken, *Beyond Good and Evil: Prelude to a Philosophy of the Future*, was originally published in 1886 and reissued by Vintage Books in 1966. The passage quoted is on p. 89 of the Vintage edition.)

2. See, for examples, Henry V. Dicks, *Licensed Mass Murder: A Socio-Psychological Study of Some SS Killers*, London, Heinemann, 1972; John P. Sabini and Maury Silver, "Destroying the Innocent with a Clear Conscience: A Sociopsychology of the Holocaust," in Joel E. Dimsdale, Editor, *Survivors, Victims, and Perpetrators*, Washington, DC, Hemisphere, 1980, pp. 329–358; Raul Hilberg, *Perpetrators Victims Bystanders*, New York, HarperPerennial, 1993.

3. Quoted in Conrad C. Crane, *Bombs, Cities, and Civilians: American Airpower Strategy in World War II*, Lawrence, University Press of Kansas, 1993, p. 144.

4. Lewis Mumford, "The Morals of Extermination, *Atlantic*, Vol. 204, October 1959, p. 39.

5. Leo Kuper, *Genocide: Its Political Use in the Twentieth Century,* New Haven, CT, Yale University Press, 1981, p. 46.

6. Leo Kuper, "Theoretical Issues Relating to Genocide: Uses and Abuses," in George L. Andreopolous, Editor, *Genocide: Conceptual and Historial Dimensions,* Philadelphia, University of Pennsylvania Press, 1994, p. 35.

7. Shigetoshi Iwamatsu, "A Perspective on the War Crimes," *Bulletin of the Atomic Scientists,* February 1982, pp. 32, 35, respectively.

8. Jack Nusan Porter, "What Is Genocide? Notes Toward a Definition," in Jack Nusan Porter, Editor, *Genocide and Human Rights: A Global Anthology,* Washington, DC, University Press of America, 1982, p. 16.

9. Frank Chalk and Kurt Jonassohn, *The History and Sociology of Genocide: Analyses and Case Studies,* New Haven, Yale University Press, 1990, p. 24.

10. Helen Fein, "Genocide, Terror, Life Integrity, and War Crimes: The Case for Discrimination," in Andreopolous, *Genocide,* p. 104.

11. As several scholars cited in Chapters 2 and 3 pointed out, engaging in total war tends to narrow the differences between totalitarian and democratic political systems. See, for example, Marjorie Farrar, "World War II as Total War," in L. L. Farrar, Editor, *War: A Historical, Political, and Social Study,* Santa Barbara, CA, ABC-Clio, 1978, pp. 171–179.

12. Quoted in Michael Sherry, *The Rise of American Air Power: The Creation of Armageddon,* New York and London, Yale University Press, 1987, p. 349.

13. Paul Boyer, "The Cloud over the Culture: How Americans Imagined the Bomb They Dropped," *New Republic,* August 12, 19, 1985, pp. 26–27.

14. Kuper, *Genocide,* p. 19.

15. Everett C. Hughes, "Good People and Dirty Work," *Social Problems,* Vol. 10, Summer 1962, pp. 3–11.

16. Telford Taylor, *Nuremberg and Vietnam: An American Tragedy,* New York, Quadrangle Books, 1970, p. 89.

17. Quoted in "Misjudgment at Nuremberg," a review essay by Istvan Deak of Taylor's *The Anatomy of the Nuremberg Trials: A Personal Memoir* (Knopf, 1993), in *The New York Review of Books,* Vol. 40, No. 16, October 7, 1993, p. 50.

18. Quoted in Ronald Schaffer, *Wings of Judgment: American Bombing in World War II,* New York and Oxford, Oxford University Press, 1985, p. 164.

19. Quoted in Richard Minear, *Victor's Justice: The Tokyo War Crimes Trial,* Princeton, NJ, Princeton University Press, 1971, pp. 100–101.

20. Michael Walzer, *Just and Unjust Wars: A Moral Argument with Historical Illustrations,* New York, Basic Books, 1977, p. 264.

21. Fein, "Genocide, Terror, Life Integrity, and War Crimes," p. 105.

22. Helen Fein, "Discriminating Genocide from War Crimes: Vietnam and Afghanistan Reexamined," *Denver Journal of International Law and Policy,* Vol, 22, No. 1, 1993, p. 33.

23. The five criteria are listed by Fein, "Discriminating Genocide from War Crimes," pp. 19–22. They are also listed in Fein, "Genocide, Terror, Life Integrity, and War Crimes," p. 97.

24. Stephen Garrett, *Ethics and Airpower in World War II: The British Bombing of German Cities,* New York, St. Martin's Press, 1993, p. 21.

25. Crane, *Bombs, Cities, and Civilians,* p. 140.

26. Robert Jay Lifton, *Death in Life: Survivors of Hiroshima,* New York, Random House, 1967, p. 57.

27. Richard Rhodes, *The Making of the Atomic Bomb,* New York, Simon & Schuster, 1986, p. 740.

28. Quoted in Kuper, *Genocide,* p. 19.

29. Uriel Tal, "On the Study of the Holocaust and Genocide," *Yad Vashem Studies,* Vol. 13, 1979, p. 18.

30. Quoted in Kuper, *Genocide,* p. 19.

31. Leo Kuper, *The Prevention of Genocide,* New Haven, CT, Yale University Press, 1985, p. 14.

32. R. J. Rummel, "Power Kills; Absolute Power Kills Absolutely," *Internet on the Holocaust and Genocide,* No. 38, June 1992, p. 10.

33. Kuper, *Genocide,* p. 33.

34. Fein, "Genocide, Terror, Life Integrity, and War Crimes," p. 97.

35. Fein, "Discriminating Genocide from War Crimes," p. 65.

36. Daniel Ellsberg, personal communication. Ellsberg was intimately involved in the development of American nuclear weapons policies, serving on the Joint Staff Study Group on Survivability of National Command and Control of Nuclear Weapons in 1960, on the Defense Department Task Force on Limited War Research and Development in 1961, and as a member of two high-level working groups reporting to the Executive Committee of the National Security Council during the Cuban missile crisis of 1962, among other relevant positions.

37. Fein, "Genocide, Terror, Life Integrity, and War Crimes," p. 95.

38. Hugo Adam Bedau, "Genocide in Vietnam?" in Virginia Held et al., Editors, *Philosophy, Morality, and International Affairs,* New York, Oxford University Press, 1974, p. 8.

39. Israel W. Charny, "Toward a Generic Definition of Genocide," in Andreopolous, *Genocide,* p. 70.

CHAPTER 12

1. Robert Jay Lifton, "Imagining the Real: Beyond the Nuclear 'End,'" in Lester Grinspoon, Editor, *The Long Darkness: Psychological and Moral Perspectives on Nuclear Winter,* New Haven and London, Yale University Press, p. 82.

2. Herbert F. York, *Race to Oblivion: A Participant's View of the Arms Race,* New York, Simon & Schuster, 1970, p. 237.

3. York, *Race to Oblivion,* pp. 230–231.

4. John Dower, *War Without Mercy: Race and Power in the Pacific War,* New York: Pantheon Books, 1986, p. 172.

5. Dower, *War Without Mercy,* p. 173.

6. Dower, *War Without Mercy,* p. 173.

7. Paul Boyer, *By the Bomb's Early Light: American Thought and Culture at the Dawn of the Atomic Age,* New York, Pantheon Books, 1985, p. 25.

8. Herbert F. York and G. Allen Greb, "The Superbomb," in Jack Dennis, Editor, *Nuclear Almanac: Confronting the Atom in War and Peace,* Reading, MA, Addison-Wesley, 1984, p. 21.

9. Herbert F. York, *The Advisors: Oppenheimer, Teller, and the Superbomb,* San Francisco, W. H. Freeman, 1976.

10. Fred Kaplan, *The Wizards of Armageddon,* New York, Simon & Schuster, 1983, p. 52.

11. Kaplan, *The Wizards of Armageddon,* p. 52.

12. Gregg Herken, *Counsels of War,* New York, Alfred A. Knopf, 1985, p. 76.

13. Kaplan, *The Wizards of Armageddon*, p. 10.

14. Kaplan, *The Wizards of Armageddon*, p. 10.

15. Kaplan, *The Wizards of Armageddon*, p. 40.

16. Herken, *Counsels of War*, p. 29.

17. Kaplan, *The Wizards of Armageddon*, p. 209.

18. David Alan Rosenberg, "A Smoking, Radiating Ruin at the End of Two Hours: Documents on American Plans for Atomic War with the Soviet Union, 1954–55," *International Security*, Vol. 6, Winter 1981-1982, pp. 18–19.

19. William Arkin and Peter Pringle, *SIOP: The Secret U.S. Plan for Nuclear War*, London, Sphere Books, 1983, pp. 45–47.

20. Herken, *Counsels of War*, 1985, p. 94.

21. Quoted in Herken, *Counsels of War*, p. 95.

22. Herken, *Counsels of War*, p. 96.

23. Quoted in Herken, *Counsels of War*, p. 97.

24. Quoted in Kaplan, *The Wizards of Armageddon*, p. 134.

25. Rosenberg, "A Smoking, Radiating Ruin at the End of Two Hours," pp. 15–16.

26. Rosenberg, "A Smoking, Radiating Ruin at the End of Two Hours, p. 18.

27. Arkin and Pringle, *SIOP*, pp. 44, 115; Rosenberg, "A Smoking, Radiating Ruin at the End of Two Hours," p. 39.

28. Thomas Powers, "Choosing a Strategy for World War III," *Atlantic Monthly*, Vol. 250, No. 5, 1982, p. 92.

29. For more on Nazi-nuclear parallels, see Robert Jay Lifton and Eric Markusen, *The Genocidal Mentality: Nazi Holocaust and Nuclear Threat*, New York, Basic Books, 1990. See also Lisa Peattie, "Normalizing the Unthinkable," *Bulletin of the Atomic Scientists*, Vol. 40, No. 3, 1984, pp. 32–36.

30. Quoted in York, *The Advisors*, pp. 156–157.

31. Robert Kennedy, *Thirteen Days: A Memoir of the Cuban Missile Crisis*, New York, Norton, 1971, p. 22.

32. Richard Smoke, *National Security and the Nuclear Dilemma*, Reading, MA, Addison–Wesley, 1984, p. 117.

33. Quoted in Martin Tolchin, "U.S. Underestimated Soviet Force in Cuba in '62," *New York Times*, January 15, 1992, p. A6.

34. Lifton and Markusen, *The Genocidal Mentality*, p. 173.

35. Daniel Ellsberg, "Call to Mutiny," in E. P. Thompson and Dan Smith, Editors, *Protest and Survive*, New York and London, Monthly Review Press, 1981, p. iv.

36. David T. Cattell and George H. Quester, "Ethnic Targeting: Some Bad Ideas," in Desmond Ball and Jeffrey Richelson, Editors, *Strategic Nuclear Targeting*, Ithaca and London, Cornell University Press, 1985, pp. 267–284.

37. This exchange is described by Powers, "Choosing a Strategy for World War III," p. 83.

38. Cattell and Quester, "Ethnic Targeting," p. 281.

39. Quoted in Michael McQueen, "Bush and Yeltsin, at Camp David, Forge Closer Ties but Reach No Specific Pacts," *Wall Street Journal*, February 3, 1992, A-12.

40. World Health Organization, *Effects of Nuclear War on Health and Health Services*, Geneva, World Health Organization, 1984.

41. Carl Sagan and Richard Turco, *A Path Where No Man Thought: Nuclear Winter and the End of the Arms Race*, New York, Random House, 1990.

42. Paul Ehrlich et al., "Long-Term Consequences of Nuclear War, *Science,* Vol. 222, December 23, 1983, p. 1330.

43. Lifton and Markusen, *The Genocidal Mentality,* p. 3.,

44. Dower, *War Without Mercy,* p. 309.

45. Quoted in Otto Klineberg, "The Contributions of Psychology to International Understanding: Problems and Possibilities," in Robert W. Rieber, Editor, *The Psychology of War and Peace: The Image of the Enemy,* New York and London, Plenum Press, 1991, p. 78.

46. Robert W. Rieber and Robert J. Kelly, "Substance and Shadow: Emnification in the Cold War," Occasional Paper No. 6, Center on Violence and Human Survival, John Jay College of Criminal Justice, City University of New York, 1990, p. 11.

47. Henry Nash, "Bureaucratization of Homicide," *Bulletin of the Atomic Scientists,* Vol. 36, No. 4, 1980, p. 25.

48. Nash, "Bureaucratization of Homicide," p. 24.

49. Roman Kolkowicz, Editor, *The Logic of Nuclear Terror,* Boston, Allen & Unwin, 1986, p. 40.

50. Quoted in Lifton and Markusen, *The Genocidal Mentality,* p. 150.

51. Hannah Arendt, *Eichmann in Jerusalem: A Report on the Banality of Evil,* Revised and Enlarged Edition, New York, Penguin Books, 1976, p. 85.

52. Herbert Kelman, "Violence Without Moral Restraint: Reflections on the Dehumanization of Victims and Victimizers," *Journal of Social Issues,* Vol. 29, 1973, p. 48.

53. Robert Jay Lifton and Richard Falk, *Indefensible Weapons: The Psychological and Political Case Against Nuclearism,* New York, Basic Books, 1982, p. 107.

54. Carol Cohn, "Slick'ems, Glick'ems, Christmas Trees, and Cookie Cutters: Nuclear Language and How We Learned to Pat the Bomb," *Bulletin of the Atomic Scientists,* Vol. 43, 1985, p. 22.

55. Cohn, "Slick'ems, Glick'ems, Christmas Trees, and Cookie Cutters," p. 31.

56. Cohn, "Slick'ems, Glick'ems, Christmas Trees, and Cookie Cutters," p. 31.

57. Nash, "Bureaucratization of Homicide," p. 26.

58. Quoted in Lifton and Markusen, *The Genocidal Mentality,* 1990, p. 213.

59. Kolkowicz, *The Logic of Nuclear Terror,* p. 38.

60. Nash, "Bureaucratization of Homicide," p. 22.

61. Nash, "Bureaucratization of Homicide," pp. 22–23.

62. Herken, *Counsels of War,* p. 163.

63. Kaplan, *The Wizards of Armaggedon,* p. 166.

64. Herken, *Counsels of War,* p. 65.

65. Herken, *Counsels of War,* p. 181.

66. Herken, *Counsels of War,* p. 181.

67. Quoted in Kaplan, *The Wizards of Armaggedon,* p. 232.

68. Kaplan, *The Wizards of Armaggedon,* p. 235.

69. Kaplan, *The Wizards of Armaggedon,* p. 121.

70. James Fallows, *National Defense,* New York, Random House, 1981, p. 139. See also, for similar conclusion by a Soviet writer, Henry Trofimenko, "The Theology of Strategy," *Orbis,* Vol. 21, 1977, pp. 497–515.

71. To our knowledge, the concept of structural violence was pioneered by Johan Galtung. See, for examples, Johan Galtung, "Violence, Peace, and Peace Research," *Journal of Peace Research,* Vol. 7, No. 3, 1969, pp. 167–191; Johan Galtung and T. Hoivik, "Structural

and Direct Violence: A Note on Operationalism," *Journal of Peace Research*, Vol. 8, No. 1, 1971, pp. 73–76.

72. William Eckhardt and Gerhart Köhler, "Structural and Armed Violence in the Twentieth Century: Magnitude and Trends," *International Interactions*, Vol. 6, No. 4, 1980, p. 348.

73. Irving Louis Horowitz, *Taking Lives: Genocide and State Power*, Third Edition, New Brunswick, NJ, Transaction Books, 1982, p. 34.

74. For a detailed discussion of how structural violence is measured, see Gernot Köhler and Norman Alcock, "An Empirical Table of Structural Violence," *Journal of Peace Research*, Vol. 13, No. 4, 1976, pp. 343–356.

75. Ruth Leger Sivard, *World Military and Social Expenditures 1993*, Leesburg, VA, World Priorities, 1993, p. 47.

76. William Eckhardt, "Civilian Deaths in Wartime," *Bulletin of Peace Proposals*, Vol. 20, No. 1, 1989, p. 92.

77. Phillips Foster, "Malnutrition, Starvation and Death," in Daniel Leviton, Editor, *Horrendous Death, Health, and Well-Being*, New York, Hemisphere, 1991, p. 205.

78. Lester Brown et al., *State of the World, 1991*, New York, W. W. Norton, 1991, pp. 16–17.

79. Ruth Leger Sivard, *World Military and Social Expenditures 1991*, Leesburg, VA, World Priorities, 1991, pp. 28–32.

80. Thomas F. Homer-Dixon et al., "Environmental Change and Violent Conflict," *Scientific American*, February 1993, p. 38.

81. Robert D. Kaplan, "The Coming Anarchy," *Atlantic Monthly*, February 1994, p. 58.

82. Kaplan, "The Coming Anarchy," p. 72.

83. Felicity Barringer, "'Repatriation' Is the Trend for Refugees Worldwide," *New York Times*, November 17, 1991, p. E4. On the rise in the number of refugees from 1976 through 1994, see Paul Lewis, "U.N. Hopes Number of Refugees Falls," *New York Times*, March 29, 1994, p. A11.

84. Judy A. Mayotte, *Disposable People? The Plight of Refugees*, Maryknoll, NY, Orbis Books, 1992, p. 2.

85. Judith Miller, "Displaced in the Gulf War: Five Million Refugees," *New York Times*, June 16, 1991, p. E3.

86. Lidia Grafova, "Twenty-five Million Foreigners in Their Own Country," *IPI Report*, Vol. 41, No. 6–7, 1992, p. 16.

87. See, for example, Richard H. Feen, "The Never Ending Story: The Haitian Boat People," *Migration World Magazine*, Vol. 21, No. 1, 1992, pp. 13–17.

88. Jasmina Knezevic and Sladjana Dimic, *Refugees in Serbia*, Belgrade, Commissariate for Refugees of the Republic of Serbia, 1993.

89. Craig R. Whitney, "Europeans Look for Ways to Bar Door to Immigrants," *New York Times*, December 29, 1991, p. 1.

90. Richard L. Rubenstein, *The Age of Triage: Fear and Hope in an Overcrowded World*, Boston, MA, Beacon Press, 1983.

91. Sivard, *World Military and Social Expenditures 1993*, p. 16.

92. William Safire, "Object: Survival," *New York Times*, November 11, 1990, Op-Ed page.

93. John M. Deutch, "The New Nuclear Threat," *Foreign Affairs*, Fall 1992, p. 134.

94. Steve Fetter, "Ballistic Missiles and Weapons of Mass Destruction: What Is the Threat? What Should be Done?" *International Security*, Vol. 16, No. 1, Summer 1991, p. 16.

95. Fetter, "Ballistic Missiles and Weapons of Mass Destruction," p. 24.

96. Fetter, "Ballistic Missiles and Weapons of Mass Destruction," p. 13.

97. Fetter, "Ballistic Missiles and Weapons of Mass Destruction," p. 23.

98. Sivard, *World Military and Social Expenditures 1993*, p. 5.

99. Leo Kuper, *The Prevention of Genocide*, New Haven, Yale University Press, 1985, pp. 171–228.

100. Kuper, *The Prevention of Genocide*, p. 204.

101. Kuper, *The Prevention of Genocide*, p. 210.

102. Kuper, *The Prevention of Genocide*, p. 211.

103. Kuper, *The Prevention of Genocide*, p. 217.

104. Kuper, *The Prevention of Genocide*, p. 218.

105. Kuper, *The Prevention of Genocide*, p. 225. See also Barbara Harff, "Humanitarian Intervention in Genocidal Situations," in Israel W. Charny, Editor, *Genocide: A Critical Bibliographic Review, Vol. II*, New York, Facts on File, 1991, pp. 146–153.

106. Theodor Meron, "The Case for War Crimes Trials in Yugoslavia," *Foreign Affairs*, Vol. 72, No. 3, 1993, pp. 122–135.

107. Kuper, *The Prevention of Genocide*, p. 219.

108. The newsletter-journal *Internet on the Holocaust and Genocide* is published by the Institute on the Holocaust and Genocide, P.O. Box 10311, 91102 Jerusalem, Israel.

109. Israel W. Charny, "Intervention and Prevention of Genocide," in I. W. Charny, Editor, *Genocide: A Critical Bibliographic Review, Vol. I*, New York, Facts on File, 1988, p. 29.

110. Charny, "Intervention and Prevention of Genocide," p. 30.

111. Charny, "Intervention and Prevention of Genocide," p. 30.

112. Charny, "Intervention and Prevention of Genocide," p. 30.

113. Israel W. Charny, "Early Warning, Intervention, and Prevention of Genocide," in Michael N. Dobkowski and Isidor Walliman, Editors, *Genocide in Our Time*, Ann Arbor, MI, Pierian Press, 1992, pp. 149–166.

114. Evin Staub, *The Roots of Evil, The Origins of Genocide and Other Group Violence*, Cambridge, England, and New York, Cambridge University Press, 1989, p. 274.

115. Lifton and Markusen, *The Genocidal Mentality*, p. 255.

116. For a discussion of the potential contribution of codes of ethics in reducing collective violence, see Craig Summers and Eric Markusen, "Computers, Ethics, and Collective Violence," *Journal of Systems and Software*, Vol. 17, No. 1, 1992, pp. 99–100.

117. Joel Primack and Frank von Hippel, *Advice and Dissent: Scientists in the Political Arena*, New York, New American Library, 1976.

118. See the summary of Kanter's work in John Macionis, *Sociology*, Fourth Edition, Englewood Cliffs, NJ, Prentice-Hall, 1993, pp. 195–196.

119. See, for example, Ann Markusen and Joel Yudken, *Dismantling the Cold War Economy*, New York, Basic Books, 1992.

120. Robert Jay Lifton, "Imagining the Real," in R. J. Lifton and Richard Falk, *Indefensible Weapons: The Psychological and Political Case Against Nuclearism*, New York, Basic Books, 1982, p. 117.

Selected Bibliography

Adam, Uwe Dietrich, "The Gas Chambers," in Francois Furet, Editor, *Unanswered Questions: Nazi Germany and the Genocide of the Jews,* New York, Schocken Books, 1989, pp. 134–154.

Alexander, Leo, "Medical Science Under Dictatorship," *New England Journal of Medicine,* Vol. 241, July 14, 1949, pp. 39–47.

Allen, Francis, "Influence of Technology on War," in Francis Allen et al., Editors, *Technology and Social Change,* New York, Appleton-Century-Crofts, 1957, pp. 353–387.

Air Force Historical Foundation, *Impact: The Army Air Forces' Confidential Picture History of World War II,* 8 Vols., New York, James Parton, 1982 [1943–1945].

Arendt, Hannah, *Eichmann in Jerusalem: A Report on the Banality of Evil,* Revised and Enlarged Edition, New York, Penguin Books, 1976.

Aron, Raymond, *The Century of Total War,* New York, Doubleday, 1954.

Ball, Desmond, and Jeffrey Richelson, Editors, *Strategic Nuclear Targeting,* Ithaca, NY, and London, Cornell University Press, 1986.

Bartoszewski, Wladyslaw T., Editor, *Surviving Treblinka: Samuel Willenberg,* Oxford, Blackwell, 1989.

Bartov, Omer, *The Eastern Front, 1941–45, German Troops and the Barbarisation of Warfare,* New York, St. Martin's Press, 1986.

Bauer, Yehuda, *A History of the Holocaust,* New York, Franklin Watts, 1982.

Bauman, Zygmunt, *Modernity and the Holocaust,* Ithaca, NY, Cornell University Press, 1989.

Beck, Earl R., *Under the Bombs: The German Home Front, 1942–1945,* Lexington, University Press of Kentucky, 1986.

Behr, Edward, *Hirohito Behind the Myth,* New York, Vantage Books, 1990.

Berenbaum, Michael, Editor, *A Mosaic of Victims: Non-Jews Persecuted and Murdered by the Nazis,* New York, New York University Press, 1990.

Bernstein, Barton J., Editor, *The Atomic Bomb: The Critical Issues,* Boston, Little, Brown, 1976.

Blau, Peter M., and Marshall W. Meyer, *Bureaucracy in Modern Society,* Third Edition, New York, McGraw-Hill, 1987.

Boyer, Paul, *By the Bomb's Early Light: American Thought and Culture at the Dawn of the Atomic Age,* New York, Pantheon Books, 1985.

Breitman, Richard, *The Architect of Genocide: Himmler and the Final Solution,* New York, Knopf, 1991.

Breton, Albert, and Ronald Wintrobe, "The Bureaucracy of Murder Revisited," *Journal of Political Economy,* Vol. 94, No. 5, 1986, pp. 905–926.

Browning, Christopher R., *Ordinary Men: Reserve Police Battalion 101 and the Final Solution in Poland,* New York, HarperCollins, 1992.

———, *Fateful Months: Essays on the Emergence of the Final Solution,* Revised Edition, New York, Holmes & Meier, 1991.

———, "The Germany Bureaucracy and the Holocaust," in Alex L. Grobman et al., Editors, *Genocide: Critical Issues of the Holocaust,* Chappaqua, NY, Rossel Books, 1983, pp. 145–149.

Caidin, Martin, *The Night Hamburg Died,* New York, Ballantine Books, 1979 [1960].

———, *A Torch to the Enemy,* New York, Ballantine Books, 1979 [1960].

Carroll, Berenice A., *Design for Total War: Arms and Economics in the Third Reich,* The Hague, Mouton, 1968.

Chalk, Frank, and Kurt Jonassohn, *The History and Sociology of Genocide: Analyses and Case Studies,* New Haven, Yale University Press, 1990.

Charny, Israel W., "Toward a Generic Definition of Genocide," in George L. Andreopolous, Editor, *Genocide: Conceptual and Historial Dimensions,* Philadelphia, University of Pennsylvania Press, 1994, pp. 64–94.

———, Editor, *The Widening Circle of Genocide: Genocide: A Critical Bibliographic Review, Vol. III,* New Brunswick, NJ, Transaction Press, 1994.

———, "Early Warning, Intervention, and Prevention of Genocide," in Michael N. Dobkowski and Isidor Wallimann, Editors, *Genocide in Our Time,* Ann Arbor, MI, Pierian Press, 1992, pp. 149–166.

———, Editor, *Genocide: A Critical Bibliographic Review, Vol. II,* New York, Facts on File, 1991.

———, Editor, *Genocide: A Critical Bibliographic Review, Vol. I,* New York, Facts on File, 1988.

———, "Genocide and Mass Destruction: Doing Harm to Others as a Missing Dimension in Psychopathology," *Psychiatry,* Vol. 49, May 1986, pp. 144–157.

———, *How Can We Commit the Unthinkable? Genocide: The Human Cancer,* Boulder, CO, Westview Press, 1982.

Churchill, Ward, "Genocide: Toward a Functional Definition," *Alternatives,* Vol. 11, 1986, pp. 403–430.

Clausewitz, Carl von, *On War,* Edited and Translated by Michael Howard and Peter Paret, Princeton, NJ, Princeton University Press, 1976 [1832].

Collins, Randall, "Three Faces of Evil: Towards a Comparative Sociology of Evil," *Theory and Society,* Vol. 1, 1974, pp. 415–440.

Committee for the Compilation of Materials on Damage Caused by the Atomic Bombs in Hiroshima and Nagasaki, *Hiroshima and Nagasaki: The Physical, Medical, and Social Effects of the Atomic Bombings,* New York, Basic Books, 1981 [1977].

Coser, Lewis, "The Visibility of Evil," *Journal of Social Issues,* Vol. 25, 1969, pp. 101–109.

Crane, Conrad C., *Bombs, Cities, and Civilians: American Airpower Strategy in World War II,* Lawrence, University Press of Kansas, 1993.

Craven, Wesley F., and James L. Cate, *The Army Air Forces in World War II, Vols. I, III, and V,* Chicago, University of Chicago Press, 1948, 1951, 1953, respectively.

Czech, Danuta, *Auschwitz Chronicle 1939–1945,* New York, Henry Holt, 1990.

Dadrian, Vahakn N., "The Convergent Aspects of the Armenian and Jewish Cases of Genocide: A Reinterpretation of the Concept of Holocaust," *Holocaust and Genocide Studies,* Vol. 3, No. 2, 1988, pp. 151–170.

———, "A Theoretical Model of Genocide," *Sociologica Internationalis,* Vol. 14, 1976, pp. 99–126.

———, "A Typology of Genocide," *International Review of Modern Sociology,* Vol. 15, 1975, pp. 204–213.

Daniels, Gordon, Editor, *A Guide to the Reports of the United States Strategic Bombing Survey,* London, Royal Historical Society, 1981.

Daniels, Roger, *Concentration Camps USA: Japanese Americans and World War II,* Hinsdale, IL, Dryden Press, 1971.

Das, Tarakchandra, *Bengal Famine 1943,* Calcutta, University of Calcutta, 1949.

Dawidowicz, Lucy, *The Holocaust and the Historians,* Cambridge, MA, Harvard University Press, 1981.

———, *The War Against the Jews,* New York, Holt, Rinehart and Winston, 1975.

Deutch, John M., "The New Nuclear Threat," *Foreign Affairs,* Fall 1992, pp. 120–134.

Dower, John W., *War Without Mercy: Race and Power in the Pacific War,* New York, Pantheon Books, 1986.

Dyer, Gwynne, *War,* New York, Crown, 1985.

Eckhardt, William, "Civilian Deaths in Wartime," *Bulletin of Peace Proposals,* Vol. 20, No. 1, 1989, 89–98.

Edoin, Hoito, *The Night Tokyo Burned,* New York, St. Martin's Press, 1987.

Elliot, Gil, *Twentieth Century Book of the Dead,* New York, Charles Scribner's Sons, 1972.

Ellsberg, Daniel, "Manhattan Project II: To End the Threat of Nuclear War," *Harvard Journal of World Affairs,* Summer 1992, pp. 1–16.

Farrar, Marjorie, "World War II as Total War," in L. L. Farrar, Editor, *War: A Historical, Political, and Social Study,* Santa Barbara, CA, ABC-Clio, 1978, pp. 171–179.

Feig, Konnilyn, *Hitler's Death Camps: The Sanity of Madness,* New York, Holmes & Meier, 1983.

Fein, Helen, "Genocide, Terror, Life Integrity, and War Crimes: The Case for Discrimination," in George L. Andreopolous, Editor, *Genocide: Conceptual and Historical Dimensions,* Philadelphia, University of Pennsylvania Press, 1994, pp. 95–107.

———, "Discriminating Genocide from War Crimes: Vietnam and Afghanistan Reexamined," *Denver Journal of International Law and Policy,* Vol. 22. No. 1, Fall 1993, pp. 29–62.

———, "Genocide: A Sociological Perspective," *Current Sociology,* Vol. 38, No. 1, 1990, entire issue.

———, *Accounting for Genocide: National Responses and Jewish Victimization During the Holocaust,* New York, Free Press, 1979.

Förster, Jürgen, "The German Army and the Ideological War Against the Soviet Union," in Gerhard Hirshfield, Editor, *The Policies of Genocide: Jews and Soviet Prisoners of War in Nazi Germany,* London, Allen & Unwin, 1986, pp. 15–29.

Foster, Phillips, "Malnutrtion, Starvation and Death," in Daniel Leviton, Editor, *Horrendous Death, Health, and Well-Being,* New York, Hemisphere, 1991, pp. 205–218.

Frankland, Noble, *Bomber Offensive: The Devastation of Europe,* New York, Ballantine Books, 1970.

Fuller, J.F.C., *The Conduct of War, 1789–1961,* New Brunswick, NJ, Rutgers University Press, 1961.

Fussell, Paul, *The Great War and Modern Memory,* Oxford, Oxford University Press, 1975.

Gabriel, Richard, *The Painful Field: The Psychiatric Dimension of Modern War,* New York, Greenwood Press, 1989.

Garrett, Stephen A., *Ethics and Airpower in World War II: The British Bombing of German Cities,* New York, St. Martin's Press, 1993.

Gault, William Barry, "Some Remarks on Slaughter," *American Journal of Psychiatry,* Vol. 128, October 1971, pp. 450–455.

Gilbert, Martin, *The Holocaust: A History of the Jews of Europe During the Second World War,* New York, Holt, Rinehart and Winston, 1985.

Goldenberg, Sydney, "Crimes Against Humanity 1945–1970," *Western Ontario Law Review,* Vol. 10, 1971, pp. 1–55.

Halperin, Morton et al., *Bureaucratic Politics and Foreign Policy,* Washington, DC, Brookings Institution, 1974.

Harff, Barbara, "Recognizing Genocides and Politicides," in Helen Fein, Editor, *Genocide Watch,* New Haven, CT, Yale University Press, 1992, pp. 27–41.

———, "Humanitarian Intervention in Genocidal Situations," in Israel W. Charny, Editor, *Genocide: A Critical Bibliographic Review, Vol. II,* New York, Facts on File, 1991, pp. 146–153.

Harff, Barbara, and Ted Robert Gurr, "Toward Empirical Theory of Genocides and Politicides: Identification and Measurement of Cases since 1945," *International Studies Quarterly,* Vol. 32, 1988, pp. 359–371.

———, "The Etiology of Genocides," in Isidor Wallimann and Michael Dobkowski, Editors, *Genocide and the Modern Age: Etiology and Case Studies of Mass Death,* New York, Greenwood Press, 1987, pp. 42–59.

Harris, Arthur, *Bomber Offensive,* London, Collins Press, 1947.

Harris, Robert, and Jeremy Paxman, *A Higher Form of Killing: The Secret Story of Chemical and Biological Warfare,* New York, Hill and Wang, 1982.

Hastings, Max, *Bomber Command,* London, Michael Joseph, 1979.

Herken, Gregg, *Counsels of War,* New York, Alfred A. Knopf, 1985.

Hilberg, Raul, *The Destruction of the European Jews, Vols. I-III,* Revised and Definitive Edition, New York, Holmes & Meier, 1985.

Hirsch, Herbert, and Roger W. Smith, "The Language of Extermination in Genocide," in Israel W. Charny, Editor, *Genocide: A Critical Bibliographical Review, Vol. II,* New York, Facts on File, 1991, pp. 386–395.

Hobbs, Richard, "The Growth of the Idea of Total War," in *The Myth of Victory: What Is Victory in War?* Boulder, CO, Westview Press, 1979, pp. 59–66.

Höhne, Heinz, *The Order of the Death's Head: The Story of Hitler's SS,* New York, Ballantine Books, 1984.

Homer-Dixon, Thomas F., et al., "Environmental Change and Violent Conflict," *Scientific American,* February 1993, pp. 38–45.

Horowitz, Irving Louis, *Taking Lives: Genocide and State Power,* Third Edition, New Brunswick, NJ, Transaction Books, 1982 [1976].

Höss, Rudolph, in Steven Paskuly, Editor, *Death Dealer: The Memoirs of the SS Kommandant at Auschwitz,* Buffalo, NY, Prometheus Books, 1992.

Hughes, Everett C., "Good People and Dirty Work," *Social Problems,* Vol. 10, Summer 1962, pp. 3–11.

Huttenbach, Henry R., "Locating the Holocaust on the Genocide Spectrum: Toward a Methodology of Definition and Categorization," *Holocaust and Genocide Studies,* Vol. 3, No. 3, 1988, pp. 289–303.

International Military Tribunal, *Trials of War Criminals Before the Nürnberg Military Tribunals, Vols. I and IV,* Washington, DC, U.S. Government Printing Office, 1947–1949.

Irving, David, *The Destruction of Dresden,* New York, Ballantine Books, 1965.

Jäckel, Eberhard, *Hitler's "Weltanschauung": A Blueprint for Power,* Middletown, CT, Wesleyan University Press, 1972.

Johnson, Paul, *Modern Times: The World from the Twenties to the Eighties,* New York, Harper Colophon, 1991.

Jonassohn, Kurt, "Famine, Genocide, and Refugees," *Society,* Vol. 30, No. 6, 1993, pp. 72–77.

———, "What Is Genocide?" in Helen Fein, Editor, *Genocide Watch,* New Haven CT, Yale University Press, 1992, pp. 17–26.

Kaplan, Fred, *The Wizards of Armageddon,* New York, Simon & Schuster, 1983.

Kaplan, Robert D., "The Coming Anarchy," *Atlantic Monthly,* February 1994, pp. 44–63.

Katz, Fred, "A Sociological Perspective to the Holocaust," *Modern Judaism,* Vol. 2, 1982, pp. 273–296.

Katz, Steven T., "Essay: Quantity and Interpretation—Issues in the Comparative Historical Analysis of the Holocaust," *Holocaust and Genocide Studies,* Vol. 4, No. 2, 1989, pp. 127–148.

———, "Technology and Genocide: Technology as a 'Form of Life,'" In Alan Rosenberg and Gerald Meyers, Editors, *Echoes from the Holocaust: Philosophical Reflections on a Dark Time,* Philadelphia, Temple University Press, 1989, pp. 262–291.

Keegan, John, *The Face of Battle,* New York, Viking Press, 1976.

Kelman, Herbert, "Violence Without Moral Restraint: Reflections on the Dehumanization of Victims and Victimizers," *Journal of Social Issues,* Vol. 29, 1973, pp. 25–61.

Kennett, Lee, *A History of Strategic Bombing,* New York, Charles Scribner's Sons, 1982.

Kerr, Bartlett E., *Flames over Tokyo: The U.S. Army Air Force's Incendiary Campaign Against Japan,* New York, D. I. Fine, 1991.

Klee, Ernst, et al., Editors, *The Good Old Days: The Holocaust as Seen by Its Perpetrators and Bystanders,* New York, Free Press, 1991.

Knox, Donald, *Death March: The Survivors of Bataan,* Harcourt Brace Jovanovich, 1981.

Krausnick, Helmut, et al., Editors, *The Anatomy of the SS State,* New York, Walker, 1968.

Kuper, Leo, "Theoretical Issues Relating to Genocide: Uses and Abuses," in George L. Andreopolous, Editor, *Genocide: Conceptual and Historical Dimensions,* Philadelphia, University of Pennsylvania Press, 1994, pp. 31–46.

———, "Genocide and the Technological Tiger," *Internet on the Holocaust and Genocide,* No. 32, 1992, pp. 1–2.

———, "The Genocidal State: An Overview," in Pierre van den Berghe, Editor, *State Violence and Ethnicity,* Boulder, University Press of Colorado, 1990, pp. 19–52.

———, *The Prevention of Genocide,* New Haven, CT, Yale University Press, 1985.

———, *Genocide: Its Political Use in the Twentieth Century,* New Haven, CT, Yale University Press, 1981.

Lane, Eric, "Mass Killing by Governments: Lawful in the World Legal Order?," *International Law and Politics,* Vol. 12, 1979, pp. 239–280.

LeBlanc, Lawrence J., *The United States and the Genocide Convention,* Durham and London, Duke University Press, 1991.

LeMay, Curtis, with McKinley Kantor, *Mission with LeMay,* New York, Doubleday, 1965.

Lemkin, Raphael, *Axis Rule in Occupied Europe,* Washington, DC, Carnegie Endowment for International Peace, 1944.

Levin, Nora, *The Holocaust: The Destruction of European Jewry, 1933–1945,* New York, Schocken Books, 1973.

———, *Thought Reform and the Psychology of Totalism: A Study of "Brainwashing" in China,* Chapel Hill and London, North Carolina Press, 1989 [1961].

Lifton, Robert Jay, *The Nazi Doctors: Medical Killing and the Psychology of Genocide,* New York, Basic Books, 1986.

———, *The Broken Connection: On Death and the Continuity of Life,* New York, Simon & Schuster, 1979.

———, *Death in Life: Survivors of Hiroshima,* New York, Random House, 1967 [reissued in 1976, 1979, 1982].

Lifton, Robert Jay, and Richard Falk, *Indefensible Weapons: The Psychological and Political Case Against Nuclearism,* New York, Basic Books, 1982.

Lifton, Robert Jay and Eric Markusen, *The Genocidal Mentality: Nazi Holocaust and Nuclear Threat,* New York, Basic Books, 1990.

Lipstadt, Deborah, *Denying the Holocaust: The Growing Assault on Truth and Memory,* New York, Free Press, 1993.

Maier, Charles S., *The Unmasterable Past: History, Holocaust, and German National Identity,* Cambridge, MA, Harvard University Press, 1988.

Markusen, Eric, "Genocide and Modern War," in Michael Dobkowski and Isidor Wallimann, Editors, *Genocide in Our Time,* Ann Arbor, MI, Pierian Press, 1992, pp. 117–148.

———, "Genocide, Total War, and Nuclear Omnicide," in Israel W. Charny, Editor, *Genocide: A Critical Bibliographical Review, Vol. II,* New York, Facts on File, 1991, pp. 229–246.

Martindale, Don, *Institutions, Oganizations, and Mass Society,* Boston, Houghton Mifflin, 1966.

Mayer, Arno, *Why Did the Heavens Not Darken? The "Final Solution" in History,* New York, Pantheon, 1988.

McKee, Alexander, *Dresden 1945: The Devil's Tinderbox,* New York, E. P. Dutton, Inc., 1982.

Merton, Robert K., "Bureaucratic Structure and Personality," in R. K. Merton, Editor, *Social Theory and Social Structure,* New York, Free Press, 1957, pp. 249–260.

Middlebrook, Martin, *The Battle of Hamburg: Allied Bomber Forces Against a German City in 1943,* New York, Charles Scribner's Sons, 1981.

Miles, Rufus E. Jr., "Hiroshima: The Strange Myth of Half a Million American Lives Saved," *International Security,* Vol. 10, No. 2, Fall 1985, pp. 121–140.

Minear, Richard, *Victor's Justice: The Tokyo War Crimes Trial,* Princeton, NJ, Princeton University Press, 1971.

Mosse, George L., *Toward the Holocaust: A History of European Racism,* New York, Harper and Row, 1978.

Müller, Filip, *Eyewitness Auschwitz: Three Years in the Gas Chambers,* New York, Stein and Day, 1981.

Mumford, Lewis, "The Morals of Extermination," *Atlantic,* Vol. 204, October 1959, pp. 37–49.

Musgrove, Gordon, *Operation Gomorrah: The Hamburg Firestorm Raids,* New York and London, Jane's, 1981.

Nash, Henry, "Bureaucratization of Homicide," *Bulletin of the Atomic Scientists,* Vol. 36, April 1980, pp. 22–27.

Nef, John U., *War and Human Progress: An Essay on the Rise of Industrial Civilization,* New York, W. W. Norton, 1950.

O'Connell, Robert L., *Of Arms and Men: A History of War, Weapons, and Aggression,* New York and Oxford, Oxford University Press, 1989.

Overy, R. J., *The Air War, 1939–1945*, New York, Stein and Day, 1980.

Palmer, Alison, "Ethnocide," in Michael N. Dobkowski and Isidor Wallimann, Editors, *Genocide in Our Age*, Ann Arbor, MI, Pierian Press, 1992, pp. 1–21.

Peattie, Lisa, "Normalizing the Unthinkable," *Bulletin of the Atomic Scientists*, Vol. 40, No. 3, 1984, pp. 32–36.

Piccigallo, Philip R., *The Japanese on Trial: Allied War Crimes Operations in the East, 1945–51*, Austin, University of Texas Press, 1979.

Poliakov, Leon, *Harvest of Hate: The Nazi Program for the Destruction of the Jews in Europe*, New York, Holocaust Library, 1979.

Powers, Thomas, "Choosing a Strategy for World War III," *Atlantic Monthly*, Vol. 250, No. 5, 1982, pp. 82–105.

Pressac, Jean-Claude, *Auschwitz: Technique and Operation of the Gas Chambers*, New York, Beate Klarsfeld Foundation, 1989.

Preston, Richard, and Sydney Wise, *Men in Arms: A History of Warfare and Its Interrelationships with Western Society*, Fourth Edition, New York, Holt, Rinehart and Winston, 1979.

Quester, George, *Deterrence Before Hiroshima: The Air Power Background of Modern Strategy*, New York, John Wiley, 1966.

Rhodes, Richard, "Man-Made Death: A Neglected Mortality," *Journal of the American Medical Association*, Vol. 260, 1988, pp. 686–687.

———, *The Making of the Atomic Bomb*, New York, Simon & Schuster, 1986.

Rosenberg, Alan, and Evelyn Silverman, "The Issue of the Holocaust as a Unique Event," in Michael Dobkowski and Isidor Wallimann, Editors, *Genocide in Our Time*, Ann Arbor, MI, Pierian Press, 1992, pp. 47–65.

Rosenberg, David A., "A Smoking Radiating Ruin at the End of Two Hours: Documents on American Plans for Nuclear War with the Soviet Union, 1945–1955," *International Security*, Vol. 6, No. 3, Winter 1981–1982, pp. 3–38.

Rubenstein, Richard, *The Age of Triage: Fear and Hope in an Overcrowded World*, Boston, MA, Beacon Press, 1983.

———, *The Cunning of History: The Holocaust and the American Future*, New York, Harper Colophon Books, 1978.

Rummel, R. J., *Democide: Nazi Genocide and Mass Murder*, New Brunswick and London, Transaction Books, 1992.

———, "Power Kills; Absolute Power Kills Absolutely," *Internet on the Holocaust and Genocide*, No. 38, June 1992, pp. 1–12.

———, *China's Bloody Century: Genocide and Mass Murder Since 1900*, New Brunswick, NJ, and London, Transaction Books, 1991.

———, *Lethal Politics: Soviet Genocide and Mass Murder Since* 1917, New Brunswick, NJ, and London, Transaction Books, 1990.

Ryan, Mark A. "The Rape of Nanking: The Genesis of an Atrocity," Minneapolis, University of Minnesota, M.A. Dissertation in History, Summer 1990.

Sallagar, Frederick, *The Road to Total War*, New York, Von Nostrand Reinhold, 1969.

Schaffer, Ronald, *Wings of Judgment: American Bombing in World War II*, New York and Oxford, Oxford University Press, 1985.

———, "American Military Ethics in World War II: The Bombing of German Civilians," *Journal of American History*, Vol. 67, September 1980, pp. 318–334.

Schleunes, Karl, *The Twisted Road to Auschwitz: Nazi Policy Toward German Jews, 1933–1939*, Chicago, University of Illinois Press, 1970.

Sereny, Gitta, *Into That Darkness: An Examination of Conscience,* New York, Vintage Books, 1983.

Sherry, Michael, *The Rise of American Air Power: The Creation of Armageddon,* New York and London, Yale University Press, 1987.

———, "The Slide to Total Air War," *New Republic,* December 16, 1981, pp. 20–25.

Sivard, Ruth Leger, *World Military and Social Expenditures, 1993,* Leesburg, VA, World Priorities, 1993.

Smith, Roger, "Human Destructiveness and Politics: The Twentieth Century as an Age of Genocide," in Isidor Wallimann and Michael Dobkowski, Editors, *Genocide and the Modern Age: Etiology and Case Studies of Mass Death,* New York, Greenwood Press, 1987, pp. 21–39.

Sorokin, Pitirim, *Social and Cultural Dynamics,* Vol. 3, New York, Bedminister Press, 1962 [1937].

Staub, Ervin, *The Roots of Evil: The Origins of Genocide and Other Group Violence,* Cambridge, England, and New York, Cambridge University Press, 1989.

Streit, Christian, "The German Army and the Policies of Genocide," in Gerhard Hirschfeld, Editor, *The Policies of Genocide: Jews and Soviet Prisoners of War in Nazi Germany,* London, Allen & Unwin, 1986, pp. 1–14.

Taylor, Telford, *Nuremberg and Vietnam: An American Tragedy,* New York, Quadrangle Books, 1970.

United States Congressional Office of Technology Assessment, *The Effects of Nuclear War,* Washington, DC, U.S. Government Printing Office, 1979.

van den Berghe, Pierre, Editor, *State Violence and Ethnicity,* Boulder, University Press of Colorado, 1990.

Walker, J. Samuel, "The Decision to Use the Bomb: A Historiographical Update," *Diplomatic History,* Vol. 14, No. 1, Winter 1990, pp. 97–115.

Walzer, Michael, *Just and Unjust Wars,* New York, Basic Books, 1977.

Weber, Max, "Bureaucracy," in H. H. Gerth and C. W. Mills, Editors and Translators, *From Max Weber: Essays in Sociology,* New York, Oxford University Press, 1958.

Webster, Charles, and Noble Frankland, *The Strategic Air Offensive Against Germany, Vol. I,* London, Her Majesty's Stationery Office, 1961.

Weinreich, Max, *Hitler's Professors: The Part of Scholarship in Germany's Crimes Against the Jewish People,* New York, Yiddish Scientific Institute–YIVO, 1946.

Williams, Peter, and David Wallace, *Unit 731: Japan's Secret Biological Warfare in World War II,* New York, Free Press, 1989.

World Health Organization, *Effects of Nuclear War on Health and Health Services,* Geneva, World Health Organization, 1984.

Wright, Quincy, *A Study of War,* Chicago, University of Chicago Press, 1942.

Wytwycky, Bohdan, *The Other Holocaust: Many Circles of Hell,* Washington, DC, Novak Project, 1980.

Yahil, Leni, *The Holocaust: The Fate of European Jewry, 1932–1945,* Translated by Ina Friedman and Haya Galai, New York, Oxford University Press, 1990.

York, Herbert, *The Advisors; Oppenheimer, Teller, and the Superbomb,* San Francisco, W. H. Freeman, 1976.

———, *Race to Oblivion: A Participant's View of the Arms Race,* New York, Simon & Schuster, 1970.

About the Book and Authors

War and genocide are the two principal forms of mass killing by governments; they have claimed more than 100 million lives in the twentieth century. The height of the slaughter was reached during World War II, and one legacy of that cataclysm is the continuing threat posed by tens of thousands of nuclear weapons. Through an examination of the Holocaust (the attempt to exterminate the Jewish people) and Allied strategic bombing (the attempt to exterminate German and Japanese civilians living in cities), Eric Markusen and David Kopf aim to promote understanding of and concern about what may be the most urgent present-day threat to human survival—the willingness of national governments to plan, prepare for, and carry out the extermination of masses of innocent people.

Markusen and Kopf strongly disagree with scholars who regard war and genocide as separate phenomena. They find that despite important differences, there are in fact striking parallels in the psychological, organizational, and scientific-technological factors that contributed to the adoption of these programs for mass killing. The dehumanization of the victims made it psychologically easier to carry out their extermination; the preparations for slaughter within vast bureaucracies diminished the sense of individual responsibility for these lethal policies; and the rationalization of the killing was aided by intellectuals who justified their actions on the basis of allegedly scientific principles and data.

The unsettling truth, according to Markusen and Kopf, is that the majority of those involved in governmental mass killings are psychologically normal and regard themselves as patriots, rather than as mass murderers. Moreover, they find that some of the same psychological factors that have accounted for genocide and total war also characterized the preparations of the superpowers for the possibility of future nuclear conflicts. The authors survey dangerous global trends that appear to support continued outbreaks of genocidal killing and conclude with reflections on the prospects for preventing such tragedies.

Eric Markusen is professor of sociology and social work at Southwest State University in Minnesota. **David Kopf** is professor of history at the University of Minnesota.

Index